A UNIQUE AND GLORIOUS MISSION

*Women and Presbyterianism in Scotland
1830 to 1930*

A UNIQUE AND GLORIOUS MISSION

Women and Presbyterianism in Scotland 1830 to 1930

Lesley Orr Macdonald

JOHN DONALD PUBLISHERS LTD
EDINBURGH

ISBN 0 85976 478 8

British Library Cataloguing in Publication Data.

A catalogue record for this book is available
from the British Library.

Typesetting and origination by Brinnoven, Livingston.
Printed and bound in Great Britain by Redwood Books, Trowbridge

Contents

Acknowledgements

This book is my work, but it is the fruit of collaboration, support and help offered by numerous individuals, groups, institutions and organisations. There are too many to acknowledge each one by name, but that does not diminish my appreciation, admiration and gratitude.

New College (the faculty of Divinity at Edinburgh University) is a congenial and diverse community. Over many years, I have enjoyed its hospitable and stimulating environment, and I record my warm appreciation to the academic, library and support staff for putting up with me in various guises! I am indebted also to staff at the National Library of Scotland, the Scottish Record Office, Edinburgh University Main Library, and other custodians of books, manuscripts and records across Scotland. Their care and professionalism are a wonderful resource, without which our history would be lost.

For permission to quote from *Arms and the Girl* by Stevie Davis, I am grateful to the publishers, The Women's Press. Many women and men took time to share their stories, recollections and insights with me, and I thank them all – their voices and faces; their laughter and tears light up historical research with humanity. I have been inspired by a long and rich heritage of women with vision, acting to change both church and world. And I have been given strength by the friendship and solidarity of hundreds of women (and some men too) – in Scotland and around the world – who are part of the creating and telling of their own history.

I have received immense practical help from those who have shared the burden and joy of caring for my children; and from others who have helped me survive frustrations and delights in the rapidly changing world of information technology.

To all of these people I owe my deepest and heartfelt appreciation for their kindness, illumination and encouragement.

Above all, I thank my dear family – parents, sister and brothers and partners, spouse and children – for their sustaining companionship, concern and love. My parents Janet and Jack Orr have been a bedrock of unconditional practical, moral, intellectual and personal support, for which

I am eternally grateful. My sister Kathryn Galloway is a woman of rare perception and passion, my mentor and soul friend. My partner Peter Macdonald challenges and affirms me with his affection, humour, wisdom, ardour and companionship. My sons Callum and Lorn shared their own gestation, birth and growing with this project: they kept me distracted, exhausted, entertained and firmly rooted while I researched and wrote. Peter, Callum and Lorn are my deepest sources of pleasure, pride and joy and help me keep everything in perspective.

This book is for all my family, with all my love.

Lesley Orr Macdonald
Edinburgh, 2000

1

Introduction

'Where is my history?'

Always it is the simple, homely things that bless and satisfy – this fire now, and Iain the dog lying asleep at her feet; the hot bread, new-baked from the oven; the taking of a book in both hands (as now, reaching for a volume of Buchanan's sixteenth-century *History of Scotland*, which she reads in the original Latin). These things – fire, bread, books – reach right back to her girlhood in Sutherland, her father also a cleric, her mother a schoolteacher, a life at once hardy and nourishing . . . The book in her hands is an early edition, as precious perhaps as the whole house over her head. When the book creaks open, and she spells the words over to herself, Buchanan springs alive into the room, she overhears the voice of a mind, speaking in the here-and-now, with all its biases, subterfuges, struggles and conflicts. *So, George Buchanan, she challenges him, What have you got to say to me?* It is all one long tale of antipathy and violence, the dog-fight of the murderous clans, the depravity of the English, the hell-fire theologians warring it out on the page; the voice of the historian, an implicated judge. *But where is my history and Isabel's?* she wonders, raising her head from the book. The voiceless, nameless women bent in the fields, at the looms, gutting the herring at the docks, hanging over the cradles, seem to crowd the margin with acts for which there is neither testament nor memorial.[1]

> – from *Arms and the Girl*, a novel by Stevie Davies

Where is my history? The question which Isla, the minister's wife, ponders, is one which I too have often asked. My own roots in the heritage of Scotland run deep. They are in working class and middle class, east coast and west coast, city and town, radicalism and conservatism. They connect me with mining communities and shopkeepers; with women struggling alone, in low paid and menial work, to support large families; and with a dynasty of church ministers. A common and centrally important factor linking my disparate antecedents was the institution and practice of presbyterianism: that form of Christianity which has had such a profound influence in shaping the character and ethos of Scotland. I believe that history is not simply a record of the past, but a resource for contemporary understanding and action, both individual and collective. In my own 'search

1

for a usable past'[2] I discovered that there was an absence at the heart of the standard texts which presumed to tell the story of Scotland: women were rarely named or discussed. They seemed only to appear as exceptions or deviants, queens or witches. The experiences and ideas of women were largely omitted. They were an undifferentiated mass, acknowledged (if at all) only in terms of their relationships to the men who were the protaganists of Scotland's development. The invisibility of women concerned and perplexed me, for I knew from personal experience, observation, and the recollections of others, that persons of female gender have always constituted at least half of the Scottish population. And surely they were deeply involved in shaping, sustaining and struggling for the people and values that mattered to them. Did women really have no history?

It has become a truism to acknowledge that the literature of human history has largely been written by, and in the interests of, the winners. The myth of universally true and objective scholarly activity has been exposed, as the motivations, privileges and partiality of historians are revealed. Research into, and analysis of the stories of marginalised, oppressed and forgotten groups, has not simply given a broader and richer picture of our past: it has radically changed the conceptual foundations and practices of historical study. The relatively new, but already quite sophisticated and multifaceted field of feminist studies, has begun the task of restoring women to history: not by inserting them into otherwise unchanged narratives, but by challenging liberal historiography to recognise that all social, political and economic orders have impinged on, and been affected by, the diverse experiences of women. This implies, at the most basic level, confronting the long-standing assumption that the absence of women from historical accounts is to be ascribed to a 'natural' order in which the biological constitution of women determines their role and functions as essentially private and ahistorical, whereas men are the agents of political and cultural change.[3] In general terms, the feminist project has argued that the invisibility and marginalisation of women has been a function, not of nature or essence, but of structures and ideologies which are constructed and maintained by human beings. To what extent have particular structures and ideologies been imposed on, accepted or resisted by women? And how much power have these factors had to limit or to liberate their human potential?

In the Scottish context, the long silence about women has started to shatter. Especially in the last decade, a number of books and articles on the history of women in Scotland have been published, and as two leading members of the growing community of interest note, in the introduction to a recent valuable collection of articles:

> This welcome development serves to underline not only the breadth of women's experience and their contribution to Scottish society, but also the potential richness of this historical seam.[4]

The conclusions reached by most of these social and economic historians, social scientists and activists about the status and experiences of Scottish women suggest that they share much in common with women in other parts of the Western industrial world. However, it has often been maintained that the post-Reformation dominance of Calvinist presbyterianism has in particular ways served to subjugate and repress the women of this country. Barbara Littlewood wrote in an article on 'Sex and the Scottish Psyche':

> In the popular imagination, Scotland is often conceived of as a sexually repressed and repressive culture, with much of the blame put on the special tradition of Protestantism which took root here. Closely linked with this is a misogny manifest in both violent and non-violent ways, in the burning of witches and the writing out of women from Scottish history. The heroes and villains of our popular history, with the exception of Mary, Queen of Scots, are invariably male, and the alternatives only replace kings, lairds and politicians with an equally male dominated roster of Red Clyde heroes. Scottish socialism offered no relief from the puritanical ethos of Calvinism; a good socialist could be just as much a patriarch in his private life as any Kirk elder.[5]

As Littlewood notes, Scottish Calvinism has been accused by many (and is still admired by others) for the masculine severity of its doctrines and practices. These, it is claimed, have promoted a patriarchal social structure (hierarchical rule of the father derived especially from Hebrew patterns of kinship organisation, providing an Old Testament model for post-Reformation family, church and state) as divinely ordained. This patriarchy, the critics argue, at worst formalised and encouraged a deep and tenacious misogyny, affecting people of all classes. However, there have been few attempts to assess the historical reality, singularity and extent of this ethos, or its impact on Scottish women. The recent standard works of Scottish church history (e.g. Burleigh 1960, Donaldson 1960, Drummond and Bulloch 1973, 1975) are examples of the historiographical neglect of women, and demonstrate little critical awareness of the potential of presbyterianism as an instrument to exercise social and sexual control over women. Texts dealing with the significance of the Scottish church in modern social history (e.g. Boyd 1980, Smith 1988 C. Brown 1987) pay surprisingly little attention to gender categories in their analyses (although

Callum Brown acknowledges this shortcoming in a brief consideration at the conclusion of his book, and has subsequently added a short chapter in the 1999 revised edition). There has been more acknowledgement of these in work dealing with particular aspects of female experience in Scotland. Christina Larner, in her study of the Scottish witch-hunt, argues that the Reformation made the practice of Christianity a personal responsibility (rather than that of specialists) for the first time. However, it preached a strongly patriarchal message about the ritual, moral and practical inferiority of women which compromised the potential egalitarianism of that central Reformed doctrine, the priesthood of all believers, and the church was determined to eliminate that which did not conform to its required pattern of female behaviour.[6] Leneman and Mitchison (1989) examine the role of church discipline in controlling the sexual and social lives of Scots in the early modern period. They maintain that the Church acquiesced in the expectation that husbands should rule their household, and might express that authority through the use of violence. There was particular censure for working-class girls and women who appeared to depart from puritanical moral standards. But they also give examples of kirk sessions which attempted to modify the extreme physical abuse of women, and demonstrated some paternalistic concern for the needs of single women and their children.[7] Sociologists Dobash and Dobash subtitled their 1979 study of violence against wives (based largely on Scottish empirical research), 'A Case Against the Patriarchy'. They contend that the Reformers, and especially John Knox, were uncompromising in their restriction of women to the roles of obedient and submissive wife and mother:

> What was manmade, enforced by men, and to the benefit of men was attributed not to men . . . but to God, and therefore both just and immutable. Religion was indeed a powerful arm of the patriarchy because it was not defined as political in nature or as manmade. It was an invaluable tool that was used most effectively in achieving what Cato the Roman had pleaded for: that husbands control their wives within the confines of the household and thus save men in general from being publicly confronted with women's pleas for change or their accusations of injustice.[8]

Dobash and Dobash also highlight the public degradation and chastisement to which women were subjected until the 19th century in Scotland, if they were seen to be 'provoking' or outwith their husband's control.

J.D. Young's *Women and Popular Struggles: A History of Scottish and English Working-Class Women 1500–1984* (1985) is an attempt to consider the impact of Calvinism on the lives of Scottish women, and he is to be commended for characterising Scotswomen as agents rather than as victims of history. But his argument that there was a clear distinction between the experiences and freedoms of Scottish and English working-class women, and that the Scottish Reformation was the source of female efforts for liberation, proceeds by assertion and repetition, rather than clear evidence or analysis.[9]

Kay Carmichael's contribution to the 1990 collection of essays, *Sermons and Battle Hymns: Protestant Popular Culture in Modern Scotland*, is entitled 'Protestantism and Gender'. It is impressionistic and includes a number of unsubstantiated generalisations, but also some perceptive commentary about the pervasive significance of the Calvinist ethos for the personal, sexual, social and economic relationships of women and men:

> The Protestant church has acted as the most powerful protagonist of patriarchy as a justification of authority. Those Old Testament images of a fierce, punitive, unforgiving and judgmental God bit deep into the Scottish psyche both in personal relationships and in institutions. Social and economic factors interacted with the church's emphasis on the women's role as being one of subservience . . . Many [men] embraced the role of tyrant with eagerness.[10]

Carmichael believes that the self-denying ethos of presbyterianism was only positive in helping working women to survive the ravages and hardships of the industrial revolution. Its legacy of guilt, repression of the sensual, and conformity is now anachronistic.

While the works cited make some attempt to consider the impact on women of Calvinism as a shaper of Scottish culture, there is almost no published research about women as church members, as believers, as active participants in the network of ideologies and institutions which constitutes organised religion, or as recipients of the religious work of others. What has been the significance of the presbyterian church in shaping the self-understanding, the attitudes, the options and the actions of Scottish women in different times, classes and locations? What have been the variations and contradictions in religious experience? Has the church been a force of reaction or change; of oppression or empowerment? Has the monolithic hegemony of Calvinist patriarchy been total, or have historical developments impinged upon and transformed orthodoxy, in theory and in practice? These questions, and others, must surely be investigated if we are to understand the similarities and disjunctions in Scottish women's lives. For presbyterian religion has been, until really very recently, one of the primary and dominant contexts within which they have been born, grown up, worked, sought recreation, formed relationships and struggled to find meaning and purpose in their lives. As a cultural shaper, it has had a bearing on all who have lived in post–Reformation Scotland, whether their roots are in Protestant, Catholic or other traditions of belief and community.[11]

The complex relationship between women and presbyterianism in Scotland is a vitally important and largely unexplored field of historical study. I hope this book, written from a feminist perspective, engages constructively with some of the big questions. Whether it answers any of them is for the reader to judge!

Are 'Women' Born or Made?

So far I have used the term 'women' in an uncritical way, and indeed the rationale of 'women's studies' has been that 'women' do indeed constitute a distinctive social group which can be categorised and analysed. This hypothesis, though it appeals to commonsense and is enshrined in language, is not unproblematic. The use of the word 'Woman' (singular and capitalised) was very popular in religious, scientific and conversational discourse throughout the period covered in this study. It presumed to signify a universal, abstract and stable category. All the qualities, defects, characteristics, and functions of 'Woman' were thereby assumed to pertain to every person of female gender, as a matter of nature. One consequence of this essentialism was that individuals who did not conform to the definition of 'Woman' were conventionally regarded as deviant, un-sexed or monstrous. Another effect was that all individual, group and class differences and distinctions were collapsed into a reified theory which purported to be timeless and universal but was actually constructed from the ideological and social material available to (and preferred by) those men who dominated the cultural expression and exchange of ideas. And their theory of 'Womanhood' was itself subject to considerable modification, through time and circumstance. Nevertheless, the widespread assumption that the qualities and characteristics of women are inherent by virtue of their biology, encouraged the habit of making sweeping ahistorical assertions about what 'Woman' could or could not do. In particular, 'Woman' was excluded from the public territory of autonomous political and economic agency, and hence, by virtue of her nature, from the making of history.

Part of my task will be to reveal and explore the mass of assumptions which so many Victorians and Edwardians made about what constitutes nature and history. But it is important to be careful about definitions and meanings, so that I do not fall into the same universalising trap. For feminists too, both then and now, have been guilty of using 'Woman' for their own ends. I take heed of the postmodern warning about the dangers of essentialism, and agree with Denise Riley that 'Woman' is in blatant disgrace:

> All definitions of gender must be looked at with an eagle eye, wherever they emanate from and whoever pronounces them, and such a scrutiny is a thoroughly feminist undertaking.[12]

That applies to use of the collective 'women', which is also historically constructed, and in relation to other, changing categories. Indeed, it is worth asking whether gender can meaningfully be isolated from other elements of identity – it is simply wrong just to assume that there is a sense of community or solidarity between all women, regardless of race, class, ethnicity or situation. Some varieties of contemporary feminism have failed to acknowledge their own biases, and have tended to build overarching theories based primarily on the experiences of white middle-class women, thus eliding the real differences between women and the forms of sexism to which they are subject.[13]

However, having entered that caveat, I will continue to use the word 'women': not to construct any grandiose or unitary theories of their oppression, but recognising that, because the subordination of women has been pervasive, multi-faceted and cross-cultural, gender is basic in human history in important ways. Yet it never appears in some pure or idealised form, but always in the context of lives which have been shaped by many influences. If, as Gayle Rubin suggests, the feminist task is to account for the oppression of women 'in its endless variety and monotonous similarity'[14], then historical work is especially important, because it takes account of specificity and diversity in different societies and periods.

I shall certainly make use of some general hypotheses as resources for analysis, but I shall try to beware of manipulating evidence to fit the theory. The whole story of Scottish women and presbyterianism (even for a 100-year period) cannot be told by using the sources which have formed the basis of my research. The records, journals, minutes and biographies to which I refer are largely the chronicles of relatively privileged, wealthy women, and of the churchmen who took it upon themselves to ponder their role in church and society. As Brown and Stephenson rightly note,

> The relationship between middle- and upper-class women and organised religion reveals very little about the very different sets of economic, social and cultural situations within which working- or lower middle-class women formed relationships with religion.[15]

I hope, nevertheless, to illustrate the importance of class (and also race and culture) in undermining the mythological unity of women and enabling some – albeit often unwittingly – to control or repress others.

A Testament and Memorial

This book is about those women who, between 1830 and 1930, were in relationship (as members, opponents, missionary objects and so on) with Scottish presbyterianism. Here, they do not all remain voiceless and nameless women who 'crowd the margins'. Many are identified (individually or collectively) and discussed as moral agents, with the capacity

> To respond creatively and critically to their environment instead of simply taking it as given. Whether symbolised religiously or otherwise, the exercise [of morality] as a critical response to life is the basic means by which human beings are creatures not simply of nature, but of history and culture. The world is not simply given but constructed.[16]

It is important to claim that potential of women to transcend the givenness of their situation. The idea that female actions (especially of care, nurture and self-sacrifice) were simply functions of their biological or divinely-ordained nature, that this confined them to personal or private responses, and that they had no capacity for real justice, was vigorously promoted during this period. Mona Caird, writing in the 1890s, observed:

> To be forced, by popular clamour, into a blind self-annihilation, is not really conducive to the health of the moral faculties; and this is why the goodness of so many women has in it a morbid quality. Von Hartmann says: "Nothing can be reasonably designated moral except a will self-determining and legislating for itself" . . . Not tenderness and sympathy for all that lives and can suffer is the underlying idea of feminine goodness, but devotion to individuals who are selected by mere accident of birth or hazard of circumstance. And this merely instinctive form of attachment is applauded as a woman's highest impulse and privilege.[17]

The values, beliefs and actions of women in Scotland were not controlled by their biology, but shaped by their historical location. They were differentiated by a range of interlocking factors which belied the monolithic understanding of 'Woman' so often and energetically proclaimed. This is a story of diverse women refuting that understanding in a variety of ways – more often in deed rather than word. In the process, they were not just responding critically to their environment, but changing it.

The period from 1830–1930 was a time of significant changes in the theology, structures, laws and opportunities which shaped the experience of women in church and society. Throughout the Victorian and Edwardian eras, the language of mission was in wide currency (in Scotland as elsewhere in the English-speaking Protestant world). Many women seized upon the concept of 'Woman's Mission' (a novel idea which was widely defined and discussed from the early 19th century) to justify and interpret their moral agency in religious work, philanthropy, social and political campaigns. Other women, both in Scotland and abroad, had to deal with that mission as its objects. They responded to the message and its bearers in a variety of ways which belie facile stereotypes of passive acceptance or belligerent rejection.

In Chapter 2 I consider the development of women's mission, in theory and practice; their work within the presbyterian denominations, and how that was related to the general industrial and professional employment of female labour in Scotland. Chapter 3 explores the involvement of women in the burgeoning foreign missionary movement, and Chapter 4 examines the official position of women within the institutional church during a century of upheaval for Scottish presbyterianism. In Chapter 5 I discuss four different movements within which Scottish women sought to challenge and change the world they lived in: the anti-slavery struggle, the temperance movement, the fight to secure higher education for women, and the women's suffrage campaign. Using these examples of female engagement with the church, and with other institutions and concerns, I consider how Scottish presbyterian culture was affirmed, contested or altered by the complex interaction of female attitudes, actions and beliefs. From this research, some conclusions about the significance of presbyterian structures and ideologies for the lives of Scottish women will emerge. In particular I discuss, in Chapter 6, whether it is possible to reach any judgement about presbyterianism as a source of liberation or oppression for women throughout the period.

This study is mainly about women in what is commonly referred to as the public realm, and I have not systematically considered the sexual, psychological, relational or spiritual dimensions of female experience. However, the boundaries between private and public, personal and social are neither natural nor immutable. Their permeability, and the interaction of apparently discrete realms was one of the realities, submerged under the weight of convention, which deeply affected women in the 19th and early 20th centuries. One of the interesting questions about the connections between presbyterianism and women's lives relates to the forms, causes and effects of individual religious experience. So there is some reference to personal and spiritual matters. I hope that as the study of Scottish women flourishes, these will be given the attention they merit.

A Godly Commonwealth?

The Presbyterian Ethos

Presbyterianism is a form of church government based on the principles elucidated by the French reformer Jean Calvin during the 16th century. It evolved as a distinctive expression of protestantism, consciously seeking to return to what was understood as the Apostolic pattern of faith, order, discipline and worship. Calvin and his followers emphasised the supreme authority of Scripture, 'In the which', as the Scots Confession of 1560 put it, 'we affirm that all things necessary to be believed for the salvation of mankind are sufficiently expressed'.[18] From this premise, Calvinists deduced that God, in his transcendent glory and majesty, could only be known by revelation through his Word. In Scripture, Christ was revealed as the divine head and authority of the universal church invisible. Only truly repentant sinners, elected by God as members of the church invisible, were predestined for eternal salvation. Christ the Saviour died to save those who were thus chosen and called, and were justified by faith. The visible church, of those who confessed Christ as Lord and were obedient to his authority, (but which could also include hypocrites and the reprobate) was of great importance. According to the Scots Reformers, the essential marks of the church as defined in their Confession of Faith (1560) were orderly preaching of the Word, the right administration of the sacraments of communion and baptism, and ecclesiastical discipline.

Calvinists subscribed to the great reformation principle of the priesthood of all believers, whereby no sacerdotal caste could stand between the individual and God, and claim to be the sole mediators of the means of grace. But Calvin's own teachings do not make much of this. His emphasis was on church structure and discipline, to be maintained by an orderly ministry of elders (presbyters). Ordained ministers exercised a teaching office of oversight and authority, and had to be well educated in order adequately to equip the Christian community. Calvin, compared with some of the other Reformation leaders, had quite a high doctrine of ordination, and believed ministers to be the sinews holding together the living organism which was the body of Christ. Their vocation would be recognised in election, examination and admission. Discipline, exercised through private rebuke, public admonition, and in extreme cases, excommunication was to be maintained in parish kirks by a body of lay ruling elders, who would live honest, faithful and circumspect lives. The authority of these officials was to be derived from the community, which would call its minister and nominate its elders. It was this principle which gave the Church of Scotland its lay democratic character and potential (and led to Disruption in 1843).

Parochial organisation was at the heart of the ecclesiastical and social vision of Scotland as a 'godly commonwealth'. But a hierarchy of ruling courts evolved, each covering a broader geographical area than the lower court, and each including both ministers and elders in membership. Church government by Kirk Session, Presbytery, Synod and General Assembly was confirmed in 1592, and established, after the political and ecclesiastical struggles of the 17th century, by the 1690 Revolution Settlement. The General Assembly, which met at least annually and exercised both judicial and legislative power, became (especially after the 1707 Union of Parliaments) a significant, if not the only, expression of corporate national identity. The Assembly was a potent symbol of the vision of the whole nation submitting to the Word of God in all aspects of its life, with the visible church as a key element in moulding the Christian character of individual, family, community and state. This social strand of Calvinism was expressed in the responsibility of local parish churches and their kirk sessions: for education, health, welfare and care of the poor, as well as for discipline. In particular, as advocates of a faith in which the Word was supreme, the reformers proposed a scheme of compulsory national education to promote literacy through a structure of parish schools.

The Reformation vision of Scotland as a godly commonwealth – of people attending to the Word of God, engaged in plain and dignified worship, submitting to discipline by representatives of their community, showing corporate concern for the poor and needy, extolling the virtues of hard work and education – clearly shaped the ethos (though not always the practice) of presbyterianism. So too did the strict scholastic Calvinist theological orthodoxy which was enshrined in the Westminster Confession, ratified by the General Assembly in 1647 as the subordinate standard of faith. It became increasingly important as a statement of presbyterian identity against the threats of episcopacy, and adherence was imposed in a strict formula which all ministers had to sign from 1711.[19] The 33 chapters of the Confession, expounding the Christian faith from creation to last judgement, recast Calvinist theology in the political context of 17th century struggles for control of the Scottish Kirk. It emphasised the doctrine of total depravity: Adam and Eve became 'wholly defiled in all the faculties and parts of the soul and body', and after this Fall, all people were 'utterly indisposed, disabled and made opposite to all good, and wholly inclined to all evil'. (WC Chap VI). It distinguished two covenants made by God: that of works made with Adam and his descendants, and that of grace made with the elect. Only the elect, and the church, belong to the order of redemption. This doctrine of double pre-destination asserted the sinner's responsibility for depravity, but also that salvation could only be by the sovereign grace of God. The psychological effect was that there could be no sure knowledge, either of salvation, or of God's love. The believer had to examine his or her life for evidence of election and worth, and seek to respond through a life of faith, obedience, and sanctification. The Westminster Confession also upheld the distinction between the visible and invisible church, and stressed the identification of the Jewish Sabbath with the Christian Sunday, which should be observed as a day of rest. These were the characteristics of puritanism.

Confessional (or Federal) Calvinism, with its stress on full doctrine, and ecclesiastical and moral rectitude, became so strongly identified with the nation that in 1707 the General Assembly affirmed its belief that the establishment of presbyterianism by the Act of Union would be a sufficient guarantor of Scottish interests after the union of crowns. Several writers have perceived a continuing tendency in Scottish life – heightened during the 19th century – to transpose national and political issues into an ecclesiastical key.[20]

In summary, then, the presbyterian ethos evolved in Scotland as a religion of the Book, through a combination of reformed theology and ecclesiology, a vision of the 'godly commonwealth', and a subsequent emphasis on strict federal Cavinist orthodoxy which formed the basis of the Catechism. This ethos was shaped and reshaped in the social and political context of post-Reformation Scotland: of Covenanters, union with England, the 'golden age' of Scottish Enlightenment, dissent and evangelicalism. It was austere, not ornate; cerebral rather than emotional in expression. It was overwhelmingly a religion of proclamation and hearing, and hence it minimised the spiritual value of sight, smell, touch and taste. It emphasised striving and rectitude; good order; seemly obedience to authority; strict observance of the Sabbath. It included appreciation of the value of community and solidarity, and a periodically expressed desire for corporate reform in national life. But ultimately the stress was on heaven and hell; on individual effort and profession to prove worthy to a judgemental God. The journalist Neal Ascherson has described the legacy of this as a fundamental contradiction between self-assertion, and self-distrust.[21]

William Storrar expands on this 'national pathology':

> For the Scottish Calvinists, their human experience became the entrails that had to be dissected for evidence that they were of the Elect, not the arena God himself had entered to assure them of his love. God's love for them became conditional upon their own moral performance, proving that they were saved and not damned. If the enjoyment of their humanity was dependent on God's love for them, and if that love was conditional and not certain, then the effect was to make their own humanity something precarious and conditional upon their own constant moral striving. If Jesus Christ did not 'pay' for the sin of all humanity on the Cross, but only for the sin of the Elect, then we'll pay for it. And we cannot be sure how sair the Lord will be with us on the Day of Judgement.[22]

Presbyterianism and Women

The Protestant Reformation in 16th-century Europe was the outcome of a long struggle against the authority, doctrines, and abuse of power of the medieval Roman church. It reflected a genuine and widespread desire to recover Biblical teaching and practice, and to make these accessible to ordinary, non-professional Christians. Reformers saw that the whole organisation and (to some extent) the theology of the church required radical reshaping to meet the changing needs and perceptions of the times. A fundamental insight was that every Christian had a vocation, and that the existence of a separate, superior estate of priests exercising spiritual and sacrificial power was a distortion of New Testament teaching. There was a new emphasis on the participation of the whole people of God in religious life. The theoretical and practical responses worked out by different reformers impinged on the lives of women in various ways, both positive and negative.

In Calvinism, women, as individual human beings, were recognised to have spiritual equality with men. They, along with laymen, were to be beneficiaries of the movement to remove the hierarchical power, and attendant corruption, of the priestly caste, and to recover liturgy and worship as the work of the whole people of God. Those who exercised the reformed ministry of word and sacrament, and leadership as elders, were officials exercising functions on behalf of the whole community. They did not mystically stand as *alter Christus*, and at least in this sense, their maleness was not essential. Calvin, and a few other continental reformers (notably Bucer) did perceive in New Testament texts, especially I Timothy 5:9f, a diaconal ministry for widows, under the supervision of men. But these tentative suggestions did not receive wide support, and the Scottish reformers say nothing of this. However, 19th-century church leaders did appeal to the female diaconate of the early church as sanction for their own endeavours to extend the official ministry of women (see Chapters 2 and 4).

The emphasis on literacy, and the right to read Scripture for oneself, was potentially revolutionary for females, who were not excluded from Knox's desire to bring education to all the people of Scotland. Those who were able to read the Bible for themselves would find in its pages two strands of tradition relating to the situation and role of women – subordinationist and egalitarian. The Hebrew history which constitutes much of the Old Testament narrative includes accounts of violence, abuse and exploitation of women. It relates their cultural anonymity, dependency and lowly status. And it presents a very partial account of cultic struggles in the Ancient Near East to replace pagan, goddess and fertility worship, with Jewish monotheism. But there are also stories of powerful, active and faithful women in both Old and New Testaments. And some of the Gospel texts affirming the worth and equality of women might have encouraged newly literate women who had not previously had direct access to the Scriptures. Their self-understanding may have been largely shaped by the extremely derogatory, if not misogynist views of the church fathers and medieval theologians, as mediated to them by priests. The ambiguity of the biblical evidence was usable in the 19th and 20th centuries by those who argued for equality on the grounds that injunctions concerning the submission of women were culturally conditioned, whereas those promoting equality reflected God's true purpose for human relationships (see Chapters 4 and 5).

The reformers were concerned about good and edifying church order, and developed that according to their understanding of biblical texts. However, church organisation was never an end in itself, but was to enable the people to hear the gospel and glorify God. The *ecclesia reformata semper reformanda* had, in principle, freedom to change in order to serve those purposes. As Calvin wrote in the 1536 edition of the *Institutes*:

> Establishing here no perpetual law for ourselves, we should refer the entire use and purpose of observance to the upbuilding of the church. If the church requires it, we may not only without any offence allow something to be changed, but permit any observances previously in use among us to be abandoned.[23]

Jane Dempsey Douglass, in *Women, Freedom and Calvin* (1986) highlights what she describes as Calvin's 'startling' inclusion of Paul's admonition regarding women's silence in church, as an example of matters in which the church is free to change (adiaphora – things indifferent).[24] This notion that the church was not forever bound to a particular mode of being, but could be moved by the Holy Spirit according to the needs of the times, was appealed to by many women and their supporters seeking change in their position within the Scottish presbyterian tradition. The relative (and sometimes competing) claims of Word and Spirit were recurring themes in debates about women's role in the church.

But the potentially revolutionary implications of the Reformation for women remained largely dormant. In practical terms the Scottish Kirk, like others within the Calvinist tradition, did not promote an expanded public role or greater freedom for women in church and society: rather the opposite. Calvin and Knox both agreed that the natural order, created by God and knowable by all people, was for women to live in submission and obedience to men. As Knox declared in his *First Blast of the Trumpet Against the Monstrous Regiment of Women* (1558):

> Nature, I say, doth paint them froth to be weak, frail, impatient, feeble, and foolish, and experience hath declared them to be unconstant, variable, cruel, and lacking in the spirit of counsel and regiment.[25]

This natural incapacity for rule, they believed, was confirmed by the authority of Scripture in Genesis and the pastoral epistles of the New Testament.[26] Knox was particularly vehement about the curse of Eve:

> After her fall and rebellion committed against God there was put upon her a new necessity, and she was made subject to man by the irrevocable sentence of God . . . As God should say: 'Forasmuch as thou has abused thy former condition, and because thy free will hath brought thyself and mankind into the bondage of Satan, I therefore will bring thee in bondage to man. For where before thy obedience should have been voluntary, now it shall be by constraint and by necessity; and that because thou hast deceived thy man, thou shalt therefore be no longer mistress over thine own appetites, over thine own will nor desires. For in thee there is neither reason nor discretion which be able to moderate thy affections, and therefore they shall be subject to the desire of thy man. He shall be lord and governor, not only over thy body, but even over thy appetites and will.' This sentence, I say, did God pronounce against Eve and her daughters, as the rest of the Scriptures doth evidently witness. So that no woman can ever presume to reign over man, but the same she must needs do in despite of God and in contempt of his punishment and malediction.[27]

Knox's intemperate *Blast* may have been a politically motivated source of embarassment for his friends, including Calvin. But in essence it expresses an understanding of women's constitution and role with which his fellow reformers would have generally agreed. Knox presumes to issue a very radical form of female subordination from the mouth of God, depriving women of the right to control their own wills and desires, as well as their bodies. For their whole natures (like the natural world in general according to Calvin's dualist cosmology) were regarded as potentially evil and polluting. It would have been as unthinkable for Knox to imagine women exercising the kind of orderly ministry of teaching and oversight which was so central to presbyterian polity, as it was distressing for him to contemplate the secular rule of queens. Indeed, if he meant his words to be taken seriously, it is difficult to conceive of anything less liberating than this divinely ordained bondage! In his attitude to women, Knox did not depart from the classical and patristic traditions which had denigrated women for centuries, but appealed to them as authorities in his diatribe.[28]

One apparently valuable element in Reformation teaching was the emphasis on the dignity of lay vocation as a valid Christian way of life. Allied to this was an affirmation of marriage, against the primacy of celibacy. Certainly Calvin spoke well of the companionship and mutuality which was possible and desirable within marriage. Yet there was a loss for women when the only vocation available to them became that of wife and mother. No longer was there the opportunity to choose an alternative life as part of a community of women in monastic orders. Celibacy at its best had given women (at least those who could afford the convent dowry) a measure of autonomy, learning and purpose. Now the only legitimate place to be a Christian woman was apparently in the home. And Calvinists developed a highly patriarchal model of domestic life, based on their reading of the Old Testament Jewish pattern. The husband and father was regarded as priest in his own home, exercising religious authority and entitled to exact obedience from other household members in the name of God. I shall return to this fundamental and pervasive feature of the Scottish Reformation legacy later.

The loss of female community as an acceptable way of life was accompanied by a more thorough masculinisation of religion. The cults of the Virgin Mary and other saints were suppressed, and that removed all female models and iconography from prayer and piety. With them went the feasts, festivals, images, processions and other features which had made Romanism a sociable and ceremonial expression of religious faith. Little of this public, sensory and celebratory dimension remained in the austerity of presbyterianism, ruled by men and worshipping a distant male God, whose stern judgement was scarcely tempered by the touch of compassionate human mercy which Catholics believed was mediated by Mary. During the period discussed here, women (especially those influenced by evangelicalism) found other ways to 'feminise' the asperity of Calvinism, and to build community with one another.

Much of the substance of this book concerns the efforts of women and men to reconcile, to overcome, sometimes to abandon, and often having to live with tensions: between the more expansive, affirming and liberating elements of the presbyterian ethos and theology, and those which were harsh, oppressive and punitive.

Changes in the Ethos and Theology of Scottish Presbyterianism 1830–1930

In 1830, the Church of Scotland, established by the State, organised on a parochial model, and with extensive involvement in the provision and administration of education and welfare, presented an apparently unitary face to the world. The Kirk, especially in the rural areas where most of the population still lived, was perceived as a cementing force in communities which tended to embody a static social hierarchy. Ministers were prominent and prestigious figures, both locally and nationally. Church affairs were considered to be of great importance. Religous belief and practice dominated the aspirations and fears of ordinary Scots. There was an identifiable Scottish presbyterian ethos which seemed to give the nation its distinctive character.

By 1930, after a century of division, the Church of Scotland was once more a unitary organisation, but with a much less central role – both practically and symbolically – in Scottish life. The intervening years had witnessed internal differences, Disruption, rivalry, and then the gradual piecing together of the shards of presbyterianism (though small fragments remained broken off).

Even by 1830, however, the singular character of Scottish presbyterianism was becoming pretty frayed. A tradition of dissent dating back to 1733 had already established several hundred congregations which at various times, and for different reasons, had seceded from the Established Church. These tended to be around Fife and the west central belt, and were dominated by artisans who found little opportunity for participation and power in a Kirk dominated by the landed and professional classes. In 1847, various groups of seceders combined to form the United Presbyterian Church: a denomination characterised by the Victorian values of thrift, sobriety, pragmatism, and also a commitment to evangelical and progressive causes. It nurtured a significant number of politicians, especially in the Liberal Party which dominated 19th-century politics.

Within the Church of Scotland, there were two 'parties' – the Moderates and the Evangelicals. Both adhered, by and large, to the theological tenets of the Westminster Confession. But the Moderates were generally more conformist, tolerant, willing to accommodate themselves with the political elite and the system of patronage which undermined the principle of ministers called by popular election. The Evangelicals were more fervent and enthusiastic in their conviction that salvation was only available through personal faith in Christ. In 1834 the Evangelicals gained ascendancy in the General Assembly, and set in train the Ten Years' Conflict against the State's right to intervene in internal church affairs. Their vision of Scotland as a nation under God found its most coherent expression and model in the work of the Evangelical leader, Thomas Chalmers. Between 1819 and 1823 he attempted to re-invigorate the old parochial model of evangelisation, education and welfare, in his massive and poverty-stricken inner Glasgow parish. He also promoted a church extension campaign within the national church.[29] Ironically, Chalmers also destroyed the possibility of that vision of a godly commonwealth by leading ministers and lay people out of the established Kirk in 1843, to form the Free Church of Scotland. From that time, presbyterianism in Scotland was profoundly divided. The new denomination devoted phenomenal resources of time, money and energy to creating the buildings and infrastructure which replicated (and competed with) those of the old Kirk. Despite its affirmation of the principle of a national church, the Free Church was *de facto* dependent on voluntarism, and hence undermined one of the tenets of the Reformation. The State assumed from the Church of Scotland responsibility for administration of poor relief in 1845, and for education in 1872. The three main presbyterian denominations became preoccupied with ecclesiastical matters, rivalries and missions, and ceded their ability to promote that truly inclusive national identity which had been at the heart of the Scottish presbyterian ethos.

The election doctrines of federal Calvinism, which had never been entirely secure from the influences of Arminianism and Universalism, came under sustained attack. In the early 1830s, Edward Irving and John MacLeod Campbell were both condemned by the General Assembly for departing from the confessional standard of the church. MacLeod Campbell preached universal atonement and assurance, and as the century proceeded, these were increasingly adopted, to challenge the supremacy of double pre-destination in Scottish theology and preaching. The influence of Anglo-American revivalist evangelicalism was significant, especially during 1859–62, and the Moody and Sankey campaign of 1873–4 (supported by clergy from all three presbyterian churches, and making a marked impact on the

Free Church). The aggressive mission strategy employed to attract the 'lapsed masses' was generally based on the more comforting and less terrifying arminian doctrines, and hastened the relative decline of the old orthodoxies – though they by no means lost their compelling power. Nevertheless, towards the end of the 19th century, church worship, and especially congregational life, did alter in many places. It became somewhat more sociable, populist, and appealing to people who found rigid Calvinism arid, tedious and difficult to understand, as well as frightening in the hellish destiny it seemed to signal for too many. It was during the Victorian era that religion was widely perceived as becoming more 'feminine' in tone and emphasis. Certainly many ministers and local congregations made more room in sermons, hymns and meetings for emotional expression, talk of God's love, and the promotion of Christian qualities which were understood as quintessentially female.

In the second part of the 19th century, new developments in science, history and biblical criticism raised profound doubts about the literal truth of the Scriptures upon which the reformed faith was founded. Within the Church of Scotland, the influence of German Idealism affected 'Broad Church' ministers, while those of the 'High Church' aspired to some of the aesthetic and liturgical qualities of the episcopal traditions. New intellectual trends also brought into focus elements of Christianity which had long been neglected: especially the Old Testament prophetic legacy, the historical Jesus and the Kingdom of God. They provided resources for presbyterians who were concerned and perplexed by the dark side of industrialisation: social dislocation and inequalities which plagued urban Scotland. These seemed to point to the failure of the churches' home mission strategy to solve social evils, and of their accommodation with the liberal individualism of a *laissez-faire* political economy. From around 1880, the churches had to face challenges, not only to traditional Calvinist orthodoxy (both the United Presbyterian Church (1879) and the Free Church (1892), after acrimonious debates, passed Declaratory Acts which modified strict adherence to the Westminister Confession. The Church of Scotland passed a similar measure in 1905), but also from collectivist socialism, Darwin's theory of evolution and its sociobiological offshoots, and the reformist Women's Movement. The presbyterian churches responded to these challenges in a number of ways, up to and during the years of the First World War. These included significant efforts to develop a Christian social and economic critique, and practical social service. At the same time, the dominant world-view in Scotland (and certainly in the churches) was imperialist, and conservative Unionism challenged the long-standing political pre-eminence of the Liberals. After the War, there was a noticeable mood of retrenchment within presbyterianism, as the conservatism of the dominant upper and middle classes asserted itself in the face of political and industrial unrest. In this context, the presbyterian churches mounted a long-lasting campaign (1923–39) against the Roman Catholic Irish immigrant population of Scotland, which was regarded as morally and ethnically polluting. Thus did the growing insecurity of presbyterian identity issue in ugly sectarian and class-conscious attacks against the threat of the 'other', to preserve an ethnic religious nationalism. The 1929 Union brought together the United Free Church (itself the result of a 1900 union between the UPC and the FC) and the Church of Scotland. But the hope that organisational unity would restore the Kirk as a central symbol and reality in Scottish life, had to reckon with the experience of the previous century. It had witnessed the dilution and fragmentation of a coherent presbyterian ethos, and the changing position of women in church and society was one of the factors which challenged the old certainties.

If 1830–1930 was a period of upheaval for Scottish presbyterianism, it was also a time of major debate about, and change in, the role of women. Several of the trends and developments in religous, social and intellectual life during the Victorian and Edwardian eras were of considerable significance for many women, as they were for the Scottish church. In 1830, women in Scotland (along with most men) had no political rights. Their legal and economic status, especially if they were married, was negligible. None had formal access to higher education or professional training. Within the church (apart from some seceder congregations where they could vote in a call) they had no official role, although some were beginning to work as Sabbath School teachers. Their parish church offered no organisations where they could meet, work and enjoy the company of other women.

By 1930, the position of women in Scotland (in theory at least, and in practice for many) had been transformed. After 1928, every woman over twenty-one was entitled to vote. Women had gained new property and matrimonial rights. Universities and professions had been opened up, and new forms of employment were available. These achievements were due to the efforts of a Women's Movement: a 'first wave' of feminism, which most scholars perceive as coming to an end some time between 1920 and 1930.[30] Women also played a much more important and active collective role in church work and affairs, and campaigns had begun to seek official parity in ministry and church government. Especially after the First World

War, there may have been, among many suffrage activists who were also church members, some feeling that the position of women in the churches represented unfinished business for the Movement, and indeed the issue appeared on the agenda of most British Protestant churches during the 1910s and 1920s (see Chapter 4). To be sure, most Scottish women were still excluded (by law, attitudes, circumstances, tradition) from full and equal opportunities in employment, politics and other aspects of life. But during those 100 years, contestation of the 'Woman Question' was high on the cultural agenda of the whole English-speaking Protestant world. And the period was marked by a largely new phenomenon in religious and public life: the self-conscious corporate agency of women. The rise of evangelicalism; the intellectual legacy of the liberal Enlightenment; challenges to doctrinal orthodoxy; the impact of new studies in physical and social sciences; the human consequences of industrial capitalism: all of these impinged on the 'Woman Question' as they did on the churches. It is part of my task to identify and discuss the relationship between women and presbyterianism in Scotland during a period of great change for both, and if possible, to observe features of that interaction which may have been distinctive Scottish expressions of a general cultural movement.

Who Tells the Story? – The Scope and Limitations of Sources

There is a wealth of archive material about women in 19th- and 20th-century Scotland. I have made extensive use of records created by women themselves: minutes of church organisations (at local and national levels), charity organisations, young women's groups, debating societies and campaigning groups; addresses, lectures and letters; magazines and journals written by women in guilds, mission agencies, clubs, colleges, and articles by women in a range of periodicals. I have also referred to autobiographies and memoirs of aristocrats, missionaries, philanthropists, political activists, evangelists, reformers, suffragettes, minister's wives and farmer's wives, doctors, servants and millworkers. These help to tell the story of how women saw themselves, what they believed in, what their hopes and dreams were, what obstructions they confronted, and what they actually did with their lives. There are also official church records of General Assemblies, Committees and Commissions, and the extensive church and local press which was such a feature of the Victorian era. These materials, along with numerous books, pamphlets and tracts published throughout the period, give some indication of the deep and enduring public interest in debating the nature and role of women. They also throw light on the extent to which the church and its representatives either shaped and changed perceptions, or were forced to react to currents and movements.

Analysis of this material is not straightforward. Motive, circumstance, censorship (whether self-imposed or external) and audience all affected what was written, whether it was kept or published, and why. Conversely, these factors also contributed to frustrating gaps and inadequacies in many existing sources; and to the absence of record for many events and people.

For all the variety and contention expressed in discursive writings about women, most comes from the pens of a relatively small number of men and women, during a time when practical literacy was far from universal. Most of them belonged to similar class and demographic groups, and occupied positions of prestige or respectability within the churches. It is very hard to hear the voices of those masses of ordinary women on the receiving end of religious prescription, mission campaigns or charitable activity: and to avoid the trap of pushing them out to the margins of history, where they exist simply as victims or objects. Nor has it been easy to find material by women who were disillusioned enough with church theology and culture to abandon it, and who then wrote about why they did so.[31]

One bias of the sources I have used is a lowland urban one. To generalise about 'Scotland' is no more acceptable than to do the same about 'women' (though I am as guilty of this as anybody). The Highlands and Islands; the North East; the Northern Isles; the Borders – they were all areas with distinctive religious identities and ways of life. Likewise the women in different parts of Scotland often had characteristic work patterns and lifestyles – as, for example, the 'fisher lassies' who were such a feature of the North coast, or the female-dominated workforce of the Dundee jute mills, or the bondagers on lowland farms. Most of the materials I have used emanated from the religious urban elite of Edinburgh and (to a lesser extent) Glasgow. That elite could be just as patronising and prescriptive about folk in rural Scotland as they could about the 'lower classes' of their own cities. I am sorry that in some respects I have acceded to the urban bias, and hope that other studies, based on more substantial local materials, will help to challenge and correct these inadequacies.

The scope of the book is also limited in that it pays little heed to the women who belonged to other faith communities within Scotland – and especially to the growing and notable Scoto-Irish Roman Catholic community. Roman Catholic women had a very distinctive religious and cultural framework, particularly in urban areas where the priest and local parish played such an important role. And these women, in their growing numbers, had to struggle with their identities as Catholics and women in a society where presbyterianism (for all its own dilemmas) was the dominant cultural force. At this stage, as far as I am aware, it simply remains an unconsidered issue, and there is surely a need for work to be done in this area.[32]

'She Struggles All in Vain Against a Divine Appointment': Patriarchy and the Domestic Ideology

The women of Scotland who acted as agents of their own history throughout this period did not do so out of a vacuum. They existed within a society in which religion, the law, political economy and literature all contributed to the promotion of a domestic ideology. Peter Gay, in his interesting study of Victorian aggression, argues that the cult of womanliness and its symbiotic opposite, the cult of manliness, were central to 19th-century bourgeois culture.[33] They both gained force from the domestic ideology which sought to encompass the whole existence of women according to the private realm of home and family, and to their relationships with men. It presented female exclusion from public participation in power and authority as natural and desirable. The evolution of the domestic ideology, and its corollary of separate spheres for women and men, was inextricably linked to the patriarchal model of family life promoted by the reformers, and to the development of liberal political theory. A study of women and presbyterianism would hardly be intelligible without understanding how important, pervasive, and obvious these notions seemed during this period (although they remained subject to controversy and change).

In 1862, a Free Church of Scotland Pastoral Address claimed:

> The institution of the family is so immediately Divine, as to have been from the beginning, destined no less to be to the end, absolutely one – a government unchanged and unchangeable, in all countries and ages of the world.[34]

In fact the government of the family was far from being 'unchanged and unchangeable in all countries and ages' but was subject to considerable variation. The writers could have been excused their ignorance about kinship organisation in the non-Christian world (despite imperial and missionary contacts with other forms of human community), but they might have had a better appreciation of the family's historical development before and since the Reformation. There was, in medieval and early modern Scotland, great diversity in the size and composition of households. During the Middle Ages, large kin groups ruled by feudal lords were the basic organising institution of society, controlling production and distribution of goods. In these patriarchal households, the lords or chiefs ruled over women, children and servants, and engaged in power struggles with one another. Marriages were contracted for economic or political gains, and the women who were thus exchanged were considered to be the property of their patriarchs. Although such households were relatively few in number, they could be very large indeed, and were a real expression of wealth and power. Within ruling families, and certainly among the peasant class, marriage could be a haphazard affair: it might be assumed on the basis of intercourse or conception, or exercised by force, or in many cases it may not have been regularised or acknowledged at all. The church struggled for hundreds of years to assert its role in the institution of marriage, and in wedding ceremonies. In any case, the Catholic Church's teaching, while making marriage a sacrament, also promoted celibacy as the ideal for devout Christians, especially the ruling priestly hierarchy. Women, too, had the option of a virginal conventual life, within which education and work were often available. And despite the severe restrictions imposed, there were some opportunities for married noblewomen to exercise power and influence, especially in the absence of the feudal lord.

The Protestant revolution replaced celibacy with marriage as the ideal condition for the exercise of Christian life, and in Scotland reformers sought to regularise marriage and make it a public event. They also wanted to promote much higher standards of marital conduct, and church courts, especially Kirk Sessions, devoted considerable time and energy to the task of surveillance and punishment for sexual misdemeanours. Adultery in particular was considered a heinous sin and crime. Church discipline was, in theory, even-handed on this matter: against the age-old double standard which expected total fidelity from women, while allowing husbands much greater latitude.[35] But Calvin appealed to the Jewish property basis of patriarchy when he demanded the Levitical sentence of death for adulterous women:

> Not only on account of their immodesty, but also of the disgrace which the woman brings upon her husband, and of the confusion caused by the clandestine admixture of seeds. For what else will remain safe in human society, if licence be given to bring in by stealth the offspring of a stranger? to steal the name which may be given to spurious offspring? and then to transfer to them property taken away from the lawful heirs? It is no wonder, then, that formerly the fidelity of marriage was so sternly asserted on this point.'[36]

All the Protestant reformers agreed that the supreme Christian duty of women was to fulfil, in submission and obedience, the role of wife, mother and housekeeper. The interpretation of Genesis 2–3 as demonstrating Eve's responsibility for the Fall of humankind was central to the enduring presbyterian perception that female subjection was imperative. As an 1840 article in the Relief Church *Christian Journal* put it:

> Had she kept her proper place, and been guided by man, instead of attempting to guide him, the great disaster would not have befallen our race.[37]

By the 19th century, it was a widely accepted protestant convention that the Reformation had been a great benefit to women, because it purified and dignified marriage. Certainly, the hierarchy of human ranks was regarded as a positive blessing, designed to preserve order against the chaos of rule by the weak or dangerous. The Christian ideal for marriage as a kind of loving despotism was based on texts such as Ephesians 5:22–23, which presented the submission of wives to husbands as analogous with the church's relationship to Christ. Mona Caird, in a series of articles published in the *Westminster Review* between 1888 and 1894, was more critical of the Protestant model:

> In breaking the back of the ecclesiastical tyranny, Protestantism undoubtedly did one great service to women, for up to this time, their fate had largely been determined by Canon Law . . . Still, all improvements being allowed for, the woman's position, as established at this epoch, was one of great degradation. She could scarcely claim the status of a separate human being. She was without influence, from the dawn of life to its close, except such spurious kinds as could be stolen or snatched . . . She figured as the legal property of man, the "safeguard against sin", the bearer of children ad infinitum . . . A man might indeed be a tyrant in his own home, in the devout belief that he was doing no more than exercising his just rights, nay, performing his bounden duties as ruler of the household.[38]

In post-Reformation Scotland, the presbyterian church made strenuous efforts to impose patriarchal rule through the combined offices of ecclesiastical and civil authority. For a range of offences, from gossiping and slander, to adultery, harlotry and witchcraft, women in the 16th and 17th centuries were subjected to punishments which were intended to silence, to humiliate, to shame, to demonise and above all to control them for behaviour which was not in keeping with the submission required by the defenders of the faith. Those who committed sexual misdemeanours, or who chose to live on their own and not in a male-headed household, were liable to particular pursuit and censure. This atmosphere of repression, abuse and contempt reached its nadir in the periodic witch hunts of the period. In 1727, the last of thousands of Scottish women was tortured and burned.[39] However, sexual control continued, and women were tragically committing infanticide (as traditional ballads like 'The Cruel Mither' indicate) well into the 18th century. However, the very levels of coercive activity by the church suggest that women were by no means wholly socialised or terrorised into acceptance of religious dictates. Leneman and Mitchison cite evidence that there was widespread adherence to traditional social and sexual customs which subverted presbyterian values, and Boyd suggests that rural laxity in particular continued to concern churchmen throughout the 19th century, by which time their powers of coercion had all but disappeared.[40]

As defenders of presbyterianism itself during the 17th-century struggles, female Covenanters displayed courage, determination and independence. Patriarchal rule was not, apparently, a hindrance to those whose persistence led the Government to decree in 1666 that husbands would be held responsible for the religious sentiments of their wives. One man complained to the Privy Council:

> Many husbands here who yield to the full length are punished by fining, cess and quarter, for their wives' non-obedience, and ye know, Sir, that is hard. There are many wives who will not be commanded by their husbands in lesser things than this.[41]

The behaviour of Scotswomen was, apparently, not amenable to being wholly defined or determined by church-imposed decrees about their role and position. The Protestant Reformation was one element in the dramatic social and political changes leading to the emergence of the modern state, which replaced the feudal household as the main organising institution of society. As mercantilism and early capitalism grew in importance, the significance of the kinship household, and the relation between lord and tenant as focus for economic production was diminished. There was a gradual demarcation of domestic and economic activity. The unitary focus for family and political life was divided and replaced by the political state and the nuclear domestic family. But each of these was rooted in patriarchal kinship, and were inextricably linked.[42]

The 17th-century philosopher John Locke was influential in developing a new ideology for political authority. He replaced competing households with the concept of a unitary state which served with the consent of propertied individuals. The family was removed from the political sphere and became privatised. But women (and unpropertied men) were not granted individual political rights. Locke believed that women were exempt from the 'natural freedom' which pertained to men, and upheld 'the Subjection that is due from a Wife to her Husband'. This is the only instance in Locke's theories of a natural difference justifying domination of one person by another. In fact, his 'social compact' is presented as a contrast with the original patriarchal compact between men and women, whereby wives consented to obey their husbands in return for protection. In both *Treatises*, Locke assumes that the natural condition of women is to be in a family, married and bearing children, for whom they are incapable of providing on their own. The resulting structures of dependence and authority, argues Locke, are created in the state of nature. The husband is in charge because he alone has the ability to control and dispose of property. Locke's main concern is the certainty of paternity and consequent legitimacy of inheritance.[43]

Although Locke was widely read in Scotland, his contractual theories differed from the characteristic philosophies of sentiment and common sense developed by writers of the Scottish Enlightenment.[44] In some respects, their emphasis on good manners, civility and sympathetic relations opened up new possibilities for women in the domestic sphere. For example, Francis Hutcheson argued for marriage as an equal partnership, which would be a training ground for moral conduct in other spheres:

> Hutcheson's insights encouraged British moralists to view the private arena of home and family as something other than a distraction from more important, civic roles. The 'little platoon' of the affectionate family is, in Burke's words, "the first principle (the germ as it were) of public affections. It is the first link in the series by which we proceed towards a love of our country and to mankind." The love between a man and a woman is the first step in the forging of this ethical chain.[45]

However, Hutcheson and also later authors perceived the roles of women and men to be highly differentiated, with the female duty and virtue of sympathy to be cultivated according to the needs and desires of husbands. Social control was to be preserved, and among the things which threatened good order were women who asserted their own rights and wishes instead of practising the art of pleasing others. James Fordyce, an influential minister whose widely read didactic works included *Sermons to Young Women* (1765) and *Character and Conduct of the Female Sex* (1776), described assertive women as 'moral monsters', 'absolute demons' and 'female furies'.[46] As for Adam Smith, his

> emphasis upon self-control and the spectatorial distance . . . caused him to emphasise the virtues of prudence, justice, temperance and fortitude. Though Smith conceded that women were more humane than men, since "Humanity is the virtue of a woman", he did not consider humanity the greatest virtue . . . For Smith, as for Voltaire . . . even a woman of erudition and genius could not overcome the fundamental weaknesses of her sex.[47]

Scotland's greatest Enlightenment philosopher, David Hume, propounded sceptical views about the limits of abstract reason, which might seem to disengage the philosophical connection between maleness and reason, but Hume's own writings confirm that he drew a conventional differentiation between male and female, public and private. He argued that reason must conform to natural propensities, and that it is always motivated by passion. But for the reflective passion of reason to be efficacious, it had to be embodied in a publicly imposed system of 'justice'. For Hume, the individual whose private interests are to be controlled by public justice is the male head of household, while women are associated with the 'private' passions whose satisfaction requires the action of men in the public realm. Women had no absolute claim to the rules of justice, because they were too weak to resist wrong. Only their 'insinuation, address and charms' allowed them to share the rights and privileges of civil society.[48] Steven A. Macleod Burns has also argued that Hume was typical of Enlightenment thinkers in assuming maleness as normative for the 'model human being', while his model female has different and inferior qualities. Chastity is the most distinctive virtue required of women, though scarcely mentioned for men: 'The smallest failure here is sufficient to blast her character'.[49] Once more, the close connections in liberal thought between male identity, legitimate offspring, and economic power are made. For although chastity is of no intrinsic value, it is required so that men can identify their own children:

> Men are induc'd to labour for the maintenance and education of their children, by the persuasion that they are really their own, and therefore tis reasonable, and even necessary, to give them some security in this particular.[50]

So the restraint exercised by women is not primarily a matter of their personal autonomy, but to secure the parental and economic interests of men. This argument resembles Calvin's position on adultery. In general, Hume's references to the nature and situation of women consistently depict them as inferior to men in both mind and body. Although he recognises that the conventional distinction between male and female is unfair to women, who are generally confined to a private realm, and unable to share in the 'artificial virtues', he simply asserts that their political activity would be contrary to common human sentiments.[51]

There was, it seems, a general failure in Enlightenment philosophy to distinguish between making a description and explanation of the inferior status of women, and a justification of that status as morally reasonable. Patriarchal authority was maintained as the male head of the family represented its interests in the public realm. From Rousseau, to Kant and Hegel, the development of the liberal belief in the natural freedom, equality and reason of individuals, who thereby must have public standing, was seriously compromised by the consistent theoretical and practical restriction of 'individual' to 'man'. John Stuart Mill was the only prominent liberal philosopher to challenge this to any degree. Indeed, the Enlightenment project tended to conceive of rationality as the transcendence of those qualities regarded as female: a state of being which was rooted in nature and particularity. This had implications for women in the 19th and 20th centuries who attempted to appeal to the ideal of sexually neutral reason to achieve individual rights, because the cultural paradigm of liberalism had defined itself in opposition to the female, and so had great difficulty in accommodating the notion that women could or should participate in the cultivation or expression of Reason.[52]

In many ways the rigorous orthodoxy of presbyterianism was not amenable to Enlightenment ideas. But the changes wrought by the 1707 Act of Union and the nascent industrial revolution; the emergence of an anglicised urban elite in Scotland's 'Golden Age'; and an evangelical revival which restated many of the 'rational' virtues in religious language, ensured that liberal humanism became a key element in the development of 19th-century politics and culture.[53]

During the 19th century, the function of the patriarchal family, as the main social unit in relation to the state, underwent considerable change, as the concept of individual citizenship took hold. Starting with the First Reform Act of 1832, political rights gradually shifted from belonging to propertied men in their capacity as family heads, towards inhering in autonomous citizens. However, although patriarchy no longer formed the official basis of civil government, the 19th-century Reform Acts were explicit in formalising the continued exclusion of women from political power. And the family remained an important ideological element in modern social democracy. The public sphere of political activity was for men; the private sphere of domestic nurture was for women; and both were under male control.[54]

As in politics, so in economic terms the doctrine of separate spheres developed and was reified in the wake of industrialisation. The rapid growth of factories and towns brought about a partition of economic and domestic labour. Home and workplace were increasingly separated for bourgeois and working-class families, and so were the contractual arrangements for labour. Capitalists employed workers on the basis of hierarchical and exploitative contracts, whereas domestic work (typically and increasingly exclusively performed by women) was subject to private and patriarchal forms of control, including moral exhortation, religious prescription and physical chastisement. In terms of the wage economy, this separation of paid employment and domestic labour inevitably devalued the latter, for it was excluded from the measure by which worth was calculated. Industrial capitalism had a highly ambivalent effect on working-class families. Women and children entered the labour market and contributed to the family economy throughout the period. Indeed, the early exploitation of their toil was an almost disastrous onslaught on the very survival of working-class families. However, at both ideological and practical levels, the division of spheres was increasingly promoted and accepted. Eleanor Gordon writes:

> Home and work were not two separate worlds, and women's participation in the labour market was more extensive than has previously been assumed. But the reality did little to diminish the force of the ideology – whose social origins became obscured so that it appeared as a natural phenomenon.[55]

And Beatrice Gottlieb summarises the evolution of post-1800 domesticity as a process of stripping away:

> The household lost one after another of its functions but the few it retained took on increasing importance, particularly those connected with nurturing, love and recreation. It is a convenient image, though the process was neither so simple nor so mechanical . . . In particular the separation of work from the household is by now a reality for almost everybody . . . There may be something in the often-heard characterisation of domesticity as 'bourgeois', since neither very poor households nor very aristocratic ones found it easy to slough off their multiplicity of functions. But much of the sentiment about domesticity as both private and enjoyable was voiced by aristocrats, and by the middle of the 19th century one of its best known advocates was Queen Victoria herself. The very poor were catapulted into their version of the new domesticity – a household likewise stripped of many functions but not so charming – by becoming industrial workers.'[56]

Among the growing urban middle classes, the tendency to see the home as both analogy and preparation for heaven was promoted to the status of a cult. By the 1830s, they were experiencing the world as chaotic, immoral, distracting. Scotland, with its poverty, squalor and degradation was a political powderkeg.[57] And yet the very wealth and power of the burgeoning bourgeoisie was based upon the exercise of competition, self-interest and aggression in the economic realm. In this confusing and contradictory world, the home was sentimentally characterised as a haven – a calm and loving retreat from anger, fear and alienation. It was a space in which the man was in control, and would have all his needs serviced by a submissive wife and unobtrusive domestic staff. Spacially removed from the industrial workplace and the miserable masses, and enjoying conspicuous new material comforts, the home was worshipped as a place of order, private virtue and spiritual reinforcement. The domestic sphere was abstracted (rhetorically at least) from the harsh public world, and the role of 'Woman' as custodian of Christian values assumed an increasing importance. Middle-class women were, in law, the property of their husbands. Their work was not meant to be economic, but reproductive, emotional and religious. It was supposedly motivated, not by the crass standards of the marketplace, but by the self-sacrificial love which was assumed to be part of 'womanly' nature:

Having confined all those virtues inappropriate within the market or boardroom to the hearts of their womenfolk, middle-class men were then left free to indulge in all those unfortunate vices necessary for successful bourgeois enterprise. The fate of women and Christian selflessness having been thus bound together, the dependency and social powerlessness of the first became the virtual guarantee of the social irrelevance of the second: once God had settled into the parlour, Mammon had free range in public life, and the exclusion of women from virtually all areas of public existence guaranteed that the tidy division was maintained. An ideal of femininity which combined holy love with social subordination not only served to suppress women, it also tamed and contained the anti-capitalist implications of Christian love itself. Domestic Christianity, like domestic womanhood, was the most comfortable kind for bourgeois men to live with.[58]

To conclude this brief consideration of patriarchy and separate spheres, I want simply to highlight the following points which, among others, undermine the claims that such a domesticity was wholly natural and benign.

1. Contrary to the 1862 *Pastoral Letter*, it is apparent that the private family extolled by these churchmen was not universal but simply one historical form of domestic and kinship relations. Nor was it monolithic, for a range of circumstances and expectations radically relativised the experience of family life. As already noted, apart from economic pressures on the rural and urban poor which made the clear division of private and public spheres a largely middle class exercise, there is considerable evidence that there was widespread resistance to, and subversion of, the strict sexual mores of the presbyterian church; that traditional courtship and more relaxed attitudes were prevalent among large sections of the working-class population. It has also been suggested that alongside the harsh – sometimes brutal – exercise of male household authority, there co-existed an informal matriarchy, whereby many strong-willed women exercised considerable power in home and community, while not challenging the broader social structures of patriarchy. In 1936, Willa Muir wrote of her countrywomen:

They carried on their shoulders the whole burden of keeping the race together. The women of the Lowlands, asking and receiving no credit for being women, developed a strength of character and a vitality on which their contentious and cocksure men depended utterly . . . In Scotland, women had less support and showed more individual character than anywhere, I think, in Europe.'[59]

2. Was the home really a refuge, autonomous in all respects from the public world? All the goods and services which provided bourgeois families with their comfortable lifestyle had to be purchased on the open market – including the domestic servants. They were wistfully supposed to be a relic of the old feudal household, but had a habit of failing to conform to their prescribed role as loyal (and cheap) family retainers, and so 'the servant problem' became a subject of endless concern and fascination.[60] And the unpaid work of wives was not just about personal care: they were deeply implicated in the process of socialisation whereby appropriate values were passed on to maintain the ascendancy of the middle and upper classes. For many women, the domestic arena was no refuge, but a space of anxiety or stress or frustration. It could also be a place of fear and violence for women and children. The sentimental idea that home was a hermetically sealed benevolent autocracy, over which the father ruled with reason and kindness, gave strength to the pernicious attitude that whatever went on within the four walls of a household was a private affair, with which neighbours, relations, the church or the state had no right to interfere. The social contract had characterised women as dependents to be protected, rather than as individuals with rights. As Victorian middle classes became somewhat more sensitive about the use of violence to maintain dominance, some measure of public concern was expressed about the apparently horrendous levels of wife-beating. The domestic ideology presented male superiority in terms of self-control and exercise of the will, rather than naked aggression. The debate about wife-beating during the 1870s contrasted these middle-class virtues with the brutality of working-class men. This was connected both with the assumed right to interfere in the private lives of the lower orders, and the contention that such depraved behaviour undermined arguments for the extension of male suffrage. For good male citizens maintained the legitimacy of the patriarchal marriage contract by protection rather than physical force.[61] Those in church circles who condemned the worst excesses of wife abuse as a crime which pervaded and sapped society, associated its committal with working-class drunkenness, usually counselled female silence and patience, and suggested that women were at least in part to blame for failing to fulfil their domestic duties satisfactorily.[62]

There was little public acknowledgement or criticism of male violence taking place in 'respectable' middle- and upper-class families (though it was alluded to in some fictional writing of the time). The domestic ideology, extolling the absolute 'yet very safe and salutary' rule of the man, and the loving helpmeet role of the women, no doubt underpinned many companionate partnerships; but it also concealed the harsh reality of cold, dreary or abusive marriage relationships.[63]

3. The two spheres had common roots in a patriachal model which shaped both private and public realms. Different strands of Calvinist and liberal thought helped generate and maintain the domestic ideology, But Knox's harsh belief that women were morally dangerous and unruly (a venerable Christian tradition) was recast, so that according to the mythology which dominated the 19th-century debate, 'Womanhood' became a potent symbol of righteousness and purity. For in the Victorian age, those 'female' traits which old-style presbyterianism had sought to discipline and control – sensuality, licentiousness, deceitfulness – were now regarded as the aberration, not the essence of True Womanhood. Peter Gay believes that the Victorians, behind the façade of the 'angelic' rhetoric, remained profoundly anxious about the potential danger and depravity of women, who were perceived in paradoxical terms as the 'powerful, weaker sex'. An Edinburgh minister expressed this in a sermon preached in 1892 when he claimed that 'a good woman is a great moral force; a bad woman is an incalculable power for evil'.[64] But the change in emphasis owed much to the evangelical revival which had gained such momentum by the 1830s, and to the developing understanding of mission as divine responsibility for all Christians.

These changes were also deeply affected by related perceptions of class and sexuality. While middle-class women were increasingly characterised as chastely confined within their genteel parlours, and their daughters required chaperones for every conceivable occasion, working-class women were the targets of concern and repression because they still claimed access to public space. In streets and parks and public houses, they were condemned for their crudeness and noise and vitality. This threatening behaviour was associated with the carnality which was denied as a possibility for 'respectable women', and females in public places were often accused of prostitution.[65] The trade in sex apparently reached epic proportions during the Victorian age (especially in Edinburgh and Glasgow) judging by the anxiety expressed in tracts peppered with statistics. It is hard to avoid the conclusion that there was a close connection between the ethos of bourgeois 'purity' and the sale of sex by poor women to middle-class men. Christopher Smout notes the Edinburgh tradition that the Rose Street brothels did their best business during the General Assemblies, though he is no doubt right to caution that this may have been just an 'amusing calumny' about the clergy.[66]

The influences of patriarchy and the domestic ideology were powerful, but not total, in determining the experience of women and men. They were accepted and resisted, transformed and subverted in all kinds of ways by individuals and groups. And the presbyterian church, in its structures and beliefs, provided one of the main arenas in which their domination and validity were tested. In that process women amply demonstrated, in various, sometimes conflicting ways, a capacity for critique and action which made them central, not marginal, to the course of Scottish history. This study is a testament and memorial of them.

Notes

1. S Davies, *Arms and the Girl* (1992) 69–70

2. L M Russell, *Human Liberation in a Feminist Perspective – A Theology* (1974) 85.

3. For methodological approaches to women's history, see e g Joan Kelly, *Women, History and Theory: The Essays of Joan Kelly* (Chicago 1984);L Nicholson, Gender and History (New York 1987); L Nicholson (ed) *Feminism/Postmodernism* (New York 1990);M Boxer and J Quataert, *Connecting Spheres: Women in the Western World, 1500–present* (1987), introduction, 3–17;E Weed (ed) *Coming to Terms: Feminism, Theory, Politics* (1989) especially section 3, 'Writing History', 81–143

4. E Breitenbach and E Gordon, eds, *Out of Bounds: Women in Scottish Society 1800–1945* (1992) 1

5. *Cencrastus* No 46 (Autumn 1993) 3

6. C Larner, *Enemies of God* (1981)

7. L Leneman and R Mitchison, *Sexuality and Social Control* (1989)

8. R Dobash and R Emerson Dobash, *Violence Against Wives: A Case Against the Patriarchy* (1980) 55

9. J D Young, *Women and Popular Struggles* (1985)

10. K Carmichael, 'Protestantism and Gender', in G Walker and T Gallacher (eds) *Sermons and Battle Hymns: Protestant Popular Culture in Modern Scotland* (1990) 226

11. Callum Brown argues persuasively for the enduring cultural significance of presbyterianism for all social classes, and especially for women in Scotland.

See 'Religion and Secularisation' in A Dickson and J H Treble (eds), *People and Society in Scotland* Vol III(1992) and 'Sprouting Wings' in *Out of Bounds* 95ff But there are few published attempts to investigate the connections between the presbyterian church and the lives of women in the modern period. *Women in Scotland: An Annotated Biography* (Women in Scotland Biography Group, 1988) lists only a few descriptive and biographical sources. There are several articles in the *Dictionary of Scottish Church History and Biography* (Edinburgh 1993). See also the chapter by C Brown and J Stephenson in *Out of Bounds* (op cit)

12. D Riley, *Am I That Name? Feminism and the Category of 'Women' in History* (1988) 2–3

13. Challenges to, and critiques of some white feminist writing and practice have come from black womanist writers in North America, and also from Latin, African and Asian perspectives. Much current feminist literature emphasises importance of context and specificity in the experience and reflection of women; and also the interlocking network of oppressions and opportunities.

14. G Rubin, 'The Traffic in Women' in ed R R Reiter, *Toward an Anthropology of Women* (1975)

15. *Out of Bounds* 95

16. R L Smith, 'Moral Transcendence and Moral Space in the Historical Experiences of Women' in *Journal of Feminist Studies in Religion* (Fall 1988) 24

17. M Caird, *The Morality of Marriage* (1897) 207–8

18. Scots Confession of Faith (1560) chap 18, quoted in J MacLeod, *Scottish Theology in Relation to Church History* (2nd edition 1946) 15

19. see A C Cheyne, 'Thoughts on Confessional Subscription' in *Theology in Scotland*, Vol II, 1 (1995) 5ff

20. Published in *Games with Shadows* (1988) 63. A C Cheyne, Ian Henderson, Christopher Harvie and others have made this point. It is one of the main themes of W Storrar's *Scottish Identity: A Christian Vision* (1990) 1976.

22. W Storrar, op cit 192

23. J Calvin, *Institutes* (1536 edition), quoted by J Dempsey Douglass, *Women, Freedom and Calvin* (1986) 46

24. ibid

25. J Knox, 'First Blast of the Trumpet Against the Monstrous Regiment of Women' in M A Breslow (ed) *The Political Writings of John Knox* (1985) 43

26. e g Calvin's interpretation of I Cor 11:4–10; 14:34, and Knox on Romans 16:13. See D Howerda (ed) *Exploring the Heritage of Jean Calvin* (1976); *The*

Place of Women in the Church (1959) Church of Scotland Study Document 29–31

27. 'First Blast' op cit 45–6

28. Calvin felt obliged to write in 1559 to Elizabeth I's secretary, distancing himself from the heated and downright offensive tone of the tract. But although he differed from his colleague in believing that female rulers should be patiently tolerated, he still considered that they were, not just unnatural, but a punishment from God for the wickedness and blindness of men. In defence of his position, Knox cites Aristotle, Cicero, Roman Law, Tertullian, Augustine, Ambrose, Chrysostom, Basil. See W Hazlett, 'Jihad against female infidels and Satan', in *Calvin:Erbe und Auftrag* 1991) ed W van Spijker. On Knox's opinions and relationships with women in personal life, the evidence is mixed. He corresponded with and counselled several, and seemed to have a reasonably high regard for their abilities and spiritual maturity. On the other hand, his unusual household arrangements (he had two very young wives in succession, and was close to his mother-in-law Mrs Bowes) aroused suspicions, and accusations of adultery and incest. His friend Archibald Hamilton referred to Mrs Bowes as Knox's 'concubine'. See John Durkan, 'Scottish Reformers', *Innes Review* XIV 1 (1994) 13ff

29. See S J Brown, *Thomas Chalmers and the Godly Commonwealth in Scotland* (1982); A C Cheyne (ed) *The Practical and the Pious: Essays on Thomas Chalmers* (1985) I Henderson, *Power without Glory* (1967) M Fry and S J Brown (eds) *Scotland in the Age of Disruption* (1993)

30. In Scotland, campaigns for women's rights, especially in politics and education, were underway by the 1860s. Throughout the English-speaking world, women collectively seeking change achieved their most notable victories during the late 19th and early 20th centuries, culminating in the extension of franchise (in Britain 1918 and complete in 1928) to women. Thereafter, most historians note a fragmentation in the women's movement, as different groups identified different priorities in the new political situation. Governments and their cultural allies (including the church) also attempted to reassert the traditional roles and functions of women; to limit and even to reverse some of the gains made before and during the First World War. I discuss this in Chapter 5. Although there is debate about the extent to which the 'feminist agenda' was continued, defeated or abandoned, most writers agree that by 1930 the Women's Movement *per se* had run out of steam. See, e g O Banks, *Faces of Feminism: A Study of Feminism as a Social Movement* (1986); C Bolt, *The Women's Movements in the United States and Britain c1790–1920* (1993); R J Evans, *The Feminists: Women's Emancipation Movements in Europe, America and Australasia 1840–1920* (1979); D Beddoe, *Back to Home and Duty: Women between the Wars 1918–1939* (1989)

31. Two examples of writing by disillusioned women: Helen Crawfurd from Glasgow was an evangelical minister's wife who became an active suffragette, peace crusader, and latterly a communist. Unpublished autobiography (nd) is in the William Gallagher Memorial Library, STUC, Glasgow. Christian Watt, from the North East of Scotland, wrote a remarkable memoir of her eventful and tragic life during her long years as an inmate in a mental hospital. She was of fishing stock married to a seaman and worked as a servant, though there were also more lofty social and family connections. D Fraser (ed) *The Christian Watt Papers* (1983)

32. *The Innes Review*, which is the journal of Catholic history in Scotland, has, to my knowledge, carried no articles about the general situation, concerns, organisations etc of Roman Catholic laywomen, although there are some recent ones about female teachers and their training, and several dealing with women religious. Books about the history of the RC Church in Scotland are similarly neglectful. Social histories are scarcely more enlightening, e g the articles about Scotland in R Swift and S Gilley (eds) *The Irish in the Victorian City* (1985). Dr Mary McHugh in the offices of Glasgow Archdiocese has been helpful, but unable to find many indexed or centrally available sources which would form the basis of such research

33. P Gay, *The Cultivation of Hatred: The Bourgois Experience, Victoria to Freud* (1993), ch 1, 4

34. Acts of the General Assembly of the Free Church of Scotland (1858–63) 489

35. See B Gottlieb, *The Family in the Western World from the Black Death to the Industrial Age* (1993) 99–104

36. J Calvin, Commentaries on Genesis quoted in K Boyd, *Scottish Church Attitudes to Sex, Marriage and the Family 1850–1914* (1980) 6

37. *Christian Journal* (1840) 10

38. M Caird op cit 81

39. For a brief and well-illustrated survey of the methods used to impose patriarchy in post-Reformation Scotland, see E King, *The Hidden History of Glasgow's Women: The Thenew Factor* (1993) 25ff

40. See Boyd, op cit (part one); Leneman and Mitchison, op cit; in an article based on urban sources, 'Acquiescence in and Defiance of Church Discipline in Early Modern Scotland', in *Scottish Church History Society Records* vol XXV, I (1993) 19ff they show there was evasion of discipline in cities too, although also harsh treatment by Kirk Sessions, especially of women, who were less able to avoid the consequences of extra-marital sex; Leah Leneman's most recent research into divorce in Scotland in the 17th, 18th and early 19th centuries offers further evidence of both men and women contravening and subverting the moral standards laid down by the Kirk. See *Alienated*

Affections: The Scottish Experience of Divorce and Separation, 1684–1830 (Edinburgh 1998)

41. quoted in J Anderson, *Ladies of the Covenant* (1857), introduction xxvi

42. For discussion on the common roots of the private and public spheres, see L Nicholson, *Gender and History: The Limits of Social Theory in the Age of the Family* (1986) ch 1,2,5

43. See A Phillips, *Engendering Democracy* (1991) 23ff; L Clark, 'Women and Locke' in L Clark and L Lange (eds) *The Sexism of Social and Political Theory* (1979); *Gender and History* 133–167

44. Barbara Benedict quotes a satire written by William Creech of Edinburgh in 1791: 'I have a wife, Sir, who has contracted a habit much more pernicious to me than the habit of swearing . . . I mean the habit of reading and writing . . . from morning to night she sits poring over some book or other, which may be very entertaining for aught I know, as I make it a rule to look into none of them. But of what use is all this to me? If I set her down to mend my stockings, she is reading Locke upon the Human Understanding . . . ' As Benedict notes, this allusion is to essential reading for the male literati of the time. Her article highlights tensions between aspirations to cultivation and gentility, and concerns about the moral dangers of women extending beyond their traditional spheres, among Edinburgh publishers of the 18th century: 'Service to the Public: William Creech and Sentiment for Sale' in J Dwyer and R B Sher (eds) *Sociability and Society in 18th Century Scotland* (1993)

45. ibid, Introduction by John Dwyer 18

46. ibid 106–108

47. ibid 158

48. see G Lloyd, *The Man of Reason* (2nd ed 1992) 50ff; S A MacLeod Burns, 'The Humean Female'; L Marcil-Lacoste, 'Hume's Method in Moral Reasoning' both in *The Sexism of Social and Political Theory* (op cit). The Hume quotation is from his *Enquiry Concerning the Principles of Morals*. Thomas Reid, the great 'commonsense' philosopher, opposed Hume's view of artificial justice. He believed that it was natural, and the concept of justice was founded upon the awareness of rights which had been violated. However, in making this point, Reid seems to adhere to the assumption that the 'person' who has this rational conception is a man: 'A man may be injured, first in his person; second in his family by robbing him of his children, or in any way injuring those he is bound to protect.' (Works 656); Reid also maintained *contra* Hume that rudeness and civilisation, ignorance and knowledge, were equally 'natural', but that the Family was the one 'Government that can be said to be purely the institution of Nature.' (Manuscripts 3061/6)

49. Hume, Enquiry . . . quoted by Macleod Burns, ibid 54

50. ibid

51. see Marcil-Lacoste, (op cit) 66–8

52. For further reading on the relationships between Enlightenment philosophy, liberal politics, and gender issues, see L M G Clark and L Lange eds, *The Sexism of Social and Political Theory* (1979); S Moller Okin, *Women in Western Political Thought* (1979); G Lloyd, *The Man of Reason: 'Male' and 'Female' in Western Philosophy* (1984); A Phillips, *Engendering Democracy* (1991); *Gender and History* (op cit); *Am I That Name* (op cit); L Anthony and C Witt (eds) *A Mind of Her Own* (1992). J Bethke Elshtain, *Public Man, Private Woman* (1981) presents a case for maintaining the liberal distinctions between private and public, and for avoiding any state intervention in the 'private' realm, whether economic or domestic;see also Sarah Coakley's article, 'Gender and Knowledge in Western Philosophy: The "Man of Reason" and the "Feminine" "Other" in Enlightenment and Romantic Thought' in *Concilium* (1991/6): 'The Special Nature of Women?'

53. On connections between evangelicalism and Enlightenment ideas in Scotland, see N Landsman, 'Presbyterians and Provincial Society: The Evangelical Enlightenment in the West of Scotland 1740–1775', in *Sociability and Society* (op cit); T C Smout, *A History of the Scottish People 1560–1830* (1969) 470–483, assesses the contribution of the changing Scottish religious ethos to the cultural achievements of Scots after 1740; M Fry, *Patronage and Principle* (1987) on the achievements and legacy of Moderatism

54. see Nicholson, op cit

55. E Gordon, 'The Scottish Trade Union Movement, Class and Gender 1850–1914', in *Scottish Labour History Society Records* no 23 (1988).

56. Gottlieb op cit 46

57. See T C Smout, *A Century of the Scottish People 1830–1950* (1986) Chs I, X

58. B Taylor, *Eve and the New Jerusalem: Socialism and Feminism in the 19th century* (1983) 126

59. W Muir, *Mrs Grundy in Scotland* (1936) 109

60. A typical, if anecdotal, comment about 'the servant problem' may be found among the records of the Ladies Edinburgh Debating Society:'In February we took up the question of deterioration of the servants of the day as compared with those of former times, a subject on which we were all qualified to speak. We only regret that no servants were present at the lively discussion, from which they might have taken some useful hints.' Ladies *Edinburgh Magazine* Vol V (1879)

61. See A Clark, 'Humanity or Justice? Wife beating and the law in the 18th and 19th centuries', in C Smart (ed) *Regulating Womanhood: Historical Essays*

on Marriage, Motherhood and Sexuality (1992). J S Mill made the connection between wife abuse, the myth of male protection, and the absence of female suffrage, when he addressed a meeting at the Music Hall, Edinburgh on January 12 1871.(The text is included in a Woman Suffrage scrapbook presented by Helen Baillie to the National Library of Scotland).

62. For example, see the article in *United Presbyterian Magazine* (1879) 33

63. Little work has been done on the history of domestic violence in Scotland. See Dobash and Dobash, op cit,King op cit. Also Frances Power Cobbe's influential article, 'Wife torture in England' in the *Contemporary Review* (April 1878) 55–87

64. see *The Cultivation of Hatred* (op cit) chap 4. The quotation is from Rev Wallace Williamson, sermon preached at a commissioning service for Church of Scotland Deaconesses, October 16 1892.

65. on the connections between female occupation of public space, and accusations of immorality and prostitution, see Littlewood op cit ; L Mahood, *The Magdalenes: Prostitution in the 19th century* (1990)

66. *A Century of the Scottish People* (op cit) 164. On the links between prostitution and the bourgeois 'double standard' of male and female morality, see Mahood (op cit); W Tait, *Magdalenism: an Inquiry into the Extent, Causes and Consequences of Prostitution in Edinburgh* (1842).

2

Woman's Mission and Women's Work

Woman's Mission

We claim for them [women] no less an office than that of instruments (under God) for the regeneration of the world – restorers of God's image in the human soul. Can any of the warmest advocates of the political rights of woman claim or assert for her a more exalted mission – a nobler destiny! That she will best accomplish this mission by moving in the sphere which God and nature have appointed, and not by quitting that sphere for another, it is the object of these pages to prove.'[1]

Thus wrote Sarah Lewis in *Woman's Mission* (1839), a widely read publication which contributed, at the outset of the Victorian era, to the debate about the nature and role of women in the English-speaking world. While many elements of the sexual ideology which Lewis and others extolled were not new, they owed their language and conceptual framework to the evangelical revival which swept through that world from the end of the 18th century. The idea that anyone, far less women, could or should have a 'mission' which might engage them in anything more strenuous than prayer or pious platitude, was fairly novel in presbyterian Scotland. In the Larger Catechism of the 1647 *Westminster Confession* there is only one reference to the subject of mission. The phrase 'Thy Kingdom Come' in the Lord's Prayer is expounded to included a prayer 'that the Gospel may be propogated throughout the whole world, the Jews called and the fullness of the Gentiles brought in'.[2] But this was a theoretical position rather than an active commitment. In 1732 the General Assembly did state that outreach at home and abroad was necessary and good, but that poverty in Scotland precluded such work. During the 18th century there were endeavours to provide Christian instruction to remote communities in the Highlands and Islands, and in 1762 the Society for the Propogation of Christian Knowledge asked the General Assembly to appoint a collection on behalf of its mission to North American Indians. But the institutional church by and large held aloof from official participation in missionary work. Opposing a motion at the 1796 General Assembly of the Church of Scotland, Rev Mr Hamilton of Gladsmuir argued

> To spread abroad the knowledge of the Gospel among barbarous and heathen nations seems to me highly preposterous, in as far as it anticipates, nay as it even reverses the order of nature.'[3]

But it was the enthusiasts, with their call to conversion and action, who increasingly found a receptive audience in a rapidly changing Scotland. Some evangelicals, especially from the skilled working class and emerging middle class, helped to create entirely new churches. Others were involved in a reforming movement within the Church of Scotland. By 1834 the Evangelicals had replaced the Moderate tendency as the dominant expression of Scottish presbyterianism. The new mood, both within and outside the Kirk, presented a dynamic challenge to the complacency and social control of Moderatism. In the first years of the 19th century the evangelical movement was often accused of being a refuge for Jacobin tendencies, intent on fomenting unrest in Scotland. At any rate, their concern for mission indicated the evangelicals' desire for change – and the wave of revival set in train new ideas which deeply affected women as well as others who had traditionally been excluded from an active role in church and State.

The concept of 'Woman's Mission' translated conventional notions of female influence into the proposition that the moral power of women was crucial to the evangelical task, and became a key component in the self-understanding and action of many Scottish churchwomen. It is important, therefore, to understand the context of the evangelical revival in Scotland, and how it affected traditional religious beliefs and practices.

While the impact of revival, and its contribution to the reshaping of church and society, was experienced in particular ways because of Scotland's unique religious, political and cultural heritage, the phenomenon happened throughout the English-speaking Protestant world (and also, in the somewhat different form of pietism, in continental Europe). Post-reformation Scotland had certainly witnessed the religious passion and sectarianism of Covenanters and seceders, but by the time of the Scottish Enlightenment their concerns were diminished in social and intellectual importance. Agricultural developments and the nascent industrial revolution brought a period of expansion, prosperity and fluidity to Scottish society.[4] A growing urban class, based on artisan skills exercised in the *laissez-faire* liberal market expounded by Adam Smith, had increased wealth, leisure and education, and was looking for opportunities to exercise power and influence in public life. It could not do so under the patronage system of the Moderate Established Church, so it is not surprising that this growing social force on the cusp of the middle classes was receptive to the new style of religion which had penetrated England through the efforts of the Wesleys and Whitefield, and had roused America, with which Scotland had many links.

Evangelicalism was a religion of personal commitment and action. Its emphasis was on the saving grace of Christ and the perfectability of the redeemed life, through the exercise of self-discipline and benevolence. It was not much concerned with the doctrinal disputes which had exercised Scotland's leading presbyterians, but it preached the validity and possibility of personal advancement to the individual who sought to overcome sin. It was a creed which owed much to the transposition of Enlightenment values – individualism, autonomy, liberty, benevolence, progress – into a religious mode, supported by Scripture. Revivalist religion was not inherently antipathetic to the need for social and political change. In the earlier years of its influence it inspired reform campaigns at home and abroad which were viewed as dangerous by the political establishment, especially in the wake of the French Revolution. The anti-slavery movement, foreign missions, temperance – these gave political education and practice to groups, including women, which had hitherto not had such involvement. Evangelicalism resonated with the experience and aspirations of the newly prosperous urban classes: both in their private lives, and in their desire for the exercise of authority. Those who responded to its attractions were able to join either dissenting denominations, or the reform party within the Church of Scotland which wanted to abolish patronage. These offered male members structural opportunities for power and status, and promoted ideas about the nature and role of women which were fundamentally conservative, and yet more purposeful, and with greater potential, than those propounded by Knox and his fellow reformers.

At the heart of this new style of revivalist religion was arminianism – the belief that all human beings are sinners, and alike are in need of God's saving grace, which is available to any person who hears the gospel and believes. This was accompanied, in different forms, by a progressive view of redemption, whereby God's saving action would lead finally to the millennium of Christ's reign on earth. It encouraged a sense of dissatisfaction with sinful self and world, but also an enthusiasm to work for the eradication of that sin, in the assurance of God's final victory over evil. The evangelical Christian was encouraged to apprehend a sense of vocation and accept that he or she had a divine duty to act for the sake of the gospel. There was a growing sense of urgency about the need to preach the good news to all before God's judgement. In other words, mission became an obligation.

This was very different from the doctrines of election and predestination which were distinctive elements of Calvinist presbyterianism. An urgent commitment to save souls was difficult to reconcile with the doctrine that God had already elected the redeemed and the reprobate. The pace and extent to which universal atonement replaced predestinarianism in Scotland is a matter of historiographical debate, and many of the prominent evangelical party members (including those who left the established Church at the 1843 Disruption, and others who stayed), remained firm in their scholastic Calvinist orthodoxy. Indeed, they were among the most vigorous opponents of Edward Irving and John MacLeod Campbell, whose advocacy of universal atonement in the early 1830s led to heresy trials and expulsion from the Church of Scotland. But the universalist doctrines which were anathema to men like the theologian William Cunningham, and the Free Church leader Thomas Chalmers, grew in popularity and influence during the middle years of the 19th century. Revivalism was a recurring feature of Victorian protestant life, culminating in the 1873 – 74 campaign of the Americans Dwight Moody and Ira Sankey, which was supported by ministers of many denominations. This made a major and lasting impact, not just on countless individuals, but on the content and style of Scottish church life and mission. As a later strict Calvinist observed, arminian revivalism was a challenge to the 'solid and serious introspection' of the Puritan tradition, and

> Those who were the advocates and fruit of the newer Evangelicalism could scarcely be reckoned upon in the day of battle to stand as champions of the Reformed Tradition.'[5]

Callum Brown argues that evangelicalism was 'not so much a theological system as a framework of response to the emergence of modern urban society'.[6] One of the key elements of that framework was the idea of woman's special mission, and although its working out was influenced by some of the distinctive historical features of Scottish presbyterianism, the idea itself was alien to Calvinist orthodoxy. It is evident that, although denominational allegiance and ecclesiastical politics were important signifiers in the identity of many, the range of beliefs and actions of Scottish churchwomen – especially those of the upwardly mobile and middle classes – were similar in important ways to those of their English and North American counterparts, and to that extent I agree with Brown's assessment that presbyterianism of the industrial period was largely 'a product of evangelicalism of the style and doctrine which took a hold amongst the English Methodists and other nonconformists'.[7]

Many writers have observed that the 19th century witnessed a process of change (long and not absolute) from the bleak rigour of Calvinist dogma towards a Christianity which was at once more sentimental and more aggressive. Domestic piety co-existed with an array of church-based voluntary and philanthropic organisations which utilised the time, money and energy of the middle classes – what the Clapham Sect in England called the 'benevolent empire'. By these means, they expressed both self-determination and religious commitment in the attempt to transform a degenerate and irreligious world in their own respectable image. The evolution of 'Woman's Mission' as part of this process was clearly posited upon the domestic ideology: the 'regeneration of the world' was to be accomplished from within that sphere ordained by God and nature to be the realm of female influence. The evangelical revival revitalised the home and family as locus for religious formation and expression. It was to be the centre for devout and pious life, the daily struggle against the forces of sin and chaos, for virtue and order. The duties of discipline and self-examination were thrust upon the family, as church courts became less able or inclined to exercise their right to public control of morals.[8] And if the patriarch was to be priest for his household, ensuring the practice of daily prayer and worship, the mother had a special duty to instruct children in the precepts of religion, so that what was taught would be 'interwoven gradually with all that is most sweet, sacred, endearing, enduring in the associations of home.'[9]

The moral power invested in women, it was argued, derived from their God-given attributes: love, compassion, self-sacrifice, patience, mildness, purity. In the exercise of these virtues as wives and mothers they were agents of God's redeeming purpose:

> The medium of our intercourse with the heavenly world, the faithful repositories of religious principle, for the benefit both of the present and the rising generation.'[10]

However, this high evaluation of women's moral worth paradoxically required them at all costs to avoid stepping beyond their ordained sphere. Their 'feminine' qualities may have been the Christlike virtues required to make the grimy world a godly place, but they could only fulfil their destiny and mission by remaining anonymous to the world:

> It was the wise intent of Providence in this arrangement to elevate her to the highest point of most excellent worth and influence, to protect her . . . source

of most transforming and benign influence upon the world from all temptation to seek more outward and vulgar forms of honour . . . Hers was to be pre-eminently intrinsic worth, essential honour, the pure moral influence of personal excellence; always unaspiring, modest and delicate, gentle and kind, full of mercy and good fruits.'[11]

Christian women were worthy of adulation in proportion to their willingness to conform to a life of self-abnegation in the service of men. Indeed, by the circular logic of the cult of 'True Womanhood', those who failed to comply were condemned as unnatural and repulsive.[12] An article entitled 'Woman's Work and Mission', published in the 1871 volume of the Free Church *Watchword* magazine argued:

> Ambition, pride, wilfulness or any earthly passion will distort her being. She struggles all in vain against a Divine appointment . . . Woman's worst enemy is he who would cruelly lift her out of her sphere, and would try to reverse the laws of God and nature on her behalf . . . Woman has her sphere and work; and she is only happy when she finds pleasure in lovingly, patiently and faithfully performing the duties and enacting the relations that belong to her as woman.'[13]

'True Womanhood' and 'Woman's Mission' were two sides of the same coin. Their advocates claimed that the former was natural and immutable, and that the latter was the working out, in obedience to God, of the former. But the quantity and content of the literature which appeared especially around the middle decades of the 19th century, suggest that its intention was prescriptive rather than descriptive. Religious writers exhorted their female readership to accept the strange combination of spiritual elevation and social subordination; for the old fear of female capacity for evil and subversion had not been consumed by the new cult, and evangelical woman-worship (like Catholic mariolatry) was reserved for asexual, submissive angels:

> If you are a pure, chaste, noble Christian woman, you will be a blessed central power in the household, mighty to raise all around you . . . If you are base, impure, unchaste, ungodly, your power will be great to pollute and pull down to your own level of degradation.[14]

It is usually the case that apologetic writings appear precisely because a set of ideas or conventions is challenged, in theory or in practice, and this was surely so with the domestic ideology. It was neither as coherent, monolithic nor uncontested as some historians have made it appear. Especially around the 1830s and 1840s, alternative models of women's rights and responsibilities were derived from the Enlightenment, from utopian feminism and from evangelical Christianity itself. The very idea of 'Woman's Sphere' was subject to a range of emphases and uses throughout the period under consideration, even for competing or conflicting goals. What for a relatively small number of women may have been an accurate description of their experience, was for others a goal, a challenge, a judgement, a convention to flout, or an irrelevance. 'Women's work' was a particularly ambiguous component of evangelical dictates. In the private sphere, the work of women was supposedly domestic and religious. It was not renumerated because man was the breadwinner who earned enough in the public domain to support his wife and household. The economic dependence of women was enshrined in the patriarchal system and upheld in law.[15] By the time of Victoria's accession, it was increasingly the case that for women of the upper and middle classes, entrance into paid employment would signify personal disaster and social anathema, and the work which expressed their divine mission – domestic, charitable, voluntary, philanthropic – was acceptable precisely because it was unpaid. However, it depended largely for its clients and goals, on the existence and labour of the mill girls, fisher lassies, domestic servants, working mothers, sweated workers, prostitutes and destitute women whose own precarious and toilsome existence relied on the wage economy which provided bourgeois ladies with their hours of leisure.

A Scotswoman named Marion Reid wrote *A Plea for Women* (1843) as her contribution to the debate about women's rights – of which she claimed that 'there has lately been a good deal of discussion' – and particularly in response to books such as Sarah Lewis's *Woman's Mission*. She was quick to point out that use of the phrase 'woman's sphere' simply begged the question, and enquired sardonically:

> If all woman's duties are to be considered as so strictly domestic, and if God and nature have really so circumscribed her sphere of action – What are we to think of the dreadful depravity of thousands upon thousands of unprotected females, who actually prefer leaving their only proper sphere, and working for their own subsistence – to starvation? Is it not shocking to see their consciences so seared that they are quite unaware of the dreadful nature of the course they are following? Ought not such wicked creatures to be exterminated? Or if we charitably allow them to cover their sins under the strong plea of necessity, what are we to think of that state of society which absolutely forces thousands of unfortunates to contradict their own nature – not by enlightening or enlarging their sphere – but by thrusting them entirely out of it?'[16]

Women's Work

Much of the the industrial revolution in Scotland was instigated and sustained on the basis of female and child labour. A growing body of research demonstrates the reality and extent of female participation in paid employment.[17] Their work was concentrated in low pay and low status jobs. In 1841, domestic service, agriculture, clothing and textiles accounted for 9 per cent of the female workforce, though the balance between these sectors differed markedly according to geographical location.[18] By 1911 that figure had fallen to 65 per cent, largely due to the development of female teaching, nursing and clerical work. In 1839, 41,000 out of 59,000 Scottish textile workers were female, and most of those were teenage girls. As the century went on, increasingly rigid census categories (which themselves reflected the doctrine of separate spheres) excluded from record the large numbers of women – single, married, widowed – who relied on casual and seasonal work. But the 1851 census returns indicated that two million of the six million adult female population of Britain were self-supporting. As an article in the 1859 *Edinburgh Review* declared:

> It has now become false, and ought to be practically admitted to be false – that every woman is supported (as the law supposes) by a father, brother or husband . . . The need and supply of female industry have gone on increasing, while our ideas, language and arrangements have not altered in any corresponding degree.[19]

The census had also shown that 42 per cent of women between the ages of 20 and 40 were single, and that women significantly outnumbered men in the population. In Edinburgh, for example, there were 47,049 men over 20, and 64,638 women. This peculiarly Victorian problem of 'surplus' or 'redundant' women (disproportionately of the genteel classes) was addressed by different arguments. Those involved in the middle class reformist Women's Movement suggested that the logical response was to open up better and more extensive educational and occupational opportunities. In 1872, the editor of *The Attempt*, a magazine of the Ladies Edinburgh Debating Society, noted:

> The remarkable preponderance of female population in Edinburgh revealed by the 1871 Census lends added weight and interest to the gallant struggles of a little band of intrepid women to secure for themselves the means [higher education] of conferring lasting benefits on the whole sex.'[20]

Others suggested mass deportation of women to the colonies, believing that it was evil to endeavour to make women independent of men, to multiply and facilitate their employments; to enable them to earn a separate and ample subsistence by competing with the hardier sex'.[21]

Such attitudes, demonstrating a firm commitment to the view that women should be, as a matter of definition, dependent and bound to the patriarchal household, were ascribed by Harriet Martineau, in the 1859 article already cited, to

The jealousy of men in regard to the industrial independence of women . . . The immediate effect is to pauperise a large number of women who are willing to work for their bread'.[22]

Most women workers endured appalling pay and conditions throughout the period 1830–1930. The overwhelmingly male Trade Union movement was increasingly influenced by the domestic ideology, and rather than fighting for the independence, dignity and equality of female workers, its officials agreed that the place for women was at home, providing services for menfolk. In general, female industrial labour (though not in the traditonal 'female' sectors) was considered to be unfair competition which undercut male wages, and the Unions campaigned for a 'Family Wage' based on the patriarchal notion of the male head and breadwinner for the household.[23] With female wages running at an average of 42 per cent of male rates, in a low-wage economy, the reality for the many women who had to provide for families was grim indeed.

Middle-class women who had to be self-supporting may have been spared the spectre of the poorhouse, but they were a source of embarrassment and anxiety for male relations under pressure to conform to the masculine stereotype as successful and solvent protectors of women. Making a good marriage had to be the ambition of mothers and the aspiration of daughters, and the social stigma of spinsterhood loomed for those who failed. The commercial ethos in Scotland had not always excluded women, married or single, from active involvement. A 19th-century biography described the subject's parentage, and noted (of late 18th-century Edinburgh):

It was customary in those days, among all grades of the mercantile community, for the wife to assist her husband in business; and in the present case she did so, and proved to him a valuable coadjutor.[24]

However, the development of male professionalisation and career structures had, by mid-century, closed off significant female access to work in medicine, commerce and serious education – fields in which women had a historical and honourable role. In the second half of the 19th century, developments in teaching and nursing provided new opportunities for training and employment, but placed women at the bottom of economic and structural hierarchies. Twentieth-century access to jobs in medicine, public service and social work was largely restricted to areas deemed 'suitable' for women, under male control.

And yet, in spite of all the hardship, the monotony, the drudgery of the double burden which was laid upon working-class women, and the genteel poverty of bourgeois women, there is evidence that female employment was not simply driven by sheer economic necessity. The 'mill girl' culture of Dundee, for example, bore testimony to the fact that 'over-dressed, loud, bold-eyed girls' enjoyed the companionship, status and freedom of their lifestyle.[25] Research by Stephenson and Brown suggests that working-class women in the early 20th century enjoyed and celebrated female solidarity in the workplace.[26] In 1914, the Church of Scotland magazine, *Life and Work* reported an address given by a deaconess who worked with some of the itinerant fisher lassies who followed fleets from the north coast of Scotland to Great Yarmouth:

> Miss Rettie said that, looking at the very strenuous life which the girls live, one was tempted to wonder why they chose it, until one remembered what an absolutely independent life it was, and for many girls therein lies the charm. They generally live and work in groups of three, and within very wide limits are allowed to do absolutely what they like. This freedom from all home restraint is one of the reasons why the friendship and advice of ladies, who go with them to the fishings every year, are so needful.[27]

Conversely, there is also evidence that the form of female working-class employment which was most acceptable to Christian philanthropists – domestic service – became increasingly unpopular among those in the job market.[28] And while middle-class employment was sometimes a matter of economic compulsion, arguments in support of opening up professional opportunities more often took the form of pleas for purposeful activity, intellectual challenge and personal autonomy. As the Scottish educationalist Louisa Lumsden claimed:

> Woman, as a human being, has surely the right, and right implies duty, to realise what is best in herself, and to devote the powers so developed to the service of Society.[29]

Lumsden's appeal to the rights language of liberal humanism indicates one direction from which opposition to the domestic ideology came. It was also undermined by the lived experience of so many women for whom private incarceration and financial dependence were never an option: those who worked alongside men in agriculture, in the fishing industry, in hotels and lodgings and pubs. The married women whose homes were in slum tenements, and whose limited personal space spilled out into the communal stairs, water closets, back courts and steamies of urban Scotland.[30] For them, homes and streets were also a source of desperately needed income – through sweated work, hawking, prostitution, charring or taking in laundry. But if the domestic ideology did not stop women from participating in the capitalist economy, it certainly affected attitudes towards, and possibilities for, working women. In Dundee, where the jute industry functioned on the basis of a substantial reversal of assigned male and female economic and social functions, religious concern was expressed in a flood of tracts and books:

> It is obvious that ere long . . . our mills will have none but female operatives, and a few boys . . . A system which is undomesticating the females in our families, and unqualifying them for those home duties, for the discharge of which God has prepared their hearts.[31]

The complex and changing relationship between the domestic role assigned to women, and their 'special mission' in a world where so many of their gender failed to conform to the myth, was deeply affected by the class divisions of the Victorian and Edwardian ages. Gerda Lerner has argued that

> The division of women into "respectable women" who are protected by their men, and "disreputable women" who are out in the street and free to sell their services, has been the basic class division for women. It has marked off the limited privileges of upper-class women against the economic and sexual oppression of lower-class women, and has divided women one from the other.[32]

The implications of this had direct bearing on the development of women's work within the churches. First, the separate spheres doctrine required assent to the principle that it was unwomanly to seek work for personal satisfaction or gain. Since Woman by nature supposedly desired only to be a good wife and mother, she could have no independent ambition, and her labour, as appropriate to the domestic sphere, would be unpaid and voluntary. This affected the style and content of work done by churchwomen, and also attitudes towards remuneration. Second, the doctrine was also the general standard by which most church workers attempted to judge and control the lives of the labouring classes: religious conversion and domestication were the means by which working women might share in the regeneration of Scottish society. Even progressive Christian women whose goal for their own class was equal opportunity preached the primary importance of housekeeping skills for women of the 'industrial classes'.[33] Third, the inherent dynamism of the mission principle, and an increasingly positive assessment of the redeeming power of women, produced tensions for some women who recognised a more liberating potential in the evangelical ethos for themselves and others. They demonstrated that the boundaries between private and public were elastic rather than rigid, and engaged in purposeful activity in a realm which fell between classic definitions of the two spheres, but which was of growing importance in the 19th and 20th centuries – the social. Christian women intervened in the social dimension, not by renouncing their central familial role (whether literal or symbolic), but by arguing that such activity was appropriate precisely because it was an extension of that role.

Women's Mission – Work in the Church

> The service of Christ in His Church, what is it but the permeating of society with that gentleness, sweetness and tact, and that sympathy with all forms of human need and suffering, which is peculiarly woman's own province, and towards which her tender nature turns as naturally as a flower turns to the sun. Her's is a unique and glorious mission; and today more than ever your Saviour and Church are inviting you, my sisters, to arise and fulfil it.[34]

Thus spoke Rev J.F.W. Grant at the 1894 Church of Scotland Woman's Guild Conference in Kirkcaldy. His combination of sentimental idealisation and evangelical fervour was characteristic of the methods adopted by those who exhorted the 'Angel in the House' to become an 'Angel in the World'.[35] If women's sphere was the home, how could they, without damage to themselves and the acceptable order of things, possibly engage with the public, male domain? The answer was not to go beyond their sphere, but simply to exert their 'blessed power' in an entirely womanly extension of domestic virtues into the villages and slums of Scotland by their personal charitable and evangelistic dealings with the poor. Protestants increasingly warmed to the idea that the unpaid protector of the hearth was quite entitled to act as the voluntary guardian of Christian values and the social status quo. From before the turn of the 19th century, individual women – often minister's relatives, or from urban liberal families – had taken it upon themselves to engage in deeds of philanthropy.[36] But the rise of evangelicalism was marked by a deliberate policy of developing agencies designed to tackle the moral and spiritual decay of the nation. The evangelicals believed that the fundamental cause of social disorder was individual sinfulness, and a plethora of educational, charitable and visiting organisations developed, especially from the 1830s to the 1860s, to engage in aggressive home mission work. It was a conscious response to the disturbing and potentially revolutionary dislocation of society.[37] For most Scottish presbyterians, including those artisans and aspiring working-class members who had found a home in the dissenting denominations, it was private morality and respectability, rather than radical political solutions, which were regarded as the means of reforming social ills. The personal seriousness and enthusiasm engendered by evangelical faith encouraged large numbers of lay Christians to believe that involvement in such work was a matter of vocation.

Women were an obvious source of labour for certain elements of this work – partly for the ideological reasons outlined above, but also because their gratuitous time and talents were available in ready supply. The arguments used to justify their involvement demonstrate the flexibility of 'women's sphere', and the fact that models of appropriate female activity varied considerably, even within the bourgeois classes. Evangelical presbyterian writers often criticised the prominent mid-Victorian definition of female gentility and refinement, which portrayed women as decorative and indolent adornments in households where all the real work was done by domestic servants. Such a mode of existence was not acceptable for morally serious Christians:

> Their lives, compared with what they might be, are an almost barren waste, a dead blank on the scale of being . . . laboriously employed in doing nothing. Their health becomes feeble, their spirits droop; they become nervous, peevish, unhappy . . . Let them learn to do all with the utmost fidelity, diligence and despatch; and always before retiring, let them call themselves to strict account for the manner in which they have spent the day.[38]

This 1840 writer lists the activities he believes are appropriate for women – domestic duties; disciplining their minds; cultivating their moral powers and affections; training and educating their children; administering relief to the needy and sympathy to the afflicted; promoting religion by assistance in Sabbath schools; offering prayers and cheering sympathy:

> In a word, securing and sustaining the elevated character and influence requisite to their successful promotion of the noblest, most valuable interests of our existence. Without this . . . they fail to rise to the proper dignity and glory of their sex.[39]

For many bourgeois women, restless and anxious to escape the stultifying confines of their parlours, religious and church work provided an acceptable opportunity to exercise purposeful activity, and gave them some experience of power and control over other people's lives outside their own homes. As the perception of female usefulness became more widespread and acceptable within church circles, there was pressure to participate in certain activities as a matter of convention. A contributor to the 1869 edition of *The Attempt* commented:

> Charity is acknowledged to be a perfectly genteel occupation for a lady. Whether as parish visitor or Sabbath School teacher, she is becomingly and usefully employed in working among the poor. These occupations are unrenumerated, hence their gentility. No matter whether a lady have a vocation for parish visiting or Sabbath School teaching, it is expected she will take her share of one or the other . . . Is it not too often the case, especially with teaching, that the work is carried on in obedience to the expressed wish of society, and for the sake of not appearing singular, rather than from any love of it in itself? Is it not performed by unloving and inefficient hands, from the mistaken idea that it is part of a lady's duty as a member of society?[40]

Whatever the response of individual women, motivation and encouragement to engage in church work was expressed, not in terms of personal development and satisfaction, but of self-giving duty and obligation in response to the saving graces of Christianity:

> To Christ you owe all. He has raised you from darkness and shame, placed you in the light and glory of immortal hopes, and called you to be a fellow-worker with Him. Your true life is not for yourself, but for Him.[41]

In the hundred years from 1830 to 1930, women's work in the presbyterian churches grew from tentative beginnings to become a significant phenomenon in Scottish religious life. Its ideological roots were the cult of domesticity and the domination of the emerging middle classes, and for the most part it remained a conservative bolster for traditional gender and class roles. But the notion and practice of women's mission also contained radical possibilities. It created space and opportunity outwith the home, which many women used creatively to learn new skills, to develop powers of organisation and (sometimes) solidarity. Experience within the churches led the most able and articulate to challenge the auxiliary functions assigned to women, and the whole concept of unquestioned male leadership. In the late 19th and early 20th centuries, voluntary philanthropy was for numerous women a springboard into education, training and employment in public service and social work. The reaction of church authorities to this development was initially one of concern, for they perceived professionalisation as a threat to their belief that women chose to work for love rather than money. Many women, in keeping with the spirit of an age preoccupied with the 'Social Question', challenged the churches' lack of adequate social and political critiques with models for the transformation of the world which were constructed upon intensely optimistic assessments of female qualities and potential. For them, women's work included the exciting new task of engaging, on the basis of their own experience and perspectives on the times, with the scriptural texts and history of their heritage. Some concluded that women's altruistic power should supersede the reign of force imposed for so long by men. They claimed to be a moral vanguard, ushering in a new Christian era of justice and love. A minority saw religion as responsible, not for the elevation of their gender, but for its continuing oppression, and they abandoned their faith.

'Everything Depends on the Lady who Presides' Voluntary Church Work c.1830–1880

By the 1830s, a network of associations and organisations committed to the recently defined home mission work of the presbyterian churches was emerging. City Missions and Bible Societies were among the first to form, and as with foreign mission, the original initiatives were non-denominational. Evangelical members of both Dissenting and Establishment congregations gave their support to such agencies, which took the offer of salvation to the urban masses. It was these organisations which were first to give women the opportunity to share in some co-ordinated way in the work of mission. Female duties were narrowly defined. In 1834, the Edinburgh City Mission Report stated:

> The design of the District Ladies' Association in aid of the Edinburgh City Mission shall be to raise a sum adequate to the support of one or more agents of the ECM.[42]

To that end, the ladies elected a small committee, and appointed collectors, all of whom had an area of the city within which they raised funds. This pattern was repeated by agencies throughout the country, and also by numerous denominational societies which were established for specific purposes: Ladies Associations for Missions to Roman Catholics; in support of Gaelic Schools; for providing Religious Instruction, and so on. In 1845, the Elders' Wives and Daughters Association was founded to collect money for the Church of Scotland Education Scheme:

> It appears to be peculiarly the province of the daughters of elders to assist, as far as in them lies, those schools which are more immediately intended for female instruction . . . [they] should exert themselves to endeavour to supply funds for endowing and maintaining schools of this description.[43]

Such associations were auxiliary bodies. They did have committee and prayer meetings, and sometimes female office-bearers. But they were always under male supervision and direction – they were reactive and supportive, rather than initiatory. And this was as far as many Christians were prepared to go, for

> Every Christian ought to be engaged in the great work of harvest. Some are marked for a more public sphere of labour, and others may labour faithfully in the more retired, but not less useful, path of duty. Among this latter class of Christian labourers may be included the female portion of our community.[44]

But there were opportunities for more direct involvement in philanthropic work directed at females of the labouring classes. The 1845 Home and Foreign Missionary Record of the Church of Scotland carried an account of the Ladies Association for Perth Female School of Industry, which aimed to train destitute girls

> Not only to habits of moral and religious feeling, but to the kind of industrial exertion which will fit them for their future position in life . . . and not, either by dress, food or education, to give them ideas and hopes associated with a higher position.[45]

Perth ladies were responsible for all the preliminary and ongoing arrangements for the School. They visited regularly, supervised the matron, and wrote reports. Similar ladies' committees took on work in female prisons, poorhouses, Magdalen institutions (for the 'rescue' of prostitutes) and other agencies for exercising control over working-class women. Linda Mahood's recent work on the methods adopted by Magdalen institutes for 'fallen women' and reformatories for girls demonstrates that their programmes of moral correction were harsh, if not penal. They were directed at girls and young women whose behaviour defied conventional middle-class ideas of female propriety, and the primary purpose was to inculcate appropriate behaviour through hard domestic labour and Scripture-based education which emphasised personal guilt and sin. Mahood concludes that this approach, combined with systematic attempts to train inmates for domestic service:

> Was part of a larger programme to control their sexual and vocational behaviour, which reflects the desire to impose a middle class social code on working class women.[46]

Some women conducted philanthropy on their own account, without formally instituting a voluntary society. One such was Mrs Blaikie, wife of a Free Church Professor of Divinity. In 1870, after a visit to Canada, the couple decided that emigration of children to work in farms and businesses could be 'a valuable outlet for the disposal of multitudes of children in our large cities who would otherwise be brought up in vice, misery and degradation'.[47] Believing that Edinburgh was already overrun with charities, Mrs Blaikie set up a Home by private subscription. It operated for twenty years, took in 708 children, and sent 301 of them to Canada. It ceased operation when it became increasingly difficult to get parental consent for the practice. The family, whose nature the church pleaded as absolute, was frequently undermined by well-meaning people who were prepared to break up families of drunken or 'unrespectable' parents – sometimes using considerable pressure and bribery. But Mrs Blaikie's scheme was not without its critics, and certainly the douce people of Edinburgh would have recoiled in distaste from scenes such as one at the Caley Station:

> Parents and friends had been invited to bid [the children] goodbye. It was a great mistake, for they made quite a sensation, and created something like a furore by abusing the promoters of emigration. One woman, very drunk, insisted on getting back her little girl and almost dragged her from the railway carriage; and Mrs Blaikie was denounced for stealing the children of honest folk and selling them to foreigners.[48]

In congregations and parishes too, women were increasingly encouraged to give their time to appropriate pastoral and missionary work. In 1850 a third of all Sabbath School teachers were female; by 1880 women teachers were in the majority. In 1830, Mrs Catherine Knox Macnab of Glasgow introduced Mothers Meetings, first to Greenock, then Glasgow, and they quickly became a ubiquitous form of women's churchwork. In 1871 the Church of Scotland's new Life and Work Committee reported that:

> There is abundant testimony to the general employment of Mothers Meetings – usually held in the afternoons. They are superintended by some experienced lady. It begins with singing and prayer, and closes with the reading and explanation of Scripture. In between there is industrial work while a lady reads a book . . . [The meeting] strengthens personal sympathy between rich and poor. Ladies become acquainted with the history and family circumstances of those who assemble, and are enabled to give judicious help to them in bringing up and providing for their children . . . Everything depends on the lady who presides.[49]

Classes were a popular form of Church work. In a country parish:

> Classes for young women are instructed by ladies in sewing, reading and the Bible, and perseveringly countenanced and encouraged by Lady —.[50]

And in a manufacturing town, a minister commended the classes held by ladies for working girls as 'a means of helpful intercourse between millgirls and people of a better culture.'[51]

Accounts of such classes, whether in official reports or in biographies, generally emphasise what was regarded as the peculiarly female ability to win the loyalty and devotion of working-class women. The following letter was written in 1879 by mill girls who attended a class conducted by Eliza Fletcher of Glasgow:

> Our beloved teacher's earnest and persuasive way endears her to everyone, and wins so many. A number have told me they have got far more good from Miss Fletcher than ever they have got from any minister.[52]

Home visiting was a crucial part of the churches' home mission strategy. The pattern of church growth which developed was of a middle-class, prosperous congregation taking responsibility for the spiritual welfare of an impoverished 'mission district'. It became ever more dependent on female volunteers. By the 1870s, according to contemporary reports, male visitors were almost exclusively ministers, theological students and professional lay missionaries. The 1875 Life and Work Report claimed that 'in cities, and generally in all populous parishes, the minister is assisted by ladies who act as district visitors', and gave the example of a city parish which had twenty elders, and 73 lady district visitors.[53]

Where it was possible to form an association of ladies, the common features appear to have been that each woman would visit, on a monthly basis, ten to fifteen families. They would keep extensive notes, and make regular reports on their district, to workers' meetings. Material assistance or relief was generally strictly regulated and restricted. Evangelicals believed in self-reliance, and not in what they considered to be indiscriminate charity. When Professor Archibald Charteris of Edinburgh University took on responsibility for the mission work of Tolbooth Church in Edinburgh's Lawnmarket, he was assisted largely by a team of ladies and the University Missionary Association. His wife kept

> Two large volumes, regular ledgers, in which a certain number of pages were devoted to each family in the district, and reports were carefully engrossed to keep them up to date. All important particulars were condensed and recorded: so that in time the Tolbooth Church possessed a family biography of all the inhabitants, and new visitors had this history to look back upon, and to guide them in their dealings with the people.[54]

But it would be wrong to assume that all female church workers were upper or middle class, even if the values of these social groups tended to shape their endeavours. One minister responded to the Life and Work Committee:

> My assistant has charge of the Parish Mission, but he would be the first to acknowledge that its success is mainly secured by his staff of workers (all ladies). Some few are of recognised social position, but the majority are pious girls and women unknown to 'society'.[55]

By 1884, after fourteen years of gathering information about lay involvement in the parochial work of the Church of Scotland, Professor Charteris, as convener of the Life and Work Committee, could write:

> When one looks clearly at work done by a congregation in aid of the minister, women obviously get most of it to do . . . The duties of elders, as commonly understood, are not exacting . . . yet elders and a few young men who teach in Sunday school are for the most part all the male allies of the minister, whereas the woman-helpers are numerous . . . The Sunday school itself is mainly taught by women . . . The Clothing Society and Mother's Meeting are of course handed over to the female workers . . . The District visiting – hardest, most trying, but most effective of all mission agencies – is as a rule entirely done by the minister and his 'lady visitors'.[56]

While neither the Free Church nor the United Presbyterian Church conducted such extensive surveys of church and mission work on behalf of their national courts, there is plenty of evidence in Congregational Reports and histories, and in memoirs, that women of the Dissenting denominations were at least as involved as their Establishment sisters. Indeed, individuals from these churches, with their greater historical involvement in benevolent and philanthropic causes (e.g. anti-slavery) and evangelical zeal, might have felt more personal and religious motivation for taking up the characteristic forms of congregational and mission work identified by the Life and Work Committee. It would be unhelpful to draw any general conclusions from individual biographies of women who were obviously considered (by family and friends at least) to be in some way unusual or exceptional. But such sketches do offer an interesting insight into their thoughts and beliefs. Agnes Renton (1781–1863), for example, was a member of a prominent Edinburgh Liberal Seceder family. Her daughter became the second wife of Duncan McLaren, who as Lord Provost and MP was a central figure in Victorian Edinburgh. Agnes was deeply interested in political reform and the Voluntary Controversy. She was involved in the Temperance, Anti-Slavery and Peace Movements in the early and mid 19th century. She visited female prisoners and prostitutes for over 30 years, and was well known in the slums of the Grassmarket and Canongate. According to her biography:

Religion obtained an early hold upon her mind, and exerted a powerful interest upon her character and conduct. From the time she distinctly apprehended that salvation is free and complete to the sinner . . . she seems to have had a greater or less measure of peace, and hope, and gratitude and love.[57]

And of her wide-ranging public and charitable work, which appears to have encroached largely on her domestic responsibilities, her son wrote:

Her's was no sentimental, spasmodic, imitative benevolence, begotten of fitful impulse, or fashion, or persuasion of neighbours, or other artificial influence. It was moved by the desire to do good to suffering or indigent fellow-creatures.[58]

Helen Lockhart Gibson (1836–1888) was born into a wealthy Kirkcaldy manufacturing family, which maintained friendships with evangelical families of many denominations. She, too, was brought up in an atmosphere of daily discussion of public and religious questions, and came into contact with the leading lights of the anti-slavery movement. In 1859, under the influence of the visiting American evangelist E.P. Hammond, she committed herself to engage in Christian work, 'to advance the Kingdom of God by faithful dealing with individual souls'. She subsequently ran Sabbath Schools, wrote and distributed tracts, held regular meetings for destitute women and mill-girls, and conducted general visitation in Kirkcaldy (where her husband was minister of Abbotshall Free Church). She also conducted open-air meetings and evangelistic campaigns, and regularly addressed audiences of several hundreds. She later helped form the Free Church Manse Ladies Total Abstinence Society, and served on her local school board. Her basic motivation for her work as, in effect, a full-time evangelist, was expressed in her diary:

Being persuaded that the cause of Christ suffers much from the unfaithfulness of his professed followers to those who are without, I have for some time past endeavoured to speak to all with whom I daily come into contact, about their soul's salvation.[59]

Like Agnes Renton, Helen gave of her personal means to support individuals and religious causes, for:

The offer of the Bread of Life could not be expected to gain acceptance, if, in the first place, no provision were made for the starving and shivering body.[60]

And, in common with other earnest middle-class Christian women, she was optimistic about the consequences of her contacts with those living in poverty:

How blessed indeed it is to have such fellowship with the poor in this world. All distinctions are broken down, when we meet as children of God. I would not give up such intercourse for all the honours this world could afford.[61]

Such accounts certainly give a one-sided view of relationships which were bound to be unequal. And both Agnes Renton and Helen Gibson were nothing if not persistent in their efforts to convert and reform individuals (although Helen Gibson's diary does indicate that some sceptical recipients of her visits and tracts put up spirited resistance). No doubt the clients of many lady visitors resented them as invasive and condescending. But an analysis which criticises their endeavours simply as attempts to secure an obedient, dependent and depoliticised working class does little justice to the convictions, effort, skills and courage of such women. Their understanding of social ills may have been simplistic, but a good number were also aware of the importance of political reform, and were not entirely quietistic in their religious and voluntary work. Mrs Renton and Mrs Gibson were both upbraided for spending too much time and affection on the 'riff-raff' of society – an interest in 'respectable sinners' would have been more becoming. Their strength of character and Christian convictions gave them liberty to act, where they believed duty required it, against the conventions of what was 'seemly' behaviour for a lady, and to risk accusations of eccentricity and singularity. It is difficult to assess the extent to which their actions carried a conscious commitment to extending or defying the bounds of 'woman's sphere', since the framework within which they and others record their stories is evangelical, and not in any way feminist. But Agnes Renton did belong to a milieu which was aware of the women's rights developments out of the radical anti-slavery movement (although she resisted the 'infidel' wing of that movement[62]), and she was the antecedent of women who were deeply involved in the Women's Movement of the late 19th and early 20th century. Helen Gibson, who was quite willing to confront men as well as women in her efforts, was also aware that her public speaking gave her a curiosity value, and that she could be spoken of as a 'female preacher'. But her criterion for success was to welcome whatever increased her opportunities for mission work and conversion. In writing their biographies, the male relatives of both women point to traits of character which were far from the insipid, superficial attractions beloved of so many propagandists of the domestic ideology. In particular, they are honoured for their intellect, courage and energy.

The period c. 1830–1880 witnessed the entry of large numbers of women into voluntary church work as an increasingly important aspect of militant home mission within presbyterianism. The purpose of their work was generally portrayed as a benevolent effort to bring a little of their supposedly heaven-like domestic world to lighten the squalor and indifference of the urban poor. In practice, these endeavours were probably as diverse in their quality as in their effect. The results of their labours no doubt varied from genuine individual conversions and affection, through the provision of some material and leisure benefits, to intrusive moral control – or a combination of all of these. In sociological terms, they contributed to the dominance of an individualistic evangelical liberalism, and to the growing ascendancy of the domestic ideology as an ideal for all classes. But the lives of working women continued to evade such tidy classification, and the philanthropists who were supposedly extending their intrinsically feminine qualities were often anything but gentle, compassionate and self-effacing. Some rather seemed to establish relationships with their clients which, being based on judgement, control, condescension and assumed superiority, reflected the image of traditional male-female relationships. For many who took part in this work, the effort was half-hearted and unreflective. For others, it was a deeply felt personal commitment which broadened horizons and gave real purpose and power to women who were able to exercise a measure of self-motivation and independence in their lives.

'A Potent Force' – Voluntary Church Work c.1880–1930

In 1894, Rev J.F.W. Grant, convener of the Church of Scotland Life and Work sub-committee with special responsibility for the recently inaugurated Woman's Guild, cast his view over changes in the position of women which had occured during the previous generation:

> It is somewhat startling to find that there is hardly a form of manual toil, or any walk of public or private life, where female talent is not heartily honoured, and does not command its deserved success . . . The great mass of woman workers [have] new opportunities of earning their livelihood, and of maintaining their own independence . . . Nor can man any more exclusively speak of himself as 'breadwinner' – three million out of six million women work for subsistence . . . Will these changes, personal emancipations, and all this development of women workers be for good or evil? If result is to be wholly good, must not the industrial and world side of women's work be accompanied and paralleled throughout by a religious movement, by a nobler personal and social ideal within the Church itself? Along with a growing recognition of her in human affairs as the co-equal and co-worker of man, must there not be a more distinct acknowledgement of her mission as an "angel of peace and love, as a power to elevate and purify and save"? Not otherwise can this great modern movement be rescued from the fatal grasp and spirit of mere secularism.[63]

In his address, Grant alludes to two major challenges which directly affected women's church work in the period c.1880–1930. He explicitly refers to the growth of the movement for women's rights – in property, law, education and professions, and politics – which had already achieved some changes in perception about the role of, and opportunities for, women in Britain. Some presbyterians were directly involved in these campaigns, and younger women were beginning to enjoy some of the fruits of their struggles. Universities had finally opened their doors to women, and new job opportunities had developed in teaching, nursing and 'white blouse' occupations. Rigid social conventions and restrictions were not as impregnable as they had once appeared. A spirit of solidarity and confidence, and a sense of achievement, were personal benefits of participation in campaigns. Even women who were not directly involved in the Movement, or who opposed it, acknowledged that horizons were expanding, whether they liked it or not. For numerous women of all classes, church worship and church-based organisations had for long provided the only significant community beyond the domestic domain. That was no longer true: organised religion would now have to compete for the time, talents and means of some of that erstwhile silent majority which it had invariably taken for granted.

Grant links the development of the Women's Movement to contemporary church concern about the encroachment of secularism in society. Dr Corbett, editor of the *United Presbyterian Record*, was more pointed in his 1890 assessment of the progress of 'Women's Rights':

> Many things have happened since first, not many years ago, that portentous expression struck dismay and bewilderment into the sober, sleepy traditionalism that never dreamed there were such things as 'women's wrongs' . . . In many orthodox circles, moreover, The Cause was often branded as radically irreligious. There was, so good Christians thought, a flavour of atheism about the thing . . . Was not this novel claim but one of many signs that the world was in a bad case, that the Bible was losing its authority, and that flood-gates were being opened through which fierce, foul streams would rush to whelm everything in chaos and death? After this the deluge, was the mournful, despairing conclusion of many devout souls, who were sure the end could not be far off when such enormities were to be seen as women in pulpits or on platforms.[64]

Corbett's wry irony captures something of the besieged doubt of church people who felt they were fighting a rearguard action against the second challenge to presbyterianism from the 1880s. After an era of supremacy, the evangelical liberalism which had dominated the Victorian age was under serious attack. Its confident prescription of personal conversion and economic *laissez-faire* individualism had failed to revive Scotland as a godly commonwealth. The country in its advanced industrial state was more complex and divided than ever. Enormous inequalities of wealth and poverty, and associated indicators of the quality of life, were beginning to shake confidence in the divine inexorability of the political and economic order.[65] Aggressive Christianity had substantially failed to raise the 'moral tone' of the nation. The development of social sciences and empirical research was beginning to reveal the systemic extent and depth of poverty, and discredit the long-held view that individual sin and character defects were its primary causes. Helen Crawfurd, as an earnest young woman married to the minister of Brownfield Parish Church in the Anderston slums of Glasgow, began to question the conventional evangelical response:

> To me, it seemed all wrong that the religious people should be so much concerned about heaven and a future life, and so little concerned with the present, where God's creatures were living in slums, many of them owned by the Churches, amidst poverty and disease'.[66]

She was deeply affected by a controversy incited by the opposition of the leading evangelical, Lord Overtoun, to the proposed Sunday opening of the People's Palace. In response, the Labour Leader published a pamphlet by Keir Hardie condemning the hypocrisy of Overtoun, whose employees endured shocking pay and conditions (including Sunday labour) in his Rutherglen chemical works. Crawfurd suggested that the pamphlet 'sowed the seeds of socialism in the minds of many of the youth of the city'.[67] Hardie himself represented many in the labour movement who, although personally connected with evangelical Christianity, were fiercely critical of the patronising cant of the institutional church. Indeed, members of the Independent Labour Party used the conceptual framework of mission and transformation to proselytise for the socialist cause. They believed that they were reclaiming the social agenda which was part of the evangelical Protestant heritage, and which had been largely abandoned by the establishment church.[68]

Many presbyterians, in their new, large and prosperous suburban congregations, simply retreated from these perplexing challenges. According to Callum Brown, they lost whatever interest they had taken in direct home mission work and concentrated on developing the social and leisure aspects of congregational life.[69] Others, especially those with personal experience of life and work in city slums, took the 'Social Question' seriously and struggled to find the theoretical and practical tools for a Christian response. In 1891, for instance, the Church of Scotland Glasgow Presbytery commissioned a report on The Housing of the Poor in Relation to their Social Condition, which took evidence and statistics from a range of sources. This kind of work certainly helped to challenge prevailing religious attitudes, but the Presbytery still perceived the social role of the church in terms of effecting the transformation of defective character:

> It is essentially the function of the Christian church to organise such agencies and to bring to bear such influences as shall move the poor to live decent and clean lives in the decent and clean houses provided for them.[70]

However, the presbyterian churches did respond to the challenge presented by the socialist analysis of injustice and prescription of state intervention, with a significant change in strategy. Utilising recent developments in Biblical studies and theology, a group of ministers – influential, though not in the numerical majority – emphasised the recovery of Old Testament prophecy and commitment to justice, combined with the incarnate love and service of Jesus, to preach a kind of ethical socialism.[71] In practice, they did not countenance class struggle, but felt that it was urgent for the churches to demonstrate loving concern in action, to counter the understandable attractions of secular socialism. Scott Matheson, a United Presbyterian minister from Dumbarton, wrote in 1893:

> [The working classes] have got to think that the Church is on the side of the strong against the weak; of capital against labour; of rich against poor; and they resent being put off with promises of justice and happiness in another world.[72]

From the late 1880s, all the presbyterian churches began to develop a strategy based on the provision of social services. While Callum Brown has argued that this was anti-evangelical, I believe that in fact it signified a recasting of missionary endeavour, which was still firmly rooted in the premise that it was possible to reconstruct both individuals and structures and create a truly Christian civilisation. Indeed, there was a millenarian confidence in the rediscovered category of the Kingdom of God which inspired a revitalised religious fervour among many presbyterians. A simplistic assessment of the relationship between political and religious culture of this period might argue that evangelicalism was essentially private and lacking the dimension of justice, while the new socialist theory was a repudiation of that in favour of public policy and collective action, and that the church responded to the labour movement by abandoning its concern for private conversion in favour of social work and ethical socialism. But to consider the private and public spheres as fixed and autonomous does not aid understanding of the complexity, fluidity and tensions of human beliefs and action. Progressive presbyterians in fact made considerable use of a familialist, rather than a collectivist model to develop their understanding of justice and the role of the State. In this model, women and their 'distinctive gifts' had a key role to play in reproducing 'home' values by intervening in the social dimension. This would, it was believed, help to preserve the influence of religion in Scottish society. Both men and women contributed to developments in the separate spheres doctrine which were in keeping with the times, and yet which were always struggling to cope with the pace of change in social and gender relations. The emergence of more formal structures for women's church work was rooted in the evangelical ideology of a distinctive woman's mission. These structures came to be regarded as an essential element in the new approach to the Social Question. However, their membership and service continued, by and large, to express an attitude towards cultural relations which betrayed the underlying conservatism of the presbyterian churches, and they failed to make much impact beyond the traditional parameters of religious philanthropy.

The Church of Scotland Woman's Guild

Dr Charteris, convener of the Church of Scotland's Life and Work Committee, and Professor of Biblical Criticism at Edinburgh University, was the moving force behind the scheme to develop a national organisation for women's work. In 1885, after fifteen years of assessing the nature and extent of lay involvement in parish life, the Committee was given authority to consider possible ways of recognising and organising work done by members. The 1886 General Assembly agreed to proceed to the formation of a Woman's Guild. Charteris was particularly interested in women's work, but the foundation of the Woman's Guild should be seen in the context of an overall strategy which he promoted to encourage lay service within congregations. The Young Men's Guild was sanctioned in 1881 'to stimulate the spiritual and intellectual life of young men, and encourage them to undertake works of Christian usefulness'.[73] Charteris believed that the consciousness of belonging to a national association would help to stimulate pride and activity in local congregations, where ministers often felt isolated by the lack of practical support from their elders. Many of the same principles informed both the Young Men's and the Woman's Guild. But there was no shortage of traditionalists who were still reluctant to approve of women acting in any but a strictly domestic capacity. Charteris had to work hard to persuade many ministers that his proposed scheme for organised women's work was acceptable. He argued, notably in the 1888

Baird lectures, published in 1905 as *The Church of Christ*, that an adequate theology of the Church as the Body of Christ must encourage the discernment and utilisation of the gifts of all its members, and not just the professional ministry. And he appealed to the New Testament for evidence that female ministries were given official recognition in the apostolic age:

> When therefore I suggest the enrolment of women who are willing workers in Christ's service I have New Testament authority. Why should we not have a Church of Scotland Association of women? Why should it not have a Centre? Branches in every district? Why should it not be an object of honourable ambition to young women to be enrolled in it? And rules and regulations requiring of all who enter it some sufficient proof of their fitness for such work as it implies?[74]

Charteris was particularly concerned that the national Church appeared to be abdicating its mission and service responsibilities to sects and non-denominational organisations – often with a distinctly proletarian ethos, such as the Salvation Army. As a constitutional presbyterian who wished to uphold the prevailing social order, he wanted the Established Church to inspire and direct a spirit of duty among upper- and middle-class women. His sentimental paternalism envisaged a focus for bringing together women of all classes on friendly terms, which would nevertheless present no challenge to social hierarchy. His plan for the Woman's Guild reflected those concerns. In 1887 the organisation was established, and its general object was:

> To unite together all women who are engaged in the service of Christ in connection with the Church, or desire to give help to any practical Christian work in the parish, as well as all who are receiving Christian teaching and looking forward to Christian service.[75]

The Guild was to have three grades. At the bottom of the pyramid were women engaged in congregational and parochial work, for whom Guild membership would introduce co-ordination, official sanction, companionship, and an element of training. No substantially new fields of labour were envisaged:

> In nearly every parish there are practical agencies carried on almost exclusively by women . . . In some parishes, such work is formally organised and superintended by the Session. But it many more cases, ministers see that female work should be further encouraged and approved. Ministers face to face with the misery and poverty of large cities feel this strongly.[76]

The second grade – the Woman-worker's Guild – was to consist of experienced workers not less than twenty-one years of age, to be enrolled by the authority of the Kirk Session, after service of at least three years. This attempt to offer incentive and recognition never really established itself. Certainly by 1897 it had been replaced by a system of awarding diplomas and badges to nominated Guild Leaders within branches.[77]

The apex of Charteris' structure was an order of Deaconesses – women of means who would be able to devote full-time service to the Church. His original plan was that they should be set apart by Presbyteries, but the General Assembly took exception to that, for it seemed to place deaconesses above ruling elders and deacons (who were ordained by Kirk Sessions) in the Church hierarchy. Instead it was decided that the setting apart would be by Kirk Sessions. It was also made clear that the deaconess would be a servant, not an official, and would exercise her office under the authority of the Kirk Session. I shall consider the order of deaconesses later in this chapter, and in Chapter 4.

Thus was born an organisation for women – conceived, approved of and under the supervision of men. It was based on the principle, as Charteris put it, that 'to minister is woman's special function; her ministry is as manifold as life'.[78]

There is scant primary source material for the first few years of the new movement, but apparently the organisation did not impose a unified structural framework on local situations. The leadership wished to emphasise the importance of individual enrolment and commitment. The Life and Work Committee received a report in 1896 that there were 380 branches with around 27,000 members, but expressed concern that many of these did not have membership cards, and that many branches had not returned detailed schedules.[79] There was much early diversity, (probably also confusion and uncertainty) with some branches emerging from already existing groups, and others being established as a result of deputation work (whereby women were appointed to the honorary task of visiting potential and nascent local branches to encourage the movement) and ministerial support. The latter feature was essential, but not always forthcoming, and in 1892 one of the Central Committee members, Rev R. Blair of Cambuslang, used the pages of *Life and Work* to encourage his less enthusiastic colleagues:

> Authorisation [of women's work] is not fully recognised by many ministers and sessions, and the development of work is slower than it would otherwise have been. The Woman's Guild is no unconstitutional movement originated and carried on outside official knowledge – but has the full sanction of our Supreme Court. It is often called the Young Woman's Guild, but it aims at including all the women of the Church . . . A Union in which rich and poor, member and adherent, can come together on common ground.[80]

In 1891, an annual national conference was introduced, as was a Guild Supplement to the *Life and Work* magazine. Both of these were crucial elements in building and sustaining momentum, and gave opportunities for those who felt tentative and uncertain about how to develop their local initiative, to share ideas and experiences with one another. They were also used by the national leadership to shape the general ethos of the emerging movement, and to develop the more intangible qualities of solidarity, purpose and belonging among women. Margaret Anderson, a female missionary in Greenock from 1863–1913, was sent as the West Church's delegate to the 1895 conference, held in Aberdeen, and her account conveys a picture, both of the event itself, and also of characteristic difficulties encountered in trying to establish a local branch of a new national organisation. She describes being given hospitality by a doctor's family in the city, and attending sessions with the eldest daughter. There was a reception given by the City Corporation, welcoming speeches, and a packed public meeting – all of which were addressed by men. Daily prayer meetings were held, and papers read on different topics. One was on 'The cause of lapsing from the Church by servant girls':

> It was a splendid paper and every conceivable cause was mentioned. The presiding lady said, "we have got the disease, now we want the remedy". We waited for a good while and were urged to say something. At last I got up and simply described the formation of the Guild in Greenock. One of the deaconesses came from Edinburgh (Miss Anderson). We had a very nice meeting indeed, tea, singing and a speech from the lady; then about sixty or seventy of us joined the Guild, gave or promised a small yearly subscription, got our membership tickets, put them safely past, and did nothing. We had an idea that all that was expected had been done. Some time after we had another lady from the Deaconess House, Edinburgh, a regular rouser, and she did give us the idle lot a few strong words. She said that every Guild member was expected to work, and every member could do something. We set to in earnest, and at that time we had about three hundred working members. We started to support a bed in the Kalimpong Hospital, work for the Deaconess House, help in the service of praise in the Church, teach in the Sabbath School, visit among the poor, help in the Dorcas Society, and other forms of service beside. We had no lapsing in these days, so I hold that work of some kind that the individual can do is the best preventive for lapsing.[81]

That the essence of the Guild was work, rather than meetings, was an important principle for its founders and promoters. And the work at Greenock West, as described by Margaret Anderson was typical: combining financial support to central Guild schemes at home and abroad, with local mission and service.

By 1900 there were 529 branches with 37,000 members, and eleven provincial councils, which brought together branch delegates for regular meetings with others in their own city or area. In the early years, Dr Charteris' wife, Catherine, was National President, and she also edited the *Life and Work* Woman's Guild Supplement from its introduction in 1891 until 1901. As a national organisation, the Guild was able to draw on and develop the talents of a number of enterprising and articulate women, offering information, encouragement and challenge to the growing numbers who were joining local Guilds. A number of central initiatives and projects were established and supported by the Guild, including Deaconess House (1887), a residential training centre in the run-down Pleasance area of Edinburgh; Deaconess Hospital (1894), which was opened to provide suitable nursing training, and offered free care to church members and others in need; Kalimpong Medical Mission in India (supported also by the Young Men's Guild); and Robertson Orphanage in Musselburgh. These were followed by a Home-House for missionary children (1900); the Guild Temperance Tent (1902), which did the rounds of fairs and shows as a counter-attraction to beer tents; a Guild Cottage (1904) 'where those who had fallen under the bondage of strong drink could be helped and strengthened'; and a Rest Home for deaconesses (1907).[82]

These agencies were supported by Guild branches around the country, and were one effective means of establishing a strong shared identity and sense of common purpose. (Although Guild headquarters occasionally chastised branches which failed to donate to any of the special Guild concerns). Some urban and rural branches also entered into partnership arrangements, which were supposed to foster friendship and practical help across geographical and class divides.

While these initiatives represent an apparently straightforward extension of the domestic concerns which were considered appropriate women's work, the leaders of the Guild were not afraid (within the traditional framework of service) to exhort more conventional or timid members to move beyond what polite society might have considered 'proper'. So Catherine Charteris rallied the 1901 conference with these rousing words:

> A great change has come in our day in the extent of women's power and influence and opportunities . . . There is however a cry on the part of some that it is not good for women, not even good for the causes in which we are interested, that we should come too much to the front. We must not forego opportunities because such an objection is taken, but we can act so as to make it visibly baseless . . . And so, if the sight of the woes of others call any of you to work beyond what have been hitherto the ordinary limits of women's

work . . . you need not fear surely to listen to the voice, nor think that it calls you beyond a woman's province: 'Whatsoever He saith unto you, Do it.'[83]

Such sentiments, however, were not enough to prevent popular impressions forming about the Guild — some of which hardened into conventions and expectations. In 1906, a contributor to the *Supplement* complained:

> Even today, after twenty years, people still imagine the Woman's Guild is a kind of class for young women, chiefly millgirls and shop girls, with a sprinkling of well-to-do elderly ladies as teachers. A more mistaken idea never existed.[84]

That particular stereotype may not have lasted, since by the 1920s the widespread view seemed to be that the Guild was mainly for older women, with girls and young women increasingly choosing to join other organisations, or opting out of church-based groups altogether. But the *Supplement* editor warned of a more enduring problem in the same year:

> There is a danger lest too much energy is absorbed in fundraising . . . We should be careful how we lift all the burden for raising money for parish needs off men's shoulders.[85]

The years of rapid numerical expansion were also those when the Social Question concerned the church, and the Guild did not ignore the issues. In 1908, a year of deep economic recession, the theme of the national conference was 'The Church's Duty to Working Women', and the President, the Hon. Mrs Scott, called for:

> A deeper and more practical interest in the condition of our people, a knowledge of our laws . . . pity for the oppressed and wronged . . . Too long have we shut our eyes to the social evils in our midst . . . Is it not time that we woke up to consideration of these problems and to the subject of social reform?[86]

But while such concern was commendable, the shortcomings of the Guild as a mass movement which could act as an agent for change are evident. The 1908 conference presents a fairly typical scenario for such meetings: an aristocrat with a social conscience addressing a largely middle-class audience about 'working women' — a species which seemed as utterly alien as the more romantic heathens in the foreign mission fields. And the main solutions proposed for their problems were the time-honoured ones beloved of their Victorian predecessors: personal conversion from sin, and improved domestic standards:

> Our most difficult duty to the working woman is to know her . . . our different training blinds us to her difficulties . . . in many there is a lack of awareness of

personal responsibility to God, and of sin as sin. Their ideal of home is sometimes painfully low, and children are in many cases absolutely untrained.[87]

It hardly surprising that such a forum did not propose radical measures for social or economic change. Indeed, the Guild sought to avoid any possibility of developing an image as a broadly political or campaigning movement, and other women's organisations increasingly filled the gap, especially after the First World War.

From the pages of the *Supplement*, and also minute books of individual branches, a pretty consistent picture emerges of the range of activities and concerns adopted by Guilds around Scotland. Reports 'from our branches' in the Supplement tend simply to list Bazaars, sales of work, and other fundraising ventures, and the beneficiaries of such events. Work parties and efforts to raise sums of money for Church schemes at all levels, were predominant. These practical skills, and the range of interests which women supported, should not be underestimated. Apart from their own local and national projects, sums were raised for the general home and foreign mission, and social work schemes of the denomination. Guild subscriptions also contributed largely to the restoration of the sanctuary at Iona Abbey in the first decade of the 20th century. Kirk Sessions did rather quickly form the habit of turning to the Guild for fundraising events, or 'lady collectors' to organise subscriptions, when they needed parish funds. Evidence suggests that many Guild branches actually began when work parties, whose primary object was to raise such funds, decided to affiliate to the Guild. Often it was the Kirk Session alone which had powers to allocate the sums raised, even although they sometimes 'allowed' the women to disburse a due proportion.[88]

Concern for family life and childrearing features in many *Supplement* articles, reflecting the early 20th-century bourgeois obsession with ideal motherhood, and also the reality that these were the primary occupations of many members. The ascription of so many Scottish ills to alcohol abuse issued in temperance work and campaigns – including support for the Local Veto Act (1913), which led to local campaigns during the 1920s, although the Church of Scotland Guild members were not uniformly active or enthusiastic about this cause (see Chapter 5). Lectures, addresses and slide shows tended to focus on foreign mission and temperance themes, although they sometimes dealt with contemporary public issues and the role of women. There were essay competitions on subjects such as 'The Ideal Home' and 'Self-denial', and baking competitions for scones and cakes. There is little indication of ordinary guildswomen engaging in the kind of direct home mission work and aggressive evangelisation which had been encouraged during the 19th century. The impression is rather of a very large group of women of all classes (but in which the leadership and values of upper and middle class dominated) using their resources to provide a network of support for a much smaller number who were directly (and sometimes professionally, as Bible women, Parish Sisters, Deaconesses, female missionaries) involved in work with the poor. Although there was much genuine charitable concern, expressed for instance in gifts of flowers, produce and clothing, and the 'twinning' of country and city branches, the evidence of some articles in the *Supplement* also suggests that some more aware women believed there was widespread ignorance and complacency about the causes of poverty and injustice, which, to be fair, the national leadership did try to counteract at conferences and in the *Supplement*.[89]

The Woman's Guild certainly gave position and opportunity to some aware and able women who attempted to inspire their sisters with a more dynamic and challenging understanding of their role in church and society. However, the lack of adequate or confident leadership was a recurring concern, and at local level, such evidence as there is tends to suggest that a great deal of responsibility for the Guild's success depended on just a few women – and often on the minster's wife in particular. Where ministers were indifferent or antagonistic to the Guild, the women felt the lack of support quite acutely. One guildswoman expressed these grievances in the 1906 *Supplement*:

> There is a want of sympathy with the Woman's Guild which prevails too frequently in the manses of parishes . . . too often a lack of comprehension of the true nature of the Guild, and a consequent lukewarmness about it against which even the most enthusiastic members find it difficult to make headway. We Scotswomen are born with a wholesome reverence for the powers that be, and we cannot bring ourselves to move in any church or parish work without the sanction and sympathy of our minister.[90]

Perhaps the Guild could have done with a healthy dose of irreverence, for the common, and no doubt largely accurate, perception was of the Guild as the repository of traditional female benevolence and usefulness within a male dominated, bourgeois institution.

Questions about the Guild's relation to women's work and struggles were raised more acutely in the wake of the Great War, during which the organisation, as the largest national structure for women, took on enlarged responsibilities at local and national levels. As the war began, the National President suggested avenues of service (like knitting socks for servicemen, and avoiding the temptation to stockpile food or money) and issued a rousing call to unity and service:

So shall we in the Woman's Guild in our National Church of Scotland be doing our part in this hour of anxiety. Let us work, and watch, and pray, assured that the issues of life and death, peace and war are in the hands of Almighty God.[91]

From 1914–1919, the Guild co-ordinated much fundraising and practical support for the war effort. It also established, from June 1918, its own War Work committee, which set up huts and canteens for women in the Service Auxiliaries and munitions factories, in different locations around Scotland. It was keen to do similar work in France, but to the committee's disappointment the War Office failed to provide an opening. There was no expression from the Guild leadership of anything other than full support for military engagement.

Traditional work and meetings of local branches were increasingly disrupted by blackout, high cost of materials, bereavement, voluntary war service at home and abroad. Meanwhile, more and more women were engaged in paid munitions, industrial, transport and agricultural jobs. One consequence of this major change in the lifestyles of so many women, was that the Central Committee of the Guild felt compelled to review its relationship to girls and young women, and in 1916 established a committee to consider this 'with a view to interesting them more fully in the Guild and its activities'.[92] In 1917 the General Assembly accepted the re-organisation of the Guild into two sections: Women's and Girls'. The latter was to be for those aged between fifteen and thirty. Its avowed intention was to attract and hold onto girls and young women who would, it was feared, otherwise remain outwith official church organisation; and to utilise their wartime experience and enthusiasm within the Guild structure. It was to have parallel executive committees, and was encouraged to develop fresh methods of study and service. The Girl's Guild was intended to serve as a training school which would channel able and eager young women into the senior Guild. This new development was a recognition that the traditional ethos and activities of the Guild, based on sewing work parties and fundraising events, were increasingly out of keeping with a new spirit emerging among young women:

> It is plain to all that the outlook for women generally has been immensely widened during the past four years, and that women's influence has never been more powerful outside the home than at present. What is the Woman's Guild doing to lead this to the highest expression? As compared with the time when the Guild was born, women today are living in a new world, and there is an urgent need that this should be reflected in new forms of activity . . . We shall never be right until Christian service on a wide interpretation (including national and social service of all kinds) becomes a chief motive of every woman in the Church.[93]

The process of reconstructing the Guild organisation continued apace throughout the 1920s, under Mary Lamond, who replaced Lady Polwarth as National President in 1920, and remained in post until 1932. Lamond built a career spanning more than thirty years in the service of the Guild: as Supplement editor, Superintendent of Deaconess House, and President. She was the convener of the sub-committee on the constitution, and was the key strategist in reshaping the Guild. The changes were designed to build a truly representative structure based on the distinctive feature of presbyterian churches – the presbytery itself. Provincial Councils were gradually replaced by Presbyterial Councils, which were to meet 'as often as possible' – sometimes monthly, as with presbyteries. Each Council sent one representative to the Guild Central Committee, and that forum, minus its male Life and Work Committee members, became an acting President's Committee, which was responsible for all internal Guild business.[94] Councils were specifically requested to defray travelling expenses, so that members who had to come from a distance would not be dissuaded or disadvantaged. (A kind of voluntary pooling system was later introduced to offset the long-standing privileged position of Edinburgh women). Council office-bearers were not to hold office for more than three years. And a new, simplified membership card was issued, along with a campaign to re-enrol every individual member in both sections of the Guild. The departmental women's work of the church – Temperance, Home Mission Foreign Mission and Jewish Mission – was also brought under the aegis of the Guild, with designated Presbyterial Council representatives serving on each of the national committees. And from 1924, the Guild was given a few places on General Assembly Committees with which women's work was deemed to have some concern.

A conferring committee, comprising leading women members of the the Established Church and the United Free Church, met during the latter years of the 1920s, and agreed to adopt the Woman's Guild as the organisational framework within which women's service should be conducted in the re-united national Church of Scotland. After the Union, by 1930, the Guild had 1176 branches and around 68,000 members, and Lamond was optimistic about the future:

> The inspiration and impetus given by the act of uniting will lead to new enterprises and fresh effort for the remedying of social evils at home and the extension of Christ's Kingdom throughout the world.[95]

No doubt the Guild leadership looked forward to a fresh injection of vigour from the substantial numbers of United Free Church women, who had developed their institutional life in a different way, and had a particular commitment to their much more extensive programme of foreign missions. They would bring significant resources of sagacity and leadership – especially, perhaps, the rather more progressive and dynamic quality to be found in the Women's Missionary College and the Girl's Auxiliary.

The Guild too, from late 1927, had made efforts to counteract a longstanding problem: an apparently chronic lack of adequately trained and confident public speakers, especially at presbytery and branch levels. Schools of Study were conducted on the art and techniques of speaking, with critiques and group discussions. These schools also gave an opportunity for women to consider the various aspects, problems and potential of the Guild. In those settings, as in Central Council, three main interlinked concerns were addressed without coming close to resolution. First, there was the overriding public perception that the Guild's main purpose was to raise church funds – especially through bazaars and sales of work. It was therefore constantly beset by narrow horizons and a weak sense of its spiritual aims and responsibilities, At the same time, work parties, which had been the main (and in many places the sole) manifestation of the Guild's presence at local level, seemed, in the words of one *Supplement* contributor, 'in imminent danger of being pensioned'. The writer continued:

> [The work party] seems to have been the natural outcome of women's desire to help, along their own special line, in days when different avenues of social service had not opened up. Sewing, embroidery and knitting were done, and sold for church funds, thus enabling both service and profit. These arts are no longer so ardently pursued. The rapid growth of 'ready-to-wear' has meant that the home made garment has gracefully retired from the struggle. Many work parties have found no outlet for their goods . . . This has led to discouragement, a refusal to sew, and the end of the work party . . . Many woman's guilds which formerly had no other activity, have tried to compromise. They are reluctant to see the work party go – it is the only thing in which many women can share – but try to meet the demands of young women by introducing a varied programme of winter meetings.[96]

But, as this article suggests, the association of Guild activity with work parties and sales had not endeared the movement to young women. The Girl's Guild had begun as a way of drawing them into the Guild, but its development as a distinctive organisation, with its own leadership, responsibilities and activities, actually had the effect of increasing the stigmatisation of the senior organisation. In 1928 the Central Committee held a special meeting to discuss 'how could it be made easier for girls to pass on from the Girl's Guild to the Woman's Guild when they are thirty', and it was clear to those involved that the older groups seemed singularly unattractive, unwelcoming and dull in their style and activity. While there was some sympathy for 'modern girls' who did not care for sewing, many in the Guild seemed perplexed about what they sometimes criticised as the 'pleasure-loving' spirit of the age.[97]

These concerns should be seen in the wider social and political context of the 1920s. The partial enfranchisement of women from 1918 gave them some measure of direct political power and potential. Both the political establishment, and women's groups themselves, had to assess and respond to the new situation. A recurring fear expressed throughout the suffrage campaign by those of differing political hues, was that women would form a separate party – or at least would tend to cast their votes in a particular direction. Despite early attempts, especially by the Pankhursts, the 'women's party' never materialised as a serious feature of political life, but as Catriona Burness has shown, existing parties did make strenuous efforts to attract female support immediately after enfranchisement. Although the Liberal and Labour parties had, in their different ways, a constitutional commitment to female equality, it was the Unionist Party which was especially vigorous in its efforts to win women's votes. Appeals were made to the 'vital contribution' of women, and to their concerns both as wives and mothers, and as citizens. The party agenda was based on the domestic premise of protecting women and family from the threat of Bolshevism, and as the bed-rock of the British Empire.[98]

Other organisations sprang up to encourage the wider promotion of female citizenship and political awareness. Women Citizens Associations were consciously designed to extend the scope and agenda of the suffrage movement. The Scottish Women's Rural Institute, founded in 1917, grew rapidly, which surprised and even alarmed politicians of this period.[99] Townswomen's Guilds and, within the labour movement, the Women's Co-operative Guild, also offered women a combination of practical and social activity, and political education. All of these, and especially, it seems, the Women's Institute, encroached on the territory the Woman's Guild occupied. *The Story of the Women's Institute Movement* (1925), written by J. W. Robertson Scott, says of the W. I. in Scotland:

> At first we found ourselves very often up against the Kirk. So many of the women had only worked for the Kirk and the parish priests (sic) did not relish them diverting their energies. In one parish the minister, his wife and a small coterie of dames have never been to a SWRI function or meeting . . . I have heard of other parishes where a similar attitude is adopted. On the other hand, I have had the greatest help often from very jolly parish ministers and their wives.[100]

A series of articles in the 1928 *Supplement* tried to show that there was no reason why women should not be members of both. But there was no escaping the fact that the Institute seemed to many rural women a much more lively and imaginative forum for the practice of traditional and new female skills. As Mrs Robertson Scott suggested:

> I find our members are keenest on the Institute because what they learn there is of use to them. They are proud of it. It thereby ranks higher than the Mother's Union, Woman's Guild and others'.[101]

Some effort was made to adapt the Guild to the higher public profile of women, in the first flush of post-1918 enthusiasm. The idea of expanded female citizenship was promoted periodically during the 1920s, at least in the pages of the *Supplement*, to encourage members to take part in the Local Option temperance campaign, and to demonstrate concern about municipal and welfare policies. Speakers on health and child development were particularly endorsed as appropriate for branch meetings. But these headquarters efforts did not seem to bear much fruit, if reports of branch activities, and presidential exhortations are anything to go by. There was little to suggest that many local Guilds were benefiting from injections of new ideas, and much which hinted that the postwar organisation was suffering from grassroots stagnation in leadership and imagination. The Guild's response to industrial unrest of the period was to reprise the old refrain about the duty of Guildswomen to eschew class conflict, and preserve their founder's aims of social harmony. In October 1920 the *Supplement*'s editorial column commented:

> At home a certain proportion of those in the industrial world seem bent on nullifying the sacrifices of their comrades who fell, and on shattering the future of the British Empire . . . Yet we must not lose heart, nor above all, lose faith; God is still in his heaven, and His hand guides the helm . . . Christian people must close up their ranks and work and pray for a better National life, for purer ideals, and worthier standards of work. Especially must the women of the country strive to create kindlier feeling between class and class, and closer trust in the love and power of our great Father. Let our Guildswomen do their part in the struggles of Peace as they have done already in the dark days of War.[102]

This kind of comment belies any simplistic assumption that the Guild maintained political neutrality, and indeed the prevailing tone of its public voice during the 1920s often reflected the domestic and imperial agenda of the Unionist party.

While there were many working-class members of the Woman's Guild, those who were most politically active in the Labour movement would not have found the church organisation a comfortable place – especially if they had tried to air class-conscious socialist views, or (what would have been even further beyond the pale of respectability) to advocate some of the pro-women legislation (e.g. on birth control) which even their male comrades in the Labour Party baulked at. The Women's Co-operative Guild was potentially a more favourable environment for discussion of such concerns, within a framework which in other ways had much in common with the Church Guild.

A discussion at the Central Council meeting held on April 11 1928 suggests that the official non-involvement position adopted by the Guild in relation to contemporary political issues was not uncontested. A letter had been received from the Edinburgh Women Citizen's Association, inviting the Guild to appoint two members to a special committee representing women's organisations. This was to plan a demonstration in the Usher Hall, 'to celebrate the achievements of electoral equality, and to arouse the interest of new voters in their citizenship'. Such an event was surely not particularly controversial, and the Guild itself had promoted good citizenship. However:

> After considerable discussion, on a vote being taken, it was decided by a majority that the Woman's Guild could not accept this invitation which was in connection with objects outwith the purpose for which the Guild exists.[103]

That rather narrow interpretation of the Guild's aims, which excluded the largest Scottish women's organisation from a symbolic and active role in promoting a respectable celebration of female equality in the political sphere, is perhaps indicative of the Guild's failure to develop its potential as a central force in Scottish public life.

By the end of the decade, the Guild retained its numerical supremacy among Scotswomen, but the traditional ethos of uncomplaining service, of older members watching anxiously over the 'welfare' of young women, and of respectful 'friendliness' between working women and their social superiors, was not the best ground upon which to build the movement of the post-Union future. Despite the concern and efforts of Lamond and her colleagues, the Girl's Guild, in its own negotiations, was eager to declare independence from its progenitor through union with the more autonomous Girl's Auxiliary of the United Free Church. And the Guild entered upon church union as a movement which claimed a huge membership, but was struggling to justify itself as a vigorous or creative force in Scottish church life.

As the major lay organisation of the reunited Church, the Woman's Guild was bound to be a significant factor in the ethos and practice of early 20th-century presbyterianism, and its very existence marked a real change in church life from the 1880s. It fulfilled an important function as focus for the social life of thousands of Scotswomen of all classes, urban and rural. But it had to contend with increasing competition from a growing range of women's groups and recreational alternatives, particularly during the 1920s. It was also a channel for the imagination and talents of many able people, who operated both nationally and locally. But evidence suggests that it failed to shift the bulk of its membership beyond a rather conventional understanding of themselves and their responsibilities as Christian women. I doubt whether the limitations of the movement could be blamed entirely on those who exercised national leadership. Most of them had no brief for challenging the fundamental gender divisions to which the Church of Scotland conformed, (although Lamond and some of her cohorts did express support for the ordination of women in the years leading up to Union).[104] But they did have a clear desire to extend the competence, confidence and participation of women within the Church of Scotland. However, the seepage of younger potential members, and the growing pressure on the church to compete for the recreational time of people for whom a greater range of religous and social options were becoming available, presented the movement with a dilemma. The most successful Guild branches were those which adapted themselves to become providers of whist drives, picnics, outings, Café Chantants and other entertainments. The more narrowly religous and paternalistic model for women's service certainly retained a strong hold, but tended to age along with the membership. Yet even by the standards of its founder, Dr Charteris, there was a lack of vision. In 1934, the secretary of the Church of Scotland Home Department described the state of women's work as chaotic, and claimed:

> It has been forgotten that the first intention of the Woman's Guild was to further active service . . . It must resist and disown the estimate of its value to individual congregations as a money making machine . . . it has far greater objectives awaiting its attention, and it can yet save itself by reaching out to these.[105]

The Dissenting Denominations

Prior to 1900, the Free Church and the United Presbyterian Church had no equivalent to the national structure of the Woman's Guild. But at congregational level the same panoply of duties was taken on by networks of individuals and associations – sometimes linked into a co-ordinating body given various designations. Enthusiasts might hire halls to run classes which were specifically evangelical and non-denominational. Others gathered for work, study or recreation as branches of organisations such as the YWCA, Scripture Union, Girls Friendly Society, and the British Women's Temperance Association. But by the 1890s there was a general feeling abroad that the times required better trained and supervised women workers within denominational structures. Dr Corbett, in the 1894 *UP Record*, specifically located the need for such service not just in personal dealings, but in campaigning against the dreadful working conditions of Scotswomen as detailed in a report of the Royal Commission on Labour. His article is a good example of the prophetic but paternalistic tone adopted by social reform Christians of this period:

> Let our women who have leisure undertake the cause of their downtrodden sisters, both young and old, and champion it as they have successfully done other causes, and a change will speedily be effected, another step forward will be taken, not simply in . . . the emancipation of women, but in that all-round amelioration and redemption of humanity which the Gospel of love is designed and destined to achieve.[106]

The United Presbyterian Synod discussed women's churchwork between 1896 and 1898, but was reluctant to suggest the establishment of any new order or department, and contented itself with the suggestion that more definite associations of 'lady visitors' with Kirk Sessions should be encouraged, to 'deal almost exclusively with special classes . . . whose cases the elders might not be able to meet so easily or so skilfully'.[107]

In the Free Church press, Mrs Anna Lendrum wrote in 1897:

> To share in the work has always been open to women – as collectors, Sunday School teachers, missionary workers and district visitors . . . Might there not be in every congregation a number of women who would perform some at least of the duties [associated with the order of deaconesses]? They are often found in city churches, but are needed just as much in smaller towns and in rural districts. At present there is very little systematic visiting by women except to collect money.[108]

The most distinctive women's association in the Free Church was one which reflected its connections in the Highlands and Islands, and the duty towards their impoverished cousins felt by urban lowlanders. The Ladies Highland Association, formed in Edinburgh in 1850 in response to the destitution caused by the potato famine, had as its object 'the improvement of the temporal and spiritual condition of the people, mainly through instruction of the young'.[109] It maintained schools and employed teachers – some of whom also acted as Free Church missionaries, with the hope of going on to become ordained ministers.

The Free Church Committee on the State of Religion and Morals, reporting in 1887, discovered, in connection with women's activities, that YWCA groups were widespread and that congregations in many fishing ports had a 'stranger women's committee, attending to cases of distress and seeking to promote the highest good of women.'[110] Guilds of Women and Ladies Associations were quite common, operating

> to render much help to the minister in the way of visiting the sick and informing him about special needs.[111]

Congregational reports, such as those of the Free College Church, Glasgow, convey an impression of women's work which matches the local picture in other denominations. Each elder's district had a 'lady collector'. There was a Young Women's Guild with an industrial (sewing) section, a literary section and a prayer meeting. In North Woodside Mission District, the work of a Bible-woman/nurse was supported by a ladies visiting and clothing society, which organised a Mothers' Meeting, a Girls' Club, a Young Women's industrial meeting, junior sewing class and cookery class.[112]

There were many in both denominations who believed that the 1900 formation of the United Free Church marked an opportunity for the further development and organisation of women's work. The first General Assembly of the new Church agreed to authorise the establishment of a Women's Home Mission Association. The new movement was inaugurated on May 29 1901, and the *UFC Record* noted:

> A wonderful spirit pervaded the meeting. One felt that a decided step forward was being taken, and that the great power of women's work for women in the Church was becoming conscious of itself and its responsibilities . . . Women can teach, visit, listen, sympathise, weep; and so long as we can do these things, God gives us work to do.[113]

Dissenting presbyterians were concerned about the failures of their home mission work at the close of the 19th century and the seepage of active lay men working in a voluntary capacity. It is not surprising that the new denomination capitalised on a growing general belief that the world was not static, but bound to change and progress. The United Free Church also affirmed the view that women had special qualities which would act as a unifying force in a society which, though divided, comprised (and shared the character of) a collection of human families. The maternal love and compassion of women could, it was claimed, serve not just their immediate families, but the wellbeing of the social fabric and the preservation of religion. There is certainly more than a hint of expediency in Principal Rainy's address to the 1903 public meeting of the UFC Women's Home Mission (WHM):

Perhaps there had been a tendency on the part of women to restrain themselves, or on the part of the Church to restrain them. There were very special reasons in the circumstances in which the Churches were now placed for such work as the Mission undertook being done. They were face to face in this country with the problem that the habits and conventions of religious life seemed, in regard to various classes of the community, to be giving way . . . These were circumstances in which they could not afford to go to work with one hand tied behind their back . . . They required all the gifts which God had given to women in order that as a united Church they might accomplish all that lay before them.[114]

There was more structural variation in the WHM than the Woman's Guild. It centred on Presbytery committees and representatives. They shared ideas and experiences, engaged in some co-ordinated local activity, and reported to the Central Committee. WHM initiatives included work in fishing stations and at fruit farms, and in the rapidly growing Fife mining villages where there was still no formal church presence. During the war, huts for female workers operated at Cromarty and Gretna.[115]

But the emphasis in the yearly WHM reports is on work done by women in congregations, towns and districts – in Sunday Schools, Bible Classes, Bands of Hope, Flower Missions, Dorcas Societies, study circles, New Year Temperance Cafés and the inevitable bazaars. Much effort and comment revolved around the problem of endemic drunkenness, while reports tend to emphasise the quiet, steady, nature of work designed to bring domestic warmth and comfort to bear in many circumstances, and for various client groups. Churchwomen were constantly reminded of the lack of 'home life' in the slums, and exhorted to ensure that the meetings and work they did should aim at the transformation of the home. A speaker at the 1909 Conference summed up the challenge which women's work in both presbyterian denominations accepted as its *raison d'être* when he described the home as 'the root and central problem of our time.'[116] Despite the high levels of involvement in such activities, congregational reports indicate that it was difficult, especially in city areas, to find enough workers for face-to-face visiting. The 1909 WHM National Conference highlighted a visitation scheme in the homes of a 'lower class' district of Dundee, conducted by what were described as 'female elders drawn from the ranks of teachers, domestic servants, clerkesses and that class known as young ladies'.[117] But the 1912 Report for Lansdowne UFC in Glasgow's West End declared:

In our Mission district many families are still without a visitor, and thus opportunities are being missed of interesting these poorer sisters in higher things.[118]

The First World War had a major impact on the range of work available to women, and the levels of responsibility they enjoyed. At local, regional and national levels, churchwomen's organisations became the co-ordinating agencies for much voluntary support and social work. Lansdowne Church WHM committee reported that

> We are to be the official representatives for our district of the national relief Fund, Soldiers and Sailors' Families Association, Health Association, Unemployment of Women Fund, and Invalid School.[119]

And within congregations, female members took on office-bearing responsibility (on a strictly *pro tem* basis, to replace absent male officials) in parish and mission organisations. But even before the War, there is evidence of a growing female solidarity fostered at least in part by organised church work. Within the UFC, the Girls' Auxiliary, founded in 1901 by two young women to promote, within their own generation, an interest in the missions of the Church, soon became a lively forum for those under thirty – young and confident women who felt that the world offered them a future more interesting and substantial than that endured by their mothers and grandmothers (see Chapter 3).

For some women in the UFC especially, there was a growing unwillingness simply to accept the *status quo* in personal life, in church and in the nation. By 1915, some of their frustrations were being expressed in answer to questions raised by a special committee on the Recognition of the Place of Women in the Church's Life and Work. Respondents felt limited in their service for the Church, by lack of representation, responsibility, consultation or control over plans and ideals for which they were asked to labour. They believed that custom, conventional views about the subordination of women, failure to realise the changes in women's position, and misinterpretation of Scripture were among the causes of the Church's denying them 'the capacity to become'.[120]

A new mood was abroad among a significant minority of presbyterian churchwomen, as a 1914 leader in the *UFC Record* recognised:

> The claim of women is now beginning to make itself felt within the Church. Many are restless and dissatisfied with their position, particularly among the younger class . . . They have hitherto been content to do what might be called the drudgery of Church work, and it is universally admitted that they have done it with a self-abnegation, patience and thoroughness beyond praise . . . But apparently the time is coming when they will no longer be satisfied to do this work, fine as it is, without some ampler responsibility than they have at present . . . the assumption is that they will wish some sort of say in the government of the Church.[121]

The churches (both Established and Free) had responded to the perceived challenge of the reformist Women's Movement by developing structures, organisations and attitudes which implied that, without a religious gloss, the growing prominence and freedom of women would be a negative (if not dangerous) influence on society. Women participated in voluntary church work in large numbers, and in traditional spheres of female usefulness. Yet one outcome of these developments, in the context particularly of pre-war suffrage agitation, was a challenge to the low status, and indeed the very concept, of allotted and subordinate spheres (see Chapter 4).

In response to the challenge of the gulf between rich and poor, religious and unchurched, and the clarion call to usher in the Kingdom of God, the busy-ness and competence of churchwomen in certain spheres of activity failed to have more than a palliative impact. Official presbyterian policy moved away from reliance on voluntary efforts of church members towards the provision of social services on a more professional and co-ordinated basis. In 1904, the Church of Scotland's Department of Social Work was established. The full-time employment of women was vital to the success of this new approach to home mission and social work. But although the Women's Movement had pressed, and begun to gain new opportunities for paid work, the churches remained thirled to traditional notions that to receive a salary was somehow rather unladylike. They were hopeful that a spirit of noble sacrifice would motivate those of private means to devote themselves to church work, and it was upon deaconesses, parish sisters and church sisters that this burden of expectation fell.

'Wise, Loving Sisters of the Poor' – Vocation or Profession?

From the 1850s, presbyterian churches began to make use of Biblewomen in their mission districts. These were mainly working-class women – often widows. But the title (which was used well into the 20th century) was subject to no standardisation or control. Individual ministers and sessions simply appointed women to take on a limited range of tasks and responsibilities, with no agreed procedures for selection or conditions. Biblewomen tended to combine, in their visits and meetings, practical sewing, cooking and nursing work, with simple scriptural instruction and encouragement.

Biblewomen were considered useful mainly because they knew, and had easier access to, women and families of their own class. However, by the 1860s, the value of full-time 'lady missionaries' was discussed (the class distinction being significant). In an article about missions among the Edinburgh poor, the 1865 *Home and Foreign Missionary Record* declared:

> In many respects, a woman is better adapted than a man for this work. She has more tact and kindness . . . She must be a lady of more or less refinement, but she must thoroughly realise the universal sisterhood of female humanity . . . Bible-women are mainly useful in so far as they instruct in shaping and sewing at mothers' meetings.[122]

One of the presbyterian concerns about the existence of Biblewomen was that so many were employed by non-denominational societies, and the need for more women of 'good social position and education' was noted in the 1881 digest of the Church of Scotland Life and Work Committee:

> There are gentlewomen in the church who would be glad of such employment . . . There has been a great recent change in the social position of nurses.[123]

The work of Florence Nightingale in transforming the image and social status of nursing, and the example of Pastor Fliedner who had established Kaiserwerth, a renowned training house for deaconesses in Germany, inspired Archibald Charteris with a vision of upper- and middle-class women who would devote their talents and means to full time Christian service 'as the chief object of their life'.[124]

The Order of Deaconesses, founded in 1887 as the apex of the Woman's Guild, was an interesting development for a presbyterian church. Charteris was well aware of the expanded role which a number of women had found within millenarian sects (see Chapter 4), and the contribution of women as helpers during the Moody and Sankey campaign (which he, unlike many of his Church of Scotland colleagues, warmly supported). The novelty of the Salvation Army's 'hallelujah lassies' also made a considerable impact in urban Scotland during the 1880s. Charteris respected the Roman Catholic conventual sisterhoods which the Reformation had so ruthlessly suppressed, but which were recognised for their effective organisation of female service. His committee was anxious to allay any fears that the Church of Scotland Order would countenance the 'evils' of that system[125] but there were undoubtedly ideological and practical similarities. Nevertheless, Deaconess House, the Edinburgh training institution established for probationers, was modelled much more on the Protestant paternalistic household. An upper-class woman, Alice Maxwell, was appointed as Head, but Charteris especially, and other men, fulfilled supervisory duties as benevolent and concerned *pater familias*. In the House, communal and worship life was overlaid by a rigorous programme of lectures, Bible study and training in practical home mission work. Oversight of the Pleasance area of St Cuthbert's parish, with 3000 of the poorest slum residents in Edinburgh, was entrusted to Deaconess House, under the overall direction of Charteris. For the privilege of this exhausting life, residents had to pay £1 a week – and many subsequently worked for a lifetime entirely at their own expense.

For although the new movement recognised the value of training and co-ordination, it remained rooted in the old ideology of women's work. The life of a deaconess, though it did not call for lifelong vows, had the character of a celibate religious vocation, and not a profession. Flora Blair of Cambuslang, in an 1892 *Life and Work* article, alludes to the perceived connection between this and their essentially conservative social role:

> The truth is, our Christianity has not kept pace with the population. The 'lapsed masses' are simply the 'abandoned classes' . . . What we need here, and what the deaconess has to give, is her religion of love; for it is only by living the true Christian life alongside the poor, ignorant and sorrowing in this world, that they will believe her about the next . . . That ladies of culture and position and intellectual power under the seal of the diaconate, should be willing to throw themselves into the work of bridging the deep social gulf, is one of the best signs of promise for the expansion of Christianity, for linking East and West Ends, and for the continued stability of the Church of Scotland.[126]

It must be said that the order did not fulfil that promise. The primary intention was that ladies of private means would work in areas of poverty. But the small number of women who elected to train as deaconesses chose a diversity of avenues in which to fulfil their calling. Some were unwilling to submit themselves to ministers and sessions, and found freedom and purpose in non-parochial training, administration and deputation work for the Woman's Guild. Others went abroad to serve as missionaries. They were seizing the first opportunity, however inadequate, to discharge official power as churchwomen, and exercised choice and initiative in doing so. Indeed, constructing the edifice of organised women's work depended to a large extent on a handful of deaconesses who occupied key positions in the early years of the Guild movement. The combination of class background, ability and (in some cases) previous education and experience of such women did not lend itself to the rise of a mass movement of unsalaried dedicated slum workers. There may have been women from less wealthy backgrounds willing to do the work, for a salary, but the areas which needed them most could not afford to pay for them.

So in 1893, the Home Mission Committee, at the recommendation of the Committee on the Religious Condition of the People, formed a new association to provide central funding and organisation for female missionaries. But even this new initiative hoped that it would get something for nothing:

> All who have worked in the poor parts of towns or mining districts must know what an incalculable blessing the help and presence of a good kind woman is . . . quietly guiding people to help themselves instead of expecting help from others. The Women's Association for Home Mission (WAHM) has been formed to employ women more generally in ministering to the poor of Scotland. Agents may be trained or not . . . [we] trust that many ladies will come forward who will require and demand no renumeration.[127]

And from 1905, the United Free Church, (which probably had more Biblewomen employed by individual congregations than the Established Church) had on its agenda the need to train, recognise and offer employment to women workers in mission and social service, arguing that:

> The Social Problem makes its appeal with peculiar force to women rich in spiritual experience, of ripe attainments in the apprehension of the Gospel message, and with ample knowledge of the conditions under which women and children of the slum population live, and calls them to consecrate their gifts and education to the service of the suffering, sorrowing and sinful'[128]

In 1916, the UFC regularised the training and employment of such workers, giving them official recognition and the title of Church Sister.

But in both denominations the central resources allocated to the development of women's work were never adequate to meet the needs and requests of poor parishes. Women from poorer working- (and also middle-)class backgrounds were largely denied the opportunity to take up training and employment,[129] while ministers continued wistfully to bemoan the ruling class refusal of vocation:

> The [United Free] Church has now responded fully to the call made to open up spheres for women's work . . . It was encouraged to think that there would be forthcoming ladies of means and leisure who would be glad to prepare for, and devote their lives as a calling, to work like this in definite spheres, at their own expense. That class has not come forward . . . This is a disappointment.[130]

By 1930 in the re-united Church of Scotland, there were 53 Parish Sisters (ex-WAHM) and 60 Church Sisters (ex-UFC). Although some of the 62 deaconesses served as supervisory and field staff for Woman's Guild projects, many in fact worked as Parish Sisters. Others were employed by the Church of Scotland's Social Work Scheme, set up in 1904. They ran institutions to extend 'an understanding hand towards helpless and hapless womanhood'.[131]

According to the rhetoric which poured out in praise of these women, in sermons and addresses; reports and magazines, they exemplified the height and glory of female service to God and His Kingdom. Theirs was an exalted calling. But if that was so, why did such a small number seize the opportunity? Perhaps the expectations of the Church were increasingly at odds with those of women themselves.

The whole edifice of female work was built on the paradox of woman's mission as self-immolation, for 'the power of absolute self-devotion is a gift given especially to women'.[132] Their lives would be ones 'of unselfish giving, not of self-seeking';[133] and their influence would be felt in 'sweetening, consoling, brightening and elevating lives that are often crushed under sore burdens'.[134] The models for this lifestyle were Jesus himself, and especially the women of the gospels. Mary was rescued from her fallen state as the object of Roman idolatry, and became worthy of emulation:

> As Mary, most honoured of women, lived a life of obscurity and sacrifice, we remember the strange fact that she was not present when Christ broke bread . . . But she is with him at the last when, abandoned by his own . . . he bows his head . . . To minister in affliction was the service left for women – the last, highest and best. In this lies the glory of the deaconess.[135]

The Christian glorification of female self-sacrifice was, in the second half of the 19th century, supported (and for many people, supplanted) by the Social Darwinism of contemporary evolutionary theory which made it ever more difficult to counter 'the saturating influence of primary maleness or femaleness'.[136] Scientists – who were becoming the new arbiters of orthodoxy – argued that the full development of the human species was based on the extreme specialisations in the functions of men and women. Many writers, of whom perhaps Herbert Spencer was the most influential, raided Darwin's theories in order to draw crude parallels between biological and social systems and structures. Spencer suggested that the psychological differences between the sexes had evolved to fit men and women for the roles they played in society. In fact, Spencer's attempt to justify separate spheres as a natural and progressive development, was based on circular reasoning. He assumed, on the premise of his own cultural experience of Anglo-saxon race, class and gender roles, what he was trying to prove – that biological fitness for respective parental functions implies radical differences between the sexes. Spencer invented one phrase which encapsulated the immense popularity and ubiquity of Social Darwinism as an expression of late Victorian and Edwardian social, political, economic and imperial ideology. He used Malthus' theory of population to argue that

> The pressure of population on the means of subsistence would lead to perfect adaptation to the conditions of existence, and to the survival of the fittest.[137]

Early formulations of biological determinism proposed that women were simply vehicles for reproduction, and on a lower evolutionary level than men. Later, as social concern was expressed in eugenic terms about quality of the race, there was a more positive evaluation of the essence of 'Woman' as 'Maternity'. Professor Henry Drummond, the Free Church populariser of Darwinism, claimed in 1889:

> It is in the endless and infinite self-sacrifices of Maternity that Altruism finds its main expression . . . All that is moral and social and other-regarding has come along the line of self-sacrifice.[138]

Even as Scriptural injunctions about the subordinate role and function of women were being challenged in the light of higher Biblical criticism, supposedly scientific theories of sex differentiation exercised immense influence. These somehow conflated the old view about the unchanging, divinely ordained nature of womanhood, with the new idea that organic change from homogeneity to heterogeneity guaranteed social progress. So, anti-feminists maintained, the Women's Movement was actually retrogressive in its efforts to secure equal opportunities, and was doomed to failure. Scottish writers Patrick Geddes and J Arthur Thomson confidently pronounced 'What was decided among prehistoric protozoa cannot be annulled by Act of Parliament'.[139]

However, many women did not attempt to refute the fashionable theories of the day, but instead seized upon a positive evaluation of the nobility and superiority of their distinctive maternal qualities as the means by which social and political, as well as domestic and religious life could be transformed. The idea of Spiritual or Philanthropic Motherhood, combined with a progressive, future-directed model of the Human Race reaching its evolutionary and religious apotheosis in a Golden Age, offered women a powerful self-image as potential saviours of a corrupt and outworn order.[140] One Edinburgh presbyterian woman claimed in the aftermath of the Great War, and in anticipation of her newly acquired citizenship:

> The most potent force of the future in recasting the moulds of civilisation, is the expansive power of woman's idealising instinct . . . If the free course of her spirit be not obstructed, there is no limit to the possibilities which this power could accomplish, even in the lifetime of those who are babes among us now.[141]

So women were not necessarily unhappy with the rhetoric of distinctive vocation, nor with being called to emulate both Jesus Christ himself, and the women of the New Testament. Recent theological interest in the Incarnation and Christology had highlighted Jesus' radical acceptance of female friendship, worth and discipleship.

But the lives of too many deaconesses and sisters bore little relation to the florid paeans of praise. Instead, their experience was characterised by isolation, genteel poverty, exhaustion and breakdown. Women of intellectual, practical and spiritual capacity discovered that their position in the church was restricted, subordinate, far removed from decision-making. The framework of vocation in fact concealed the reality of exploitation and marginalisation for women through whom the church vicariously expressed the courage and compassion of the gospel. With scant resources or authority, and little useful support, they often provided the only meaningful point of contact between the urban poor and the presbyterian church. Those who depended on the work for their livelihood received a salary which was

> Utterly inadequate to provide lodging, food, clothes . . . and insufficient to prevent anxiety from shadowing these faithful women and from depressing their brave hearts . . . The Church must wipe away the reproach of being a party to sweated labour.[142]

Such conditions were hardly designed to attract able young women whose expectations and opportunities had improved considerably since the 1880s, and especially those with degrees and access to professions. Attitudes towards the recognition and evaluation of women's work were changing. Even that archetypal angel of mercy and dogsbody, the minister's wife, felt able to express a grievance. One shared this story in the 1906 Guild *Supplement*:

> The minister has an easy time compared to his wife, who has to bear the double burden of parochial work and home duties . . . I heard of an old man complaining to a lady of the minister's wife. The lady listened, and then enquired what salary she received – 'Salary? It's the meenister's wife I'm speaking o" – 'So am I – I thought you probably paid her a salary, and so had a right to grumble she was not earning it!'[143]

The churches were slow to recognise the reality that they were in competition for the full-time trained services of women. At first, they tended to criticise professional women in secular philanthropy for being hard and mercenary – lacking the graces which they fondly believed were a feature of the old amateurism. And they appealed to women's absolute obligation to reciprocate for the emancipation which Christianity had secured their benighted sex, by giving their all for the sake of the Church. But as jobs in social work, medicine and public services opened up with the growth of State welfare, and extended especially during the war years, the threat began to dawn:

> The Church should take into serious consideration the fact that there is a tendency among able Christian women to seek opportunities of service in public and philanthropic activities because they find in such forms of service larger scope for the exercise of their special gifts and qualities.[144]

In the early years of professional education and employment for women, most opportunities were predicated on the tenacity of the domestic ideology. Career structures and the nature of work available for men and women respectively were patriarchally determined. The increasing prestige and specialisation available to men depended, especially in teaching, medicine and office-based employment, on recruiting a large workforce of subordinate, 'hands on' women without access to proper career development, equal pay, or to top decision-making positions. The Church mirrored and accentuated this pattern, with its ambivalence about the professional status, and potential threat, of deaconesses and sisters. Its theology of women's ministry underpinned a gender hierarchy in which the subservience of female workers to male ministers and Sessions was institutionalised. So the United Free Church Moderator of the UFC told new Church Sisters in 1917,

> This, we are told, is an age in which work is passing into the hands of women . . . But I should like to remind you and this House that you are not being called to take the place of men or to do the work for which men cannot be found.[145]

Increasing numbers of theologically literate and competent women must have agreed with Elizabeth Hewat (who in 1926 graduated in divinity from New College, Edinburgh) when she wrote:

> Can one feel that the limited, tentative action so far taken by the Church is in any way commensurate with the greatness of the change wrought by the Women's Movement? The situation, it may be said, has been adequately met by the foundation of Deaconesses and Church Sisters . . . [but] one cannot help feeling that such orders . . . are built theoretically on uncertain foundation, in so far as they ignore the basic question of the place of women in the existing framework of Presbyterian polity . . . It goes against the grain to use words like 'inferior' or 'subordinate' in connection with Church service . . . Yet facts are facts, and the fact remains that women in the Church hold a subordinate

position. And the women of today ask why . . . Of one thing they are certain, and it is this, that it is not Christ who is barring the way.[146]

Hewat, like others, found some measure of job satisfaction and responsibility in the mission field. She became professor of history at Wilson College, Bombay, and an elder in the Church of South India long before that was possible in Scotland. But an increasing number of Christian women sought greater latitude and financial recompense outwith the institutional church.

An Old Tale

At the Assembly which marked the union of the two main presbyterian denominations, on October 3, 1929, Dr Norman MacLean moved that:

> The Assembly resolve to record their gratitude to God for consecrated women who have devoted their lives to the service of their Lord at home and abroad, and for the continuing development of women's work in the Church'.[147]

As the *UFC Record* summed up succinctly,

> It was an old tale he told, of incalculable service rendered to the Church, and of her debt owed to selfless devotion.[148]

The one hundred years between 1830 and 1930 witnessed a significant feminisation of patriarchal Scottish presbyterianism. The religious framework which had once confined women to strictly private lifestyles offered sanction and encouragement to engage, one way or another, with the public domain, and many thousands of women were inspired, cajoled or otherwise motivated to do the work allotted to them. It provided opportunities for friendship, challenge, purpose, and the learning of new skills and confidence. It was clearly a source of power and personal liberation for certain individuals throughout the period. As a potential threat to the *status quo*, women's work was stubbornly contested by a minority of presbyterian men and women who refused to countenance each new development until it became part of the unquestioned fabric of the institution. Others accepted the changes without excitement, while some were enthusiastic promoters of new organisations and attitudes to women's work.

But the feminisation of the church must be measured largely in terms of service rendered, rather than status bestowed – as a fairly successful attempt to draw on female labour and goodwill without giving up the male monopoly on official power. There was a price to pay. Firstly, as tenacious propagandists for the domestic ideology in its more conservative forms, the presbyterian denominations eventually alienated many of their more creative and ambitious women members. This is a feature of the period which requires more research, but the concern was expressed with such regularity in Assembly debates, church press and committee meetings that it must have had some grounding in reality. Most such women may not have left the church, or given up their religious beliefs, but in practical terms their motivation and energies were directed elsewhere – in work or campaigns or ways of life which were regarded with indifference or antagonism by the religous establishment. A smaller number did appear to reject the church entirely, and discontent about the position of women was one reason.[149] Despite attempts to get the church to reckon with the Women's Movement (especially 1890–1920), they felt stifled and frustrated by the limitations of traditional church women's work. By the 1920s, the more progressive male supporters of women's rights had died, or moved elsewhere, or been marginalised by the ecclesiastical retrenchment of the churches in the years before reunion, and it was an optimistic female leader who could claim, in 1928, that:

> In facing the Social Problem in Scotland, we have in our new political power, a weapon to use for the glory of God, and in the Union, a new fellowship to work for his Kingdom.[150]

Secondly, the utilisation of women workers failed to solve, or indeed seriously to address, the perplexing constellation of religious and social questions thrown up by industrial Scotland in the wake of the evangelical era. Their employment was based on a class-shaped and sentimental ideology of womanhood (forcefully endorsed by even the most committed proponents of Christian ethical socialism),[151] and an abdication of collective responsibility for injustice in a Christian culture. By 1928, the efficacy of a parish sister could still be measured in terms suspiciously similar to the self-righteous individualism of 19th-century evangelicalism:

> What our poor and non-churchgoing people need is religion, and they don't know it . . . The Gospel would be good news to them if they saw religion in action . . . embodied in a person. They will see in her a level of life higher than their own. They will admit its superiority and will want to be like her. But they have not the power.[152]

The actual, as opposed to the mythological, parish and church sisters, were often much more realistic and respectful of the fortitude of the poor. They recognised common human frailty and, although often overwhelmed by the personal and structural dis-ease which they faced, did what work they could with compassion and imagination.[153]

But by the 1930s, the strategic failure of women workers was apparent. There were criticisms that many Sisters had become little more than congregational assistants to ministers – that they were denied scope to fulfil their calling among the poor and depressed of parochial Scotland, and were also relieving Woman's Guild members of their traditional congregational responsibilities.[154] As for the impression that most ordinary working people had of the volunteer church ladies who decided to take an interest in them, perhaps Chris Colquhoun, heroine of Lewis Grassic Gibbon's trilogy, *A Scots Quair*, might have the last word:

> Syne Miss McAskill was asking Chris, sharp, Are you fond of social work, Mrs Colquhoun? and Chris said Not much, if you mean by that going round and visiting the kirk congregation. Miss McAskill raised up her brows like a chicken considering a something lying on the ground, not sure if it was just a plain empty husk, or an interesting bit of nastiness, like. Mrs Geddes said she was very disappointed, she'd hoped they'd have Mrs Colquhoun to help – with the work of the WRI, she meant, and why didn't Mrs Colquhoun like visiting?
>
> And suddenly Chris understood her and hated her – she minded the type, oh, well, well enough! So she smiled sweetly at her and said Oh you see, I wasn't always a minister's wife. I was brought up on a croft, and married on one, and I mind what a nuisance we thought some folk, visiting and prying and blithering about socials, doing everything to help us, or so they would think – except to get out and get on with the work![155]

The ideology of womanhood was not a fixed and unchanging reality, but was shaped and challenged by historical developments. In a variety of ways, it was espoused, subverted and circumvented by churchwomen of different classes and times. It certainly produced some tensions and feminist offshoots. But the overall impact on the institutional presbyterian church was conservative. In all the main denominations, structures were modified to incorporate women's work without risking any fundamental changes to the patriarchal, stereotypical and bourgeois character of Scottish presbyterianism. Annie Small, ex-missionary and principal of the UFC Women's Missionary College, which was founded in 1894, was a loyal but critical and visionary member of the Church. She wrote in 1931:

> I was never a member of the Church at home until the end of my missionary service (1892) and entered therefore upon membership as a woman of considerable experience . . . The conditions of Church service at home amazed and shocked me . . . The great proportion of work in many congregations is done by women, silently and unobtrusively, without even the pretence of comradeship on the part of men . . . In due time the Church must realise that

true and perfect comradeship must inevitably express itself through true and perfect colleagueship.[156]

Notes

1. S Lewis, *Woman's Mission* (1839) 11–12

2. Larger Catechism, *Westminster Confession* (1647). The Confession shaped the doctrine, polity, education and worship of Scottish presbyterianism after its legal restoration in 1690

3. quoted in D Mackichan, *The Missionary Ideal in the Scottish Churches* (1927) 80

4. See T C Smout, *A History of the Scottish People 1560–1830* (1969) part two

5. J MacLeod, *Scottish Theology in Relation to Church History* (1943) 315

6. C Brown, *The Social History of Religion in Scotland since 1730* (1987) 136

7. ibid 141

8. Leneman and Mitchison *Sexuality and Social Control 1650–1780*, (1991) and K Boyd *Scottish Church Attitudes to Sex, Marriage and the Family 1850–1914* (1980) chart the diminishing exercise of Kirk Session public discipline

9. Acts of the Free Church General Assembly 1858–63 491

10. W Wilberforce, Practical View 453, quoted in B Taylor *Eve and the New Jerusalem* (1983) 126

11. *Christian Journal* (1840) 17

12. ibid

13. *Watchword* (1871) 81

14. *Life and Work* (1890) 51

15. A series of Acts in the second half of the 19th century transformed the dependent chattel status of married women. The 1861 Conjugal Rights (Scotland) Amendment Act declared that after judicial separation, or a protection order granted to a deserted wife, all property acquired by the woman thereafter belonged exclusively to her. The Married Women's Property (Scotland) Act 1877 gave wives the right to keep their own earned income, unless from a business owned jointly with the husband. By the 1881 Married Women's Property Act, 'the whole moveable or personal estate of the wife, whether acquired before or during the marriage shall, by operation of law, be vested in the wife as her separate estate and shall not be subject to the jus mariti.' However, the husband retained power of administration, and his consent was required if she wished to dispose of her property, until the

Married Women's Property (Scotland) Act of 1920. (see The Law of Husband and Wife in Scotland eds E M CLive and J G Wilson (1974) 287–9)

16. M Reid, *A Plea for Woman* (1843 reprinted 1988) 14 See Helsinger Sheets and Veeder, *The Woman Question* vol I, 'Defining Voices' for more on Sarah Lewis's influential text and Marion Reid's critique.

17. See E Gordon and E Breitenbach, (eds) *The World is Ill Divided – Women's Work in Scotland in the 19th and Early 20th Centuries* (1990); E Gordon, Women in the Labour Movement in Scotland 1850–1914 (1990); R Rodger, 'Employment, Wages and Poverty in Scottish Cities' in G Gordon (ed) *Perspectives of the Scottish City* (1985); A J McIvor, 'Women and Work in 20th century Scotland' in *People and Society in Scotland* Vol III 1914–1990 (1992)

18. See Gordon (1990) for statistics. Rodger (1985) gives detailed tables which demonstrate the regional variation in female employment over a 90 year period

19. *Edinburgh Review* (1859) 293 ff

20. *The Attempt* (1872) 30

21. W R Greg 'Why are Women Redundant?' in National Review (1862) 454–5 quoted in M Poovey, *Uneven Developments: The Ideological Work of Gender in mid-Victorian England* (1986) 4

22. Edinburgh Review (1859) op cit

23. See Gordon (1990) op cit, and 'The Scottish Trade Union Movement, Class and Gender 1850–1914' in *Scottish Labour History* 23 (1988) on trade union attitudes to female labour

24. H Renton, Memorial of *Mrs Agnes Renton* (nd) 2

25. *People's Journal* Oct 14 1922, quoted in W M Walker, *Juteopolis: Dundee and its Textile Workers 1885–1923* (1979) 40

26. See J Stephenson and C Brown, 'Women's Memories of Work in Stirling c1910–1950' in *Out of Bounds*

27. *Life and Work* Woman's Guild Supplement (1914) 67

28. Stephenson and Brown, op cit, see also *Uncharted Lives: Extracts from Scottish Women's Experiences 1850–1982* (1983); T McBride, *The Domestic Revolution* (1976) E Higgs, 'Domestic Service and Household Production' in A V John (ed), *Unequal Opportunities* (1986)

29. L Lumsden, 'The Position of Women in History' in *The Position of Woman, Actual and Ideal* (1911) 63

30. J Melling, *Rent Strikes: Peoples' Struggles for Housing in West Scotland 1890–1916* (1983) and Edward Gaitens' novel of life in the Gorbals, *Dance of the Apprentices*, (1948) give some flavour of this.

31. Rev G Lewis 'The Tavern Bill of Dundee': Course of lectures on the physical, educational and moral statistics of Dundee (1840) 3, quoted in W Walker op cit

32. G Lerner, *The Creation of Patriarchy* (1986) 139

33. Middle class feminists who were pioneer members of the state school boards from 1872 campaigned vigorously for the teaching of domestic education to working class girls. See Chapter 5

34. *Life and Work* (1894) 116

35. For a helpful outline of different formulations of the ideology of 'true womanhood', see Helsinger, Sheets and Veeder, *The Woman Question: Society and Literature in Britain and America 1837–1883* (1983) Vol II, introduction. They have identified four 'competing, though not mutually exclusive myths or models for woman's place in society' – Angel in the House, Angel Out of the House, the Female Saviour, and women as free and equal agents. 'Angel in the House' is the title of a mid-century poem by Coventry Patmore.

36. See e.g. *Autobiography of Mrs Eliza Fletcher of Edinburgh* (1877) ed Lady Mary Richardson. She belonged to the liberal/intellectual milieu of Enlightenment Edinburgh

37. For discussion of the political situation see T C Smout, *A Century of the Scottish People 1830–1950* (1986) Chap I, X

38. *Christian Journal* (1840) 213–4

39. ibid 214

40. *The Attempt* (1869) 159

41. Sermon preached by Rev W Williamson, at a service to commission deaconesses, at St Cuthbert's Church Edinburgh, October 16 1892

42. Edinburgh City Mission Annual Report (1834)

43. *Home and Foreign Mission Record* (1850) 263

44. ibid

45. HFMR (1845) 13

46. L Mahood, 'The Domestication of 'Fallen' Women: The Glasgow Magdalene Institution, 1860–1890', in D McCrone, S Kendrick and P Straw (eds), *The Making of Scotland: Nation, Culture and Social Change* (1989) 158

47. *W Blaikie, An Autobiography* (1901) 314

48. ibid 327

49. Reports of the Schemes of the Church of Scotland (1871) 396

50. Reports of the Schemes of the Church of Scotland (1884) 371 ff

51. ibid

52. C A Salmond, *A Woman's Work: Memorials of Eliza Fletcher* (1890) civ (not the same Eliza Fletcher as cited in note 36!)

53. Reports of the Schemes of the Church of Scotland (1875)

54. A Gordon, *Life of Archibald Hamilton Charteris* (1912) 162

55. Reports of the Schemes . . . (1884) op cit

56. *Life and Work* (1884) 33

57. H Renton op cit 84

58. ibid 66

59. W Gibson, *Not Weary in Well-Doing: The Life and Work of Helen Lockhart Gibson* (1888) 32

60. ibid 96

61. ibid 66

62. Renton op cit see 127

63. *Life and Work* (1894) 116

64. *United Presbyterian Magazine* (1890) 70

65. See S J Brown, 'Reform, Reconstruction, Reaction' in *Scottish Journal of Theology* (1991) 489–517

66. See Helen Crawfurd's unpublished autobiography 46 (copy held in the William Gallacher Memorial Library, STUC Headquarters, Glasgow. I am very grateful to Audrey Canning for her interest, help and cups of tea.)

67. ibid

68. See M A McCabe's unpublished PhD thesis 'Evangelicalism and the Socialist Revival' (Edinburgh University 1992) for discussion of the connections between evangelicalism and socialism during this period

69. C Brown op cit 179ff

70. Glagow Presbytery Report on The Housing of the Poor (1910) 10

71. see S J Brown op cit

72. A Scott Matheson, *The Church and Social Problems* (1893) 12

73. *Life and Work* (1882) 75

74. *Life and Work* (1884) 33

75. *Church of Scotland Year Book* (1887) 73

76. *Life and Work* (1888) 108

77. See WG Central Committee minutes, April 8 1897 (SRO CH1/38/1/1)

78. *Life and Work* (1893) 27

79. See WG Central Committee minutes, June 9 1896

80. *Life and Work* (1892) 48

81. M Anderson, *Memories of 50 years Mission Work in the West Parish of Greenock 1863–1913* (1914) 56–7

82. See *Church of Scotland Year Book* (1912) for details of Woman's Guild initiatives

83. *Life and Work*, Woman's Guild Supplement (1901) 95

84. WG Supplement (1906) 97

85. WG Supplement (1906) 73

86. WG Supplement (1908) 57

87. ibid

88. For example, Dalkeith Parish Church Ladies Work Party, founded 1904, stated in its Constitution that 'the minister and Kirk Session alone shall decide how to allocate the funds' raised at the annual Sale of Work. In 1907, the minister 'was asked to impress on the Kirk Session the desire of the ladies that part of the contribution should be allotted to the Social Scheme of the Church of Scotland'. And in 1908, he informed the Work Party that 'the Kirk Session desired the Work Party to allocate £20 amongst Church schemes as the members might feel inclined.' See Dalkeith PC Ladies Work Party Minute Book:SRO CH2/84/78

89. See eg articles in Supplement: (1906 86,95) on the need, not just to relieve poverty, but to prevent it through education and public service; (1912 69) on the National Insurance Act and its effect on women; (1920 31) on women's new civic responsibilities: 'The training and education of women especially, have tended to foster in them a habit of deploring existing evils and of labouring to mitigate their effect on individuals without any effort to remove them. 'They' ought not to allow such things, they remark, without considering who 'they' may be. Now 'they' has become 'we' and the sooner we women recognise that the better'.

90. WG Supplement (1906) 97

91. ibid (1914) 103

92. Reports of the Schemes of the Church of Scotland (1916) 416

93. WG Supplement (1918) 56

94. See minutes of WG Central Committee and Constitution sub-committee, 1919–1920

95. *Life and Work* (1930) 28

96. *Life and Work*, Women's Work in the Church (1928) 59

97. Comments to this effect feature in WG Committee minutes, and also in a number of articles which appeared in the Supplement during 1928

98. See *Out of Bounds* (1992) 152ff

99. Professor Martin Pugh made this point at a conference on 'The March of the Women', held in St Andrews, April 29 1995

100. J W Robertson Scott, *The Story of the Women's Institute Movement* (1925) 236

101. ibid 238; See also the articles in *Women's Work in the Church* (1928) 5,

102. WG Supplement (1920) 39

103. WG Central Committee minutes, April 11 1928

104. See e.g. *Women's Work in the Church* (1929) 17: 'It may be that the future will even see women ministers everywhere! Without entering into the controversial, surely spiritually minded and studious women, who look on the ministry as a 'vocation', not merely as a 'profession', could be a great power for the good. Many are 'ministering' now in the truest sense of the word, and nobody can afford to ignore the divine call if it comes.'

105. A H Dunnett, *The Church in Changing Scotland* (1934) 127ff

106. *UP Magazine* (1890) 51

107. United Presbyterian Church Synod Report (1898) 29

108. *Youth* Magazine (1897) 13

109. *Free Church of Scotland Yearbook* (1888) 99

110. Reports of the Free Church of Scotland (1887) XX 34

111. ibid

112. See Reports of Free College Church, Glasgow (1880s)

113. *United Free Church Record* (1901) 333

114. *UFC Record* (1903) 321

115. The Report of Women's Home Mission (1916) gives descriptions of the characteristic initiatives undertaken during the war years

116. *UFC Record* (1909) 312

117. ibid

118. See Reports of Lansdowne United Free Church, Glasgow (1912–18)

119. ibid 1915

120. Reports of the UF Church (1915) XXVIII App 1 11–17

121. *UFC Record* (1914) 151

122. *HFMR* (1865) 146. In a further article, the same author calls for 'Christian ladies to arouse themselves from that epicurean selfishness which is the besetting sin of the age . . . In their attempts to reach and purify the home life of the people, ladies would have in many ways the advantage over their

poorer sisters who have to work for their daily bread. To their efforts no mercenary motives could be attributed' 220

123. Reports of the Schemes . . . (1881) 359ff

124. *Life and Work* (1884) 33–4

125. See correspondence in HFMR (1868) 61, 90. Also Life and Work (1886) 97

126. *Life and Work* (1892) 94

127. *Life and Work* (1893) 212

128. UF Church General Assembly Proceedings and Debates (1905) 253

129. Some women with no personal means were supported through training at the Missionary College. The Girls Auxiliary sponsored a few parish sisters in later years

130. UFCGAPD (1909) 220

131. *UFC Record* (1929) 419

132. *Life and Work* (1890)

133. WG Supplement (1906) 73

134. *HFMR* (1893) 3

135. *Life and Work* (1892) 48

136. J A and Mrs Thomson, 'The Position of Woman Biologically Considered' in *The Position of Woman Actual and Ideal* (1911) 4. J Arthur Thomson, working with Patrick Geddes, wrote *The Evolution of Sex* (1889), which was almost as influential as Herbert Spencer's work in popularising sociobiological theories of gender differentiation

137. H Spencer, 'A Theory of Population Deduced from the General Law of Animal Fertility', *Westminster Review* (1852) 498. Quoted in J Sayers, *Biological Politics* (1982) see Chapter 3: 'Social Darwinism and the woman question'.

138. H Drummond, *The Ascent of Man* (1889) 278

139. P Geddes and J A Thomson, *The Evolution of Sex* (1889) 247. In spite of the implications of their views, these men, and certain other theorists, were not by any means totally opposed to women's rights. Geddes was a real polymath who made a considerable contribution to Scottish intellectual and cultural life.

140. See e g E Pearson, 'Spiritual Motherhood and Philanthropic Service' in *The Position of Woman* . . . op cit 135–148.

141. *UFC Record* (1918) 87

142. WG Supplement (1919) 179

143. WG Supplement (1906) 96

144. Reports of the UF Church (1915) XXVIII

145. UFCGAPD (1917) 264

146. *Life and Work* (1931) 138

147. *UFC Record* (1929) 468

148. ibid

149. It is difficult to establish how many women actually left the church, or for precisely what reasons. Helen Crawfurd, Helen Fraser and some others who were involved in the suffrage movement did so (though not always at the time of that campaign), and expressed resentment and rejection of the constraints under which women were placed by institutional religion. Many within the churches who sought more equality and latitude argued consistently, especially into the 20th century, that the church was losing intelligent and capable women members, though they gave no names or figures. I make further reference to these in chaps 4 and 5. Whatever the reality, there was a widely held perception that some women left the church for these kinds of reasons.

150. *UFC Record* (1928) 312

151. See, e g David Watson, *Perfect Womanhood* (1906), A Scott Matheson op cit chap 12

152. *Life and Work*, Women's Work Supplement (1929) 25

153. See e g WG Supplement (1902) 57f

154. See Dunnett (1934) op cit Ch XI 127–134

155. Lewis Grassic Gibbon, *Cloud Howe* (1933)

156. *Life and Work* (1931) 145

3

Women and the Foreign Missionary Movement

Introduction

The rights of woman! what are they?
The right to labour and to pray
The right to comfort in distress
The right, when others curse, to bless
The right to love whom others scorn
The right to comfort all who mourn
The right to shed new joy on earth
The right to feel the soul's high worth
The right to lead the soul to God
Along the path the Saviour trod.
Such, women's rights! and God will bless,
And grant support, and give success.[1]

The organisation and conduct by women of work in the foreign missions of the Church was one of the most distinctive and significant aspects of evangelical religious life in the 19th and early 20th century Anglo-Protestant world. The foreign missionary movement was inspired in part by the characteristic twin beliefs of revivalist evangelicalism – arminianism and benevolence. The corollary of the conviction that all human beings are equal in sin and guilt before God was that those who accepted the gospel and were redeemed, were also equal by virtue of their conversion. The urgent desire of evangelicals was to preach that good news, not just to individuals, but to nations: for their vision was of a Christian civilisation which would perfect and save the whole world. 'Religious and moral interests are our first concern' commented Wilberforce during a Parliamentary debate about missions, 'but of course what we recommend tends no less to promote temporal wellbeing than eternal welfare'.[2] The global system of slavery, which for many converted Christians was the paradigm of sin and spiritual darkness, threw into sharp focus their moral responsibility. They believed that in both anti-slavery legislation and foreign mission, Britain could act as a mighty power, not only atoning for national guilt, but vindicating Protestant Christianity as a progressive force. As such, it was not just a matter of individual faith, but of commerce, imperialism, culture and lifestyle. In Scotland, Adam Smith's free trade theories were invoked against slavery and in support of world-wide British expansion. Among the emerging artisan class were many evangelicals who were inspired by the possibility of self-improvement and of contributing to global progress – especially in the places where trade routes had planted British influence. By the turn of the 19th century the scene was set for Britain to fulfil what became seen as a God-given task to liberate and save the world. At first, the model of conversionism which informed foreign missions accepted the potential equality of all human beings, regardless of race, and concentrated on attempts to develop indigenous communities which demonstrated the benefits of Western civilisation. Later, under the influence of Social Darwinism and high political imperialism, missionaries generally came to accept the belief that humankind was a hierarchy of races, in which the evolutionary destiny of the Anglo-Saxon race was to embody the highest form of civilisation and progress. The model which dominated late 19th- and early 20th-century mission work was trusteeship – based on the idea that people of other races were inferior and needed to be looked after.[3]

Scotswomen who participated in the foreign missionary movement initially did so because of their relationship to the first male missionaries (though wives and sisters very often shared these men's sense of vocation). But their involvement fairly quickly came to be based on the distinctive premise of 'women's work for women'. Under that banner, women were recruited as pioneers to demonstrate and inculcate the blessings of Christian civilisation to pagan, infidel or savage females. Later, and in much larger numbers, they shared in the perceived Providential white burden of educating and caring for Indian, African and Caribbean women and children under colonial rule. For the hundreds of presbyterian Scotswomen who ventured beyond their native shores, and the many thousands who developed a complex structure and culture of support at home, the foreign missionary movement respresented the logical (and glamorous) outcome of Woman's Mission. I concluded the previous chapter with a quotation from Annie H Small, in which she draws a clear distinction between her negative view of Scottish church life, and her positive experience as a Free Church missionary in India. In the same article, she wrote:

> In the mission community we were a team – we aimed at co-ordination and the balanced interrelation of all departments, guided by constant consultation.[4]

Small valued the co-operation and authority which she implies were enjoyed by women in the field, and mission work certainly offered women opportunities for personal and professional development and autonomy which would have been unimaginable at home. But the poem at the head of this chapter, used by Emma Pitman Raymond in her widely read *Heroines of the Mission Field*, published in 1880 at the start of the massive expansion in women's foreign missions, suggests that the cult of true womanhood had a central ideological role in the development of the movement. 'The Rights of Woman' presents, as the context for women's missionary endeavour, an implicit rejection of the claims of the contemporary Women's Movement, in favour of a classic exposition of self-abnegating religious service. In fact, from the outset in the 1830s, the doctrine of separate spheres was a fundamental aspect of the foreign missionary enterprise. As a basic tenet of the civilisation which was to be exported around the world, it was bound to be. Women were exhorted, in the light of their elevated status as Christians, to take responsibility for spreading the gospel to their degraded sisters in the East. Only women could fulfil this obligation, for only they could witness effectively, by teaching and example, to secluded or savage females. And the task came to be regarded as crucial, for without women, converted and domesticated according to the Protestant Christian ethos, heathen societies could never be civilised in the image of the evangelising nations. The domestic ideology, which constrained so many women in Scotland, was also the basis of outreach and emancipation proclaimed by missionary women. Scotswomen in increasing numbers accepted and rejoiced in what they regarded as their special and distinctive task.

The foreign mission field in one sense offered quintessential work for evangelical Victorian women – the epitome of their God-given role as 'Angel in the World'. But the complex dynamics of race, gender and class in very diverse places, times and circumstances challenged and frequently undermined the very ideology which informed that work.

Exposure to different beliefs and practices in the Southern Hemisphere disturbed and shocked Scottish missionaries, who found it difficult to come to terms with men and women acting counter to bourgeois Western mores and values. In Southern Africa, for example, men did all the sewing whilst women engaged in hard agricultural and construction work:

> Women of Nyasaland were not only ignorant of women's work, but required to be taught how to act generally. They were deficient in washing and household work, and many were uncleanly, lazy, disobedient, deceitful and untruthful.[5]

Most missionaries proceeded on the unquestioned assumption that Christianity in its Anglo-Protestant form represented the highest development of civilisation, and that their duty was to inculcate that in all aspects of life, including dress, marriage roles and morals. In this respect the evangelical attitude to people of other races and habits was similar to their view of Scottish working people who did not conform to a 'respectable' lifestyle. But the fact that domestic arrangements and structures were pluriform and culturally conditioned led to some interesting consequences in situations where the gospel they preached was not embedded in the social fabric, but was at every level a strange intruder.

1. In Scotland the domestic ideology was a conservative ideal which in various ways exercised control over women's lives. By contrast, in its Western, Anglo-Protestant form, it represented a radical attack on other cultures. Women who, at home in Scotland, were expected to exercise a cohesive and unifying influence became, in the field, agents for social change. The spheres in which they contested might seem genteel and unspectacular – schools and dispensaries and homes – but they brought values which directly collided with prevailing norms in Africa and Asia. The confrontational role was a novel one for Scottish women, and some revelled in a militant enthusiasm for transforming the lives of indigenous women.

2. If women missionaries were engaged in racialist and cultural imperialism, they were also exposed to the possibility of cultural assimilation. Involvement in places so far removed, in every respect, from Scotland, provoked in some a critical perspective which enabled recognition of the good and valuable in other societies, and a deprecation of what was inappropriate, arrogant or unjust in missionary or imperialist practice. Mary Slessor, an ex-mill girl from Dundee, rejected a mission life modelled on bourgeois conventions, in favour of a simple lifestyle influenced by West African patterns. Her bare feet, bare head, cotton shift and mud hut were external symbols of an intelligent (though critical) understanding and solidarity. A deputation from Scotland recommended that she continue thus, 'because she prefers this manner of life to being associated with another white person on a station'.[6] Although the working-class Slessor was atypical because she was socially more uncomfortable with the stifling manners and attitudes of compound life than in her down-to-earth dealings with local tribes, others were also challenged by the conjunction of two cultures. Annie Small recalled:

> As between Britain and India in their mutual relation I was on the side of India every time . . . I criticised hotly our British restlessness, acquisitiveness, self-

assertiveness; our talk of commerce while intending conquest, our attempts to gloss over our not very admirable ambitions with a hypocritical profession of desire for the good of India . . . Our national manners aroused my fierce indignation also. When one heard a lordly young Britisher issuing his orders, often in execrable Urdu, with insulting epithets, to an Indian double his age, and probably with twice his brains . . . shame took hold of me.[7]

Others were content to replicate a Scottish way of life in mission stations, and never challenged (even if they recognised) the conceptual or political framework for their endeavours. But it is possible to argue that the more imaginative and critical women at least raised some important questions about the nature and value of the civilisation they were exporting. On the whole, though, even missionaries who developed an apprecation of, and affection for other places, languages and cultures remained publicly loyal to both church and state.

3. Missionary women themselves made a direct impact upon those with whom they came into contact, both on mission stations and in local communities. As examples of the message they sought to convey about the place and role of women in Christian life, they were confusing, to say the least. Whatever the circumstances they might have left in Scotland, in the mission field their primary function was neither strictly domestic nor maternal. Many were adventurous, independent, competent and indomitable. Even those who were more conventional and modest in their aspirations presented a puzzle to people who were told that the highest duty for a woman was to provide moral and domestic support for a husband and family. The language used to describe women missionaries in tributes and biographies is usually quite striking in its evocation of individuals who displayed, not just the traditional 'feminine' attributes of the time, but also so-called 'masculine' qualities. The American theologian, John B Cobb Jr, in attempting to explain his surprise at realising the extent to which patriarchal society has undermined the self-confidence and completeness of women, has written:

> I believe the deepest reason . . . is that the image of woman I formed in childhood was based on what I now see as quite a special case: Protestant women missionaries . . . Such women were not the sort who derived their identity from relationships with men. Presumably they required more courage for their solitary adventures carving new institutions in distant lands than did the men who rarely went without wives. Several such women were part of my childhood.[8]

The integrated personalities of women who demonstrated independence, compassion, love and courage, evaded facile gender categorisation, and were rewarded with great fondness and respect by the communities in which they served, were powerful countersigns to the rhetoric of separate spheres. Even missionary wives did not always conform to the conventional pattern of domestic relationships. They typically participated actively in mission work, while many of their domestic and childcare responsibilities were delegated to servants within the station, and to relatives or schools back in Scotland.

4.By the 1880s, as the number and range of opportunities for female missionaries grew, and as they became the dominant numerical force in the field, it became increasingly difficult to maintain any meaningful lines of demarcation between male and female missionary spheres. In 1901, J.W. Jack argued in his book *Daybreak in Livingstonia* that appropriate roles were clearly defined:

> To *men* belongs the task of opening a way for the gospel, making straight in the desert a highway for God, striking vigorous blows at the citadel of heathenism, superintending various agencies, planting the standard of the gospel, and accomplishing other deeds of strength and wisdom. But to *women* belongs the quiet, patient labour in the homes of natives, striving to win the hearts of wives and mothers, and to gain the love of the children. Let women hear the tender call of Christ to the foreign field![9]

But Jack's picture of the male shock troops of muscular Christianity backed up by the female devotion to sentimental family values was, by then, based more on wistful nostalgia than on accurate description. For women were already doing all that he listed as male duties – in exploration, education, preaching and teaching, contruction and medical service – as well as the more traditional women's work. By the turn of the century they were in the vanguard of a social-service, rather than a strictly conversionist, approach to foreign missions. And in 1910, the Report of the Edinburgh World Missionary Conference went so far as to claim that the slogan, 'women's work for women' was a fallacy, which

> has served to narrow the conception of the mission of Christian womanhood to the great loss of the whole movement. A vision of the place of women in the building up of the whole fabric of national life, and a statesmanlike conception of the way to realise that vision, is urgently demanded.[10]

5. Missionaries were white women. They entered the field as symbols of a white culture which was always supremacist and became increasingly racist. Their relationships with non-white individuals and structures were affected, if not wholly determined, by these realities. In particular they had to confront assumptions about the 'essential nature' of Woman with the

reality of fragmented and highly differentiated female experience. Initially that was explained by reference to indigenous savagery or heathenism, but latterly many missionaries accepted the widespread theory that women of colour (especially in Africa) were congenitally inferior and in need of special kinds of care, treatment and education. By the 1880s, under the influence of racial theory developed by writers such as Herbert Spencer and Benjamin Kidd, it became accepted wisdom that so-called higher races – especially those of northern Europe and their American descendants – were naturally superior to others, over whom the Anglo-Saxons were destined to expand and rule. On the other hand, there were also female agents who went out of their way to affirm the equality and potential of the women they encountered, and extended them opportunities (based on the conversionist model) which were not always available to women back in Scotland. Their vision of what would liberate the women they worked with was largely shaped by the project of Christian civilisation, but was not always totally insensitive to local circumstances and traditions. The relationship between class, culture and race in female missions was complex and changing. But on the whole, it tended to be based on the fallacy that the white, bourgeois model of womanhood was normative – the standard according to which the practical worth and morality of all others would be judged.

6. Changes in the field affected, and were reflected in, changes at home. The female missionary agencies were the first and in many respects the most important large-scale presbyterian organisations for women. They did not always enjoy an uncomplicated or harmonious relationship with their fieldworkers, but together they constituted a network of information and support, which received regular injections of fresh ideas and challenges. The women at home, too, gradually developed new skills and confidence as their operation expanded along with their global perspective. They played a key role in the overall missionary movement, as the main fundraisers, collectors and publicists for general (ie male) as well as specifically female work. But their treatment by the church at large, and certainly by the power structures was often patronising or contemptuous. Within the three main presbyterian denominations, different approaches were taken to the organisation and employment of women missionaries. Different incidents and developments suggest that the extent to which it was an advantage for women to operate independent of church courts and male leaders, was never a settled question. But there was certainly political and literary capital in maintaining the rhetoric of a uniquely female missionary task, even when missionary reports told a different story.

The tensions arising wherever realities collided with the ideology which had provided the women's missionary movement with its *raison d'être*, were neither progressively nor completely resolved during the period 1830–1930. One recurring problem was the question of authority and responsibility within mission stations. Some notable women learnt to their cost the acceptable limits of female assertiveness within the hierarchy of a mission. Others enjoyed the support of more flexible colleagues and committees. In any case, records reveal a level of bitterness and acrimony in mission politics (both within stations and between missionaries and home committees) which might have shocked supporters for whom missionaries were heroes and heroines of the faith. One notorious example which did become public was the Calcutta Mission Scandal of the early 1880s. A leader in *The Scotsman* of May 31, 1884, concluded that printed reports always gave a rosy impression of pious missionaries and effective management:

> It has often been suspected that behind these conventional pictures there was another aspect of mission affairs bearing a closer resemblance to imperfect human nature. Mr Hastie and Dr Scott have betweeen them rent the veil, and the seamy side of missions is revealed to the profane view of heathen at home and of mild Hindoo.[11]

The story of Scottish presbyterian women and foreign missions is complex and fascinating. It offers valuable insights into a range of female responses to the potent ideas of women's sphere and mission as those were tested and preached in Scottish and foreign contexts. There is a huge resource of printed and archive material awaiting a much more intensive study.[12] What follows is simply a general survey of the origins, development, opportunities and difficulties encountered by the movement within the Scottish churches. By referring to individual examples and notable events, I hope to give substance to my assessment of the movement's central significance in the changing relationship between women and presbyterianism.

The Origins of a Scottish Women's Missionary Movement

> Come, as many as you will . . . the fact is appalling, that none will come over to aid us! The cry has been made with tears and supplications.[13]

So wrote Margaret Bayne, wife of Dr John Wilson, who had gone to Bombay with the Scottish Missionary Society in 1828. It was the inspiration of the work she did during the seven years she survived before an early death in India, and the appeal made to her two sisters in Scotland, which led to the establishment, in 1837, of the Edinburgh Ladies Association for the Advancement of Female Education in India. In the early years of the 19th century, pioneering Scots missionaries went to Africa and India with non-denominational societies. They often took wives or sisters with them. And from the beginning, women supported this new movement with money and prayers. As early as 1797, a female correspondent to the *Scots Missionary Magazine* was calling for a more active involvement in societies:

> Why are females alone excluded from all ostensible share in these labours of love? It cannot be denied, that some among them possess both ability and inclination suited to the purpose . . . The common accounts of receipt and expenditure, together with minutes of proceedings etc might, I think, be easily accomplished by females in the middle classes of life; and I doubt not some of their married brethren would kindly assist in any matter of difficult emergency.[14]

In 1800, the Northern Missionary Society, based in Inverness, established a Women's Society which raised and allocated its own funds, and organised meetings, sermons and collections. By 1820, the *Missionary Magazine* was carrying reports of ladies' auxiliary associations in towns like Peebles and Lanark.

However, it was not during these years of inter-denominational activity, but after the Church of Scotland had sanctioned foreign mission work, that the direct participation of women as agents in their own right began. As model and inspiration, Margaret Wilson was an impressive character. She was an exceptionally gifted woman who had enjoyed the unusual benefits of an education to the highest standard (she joined in classes at Aberdeen University for several months). In the strange, often hostile climate and culture of Western India, she attempted to make full use of her talents. The biography written by her husband – a four-hundred-page eulogy of her intellectual and spiritual capacities – conveys a vivid (if verbose) impression of her achievements. In the funeral sermon he preached in 1835, Dr Wilson summed up Margaret's contribution to the pioneer mission:

> The difficulties arising from superstition, custom and corrupted feeling, which are in the way of female education, she found to be numerous and formidable, but she resolved to encounter them . . . She instituted and organised six female schools; she trained teachers; she visited scholars and parents at home. She taught several adult females to read. During my long journeys she managed, with much fidelity and prudence, the general concerns of the mission, and she always freed me from many secular cares connected with its business. She was its principal attraction to many native visitors. She wrote several striking papers in native periodicals – and did much translating and writing in Marathi . . .

Amidst all these personal exertions, she ever communicated with me the most valuable counsel, and the most exciting encouragement in my work.[15]

Margaret pleaded with her two sisters to join her in her work. Instead, they travelled to India after her death, and at their own expense, to continue her labours. Captain St Clair Jameson, a Scottish soldier in India who had admired Margaret Wilson's efforts, wrote early in 1837 to a female friend in Fife:

I am in hopes soon to send you a very strong appeal on behalf of native female education in Bombay which, I doubt not, your favoured sex in general, appreciating the advantages they possess over the degraded females of the East from their moral and religious education, and the benefits of institutions which owe their rise to Christianity, will respond with feelings of sympathy and actions corresponding to its importance. Some few friends of the cause here are in hopes of getting ladies in Edinburgh to form themselves into an association to aid in promoting Female Education in Western India, and it is believed that the fact of the Misses Bayne leaving to take up labours . . . will have an effect on the public mind.[16]

A meeting held on March 8, 1837 filled the Queen Street Religious Institution, and several men addressed the gathering. A committee of twenty-two New Town ladies was formed, with male office-bearers, to further the aims of the new organisation. These included:

To give a religious and general education to the Females of India. For this purpose it shall raise funds, procure information, form auxiliary branches throughout the country, and procure the services of well qualified teachers. These teachers shall be appointed by the General Assembly's Committee, and shall be under the superintendence, and their operations under the control, of the missionaries of the Church of Scotland in India.[17]

In 1839 the Glasgow Ladies Association for promoting female education in Kaffraria was formed, because 'women accustomed to savage life needed much Christian training, which only Christian women could give, to fit them for their proper place in home and Church'.[18] Unlike the Edinburgh Ladies Association, it was not connected with the Church of Scotland, and it remained autonomous until 1865, when it entered into partial union with the Edinburgh Ladies Society in connection with the Free Church.

These societies were among the first in the English-speaking world to organise and support female agents. They preceded North American initiatives by thirty years, and according to many contemporary sceptics, they were indeed premature, for the state of Indian and African society, they argued, was incompatible with the employment of 'unprotected females'. They must either marry or die. In the first tentative years of the new venture, one or other of these fates befell most of the pioneer agents. Those who succumbed to matrimony were automatically deemed to have resigned, though most married other missionaries and in fact continued their labours unpaid. Whereas it was expected that male missionaries would enjoy the companionship and support of marriage, females were required to repay their expenses if they married within five years of appointment. Thus at an early stage, the principle was established that those who were to teach heathen women about the blessings and family ideals of Christianity were themselves to be single and childless.

Another early difficulty for the Ladies' Associations was finding women who were physically and mentally suitable for the work to be done. There were complaints from India that the Scottish Ladies Association (SLA) had engaged

> persons quite unacquainted with any practical system of tuition, and who have even in some instances displayed little tact and indeed no great inclination or fixed resolution to acquire a method.[19]

The SLA responded by introducing new rules. These included the requirement that all candidates should answer in writing a set of approved questions; that they should produce medical certificates of good health and fitness for an eastern climate; that they must possess or acquire a knowledge of schoolkeeping, and take preparatory training as required by the committee. It is hardly surprising that well qualified candidates were so rare, when the general standard of female education in Scotland at the time was lamentably far removed from that enjoyed by Margaret Bayne, and Normal Schools (which trained teachers) had only recently made training and certification available to women.

Problems in the field were compounded by hindrances at home. As an 1885 historical sketch recalls:

> The ladies in 1837 had but a faint idea of the difficulties in India . . . But they were sure to be aware of obstructions to their work at home. The Church of Scotland was in the midst of the ten years conflict. The ordinary scale of Christian liberality was far down. Dr Chalmers had inaugurated his Church extension scheme at £50,000, and Dr Duff was pleading for Foreign Mission among men. In fact the ladies, at the outset, got little countenance from the Church generally.[20]

Indeed, they could not raise enough funds even for the modest demands made upon them from India. They were widely suspected of undermining the effect and prosperity of the Church's officially sanctioned mission schemes. All the public and executive offices of the Association were carried out by men; but even the tasks of fundraising and publicity among women were new and uncomfortable for many of the female members.

Nevertheless, they persevered, and much had been learnt by those concerned with women's foreign missions when the 1843 Disruption divided the SLA. Most members of the Association joined the Free Church, and from 1843 two organisations existed: the continuing Scottish Ladies Association for the Advancement of Female Education in India, and the new Female Society of the Free Church of Scotland for Promoting the Christian Education of Females in India.

The Development of Women's Work in Scottish Mission Fields

> It is to improve, to teach, and if possible to convert [Hindu women] that is the object of the SLA – to make them obedient daughters, better wives and fitter mothers – and what philanthropist can gainsay such a purpose?[21]

In the years following the Disruption, women served in Scottish mission fields under the auspices of the three main presbyterian denominations of Scotland. Until the 1880s, the numbers of single female agents were small. Much of the work attempted was fitful, or effectively sustained by missionary wives and locally appointed workers. The Church of Scotland Association had particular difficulty in raising adequate funds and finding candidates from within the denomination. Its efforts were concentrated in Calcutta, Madras and Poona. The Free Church Society, which took with it most of the missionary enthusiasts after 1843, was able to employ more workers – by 1880 it had appointed a total of fifty agents. From 1865 the partial union of Glasgow and Edinburgh Ladies Societies to form the 'Society for Female Education in India and South Africa' widened the field of operations and achieved General Assembly recognition as being 'in immediate connection with the Foreign Missions of the Free Church'. But it too struggled to raise sufficient funds, which remained separate from those collected (largely by women) for the Assembly's own scheme. Women who served on behalf of the United Presbyterian Church were under the direct jurisdiction of the Synod's Mission Board, which in 1881 itself established a Zenana Mission. Prior to that, there were no single women in India, and only a handful in Africa. Only from 1886 did women participate directly in the management of female agents employed by the Board.

From 1880–1930, there was a tremendous expansion in opportunities for women missionaries, as the denominations finally adopted, officially or otherwise, a policy of having female agents employed at every Scottish mission station, and as new fields were opened up in parallel with high political imperialism. By 1930, in the newly united Church of Scotland, there were 256 single women missionaries (plus 193 wives, many using professional skills) at work throughout India, Africa, China and the Caribbean. The total male agency was 253.

Changing Tasks and Responsibilities in Different Mission Fields

The titles of the original female missionary societies indicate that the first perceived need for work among women was educational. This was less a matter of intrinsic concern for their improvement, and more to do with their influence over men who were seen as the shapers and controllers of society. Their socialising role as wives and mothers was recognised. As an article in the Church of Scotland's *Missionary Record* claimed;

> It will be in vain that we make Christian converts of men, whilst girls grow up in heathenism. Unquestionably, one of the chief causes of moral degradation of Asiatic, in comparison with European society, is the miserable state of ignorance in which women have been brought up.[22]

Scottish women used different approaches, with varying success, to combat that 'miserable state of ignorance'. Initially, the most fruitful method in India was the establishment of institutions for outcastes and orphans, for such girls were not subject to the seclusion, early marriage, and caste laws which determined the lives of caste Hindus and Muslims. Margaret Wilson's bazaar schools in Bombay provided the nucleus of a Christian boarding school – the first for girls in Western India. Others were established during the 1840s in Madras, Poona and Calcutta. They offered the best hope of developing a full programme of elementary, and in due course higher, education. By the 1880s, Free Church boarding schools offered a curriculum up to university entrance. One Calcutta student, Chundra Mukki Bose, was the first female MA graduate in India. Orphans could also be given teacher training, for, as Christina Rainy pointed out in 1887:

> All missions are beset with particular difficulties in procuring and employing young women as teachers. Old maids are a Christian institution not yet tolerated by the natives of India. Even Christian parents deem it a disgrace not to have daughters married by twenty.[23]

A more daunting challenge, then, was to confound centuries of Hindu tradition and rigid social structures. Mr Anderson of the Free Church Mission in Madras argued in 1843:

If caste girls are not reached, every scheme that aims at India's amelioration must in the long run prove abortive. Pariah girls may be obtained in any numbers.[24]

And it was in Madras that the first day school for caste girls in India was established, by Mrs Braidwood of the Free Church. Attendance was induced by the offer of a farthing a day to each pupil, but objections and wild rumours greeted its appearance. By 1847 there were over four hundred pupils, but the worst suspicions of high caste Hindu society were confirmed when that year five girls became baptised Christians. There was violent local opposition; the girls had to come to live in the mission house, and with them began the Christian Girls Boarding School. But the day school eventually recovered, expanded, and within twenty years was charging fees instead of offering inducements. By 1870 there were six schools in the city, and others in the surrounding district, run under Free Church Society auspices. Similar efforts to create and maintain viable caste education were repeated in other Indian stations, and indigenous opinion became less hostile. In Calcutta, an 1861 editorial in the *Indian Field* declared:

> We congratulate Dr Duff and the country on the success of his school to educate the Hindu females. When we see the effect of education on these young creatures – how it has already made their eyes to sparkle and their countenances to beam with lively intelligence, and thereby added even not a little to their natural graces . . . we cannot tell how our heart yearns, in the intense longing for the universal enlightenment of the Hindu female mind.[25]

Scottish presbyterian women were among the key pioneers and providers of female school education in India. It was a notable achievement that within sixty years, a few Indian women had moved from a position of total, enforced ignorance, to the possibility of university education and professional training before women in Scotland had achieved those goals. But by 1881, only one out of every 849 girls had access to any form of instruction. Miss Kind, a SLA agent in Bombay, wrote of the main cultural obstruction which hindered the value of schools:

> What I deplore is, that the girls, on account of early marriages, are left such a very short time under the influence of Christian education.[26]

The system whereby girls, who could be betrothed as young as three and commonly by the age of twelve, were thenceforth obliged to live in the total seclusion of their in-laws' household zenana, was by no means as universal as Western writers made out. Nevertheless, it did present a formidable obstacle to the development of female education and evangelisation in India. The Free Church Society in Calcutta, and later the

Church of Scotland Association in Poona (one of the centres of Brahmanism), were among the pioneers of organised zenana missions.

As early as 1840, Rev Thomas Smith of Calcutta had published an article proposing a plan for zenana education, which he submitted to his local Missionary Conference. Back in Scotland, the fathers and brethren of the General Assembly found it impossible to countenance such a scheme. In 1853, Mr and Mrs Fordyce arrived as agents of the Free Church Ladies Society. For two years, they worked alongside Smith to plan and publicise zenana missions, which they considered the only realistic way to stimulate and sustain widespread and effective female education. Smith offered to introduce Mrs Fordyce and a colleague, Eliza Toogood, to 'a few native gentlemen who would admit ladies to their zenanas to teach their wives and daughters'.[27] In 1855, the two women made their first visits into a strange and previously impenetrable world:

> Many thought we were attempting the impossible, but we told ourselves, 'this is the beginning of a new era for India's daughters.'[28]

All this was reported to the Ladies Committee in Edinburgh, but not by way of seeking sanction or funding. The whole business was viewed in Calcutta as a doubtful experiment, and the Fordyces felt they could not ask for donations until they could claim some success. But in September 1855, the Bengal Missionary Conference heard a report of seven months' work by Miss Toogood and Isabella Marr. The following resolution was passed unanimously:

> They rejoice in the hopeful commencement of the zenana school scheme, both as a sign of progress and as a NEW MEANS for the elevation of women in India.[29]

Similar schemes were organised in different places by agents from different Western societies, and Scots were happy to take their share of the credit for initiation. Zenana work quickly came to be promoted, not only as a new epoch for Indian women, but as the distinctive form of women's missionary work, for which new money from Scotland ought to be forthcoming. 'Zenana' became synonymous with any work done by female missionaries, and the United Presbyterian Church used the word in the title for its new department, established as a committee of the Mission Board in 1881.

By the 1880s, a flood of sentimental literature was in circulation, romanticising zenana missions, emphasising the vast gulf between the blessings imparted upon women by Christianity, and the dreary oppression endured by their Indian sisters; and promoting the work as the key to heathen conversion and civilisation.

The reality was somewhat different. Annie Small, for example, held a low opinion of such publications, and the foolish or ludicrous impressions and questions which arose from them.[30] Zenana work was often experienced as tedious and extremely frustrating. The basis on which entry to households was negotiated placed workers in a weak position. As Mary Pigot wrote of Church of Scotland efforts in Calcutta:

> The desire for some culture among their women is so keen that, notwithstanding the rooted prejudices against Christianity, the Bible is tolerated for the sake of secular education. And in Poona, 'Instruction is given in anything, as long as the Christian religion is accepted as part of it.'[31]

Reading between the lines of letters and reports, the impression conveyed is of male caste Hindus taking advantage of missionary fervour to provide the women in their households with a gloss of the Western-style education and refinement which, in many circles, was becoming something of a status symbol. Christian instruction was tolerated, graciously (especially in the form of singing) or otherwise; but as an evangelistic method, its efficacy was far from proven. Women who were known at home as zenana missionaries in fact were likely to be spending only part of their time in direct visiting and teaching of women in their homes. From the 1880s, as the institutional base and commitments of each mission station grew, administration and superintendence of schools and teacher training facilities were more common tasks for European agents. Likewise, the zenana work was increasingly delegated to Indian Biblewomen, who after all had distinct linguistic and cultural advantages in prosecuting the task – although their Scottish employers were greatly exercised by the concern that their teaching and witness should impart the right message. It is difficult to find evidence of zenana converts who were able in turn to Christianise their households. But the missions persevered, and into the 20th century, as school education became more acceptable and accessible for girls, the Scottish societies certainly viewed zenana work as primarily evangelistic rather than educational. But one clear consequence of this more intimate contact between European and Indian women was the development of female medical missions.

The Work of Medical Women in India (1929) describes the circumstances which led to this new departure, which was radical in its implications for both Indian and Western women:

> Most [pioneers] came to India as zenana missionaries, and scattered in different

parts of the country, came to the same horrifying realisation of the fatal and almost unspeakable tragedies, which were common events in the zenanas they visited. They saw their pupils dying in childbirth without any advice other than that of the dirty and ignorant old dai. They saw precious babies snatched away by pneumonia or dysentery, untreated, because their mothers could not take them to a male doctor. They saw the women sinking into chronic illhealth and fatal disease unrelieved, but when advised to go to the hospital, holding up their hands with horror at the idea of consulting a man . . . Medical books were begged from friends and the first furlough was often the opportunity of haunting hospitals . . . Unfortunately, there were not many facilities in those days of the sixties and seventies for giving medical knowledge to women . . . Institutions began to spring up where a short training in medicine and midwifery was given to missionaries.[32]

Evidence from Scotland bears out this general picture of women responding in piecemeal and practical ways to perceived and urgent need. The *Free Church Monthly*, March 1889, gives an account of its medical missions in India. In 1860, Mrs Smith began zenana work in Serampore, but

> sad experience led her to develop into a medical missionary to women, as far as that was possible without qualification. What she witnessed, and often in vain tried to relieve, can be told only to women . . . Mrs Smith gave up her little leisure to plead for 127 million women of India – that they should have Christian physicians of their own sex.[33]

Dr Alexander Duff, the pioneer and leader of the Free Church missionary movement, was willing to concede the importance of medical work, but more ambiguous about whether women should actually be entitled to full qualification as doctors:

> If a female missionary knew something of medical science and practice, readily would she find access, and while applying medical skill to the healing of the body, would have precious opportunities of applying the balm of spiritual healing to the worst diseases of the soul. Would to God that we had such an agency ready for work! Soon might India be moved in its innermost recesses![34]

The first Scotswoman to take a full medical course and qualify for entry onto the Medical Register was Jane Waterston, who trained between 1874 and 1879 with the intention of working in Central Africa. She was scathing about the willingness of the Ladies Society to employ agents without full training:

> I simply detest the fashion in which the Edinburgh coterie does its work. They train so-called medical missionaries at some expense and send out agents to India . . . But when a woman works for some years on a pittance and then

spends hundreds on a complete, instead of a sham medical training, and at the end is a woman with considerable knowledge of life as well as of Mission work, instead of a raw girl with no experience of any kind, there are no funds to send her out. Rawness, greenness and cheapness are the things they want, and very dear they have proved to be.[35]

The Free Church never officially utilised Waterston's skills as a physician. She spent most of her long life as a private general practitioner in Cape Town, where she was involved in and honoured for a range of medical and public services.

The first female doctor in India was an American who began work in 1869. At that time it was not possible for women to gain medical qualifications and licences in Britain, but the campaign for these was just beginning. The fact that missionaries argued for women doctors on the grounds of service, benevolence and evangelistic opportunity (and not in terms of personal and professional fulfilment) no doubt helped secure the support of many church people in the struggle for female medical education during the 1870s and 1880s, as indicated by the 1889 *Free Church Monthly* article:

> Long opposed by teaching and licensing bodies in the UK, Christian women yearning to relieve the misery, bodily and spiritual, of millions of their sisters in the East, were driven to America or Switzerland for training . . . Now the first woman medical missionary has been sent by the Ladies Society to Madras.[36]

And although women continued to be offered, and to embark on, para-medical training, all of the Scottish societies eventually agreed with Dr Lowe of the Edinburgh Medical Missionary Society, about the necessity for missions to be headed only by fully qualified physicians:

> It is most inadvisable to send out partially trained ladies to undertake medical mission work on their own responsibility . . . the heathen to whom they are sent have the right to expect skilful aid, and especially in times of emergency when all other help has failed.[37]

Dr Letitia Bernard, who went to work for the Church of Scotland SLA at Poona in 1884, was the first representative of the new movement. She was followed by presbyterian women – Matilda Macphail, Agnes Henderson, Jean Grant and others – whose impact, as first generation female doctors, was considerable in Scotland as well as India. A tribute to Dr Macphail at the end of her long career in Madras recalled that

> Her care for those whom she attended was without bound . . . Government doctors, members of the Indian Medical Service, have spoken with glowing

admiration of her marvellous powers . . . Time and again Dr MacPhail has been consulted by Government; in every endeavour to promote the medical education of women, she has taken an important part . . . Her medical skill was so highly esteemed that exercise of it took her to the furthest parts of the Presidency.[38]

That commendation gives some indication of the range and scope of opportunities available to medical women working as missionaries. Such pioneers not only practised medicine, but established dispensaries, raised funds to build hospitals, and occupied prominent positions of responsibility. Scottish doctors were particularly noted for their training of nurses, and for the encouragement they gave to local women who wished to study medicine.[39]

Female medical missions quickly became a strategy in which immense hope was placed, as offering an effective entrance into the confidence and obligation of those women and their families who received treatment. Medical work represented perhaps the greatest cultural challenge to Indian tradition, and yet its effects (notwithstanding many misunderstandings and unrealised expectations) were generally positive. So female physicians were particularly highly regarded, both in the field, and also at home, during a period which witnessed the steadily increasing dominance of women as the major mission agency.

In India, the main stages in the development of women's work were determined by response to a highly complex and religious society, under a well established colonial regime. In Africa, the main concern appears to have been to challenge what was regarded as the unrestrained savagery of tribal society. As early as 1839, the Glasgow Missionary Society had declared that, by evangelism and Christian education, they hoped to

raise the female character above mere animal propensities and brute labour, to induce in them the habits of industry and the wearing of modest and suitable clothing, to make them acquainted with their high destinies in another world, and so to give them a sense of self-respect.[40]

The outward appearance, lifestyle, and apparent subjugation of women in West and Southern Africa certainly presented a challenge to the earnest Victorian women who first ventured into the 'dark continent'. With their voluminous clothing, bourgeois conventions, and all the trappings of the domestic ideology in their baggage, the task they set themselves seems as enormous in retrospect as it must have seemed at the time. When Mrs Waddell and Euphemia Miller of the United Presbyterian Church first arrived at Old Calabar, West Africa, in 1849, and saw the unclothed state of the women, as well as their manners and customs, such was the shock to their sensibility, that the two devoted women fell into each others arms in an agony of tears. The elder lady was the first to regain calmness, and comforted her young companion by reminding her, 'We have come to raise them up from their degraded state; let us be strong and labour.'[41]

The juxtaposition of such opposing images, and the aim which gave such missionary women heart, has led to accusations that they were simply agents of crude cultural imperialism. Certainly women who found their way to Africa were (at least in the first generation) lamentably ill-prepared, and rarely questioned the assumed superiority, not just of Christianity, but of Western values and lifestyles. Nor were they in the habit of criticising the principle of British rule. But they responded with courage and compassion to what they observed, and were honest champions of women against practices which by any standard were cruel. In West Africa they confronted polygamy, slavery, twin deaths, wife-fattening and other customs which oppressed women, by using a range of confrontational, diplomatic and compassionate strategies. Mary Slessor (who served in West Africa 1878–1915) was the best known of the Old Calabar women, and she was certainly an individual of outstanding intelligence, insight and guts who directly opposed ritual acts of brutality, mission officials, European traders and imperial agents with equanimity. But she was preceded by a generation of women who, though more conventional in outward appearance and lifestyle, displayed similar character and forbearance.

While the ultimate aim of most women in Africa was to reproduce an indigenous Christian community in the monogamous domestic image of Scottish home life, the range of tasks they undertook was generally much wider, and less easily defined, than that of Indian missionaries. They were not confined to working with girls and women, and commonly taught mixed sex and age groups in their little schools. They often came into direct contact with tribal chiefs and authorities, and although they encountered much amused disdain and contempt, they could also find themselves in positions of considerable power, if they won chiefs over on certain issues and practices. Of Mrs Louisa Anderson, it was said that she

> ruled her household with a rod of iron, and even the chiefs of Duke Town trembled before her. Sometimes they resisted the missionary, but yielded to his wife. One old chief commented: 'I tell you for true, them woman be best man for mission!'[42]

That little vignette conveys some impression of the attitude adopted by many missionaries, who regarded the people they worked amongst – even

political and cultural leaders – as somewhat like disobedient children
requiring to be subdued.

Single women could quite regularly find themselves in charge of out-
stations, with responsibility for all aspects of mission work, and with only
occasional visits from an ordained missionary. From her Old Town base,
'Mammy Sutherland' (the ex-Miss Miller) conducted Sabbath meetings,
organised schools, gave refuge to twins, widows and orphans, and went on
occasional exploratory sorties to places where she was the first white person
to be seen:

> I have reached a place which I have long wished to get at, on the great Qua
> River. I got to it with my alphabet boards and books, and was kindly received
> by the people.[43]

In 1852, the UP *Missionary Record* carried a report of 'Miss Thompson's
labours among the Fingoes' which encapsulates the image of the lonely
Scottish woman missionary in Africa:

> She lives four miles from the nearest European in a small wattle and daub
> cottage, with a schoolhouse adjoining. There are fifty pupils of both sexes, aged
> from four to forty years. Twenty-four can read the Bible in Caffre, eight can
> read English. She has also been assiduous in training them to the habits of
> civilisation – how to build houses, and teaching the females to sew, knit, make
> butter, and bake bread. Mr Calderwood and a minister from Lovedale lead
> worship on the Sabbath. Here there is a single person – a female – separating
> herself from all civilised society, and casting in her lot with a tribe of barbarians,
> and devoting her whole time and energies to promote their social and spiritual
> benefit. Piety, decision of character, vivacity, obligingness, method, patience,
> firmness, perseverance, zeal and consistency have won her respect, confidence
> and affection.[44]

Mary Slessor not only lived among the Okoyong people (who were
previously considered too dangerous for white people to meddle with),
but was appointed first Vice-Consul in 1892, and thus became responsible
for mediating and adjudicating colonial justice among indigenous groups.
From 1903 her main work (in the face of much opposition) was exploratory
and itinerant, and she rejected as inappropriate the organisation of large
mission stations with presbyterian-style churches, arguing that

> there is the essential need for something in-between, something more mobile
> and more flexible than ordinary congregational methods.[45]

Slessor also became increasingly concerned to promote economic self-
reliance and independence for women from the servility, degradation and
destitution which tribal custom imposed on them – especially widows.

Although her Christian faith was unshakeable, she was not bound to scriptural literalism, but allowed anger at the way men treated women to influence her vigorous dialogue with the Bible. In one of her copies, against the Pauline text commanding that wives should be subject to their husbands, Slessor scribbled 'Na Na Paul laddie! This will no do!'[46] She proposed a women's settlement, where they could build their own huts and farm their own land. Although her plan did not bear full fruit in her own lifetime, Agnes Arnot (the first 'Mary Slessor Memorial Missionary') developed this work. In 1918 she wrote home:

> The new buildings are being erected – a school and women's meeting house, a dwelling house, and three double houses for girls, and we hope to occupy them in the near future. One is to be a house of refuge for young Aro widows, who seek our protection and help in their pitiful position under Aro law, and for any others who need sanctuary. Also for churchwomen from various districts . . . who will stay for a few days, talk with the girls and give them advice about their position as Christians.[47]

Other women who went to work in Africa pushed out the boundaries of their own work and ideals, and of commitment to the rights of women from apparently conventional starting points. Jane Waterston from Inverness went to Lovedale – the flagship of the Free Church's Southern African mission – in 1867. At the age of twenty-three she established and superintended the girls department at the famous boarding school, where 'from the start, she began to impress on the school her own vigorous and original personality'.[48] Although her declared aim was 'Not to turn out school girls but women . . . Homes are what are wanted in Kaffirland, and young women will never be able to make homes unless they see and understand what a home is',[49] the academic standards and achievements of the school were high. Waterston was proud of the fact that:

> The girls were ambitious to get on so as to be up to the boys . . . It was at Lovedale that boys learnt that girls were not beasts of burden but their friends and companions.[50]

But Jane Waterston was not content with her undoubted success at Lovedale. As early as 1869 she wrote,

> I am happy here in everything but one, and that is these poor wretches of women up country. I am a woman myself and it haunts me more than I can tell you, the thought of these poor women whose present life is misery . . . The question of responsibility for these black sisters rests heavily with me.[51]

In 1874 she returned to Britain to begin medical studies, with the firm conviction that she would serve as a doctor in the proposed Central African mission which was established as Livingstonia in 1877. She was one of the first twelve women to study at Elizabeth Garrett Anderson's London School of Medicine, where she was highly regarded and offered a post teaching anatomy. But in 1879 she returned to Africa. Her sojourn at Livingstonia was short and extremely ill-fated, due to circumstances oulined below. In 1880 she went back to Lovedale, where for three years she worked unofficially, and by 1882 she was treating 7038 patients. But the Free Church Mission Committee would not countenance a medical mission there, and so Waterston was lost to the mission enterprise.

Marion Scott Stevenson went to Gikuyu, Kenya, as an unpaid missionary in 1904. By 1910 she was in charge of the educational work at Tumutumu – a new station five days' journey away. The Phelps-Stokes Commission on African Education gave her a glowing report:

> We can assure the Government that they will travel far and wide throughout the world to find a better educational worker than Miss Stevenson. Considering the time that the Mission has been organised, it would hardly be possible to discover a more brilliant system of village education. Miss Stevenson directs the school activities at headquarters as well as the supervision of no less than 43 little out-schools surrounding it.[52]

Stevenson was also an enthusiastic itinerator. Her biographer claims that she spent 483 out of her 583 last days sleeping under canvas, and moving, through scorching and difficult terrain, from village to village to work with women and girls.

Medical missionaries in Gikuyu became embroiled in an issue which had serious cultural and political ramifications. It marked an early clash between feminist imperialism and the apparent mysogyny of local ritual, over a practice which remains widespread and highly controversial. Scottish nurses and doctors were puzzled at the difficult labours, stillbirths, and infertility among the women they attended. By 1906 they had identified female circumcision (more accurately described as genital mutilation) as a major cause, and they began a campaign against it. This outraged Gikuyu people, for whom circumcision was a rite of passage, and the Christian stance presented converts with a real ethical dilemma. In 1922, some Christian student nurses witnessed a death during childbirth, the doctor explained its cause, and as a result they declared their opposition to female circumcision. Five nurses vowed to the local chief that they would never have their daughters circumcised, and three of them explained their position to the British District Commissioner. Women members of the Presbyterian Church of East Africa then formed an organisation to shelter and protect girls. They called it Kiama kia Ngo (Council of the Shield), and the title was not just symbolic. Sometimes women had to arm themselves with machetes, and even so, many girls were kidnapped and forcibly circumcised. Nyambura Njoroge writes:

> The Gikuyu circumcision controversy reached its height in 1928. Through the Kiama kia Ngo more Christian women from other mission stations and societies joined in resisting the degrading operation. Later, the woman's organisation merged with the girls' guilds and Bible study groups which missionary women had begun in various mission stations. By taking action against female circumcision, the women of the PCEA carved out an 'independent space' within the larger church . . . It is unfortunate that the church adopted the name used by the Church of Scotland [Woman's Guild], dropping the original name which signified women's struggle for wholeness and dignity. All the same, the women of the PCEA have never lost sight of their struggle, for it is through this "space" that they continue to fight for the full participation of women in the church and its ministries.[53]

This story illustrates some complex consequences of the female missionary presence. They certainly used their Western medical knowledge and moral standards to judge a practice which was of deep ritual significance to indigenous people. But the Scottish women's stand against circumcision enabled local women to understand the practice as something which damaged and endangered female quality of life, and they chose to defy their own culture and assert their rights. They were empowered, not only to show solidarity with one another, but to struggle for dignity and worth in the church as well. It is interesting also that Njoroge, as a Kenyan feminist historian writing in the 1990s, should affirm the importance of the female missionary contribution to the lives of the women among whom they worked, in the context of an article which concludes that

> We need to revisit our history in order to critically reflect on the question of African Christian womanhood on a continent in which the social status of women is not taken seriously.[54]

The establishment of mission fields in China was a later development in the Scottish mission story. The first single woman to be sent there was Barbara Pritty of the UPC Zenana Mission in 1889. The generally low status of Chinese women was compounded by particular challenges – footbinding, complex languages and a volatile political climate. Without the support of a colonial government, missionaries were much more vulnerable at the basic levels of acceptance and survival, as they discovered during the 1900 Boxer Rebellion and the inauguration from 1912 of the Republic. But these circumstances made the development of an indigenous church much more important, and in addition to educational and medical work, Scottish women shared in preparing Chinese Christians for leadership and evangelism. In 1927 the Moukden Theological College began to take women as regular students, and Elizabeth Macgregor, along with a Chinese colleague, trained female evangelists there. During the 1920s, the Manchurian church, which emerged from a union of fifteen churches and missions, also opened all its Courts to women. As an elder remarked,

> 'Paul has told us we are all one in Christ, there is neither Jew nor Greek, and we follow that; there is neither bond nor free, and we follow that; there is neither male nor female – why do we not follow that? Where are the women?' and he pointed round the assemblage of men. So women were also made eligible for election to Church courts.[55]

Under the banner of 'women's work for women', then, Scotswomen engaged in a wide range of tasks and responsibilities which offered able and innovative individuals levels of independence, professional development and authority which they could never have aspired to back in Scotland. As the *UFC Women's Missionary Magazine* acknowledged in 1918,

> The inspiration of Miss Slessor has fired the women of the Church, and many intrepid spirits have followed her into the wilds . . . Women missionaries are to be found, doing the work of men; teaching, healing, preaching, laying foundations of new industries, introducing new forms of agriculture, and renewing the life of people through their homes. The Church at home debates whether women may rightly serve as deacons, while the Church abroad thrusts almost the whole office of ministry upon them . . . Some are lonely, in danger, and all are weary and overstrained, but none is timid or regretful of the choice of her life-work. As one has just written from the remotest of our stations: 'I am so well, and enjoying life and work so thoroughly. I had far rather be building mud-houses out here than doing deputation work at home – a thousand times more. It is the people at home who ought to have the sympathy.'[56]

The Justification for Separate Women's Work

In 1884, Miss MacInnes of Glasgow addressed the UPC Zenana Mission Ladies Conference, on the subject, 'Woman's indebtedness to Christ a reason for engaging in zenana work'. She claimed:

> There is good reason why every Christian woman should take a prominent part in telling the Good News. For it is to the incarnation of God's dear Son that she owes everything that is elevating in her lot . . . Above all, let our girls

be impressed with the supreme importance of the missionary enterprise. Let them know that it is the noblest cause in which anyone can engage . . . Then when the church's sons shall eagerly press forward to enrol themselves in the army of the conquering Christ, so also, her daughters, realising that woman's true position in the church as in the family is that of 'help-meet', shall go forth in joyous bands, strong in numbers as in love, bearing with them into the dark and suffering homes of heathenism the gifts of healing and the lamp of light.[57]

The impact of the doctrine of separate spheres on the work of foreign mission is clearly seen in three inter-related justifications for distinctive women's work. They were all utilised in writing and discussion about such work from its outset until, in the first decades of the 20th century, they began to be challenged by those with first-hand experience. First, Scottish women were continually exhorted to recognise, and give grateful thanks for, the exalted position which their sex enjoyed in Christian lands. As a rhetorical device, the contrast which was drawn between the comparative situations of women in different cultures was a powerful tool utilised to great effect by advocates of the domestic ideal. Could the 19th-century evangelical woman fail to be moved by the following?

> Two pictures arise before the mind's eye – one of an English wife, the other of a Hindoo wife. The English wife sits in the bright, warm, cosy sitting room – herself the centre of all the household joy. The Hindoo wife is shut up in her apartments like a prisoner, or waits upon her lord and master like a slave . . . Two more pictures arise – the one of an English bride, the other of a Hindoo bride. The one wooed and wedded for her own sake, goes with the husband of her affections and of her choice to a home sanctified by love. The other, a poor, timid, crying, terrified child, whose age varies between five and twelve years, is bought and sold for money, carried off forcibly from her childish home to dwell among strangers, who may or may not be kind to her – the child-wife of a man who esteems women as a polluted, worthless race, expiating in their sex the sins of a former life.[58]

Such literature was hardly designed to excite much recognition of the common oppression suffered by both Indian and Scottish women of the period; nor to challenge the less rosy reality of Western marriage and family life concealed behind the sentimental idealism of the visions conjured up by Emma Pitman Raymond and her ilk. What it did was to confirm for readers the assumed superiority of Christian civilisation in which the 'natural' order of gender relationships prevailed, over the 'unnatural' practices of other religions and cultures. The purpose of such writing was to instil a sense of obligation in evangelical women to share their blessings with benighted sisters in distant lands.

The second reason advanced for women's missions was the urgent need to alleviate social and spiritual suffering. Individual acts of compassion, and later social welfare strategies, were central manifestations of the ethos of 'true womanhood'. In the foreign mission context, the possibilities of such womanly action were extensive and potentially radical. Not just friendship and relief of suffering, but also liberation and transformation of life were on offer. As Mrs Parker of the UPC Zenana Mission in Benares told a meeting:

> In order to reach the poor and downtrodden amongst the despised daughters of India, Christian women preach every day in religious festivals, streets and villages. The emancipation of Hindu and Mohamaden women can come only through the Gospel of Him who has done so much to elevate, and to place her in the position she occupies in Christian lands as equal and helpmeet of man.[59]

Yet even in this expression of female solidarity, and the recognition that only women could thus minister to other women, there is a hint of the third reason for women's mission to women. For the equality and emancipation on offer was that of helpmeet to man. The importance of female conversion lay, not just in its inherent redemptive value for individuals, but more particularly because only Christian women would be able to influence and service new and potential male converts according to the domestic precepts which were fundamental to the evangelical gospel. As at home, so abroad, women were considered primarily in terms of their relationship and usefulness to men. The Church of Scotland Foreign Mission Report of 1855, in commending the work of the Ladies Association, made this clear:

> Who can calculate the influences yet to be exerted by her who, touched by the power of God's grace and rescued from superstition and degradation, is enabled as sister, mother, wife, to exhibit in her appropriate sphere, all the graces and proprieties of the Christian character.[60]

And as an enthusiastic new missionary, Mary Slessor wrote in her first letter home from Old Calabar:

> Something more must be done for the women here, if we are to raise the men . . . they are the great drawback to our success.[61]

The conceptual equation of female equality with an auxiliary and circumscribed role permeated 19th-century missionary culture. In fact it was widely advocated as positive and Biblical by women in the movement. In 1891, the Free Church Ladies Society decided to call their new magazine *The Helpmeet*, because:

This name, first given to woman by her Maker, indicates her legitimate sphere, as the associate of man in work and worship – one specially fitted to help him . . .Yes, sisters in Christ, of whatever age or condition, may we not, every one of us, rejoicingly believe that He has set us in His Church to be 'helps', and that He is able to make us meet for His own use.[62]

What were the effects of this ideological justification for women's special mission? It certainly shaped the aims of the work attempted in the different mission fields. Whatever the particular challenges of each situation, female agents strove to inculcate the values and activities associated with the role of Christian wife and mother. The material and moral conditions of homelife were important – bourgeois Western notions about cleanliness, clothing, cooking, childcare and division of labour were criteria for judging the success of the enterprise. Christina Rainy remarked on her 1887 tour of Free Church work in India:

> We are raising up Christian wives and mothers who may become a power for good. On going to Toondee, I was quite struck with the nice tidy houses, well trained children, and modest, womanly bearing of the young married women who had been educated at Pachamba.[63]

African missionaries often commented that Christian men asked them to train up their wives, and Agnes Arnot in Calabar perhaps revealed more than she intended about the reality of 'Christian marriage' when she commented in 1918:

> There is no greater need than the development of pure home life on a Christian foundation. These girls have everything to learn . . . In heathen homes there is always someone a little lower in the social scale to do the drudgery, but in a Christian home there is but the one. In every way we are trying to train our girls for this.[64]

An uncharitable assessment might discern that this lays bare the truth of 'women's work for women': Scots presbyterian drudges encouraging other women to accept the domestic shackles of Christian marriage while pontificating about elevation and equality. But the reality was more complicated and positive for both groups of women. It is important to acknowledge the real and life-transforming advances which the Scottish brand of feminist imperialism brought to many thousands of women – in the shape of educational opportunities, medical treatment, personal compassion and respect and a sense of their own human worth. Likewise, the missionary women themselves (at least a significant portion of them) were far more than subordinate servants of the cause, modelling and teaching acceptable womanly spheres of activity as prescribed by evangelical Christianity and Victorian morality. Throughout the period, there were Scottish women whose qualities, actions and lifestyles belied the helpmeet role which the female societies claimed for themselves. They all shared to some extent the concept of Christian woman as moral guardian of society. But another fundamental belief was in the equality of every human soul before God. Salvation or damnation was a matter of inescapable individual responsibility. Mrs Ross, the Church of Scotland chaplain's wife who helped initiate zenana work in Poona, described the women who engaged in this mission as being shaped by 'a strong sense of individual responsibility before God', and recalled a conversation with a zenana woman:

> You Hindus always look upon yourselves as belonging to a class, as community, nation, caste or family; but God deals with people as individuals; the husband cannot answer for his wife, nor the parent for his child. The day will come when you must go forth alone to meet God – you know that you must die alone.[65]

Missionary women, like their peers in Scotland, may have failed to understand the importance of class and community in shaping their own society and presumptions, but both for themselves, and for the women they worked with, this individualism was an important corrective to the pervasive denial of female personal autonomy. And presbyterian Scotswomen were not slow to show respect for the individual (including themselves), even when that conflicted with convention or propriety. Perhaps they had an advantage over, for example, their Anglican sisters, because personal accountability tended to count for more in the Scottish cultural and religious heritage than right order. The Anglican Church Missionary Society Regulations made it quite clear that female agents' work was subordinate and circumscribed:

> Being a woman as well as a missionary, each sister has assigned to her, a distinct limit of service, and a definite sphere.[66]

Scottish women may, on many occasions, have had reason to doubt practical recognition of their status and liberty of action, but they were never explicitly subject to rules which restricted them in this way.

While there were always individual women who, in their missionary work, effectively contravened or ignored the doctrine of separate spheres (even while upholding it in theory), it was only in the 20th century that it began to be challenged as a principle. The numerical female superiority at mission stations, the expansion of their roles and responsibilities, the improved standard of their education and professionalism, the impact of the Women's Movement – all of these factors tended to make the understanding of women's work as auxiliary and separate increasingly obsolete and misleading. As the report of the 1910 Edinburgh Missionary Conference argued,

> In the field, work which once seemed so distinctively for women is not now so clearly differentiated. Christian effort for both men and women presents a far more united front. Many urge for an end to the 'artificial division' between the work of general and women's societies.[67]

Supervision and Jurisdiction of Women Missionaries

It was over questions of management and authority that these issues came to a head. By the 1910s, they were firmly on the Churches' agendas as structural and organisational matters, but the politics of gender recurred periodically at different times and places. It may be illuminating to consider three individual cases of assertive women in potential or actual conflict with their colleagues and societies, and representing the three main Scottish presbyterian denominations.

Jane Waterston

Jane Waterston, the first Scottish female missionary (probably the first Scotswoman) officially to qualify as a doctor, belonged to an Established Church family, but served with the missions of the Free Church in Lovedale and Livingstonia, South Africa. Her family did not support her vocation, although she ended up supporting them financially after her father's bank crashed in 1878. She was a forthright person who was never afraid to express her strong views. As such, her mixed fortunes as a missionary depended largely on her male colleagues and their ability, or otherwise, to comprehend and value a capable and unconventional woman.

At Lovedale, she enjoyed an excellent working relationship with Dr James Stewart and formed a lifelong friendship with his family. The founder of Lovedale, William Govan, had told Stewart that the proposed Female Institution 'should be presided over by a male head',[68] but when Waterston was appointed in 1867, she was given a free hand to develop the school as she saw fit. During her eight years there, with the support of Stewart, she established a successful and renowned institution. Although Waterston enjoyed her position of authority and respect at Lovedale, she had much to say in criticism of other local missionaries, of Dr Duff and the Foreign Mission Committee, and of the Ladies Society. As she commented in one letter:

That Mound, it deserves its name for I think plenty of good work gets buried there.[69]

Her main complaint concerned the poor terms and conditions offered to female missionaries. Although she demurred in a ladylike fashion at the salary first offered in 1866, writing, 'I am very glad to hear that it is to be no more than £80 . . . and the allowance for outfit I would like to be as small as possible', by 1869 she had discovered the harsh reality:

> I have considered the LSD and find that I am just living at that rate at present . . . A woman's life can never be the broad, strong thing a man's may become, but still, you might allow her to do what she can in the way of living. I like to live. I don't like to exist.[70]

And not every male missionary had such high regard for her as Dr Stewart. He wrote to his wife in 1871:

> Dr Dalzell and Miss Waterston did not get on well. He has not sufficient esteem for the sex as a whole to please her. When she came out with her strong views about women's rights and women's ability, then he would rap out something about a 'philosopher in petticoats' – one of his expressions to her – and so they went on.[71]

In 1874 Jane Waterston returned to Britain to train as a doctor. It was her ambition to work as a medical missionary in the proposed Central African Station, which in 1877 was established as Livingstonia, with Dr Robert Laws in charge. Her time in London brought new challenges and a strengthening of feminist convictions. In 1878 she confidently stated her terms for going to Livingstonia (in the face of attractive offers for employment in London). She made it clear that she considered that her main work would be medical, but that she should also be the head of any female department or school, with full powers and financial control. She upset the Society by asking for a salary of £200 to be paid in advance, along with passage and expenses, claiming:

> I make these two conditions from personal experience of unpleasantnesses and inconvenience of a difficult arrangement.[72]

She arrived in Livingstonia in November 1879 on a five-year contract. She left in April 1880. Her time there was an unmitigated disaster. Laws treated her with uncomprehending hostility – an attitude which was reciprocated. Neither he nor his colleagues could understand or cope with her opinions and manner. He refused to acknowledge or value her educational and medical experience (which was greater than his own), and relegated her to teaching elementary subjects and sewing. He took all the credit for establishing the medical practice of the mission, though she claimed that she undertook 'the heavy end of the medical work'. Waterston was incensed at the insinuations that she was there mainly to procure a husband; she felt lonely and ostracised. Perhaps her worst crime, in Laws' opinion, was her continuing criticism of the basis upon which he had established relationships with the local people. She felt that his harsh regime of discipline and corporal punisment was a reproach to the mission and to Christianity itself. Only a few weeks after her arrival, she was writing to Stewart:

> It is the gun and not the Bible that they rely on at Blantyre [a nearby Church of Scotland mission] and even here . . . I can't believe that this is the Gospel . . . It is a terrible pain to me to find the thing I had looked forward to and worked for turns out to be a very apple of Sodom.[73]

The extent of her bitter disillusionment is clear in a letter dated February 14, 1880:

> I have resigned . . . I will never repent having come here but once, and that is to the last day of my life, for it has shattered my faith in God and man and I fear I will never recover it . . . I have got a horror of religious humbug that will last me the rest of my days. I just hate being up here. It is my profession and the use that it has made me able to be of, that has kept me alive and prevented utter despair.[74]

The Foreign Mission Committee, who had found Waterston problematic in the past, struck her off the register of missionaries and demanded that she repay her passage and outfit, although she had returned to Lovedale and intended to see out her contract by engaging in medical work there. James Stewart was stalwart in her support, and wrote to a Glasgow man who was prepared to make a private contribution to help her establish a hospital:

> Her feeling against the Committee for their very summary justice in cutting her off is very strong. It is possible Laws' letters may have had something to do with their precipitousness. He did not like her and she just as cordially detests him. Placed up there as she was, a lonely woman – and seeing more clearly, I fear, than any of them that their general policy towards the natives was to be a disastrous one – there was nothing left for her but to come away . . . Now though she is reckoned to be difficult to get on with, I get on with her very well. She does her work excellently, is thoroughly loyal . . . she can be trusted implicitly and is in reality a splendid doctor.[75]

The Foreign Mission Committee would not sanction a medical mission at Lovedale, and in 1883 Jane Waterston moved to Cape Town, where she became a prominent doctor and citizen until her death in 1931. She apparently also recovered her faith enough to become a loyal member of St Andrew's Church. In 1929, an honorary degree of LLD was conferred on her by the University of Cape Town. The citation said of her:

> She has been a jealous fighter for the prestige of the medical and nursing professions, but the most authentic record of her life's work will be found written in the "humble annals of the poor" by whom her deeds of mercy and healing will long be remembered.[76]

Mary Pigot

Mary Pigot was a Eurasian woman who was first employed by the Church of Scotland Ladies Association in 1870 to take charge of their work in Calcutta. She became well known on her first furlough to Scotland, 1875–6, when she spoke at over forty meetings around the country on behalf of zenana work, which she claimed was woefully underfunded. She was the first agent to address public meetings on her own behalf, instead of sitting mute while men did the talking.

But her main impact, and notoriety, was achieved as the instigator of a libel case which shook the Church of Scotland Foreign Missions, and indeed the whole institution, to their foundations during the early 1880s.

For lovers of scandal, the Calcutta Mission Case had everything: sex, race, class, power struggles, violence, internecine presbyterian rivalry. It is difficult to find clarity or to draw conclusions from the morass of legal and ecclesiastical documentation. But the crux of the matter was a bitter personal conflict over issues of authority between the heads of the Male and Female Missions in Calcutta, which had direct results for the management of women's work both at home and abroad.

As a voluntary agency, rather than an integral part of the Church's official Mission Scheme, the Scottish Ladies Association and its agents were not under the jurisdiction of the Foreign Mission Committee or its field management. However, arrangements were made whereby supervision and financial control were carried out in consultation with the local Corresponding Boards (which consisted of ministers and elders of the colonial church, plus male missionaries). This arrangement had apparently operated quite harmoniously in Calcutta, and Pigot was on friendly terms with her male counterparts, until 1879, when William Hastie arrived to take charge of the General Assembly's Educational Institution in the city. Within two months:

In consequence of the machinations of [Hastie], who desired to place the Female Mission in subordination to the Corresponding Board, which [Pigot] resisted, a spirit of alienation appeared between members of the Board and Mary Pigot, who resigned.[77]

The SLA refused to accept her resignation, claiming that she was employed by them, and not by the Mission in Calcutta. She stayed on, but all connection with the Corresponding Board was severed, except that money was still channelled through the treasurer. Pigot believed that Hastie was engaged in an active campaign either to subordinate her or get rid of her altogether – and this feeling was exacerbated when Georgina Smail, who arrived in 1881 to act as her assistant, soon began to criticise Pigot's character and management, and refused to fulfil her contract. The SLA at home were anxious about what was happening, and invited Hastie to exercise his influence to restore harmony. He wrote a Memorandum to the SLA, and in the meantime Pigot sought leave to go to Scotland so that she and George Gillan (chaplain at St Andrews Kirk, Calcutta, and Corresponding Board Secretary) could be interviewed in the presence of the SLA Acting Committee, in an attempt to resolve the situation.

When she arrived in Scotland, Pigot discovered that

Georgina Smail had written to various SLA members, bringing charges of a serious nature against her, and that William Hastie had sent a Memo, alleging amongst other things, that his missionary efforts had been most seriously impeded and bitterly opposed by influences operating from the Female Branch of the Church's Mission.[78]

The SLA asked a number of prominent churchmen to investigate the charges against Pigot, and they exonerated her. However, in November 1882, Hastie sent documents to Dr Archibald Scott, convener of the Foreign Mission Committee, which he claimed provided authenticated evidence of immorality and malpractice by Pigot. In Scotland, Scott handed over the documents (which were letters solicited by Smail's sister, Mrs Annie Walker), to Pigot, and told her to vindicate herself, or else she would be prevented from returning to her duties as Superintendent.

It was on this basis that Pigot brought a libel action against Hastie, filed in Calcutta High Court on March 21, 1883. She claimed that he had conspired with Smail and Walker to discredit and damage her reputation and livelihood. The Judge found that there was malicious intent on the part of Hastie, but also that his defence had substantially succeeded, because allegations of immorality, impropriety and ill-treatment of orphanage pupils by Pigot were found to be true. He gave the verdict to the plaintiff, but awarded token damages, and instructed each party to pay costs.

Pigot went to the Court of Appeal, and the judgement was reversed. Hastie was ordered to pay damages. He was suspended by the Foreign Mission Committee and spent time in Calcutta jail because he was unable to pay his debts. Eventually he had to declare himself bankrupt. Mary Pigot, though apparently vindicated, was never re-appointed, although some of her Scottish supporters set up a pension fund on her behalf.

In bare outline, that was the Calcutta Mission Scandal. But it was the detail of scurrilous allegations which appealed to the salaciousness of the public in Calcutta and in Scotland. Mary Pigot was accused of having affairs with James Wilson, Professor in the Institution, and with Kali Churn Banerjee (a high profile convert of the Free Church Mission in Calcutta, and scourge of William Hastie in a dispute over which Church had the right to claim Dr Duff as founder of its mission). Both men were married. More seriously, Pigot was also accused of keeping the orphanage in a filthy condition; of beating and imprisoning certain girls; and of providing inadequate food and clothing. She had resolute supporters in both Scotland and India, but the SLA eventually came to the conclusion that her management practices were not satisfactory, which they attributed largely to overwork and ill-health. The Committee never accepted the imputations on her moral character, but most members of the scandalised public (including supporters of the SLA) did not believe that there could be so much smoke without fire.

However, William Hastie himself was no blameless paragon of virtue (in spite of the efforts of his biographer to make him seem so[79]). As the Secretary of the Foreign Mission Committee wrote in a private letter to Scott,

> His infirmity of temper, his intense self-conceit and his want of common sense in my view more than neutralise all his splendid qualities.[80]

His language was invariably intemperate, and he described Pigot as an illegitimate half-caste, a whore, and 'that abominable woman'.[81] He held a very exalted view of his own status as male ordained missionary, and while he may have been justified in criticising aspects of Pigot's management, his proposed solutions were not diplomatic. He recommended in his memo of 1882 that the Corresponding Board should be official correspondent, should control finance, sanction appointments, and have power of summary discharge over all non-Scottish SLA Agents. He proposed a Board sub-committee with the right to visit and oversee all departments of the Female Mission, and with sole power of management; concluded that he was 'entirely opposed to the policy of separation and independence pursued by the Ladies ever since I came to India'; and claimed that 'these powers seem to me moderate and reasonable'.[82] The SLA (or more accurately, the small group of men with whom they consulted about complicated situations) had been struggling for years to find appropriate mechanisms for local management. They did not agree with Hastie, and suggested instead a consulting committee, elected from within the Corresponding Board, with the Lady Superintendent as a full member, claiming that:

> Any lady competent to take such superintendence and of such sufficient age and strength of character to leave home for the field, and to have charge of such a Mission, is not likely to be willing to be virtually under the orders of the Corresponding Board.[83]

When Hastie received their response to his memo, he was scathing and contemptuous. In a letter to the Corresponding Board, he was critical of the educational thrust of the Female Mission's work. He thought its priority ought to be promotion of Christian family life, rather than

> entering upon the exciting career of striving to come up to a native institution in producing a set of Hindu Blue Stockings.[84]

And he was sarcastic about the 'logic of the whole report which seems to be founded on some new feminine system that may have been worked out in Edinburgh of late.'[85]

The Judge at the High Court concluded:

> What appears to have weighed much with William Hastie was a feeling of annoyance that the Ladies in Scotland were, for some reason or other, desirous that he should have practically no part in the control and guidance of the Female Mission. As head of the Male Mission, he seemed to consider he ought to have had more direct control, by virtue of his position . . . his pride had been mortified, and a condition of things had arisen between them, which animated Hastie with the desire, either to get rid of Mary Pigot, or to place her under close subjection.[86]

The repercussions of the whole sordid affair, apart from its effects on the individuals involved, and on the reputation and finances of the already beleagured Foreign Missions of the Established Church, directly affected the Ladies Association and its operations. An overture came before the 1883 General Assembly, asking that the whole subject of management be taken into consideration. Dr Scott described the events leading up to the libel action, and then, as *The Scotsman* of 30 May reported:

> He ventured to add that agents of the SLA should be supervised by the same body as supervised the missions of the Church. This trouble would never have

occurred had the SLA had the benefit of the protection of a proper board. Foreign Mission Committee representation should be increased on the SLA committee, and the convener should preside at all meetings of the acting committee of the SLA, and so get rid of the anomaly of the ugly word, 'chairwoman'.[87]

Apart from the central clash of two opinionated and apparently imperious personalities, the SLA as an autonomous organisation was on trial, and found wanting by many in the Assembly who were only too ready to sneer at a group of women who seemed to prevaricate and lack decisiveness. There was, apparently, much laughter during the 1883 debate about the competence of women to manage missions, and their admirably ladylike, and yet feeble inclination to turn to their husbands and other men for solutions to intractable problems. For those men there was also criticism. The leader in *The Scotsman* of June 2, 1884 (at which Assembly Hastie argued against his suspension in an epic eight-hour speech) exemplified the patronising attitudes which were so much in evidence:

> A man of real business ability would have known how to deal with conduct of this kind . . . and would never have let the case drift among the good, but not always wise, women who seem to be regarded as a mainstay of the mission. There is no doubt one excuse to be pleaded. The ladies do not seem to have been much more unwise than those of the other sex with whom they were associated . . . The public may be excused for thinking that the management of Foreign Missions has of late been given over to old women all round.[88]

Mary Slessor

Mary Slessor was a working-class woman whose early experience was as a mill worker in Dundee. Her father was an alcoholic, but her mother was a pious member of the United Presbyterian Church who was determined that her son should serve as a foreign missionary. Mary was a self-confessed 'wild lassie' in her teens, but her character and intelligence were recognised by her teachers and church elder. After the death of her brother, Mary began to consider her own vocation to the mission field, and she applied to be an agent at Old Calabar, where she arrived in 1876.

She was a plain speaking and down-to-earth individual, and was at first extremely frustrated working within the conventions of life in the mission compound of Duke Town, which involved polite pleasantries with the colonial community and with the wives of chiefs. She wanted instead to make contact with the ordinary people who belonged to the tribes of the surrounding country.

Her life as a missionary was marked not only by recurring disease and ill-health, but also by a succession of disputes with her colleagues and the UP Missionary Board in Scotland about how her time and talents were to be deployed. The latter had certainly not employed her to adopt African food and lifestyle (and numerous children too); nor did they envisage that any woman would choose to spend her time living on her own among notoriously fearsome peoples such as the Okoyong or Aro. But Mary was a woman of iron determination and resolute faith in a God whose will for her superseded any personal or ecclesiastical discipline.

Fortunately, her colleagues at Calabar were sufficiently perceptive and flexible to recognise that it was in their own and the mission's best interests to let Slessor have her way. In 1886 the senior missionaries, Anderson and Goldie, at first opposed the seemingly outrageous suggestion that she should live under tribal conditions with the Okoyong. But Slessor persisted, and also made several preparatory visits. In 1887 the local mission agreed to her plan, and 18 months later, so did the *Mission Board* in Edinburgh. In 1892, her knowledge and involvement with the people was such that she was appointed Vice-Consul by the colonial government to supervise the work of the newly established 'native' courts. In 1895 she submitted a lengthy report of her work, which was published in the Mission Record, and declared that it was time to move further inland to open up Itu territory, leaving the Okoyong to ordained missionaries.

And so her career went on, as she pushed deeper into new and unexplored lands. Her style was that of a dynamic initiator, rather than detailed organiser. She presented her schemes and suggestions as declarations of intent, and left the mission authorities to respond as they saw fit. But as they saw the fruits of her uncommon gifts and personality, and as her fame grew, they were expedient enough, in general, to let her develop her own career (and the achievements of their mission) as she pleased. Her most radical proposal was made in 1903. She believed that the time had come to fulfil the original intentions of the Calabar mission – that Africans should be their own evangelists – rather than concentrating on setting up large stations and churches according to incongruous Scottish models:

> I think that it is an open secret that for years the workers here have felt that our methods . . . were far from adequate to overtake the needs of our immense field . . . The scattered, broken units into which our African populations are divided..make it necessary for us to pay more than an occasional visit . . . even if that visit results in a school or church being built. Many plans suggest themselves, Church members organised into bands of two or three or four to

itinerate for a week over local neighbourhoods; native teachers spending a given number of days in each month in the outlying parts of their districts; trading members of the church undertaking service in any humble capacity on up-river trading stations . . . in these and many other ways the gaps may be bridged . . . and communications be opened without the material expense which the opening of new stations involves.[89]

Slessor proposed a survey which she would undertake herself, by canoe, to assess possibilities for expansion. The Mission Committee of the United Free Church had already banned further development in the Cross River area, but the plan was sent for their consideration. In the meantime, Slessor took her senior colleague, Mr Wilkie, on a tour of the proposed new territory, and he reported to Scotland that this was a great opportunity and Mary Slessor should receive full support. In *The Expendable Mary Slessor*, James Buchan comments:

> A less democratic church might well have insisted that even a famous missionary must toe the line. But . . . what Mary was saying made sense, and the FMC, with even less money to spare since the union, decided to take her up on her offer . . . This on the face of it was a very good bargain for her church. Its mission would expand its operations at no cost to anybody except the Africans and its expendable Miss Slessor. She, it seemed, was determined to go her own way and whatever happened to her would therefore be her own responsibility. So Mary spent the rest of her life, in WP Livingstone's words, 'dragging a great Church behind her' into Africa.[90]

Mary Slessor's disregard for standard mission behaviour derived in part from her own experiences in the factories and streets of Dundee. But had she remained in Scotland, her tremendous gifts and potential would surely have been frustrated, and perhaps entirely stifled, if channelled within the constraints of teaching or home mission work. Indeed when she came home on furlough, Slessor the explorer and dispenser of colonial justice was diffident and uncomfortable in church circles. But in the life she developed for herself in West Africa, she demonstrated the truly liberating possibilities of foreign mission work for women.

A common feature linking these three examples of forceful women in relation to the authority they sought and gained for themselves in very different circumstances, is that the only available local frameworks of management and support were those designed for and controlled by men. While many women enjoyed considerable personal autonomy, cooperation and encouragement, the structural inequality of their position was eventually recognised as anomalous. In the 1901 regulations for the Women's Foreign Mission (WFM) of the UFC, agents were placed under the supervision of local Mission Councils, but were allowed to speak and vote when their own work was under review. However, dissatisfaction with this arrangement was widespread by 1915, when the whole question of women's position in the Church was under consideration. Professor A H Hogg of Madras pointed out the inequality of status assigned to women:

> While there is no provision for giving women a share in the discussion and control of men's work, women missionaries are set under the control and supervision of Mission Councils which are local representatives of the (men's) Foreign Mission Council . . .The separation between men's and women's work is artificial . . . Hence any system is mischevious that restricts to men consideration of any given problem.[91]

It was proposed that women missionaries should become full members of Mission Councils, on the same terms as men (including the possibility of co-option for women – notably wives – who had responsibility for aspects of work, but in an honorary capacity), except when Councils exercised presbyterial powers. Women missionaries were overwhelmingly in favour of this. Men were less universally enthusiastic, and several Mission Councils suggested other compromise measures. But the proposal was passed at the 1916 General Assembly.

Throughout the first decades of the 20th century there was a growing mood in favour of doing away with separate female missionary societies, and in the post-1929 Church of Scotland, women's mission was incorporated into the Foreign Mission Committee, thus marking the end of almost a century of independent organisation. An article in the 1912 *International Review of Missions* outlined both the opportunities and potential drawbacks of this new order:

> The separate women's missionary society works in unsuspected isolation at a time when fresh light from God is streaming on the essential unity of humanity, which can no longer be segregated by race, class or sex . . . Many sided problems call for all available insights, both of men and women – new issues in the field belong to the body politic – their administrative treatment must be in the hands of men and women combined . . .The absence of co-operation is not satisfactory to woman missionaries. At least women in separate societies can administer their own work, and develop without interference, and to ask them to exchange this realm of influence for an uncertain place in joint administration is unwelcome. But true administrative co-operation would be welcome.[92]

On the whole, the post-1929 incorporation of women's work into the general administrative structure was experienced as a loss of power, as direct control was replaced by tokenism. It was disengenuous to assume 'the essential unity of humanity' without taking due account of the disadvantage, lack of power, and exclusion experienced by those who did not conform to the normative male, white, Western and middle-class image of that humanity.

On the Home Front – Women's Missionary Associations in Scotland

> One innovation after another! Envelope collections, missionary prayer-meetings, speechifying ladies![93]

There were certainly those within Scottish presbyterianism who believed that the organisations which supported female missionaries abroad represented innovations in the activity of women which were faintly ridiculous, or even rather threatening. That they had an impact on the lives of thousands of presbyterian women is undeniable, but the case for arguing that the impact was radical or transforming is much less clear cut. As the societies progressed and grew in size and complexity, they did extend the range of skills and activities of those who were involved, especially in leadership and advocacy. But they remained firmly embedded in (and indeed came to exemplify) a female evangelical culture which did not reject, but expanded the boundaries of, the concept of woman's sphere. However, that does not preclude recognition that for many individuals, and certain groups, involvement in the missionary movement required substantial personal change, growth and courage in particular situations. And for some it inspired deeper awareness of, and challenge to, church and societal structures which restricted opportunities and justice for women.

The history of the women's associations is marked by continual struggles for two basic necessities – recognition and money. The general reluctance of Scots to give adequate countenance and support to Foreign Missions was magnified in the case of female missions. The Established and Free Church ladies' societies were voluntary agencies (although individual ministers gave them help and support) and they could not make appeals for money through official church channels. And in the first years of their existence, they were constrained in the methods available to publicise their cause. All the associations began as groups of women in one town or city, without the benefit of a national organisation or network. Difficulties in travel, communications and female mobility meant that in practical terms their decision-making powers remained with members in Edinburgh or Glasgow. They did recognise the need to publicise the cause of female missions around Scotland, and to set up fundraising auxiliaries in different parts of the country, but accepted that men would have to act as their agents in this work, which was not regarded as seemly for women. A male deputy was appointed by the pre-Disruption Edinburgh Ladies Association, and in 1844 Captain Jameson advised the new Free Church Society:

> Your secretary should be a gentleman, and not on any account a lady . . . Not that ladies of the Committee should not do all in their power to promote its interests by active and vigorous correspondence all over Scotland.[94]

Indeed, letter-writing to friends and relations, and the seeking of personal donations, was the main early activity of members. As auxiliaries grew and awareness of women working abroad developed, other ways to support the work were adopted. In 1850 it was first proposed that an individual or group (such as a Sunday School) might choose a project or person to sponsor. In 1853, a collection of 'fancy work' (sewn and knitted goods, toys etc) was sent in a box to Calcutta, and the 'mission box' soon became a mainstay of home effort. In churches and manses all over Scotland, hundreds of work parties became regular features on church calendars. (They provided the basis for many a local branch of the Woman's Guild from 1887, and were no less ubiquitous in the Dissenting denominations). Some of the goods they produced were for sale in bazaars (often to expatriate Britons), and some were for use at the stations.

At these work parties it was usual for extracts from missionaries' letters, or some other appropriate literature, to be read aloud. Local groups were supplied by a network of letter-copiers, who in the Free Church Society formed the basis of a national organisation, and were sometimes directly inspired to volunteer for service themselves.

Missionary publications were also deemed a suitable avenue of communication for women. In 1844 the SLA entered into an agreement with the *Missionary Record* to include information about its activities. The Free Church Ladies Society actually produced its own magazine, The *Eastern Female's Friend*, from the same year. In 1859 the Church of Scotland SLA published a quarterly, *News of Female Missions*. The first issue carried an appeal for a thank-offering fund after the Indian Mutiny. As a direct result an orphanage was built at Sialkot.

In the mid-Victorian years, then, foreign missions were the focus for considerable church-based activity. A few women were engaged in organisational and literary enterprise, while many more shared their traditional skills on behalf of the movement. David Smith Cairns (later a Professor at the UFC College in Aberdeen) recalled his childhood in a Borders manse:

There were countless tea-parties with the women of the church – always for some practical objective. [My mother] had a deep interest in Foreign Missions so we saw and heard a good many missionaries. We in Stitchel had a special interest in Calabar. Under the leadership of my mother, women made garments for Calabar children and their mothers. I remember a great display of all these in the old church, which was festooned all around. These were despatched in a large wooden trunk on the Smith Elder steamer. In return Calabar people sent home hampers of tropical products . . . All these things humanised and popularised the mission idea for children and plain folk, long before one could really understand it.[95]

But although women throughout the country were beavering away on behalf of missions, it was hard for the female associations to ensure that support was directed specifically to their work, as long as they had a low public and official profile. To counteract the former problem women broke genuinely new ground within church circles, by engaging in progressively more extensive levels of public address and debate. During Mary Pigot's 1875 tour of Scotland, she directly campaigned for contributions to the Calcutta zenana scheme. In a 1900 article, Christina Rainy wrote of this general development:

With much misgiving, women began to speak, first to little gatherings of their own sex, then to mixed meetings; and finally to congregations and presbyteries! Some were shocked, but even the shock wakened them up. The speakers did not like it, but necessity was laid upon them.[96]

The difficulty, and yet also the resolution, with which prominent women like Rainy accepted these developments was recognised by Annie Small, who claimed that Rainy was 'a conservative by instinct and a radical by principle':

She loved the ancient paths, especially for women . . . But when, on the other hand, the need for missionary information throughout the Church seemed urgent, Miss Rainy threw herself wholeheartedly into the business and planned a crusade concerning which she wrote to me that we must be 'willing even to ascend the steps of the pulpit that we might reach larger audiences, even to visit Presbyteries, should these exclusively masculine bodies vouchsafe their permission or invitation!'[97]

And Mrs Sutherland of Calabar demonstrated the changes in her own lifetime:

During some of her earlier visits home her information was mostly imparted in private family circles; aft rwards, friends held drawing room meetings for her; then came public women's meetings, and the last time she visited this country, she addressed several large general meetings.[98]

In order to achieve public recognition and acceptance, the women's organisations had to tread a fine line between gaining the sanction (or at least commendation) of the General Assembly, and maintaining their autonomy and distinct purpose. They also evolved different degrees of internal control, while never entirely dispensing with the services of men in key practical and policy-making positions.

The Edinburgh Ladies Society of the Free Church, and its counterpart in Glasgow, which had no official links with any denomination, both struggled to make much impact on public awareness and purses before their partial union in 1865. In that year they agreed to exchange minutes and notify appointments to each other and to the Foreign Mission Committee of the Church. They also decided to pool their resources in a common fund, and to place agents under the express control of local Mission Councils.

The Assembly thenceforth annually commended the duly constituted 'Society for Female Education in India and South Africa' to the liberality of the Church, but this bore little fruit until 1883, when the Society obtained Assembly sanction to form Presbyterial Auxiliaries. These were developed from the informal district associations, which in turn had brought together letter copiers to share information and support. The 1883 deliverance resulted, according to the 1884 report, in an increase of eighty-three congregations contributing to funds, bringing the total to 342 (which was still only a quarter of all Free Church congregations). Income that year went up by £900. A national meeting of women from the various presbyteries evolved into an annual delegate Conference, and in 1885, the previously self-selecting Edinburgh Committee put its election in the hands of the conference. In 1892, the Glasgow and Edinburgh committees, which had retained responsibility for work in Africa and India respectively, resolved to unite. The Society was renamed the 'Women's Foreign Missionary Society of the Free Church of Scotland', and it submitted its Annual Reports to the Assembly. But it transacted its business independently of the Foreign Mission Committee, and all members, except for President, Vice-President and Secretary, were women. Between 1883 and 1900, the number of European workers employed increased from twenty to seventy, and those appointed locally at stations from one hundred to four hundred. By 1900, the home income of the Society was over £16,000, and it raised around £9000 abroad in fees, government grants and local contributions. This increasingly sophisticated and complex business operation was sustained and stimulated by a network of enthusiastic and competent women, who nevertheless felt that the burden fell unfairly upon them. The 1896 WFMS Report claimed:

It is evident that Free Church women are developing business powers which were hardly suspected 20 years ago. Perhaps there is room for improvement still . . . Let us be well assured that in wisely enlisting the sympathies of all our ministers and people, we are really conferring a benefit on them. One Presbyterial secretary writes, 'The meetings of women in our different congregations have been helpful, not only in fostering interest in Foreign Missions, but also in stimulating us in reference to all the different departments of congregational life and work.'[99]

The Ladies Association of the Established Church also evolved a structure based on an acting committee supported by, and passing on information to, groups which met at congregational, presbytery and national levels. After years of struggling to meet its financial commitments and to encourage popular support for its efforts, the Calcutta scandal brought the SLA into the purview of the Church at large in a negative light. Organisational changes placed it much more directly under the control of the Foreign Mission Committee (FMC), but the mid-1880s also witnessed a marked increase in interest and activity at home and abroad. By 1885, the acting committee and sub-committee for each station, for finance and for publications, were under the overall chairmanship of the FMC convener. There was a sub-committee of the FMC which was to 'advise and co-operate with the SLA', and also a group of male financial advisers elected from the FMC. On the other hand, a full-time female organising secretary – Helen Reid – was employed, and she was particularly successful in developing the association at parochial and presbyterial levels. As the Woman's Guild grew within the Church of Scotland, those involved in foreign missions shared their experience with, and were integrated into the framework of, the movement. In the 1920s, a few members of the Women's Foreign Mission finally found their way into token membership of the Assembly's Foreign Mission Committee.

In the United Presbyterian Church, the Zenana Mission Committee, formed in 1881, was an initiative of the Foreign Mission Board, which appointed a sub-committee of eight men to consider the employment of single women in India. It was they who sought the assistance of women to promote the scheme and help raise funds. In 1884 a Conference was held to bring together local representatives of concerned women, and in 1886 a 'Conference Committee' of eight women was appointed to co-ordinate information and arrangements. Eventually this small group became associated with the Zenana sub-committee to form, in effect, the executive of Women's Mission work (including, after 1886, all female agents at Calabar). These women were invited to attend the Foreign Mission Board itself when decisions they had taken were under review.

Miss Adam, who was convener of the Conference Committee and the only woman invited to address the UPC Jubilee Conference in 1897, told that gathering:

> The Conference Committee now helps with all administration; conducts regular correspondence with each missionary and Presbytery Secretary; regulates mission boxes; organises visitation work by those on furlough, and publishes the *Zenana Mission Quarterly*, which was first issued in October 1887. It is well managed and with a credit of £220. The work at home is important. Women's work has brought a fuller life into many a heart. One writes, 'I am conscious of my relations to the whole world. I feel that with my own hand I am unlocking forces which will speedily bring the world to its Lord and Christ.'[100]

While these developments gave some scope to women to participate in structures which deliberately mirrored those official presbyterian institutions from which they were excluded, all the societies depended upon the support and active involvement of men, whilst the Free and Established Church bodies enjoyed none of the real benefits of being official schemes of the Church. Leadership positions were still largely occupied by women from Edinburgh and (to a lesser extent) Glasgow, who were usually the wives, sisters and daughters of prominent ministers and other advocates of the foreign mission cause. And their efforts did not enjoy the unqualified support of church members. Mrs Watson of Dundee feared that they were

> much inclined to consider the newfangled 'Zana' scheme as an unreasonable fad being urged upon them by ministers and a few rich ladies in want of something to do . . . When missions are the object [of fundraising], people are smitten with cold indifference or even provoked to anger . . . 'Dinna ye give to those missionaries; they're just an idle lot, and Christian natives are all hypocrites.'[101]

The 1900 Union of the United Presbyterian and Free Churches provided an opportunity to review the methods employed by proponents of women's missions in both denominations, and to consider ways of combining the advantages, as they perceived them, of both. Christina Rainy of the Free Church was a corresponding member of the UPC Conference Committee, and she wrote in *The Helpmeet*:

> I can testify from personal observation that while the ladies exercise all legitimate influence in management, there is an advantage in having the gentlemen of the Mission Board taking their own share of responsibility, were it only because you thus have the leading office-bearers of the Church prepared to explain and defend the decisions arrived at, should these be challenged in

Church Courts or elsewhere, and also as it tends to unify the administration of both sides of the work.[102]

The regulations for the Women's Foreign Mission of the United Free Church established a a Central Committee, consisting of 40 members (26 ex-FCS, 14 ex-UPC) elected annually by a representative conference, plus ten representatives of the Foreign Mission Committee. A number of members were associated with the FMC when it considered and confirmed the minutes of the WFM. Subject to these provisions:

> The WFM Committee shall manage its business, select and correspond with missionaries, and administer funds connected with its own department.[103]

And in 1916, the UFC Assembly passed a resolution which gave a small number of women full voting membership of, among others, the Foreign Mission Committee. It also authorised the addition of women to Presbytery Committees, 'as they see need.'[104] Two other developments are worthy of note. One emerged from within the movement, as the initiative of women who had been involved in the promotion of mission work for a long time. The other brought new blood, ideas and challenge into the organisation, both at home and abroad. Both were connected with the growth in opportunities for the professional training and higher education of women.

The Women's Missionary College

Christina Rainy and her friend Mrs Cleghorn (daughter of Lord Cockburn), provided the inspiration and practical backing to establish a College in Edinburgh. For some time they had recognised that Normal Colleges and private para-medical institutions were of limited value in offering adequate preparation and encouragement to women who claimed a missionary vocation. As the work grew in scale and complexity the fallacy that earnest piety was sufficient qualification for such women was ever more evident. Discernment and development of appropriate character and skills had to be undertaken systematically.

In 1894 the new College opened in George Square, near to the Rainy home, with Annie Small as Principal, and three students. In 1897 it moved to Atholl Crescent, and in 1908 it took up residence in purpose-built accommodation at Inverleith Terrace. Its general aim was:

> To provide, in view of the complexity of the modern situation, an adequate general preparation for women who are anxious to devote themselves to religious work at home or abroad.[105]

The College, which attracted students from many denominations and nationalities, was ahead of its time in the quality of theoretical and practical education, and of corporate life, which it offered. It played a pioneering role in the international missionary movement which coalesced at the 1910 Edinburgh Conference and influenced many subsequent developments. It owed its success largely to the vision and creativity of Small. She combined intellectually advanced teaching in Biblical criticism, comparative religion, languages, sociology and methodology; with an imaginative programme of practical experience and group work. These elements were underpinned by a community life which emphasised solidarity, individual character and tolerance, rather than the uniformity, obedience and conventions which characterised so many female residential institutions. She had a truly global perspective, accepting no rigid divisions between sacred and secular; Protestant and Catholic; 'civilised' and 'heathen'. One former student recalled:

> The curriculum was designed on a very liberal scale, and on attractive as well as practical lines . . . Looking back and considering the very Victorian character of her education and ours, I am filled with admiration at the sweep of the curriculum and its adequacy, both in conception and realisation. We left with our minds opened in many useful and essential directions . . . She did not try to force us all into the same mould: charity, toleration, fellowship, this was the spirit which she inculcated, and in which she herself lived.[106]

The Women's Missionary College continued to develop its system of training after Small's retirement in 1913. Staff members were committed to the affirmation and increased participation of women in church life. The spirit of sisterhood and mutual support which was imbued in alumnae around the world cannot fail to have influenced the attitudes and actions of those concerned with female missionary work in the first thirty years of the 20th century.

The Girls Auxiliary

In 1901, two young Edinburgh women attended a missionary conference held by the presbyterial committee of the UFC Women's Foreign Mission. No one else present was under thirty, and they decided they should do something to interest young women in the mission work of the Church. Eleanor Lorimer recalled in 1951:

> The Girls Auxiliary was born to link the more go-ahead girls to the direct service of our own Church . . . Missions generally had become the province

of old ladies or of very pious and rather 'stuffy' girls . . . The Church in that day did not use girls as such: it merely set them to help mildly in organisations run by other people.[107]

The 'go-ahead girls' in fact belonged to the first generation of women to enjoy the benefits of university life and education. Most of the original GA leaders had experience of debating societies and the British Colleges Christian Union, which became the Student Christian Movement. The SCM was a notable early training ground in ideals of equality and comradeship between men and women and a channel, through the Student Volunteer Missionary Union of Britain and Ireland, which first met in Edinburgh in 1892, for commitment to 'world evangelisation in this generation'. The Girls Auxiliary quickly developed into a national network of young women aged between fifteen and thirty who engaged in prayer, study, debate and fundraising for the work of WFM. By 1922 there was an office, a full time secretary, 14,000 members and six 'Girls' Own Missionaries' supported in different fields.

The GA injected new life into what seems to have become a rather moribund and unimaginative home organisation. It brought both older women and other young church women into contact with some of the more progressive currents and developments in the Women's and Foreign Mission movements. And it provided a forum for some serious discussion about the nature and purpose of mission and the role of women in church and society. However, the ideas which were considered progressive during the Edwardian period were heavily influenced by Social Darwinist understandings of race and gender. With the influx of large numbers of middle-class women (and also men from higher social classes than had previously sustained foreign missionary endeavour) came a new emphasis for evangelism: the optimistic sense of national and racial destiny to conquer the world for Christianity:

> Nowadays we must link on the Imperial to the missionary idea. It is our duty, not only as Christians, but as fellow-subjects of the British Empire, to send the best gift we possess to these lands.[108]

Middle-class Scots who believed in the essential goodness and glamour of the British Empire were perhaps more excited at the prospect of contributing to its benign rule over benighted people, than with struggling to solve the intractable problems at home. The development of sophisticated mission compounds and institutions concentrated in areas which had been incorporated into the political Empire, led also to the widespread abandonment of genuine attempts to build up indigenous churches. Instead, increasing numbers of white agents with professional skills ran the religious and philanthropic services of missions. And women, having recently gained access to medical and teaching qualifications, were prominent in determining their ethos. At this time there is little evidence of missionaries engaging in any radical critique of imperial political economy.[109]

The feminisation of the missionary workforce at home and abroad met with a range of male reactions. A minority were genuinely supportive and welcomed every change, including increased participation in management and decision-making. Others adopted attitudes ranging from mild derision and scorn to outright hostility – especially when women sought entry into the hallowed portals of exclusively male bastions. On the whole, male support was conditional on women accepting their ascribed auxiliary status, especially in the home organisations. In 1884 Principal Rainy commended the work of the Free Church Ladies Society in terms which may have reflected awareness of troubles in the Established Church, but which nevertheless seem rather insulting to his own sister Christina, and other capable women:

> There was in some quarters no adequate appreciation of the importance of women's work. People failed to remember that half the mission field was work among women. He dared say that as this work was in the hands of the ladies, there might be a polite feeling on the part of the male classes (laughter) that the work could not be very complete or well done. But he might comfort the Assembly by telling them that though the Ladies Society gathered the funds for the support of their agents, yet all their arrangements were sanctioned by the Foreign Mission Committee. In their work they had also the guidance of some of the very best elders. When sent forth to work, their agents did not work at their own hands, but under local mission councils in the field. So there was every reason to believe that the work would go on in a well regulated way.[110]

A Ladies Society *Women's Work* pamphlet, 'Doubts and Difficulties Dispelled – A Dialogue', took the form of a dialogue involving several women and men from a country parish meeting in the Edinburgh parlour of a former member during the 1884 Assembly. While the dialogue is, no doubt, a construction, it is reasonable to assume that it reflects the range of male attitudes which women in the Ladies Society encountered. The pamphlet was clearly intended to serve as both resource and encouragement to its readers, who would have to promote the cause of female missions at parish level, after the Society had been endorsed at the 1884 Free Church Assembly. At the very least, it reveals the way in which male attitudes were perceived by women activists:

M – But why does not the Foreign Mission Committee undertake both sides of the work?

W – We are able to create more interest, and raise more money, by co-operating with men in this great enterprise . . .

M – But did you ever hear of any other church that managed its foreign mission so..?

W – Nearly all Presbyterian Churches do so

M – Some of us have our doubts about the management of the Society

W – What do you find fault with?

M – I heard you lost several good agents who offered you their services, and were afterwards picked up by other societies. This is what comes of the 'monstrous regiment of women'!

W – What you refer to applies to the FMC as well as to the Ladies Society . . . (There follows a discussion about raising interest and funds) . . . The missionaries on furlough are all very ready to help. At all events, we could perhaps send a lady to address the women of your congregation.

M – One innovation after another! Enveloped collections, missionary prayer-meetings, speechifying ladies!

W – (aside) It is lucky we did not mention our Presbyterial Auxiliaries

M – All I can say is, that you have a talent for inventing jaw-breaking names. No wonder people are afraid of you!

W – Auxiliaries are simply meetings of ladies who reside within the bounds of a presbytery, for mutual consultation and encouragement . . .

M – They will soon tire of it!

W – (aside) You will see that we meet with a good deal of discouragement.[111]

There were frequent complaints that the courts of the church either lacked interest in, or were actively antagonistic to the work of the societies. And although changes in the UF Church theoretically entitled women to representation on certain committees, the 1918 Report of the WFM claimed:

Presbyteries have been slow to follow the Assembly recommendation to appoint representatives of WFM to serve on committees for Foreign Mission – only Dunoon, and Irvine and Kilmarnock have done so, although the secretary of the latter's WFM says "We have not, so far, been called to any meetings". In Edinburgh, representation has been increased from four to eight at the presbytery's request. For the rest, co-operation between FM and WFM rarely goes beyond the sending of a report once a year – or the occasional social evening.[112]

This grudging attitude, with its reluctance to concede competence as a female attribute, and unwillingness to accept female enterprise on equal terms, co-existed with an underlying fear, occasionally expressed, that women were trying to set up their own church, in competition with the real thing. There were many men who recoiled at the very idea that their age-old monopoly on ecclesiastical power was under threat. Lady Frances Balfour, who was a staunch supporter of both the Church of Scotland and the Women's Movement, recalled:

> Which of us, acquainted with the church history of our day, but remembers the General Assembly when women missionaries were first invited to stand by their fellow workers and be addressed by the Moderator . . . It was a great shock to the Fathers and Brethren, that their sex should not disqualify them from standing in the Assembly.[113]

Nevertheless, there is little to suggest that the women's missionary organisations perceived themselves to be in the vanguard of the struggle for women's rights. Although it can be argued that missionaries were exercising a kind of feminist imperialism in alien cultures (for example, in promoting female literacy and opposing cultural practices such as foot-binding or female circumcision) its basis was the essentially conservative domestic ideology, allied with the conviction that Christianity was a beneficent influence on the position of women. The leading lights of the movement had close personal ties with eminent churchmen, and a reverence for presbyterian traditions. Most missionary candidates and home supporters expressed their motivation firmly within an evangelical framework. Agnes Cunningham was typical:

> My heart having been led to take a deep interest in the Mission field in early years, and having been brought to personal knowledge of Christ as my Saviour, I longed to go and tell those who know not Christ, of his love and saving power.[114]

It is not helpful to adopt the approach of some social historians who underestimate or ignore the reality and strength of religious faith as a motive force in individual and corporate life, and who regard it rather simplistically only as a socio-economic framework. First and foremost, it was a deep and genuine Christian conviction which induced most missionary women to undertake and thenceforth to expand the boundaries of work abroad. On the whole, there is little evidence to support any suggestion that missionary fervour was used by those directly involved to justify pre-formed arguments about the changing role and rights of women. It was the reverse process which characterised the changing experience of so many women – they found courage to push back the boundaries of their 'sphere' precisely so that they could be more effective in their Christian vocation.

But if the women's foreign missionary movement did not adopt a conscious feminist position, it offered plenty of grist to the mill of Christian women who were involved in the reformist campaigns of the late 19th and early 20th centuries. Helen Reid, for example, was deeply involved in the movement for the higher education of women, and edited *The Attempt* magazine, before she became SLA secretary. She remained a political conservative throughout. From around 1870 the same Edinburgh establishment names crop up frequently in connection with a range of social and philanthropic causes, including female suffrage and foreign missions. Commitment to these was apparently quite compatible with traditional church membership and activity.

But dissatisfaction with the Church itself in its attitudes toward and limitation of women was also felt and increasingly expressed. Those who experienced obstruction and petty restrictions abroad, and conversely those who felt that church life at home compared unfavourably with opportunities in the field, both made some impact through the network. The patronising and contemptuous attitudes of so many presbyterian men towards the societies also aroused much irritation and reaction.

These rumblings of dissent, allied to a growing sense of history and achievement within the mission organisations, and the new input from such as the Missionary College and the Girls Auxiliary, certainly stimulated a significant minority, in the first decades of the new century, to make an explicit connection between the Women's Movement and Foreign Missions. Mary Williamson, daughter of the minister at Dean Parish Church, Edinburgh, gave an address to the Scottish Churches League for Woman Suffrage, meeting in March 1913. The hints here of imperialist maternalism, of millenialism, and of warning to forces of reaction within the Church, are all characteristic of the mood within the pre-war generation of progressive churchwomen:

> The student of history cannot fail to be struck by the correspondence between the Women's Movement in the west and the type of woman missionary required at the front . . . All over the east women are being educated and emancipated . . . Who will direct this Women's Movement in the East and prevent its new found liberty from degenerating into license? The Woman-Statesman is required, but how shall she free and guide others unless she herself is free? Where can missionaries find better training than in the Women's

organisations of the west. Is the close connection between the Women's Movement and Foreign Missions not providential? Should not this consideration give pause to those who, either by active hostility, or by indifference to the cause of women at home, are hindering the progress of God's Kingdom in other lands?'[115]

The Significance of the Scottish Women's Missionary Movement

We thought of our whole lives from infancy upwards as an adventure – a reaching forth into the unknown . . . [We] spoke of the need for adventurous spirits in the high places of the field: to go forth, like knights of old, to succour and heal.[116]

Foreign mission work was, as it changed and developed from 1830–1930, a symbolic expression of what it meant to be a Scottish presbyterian woman. It espoused and gloried in the idea of a distinctive ministry. It affirmed apparently conservative values relating to gender, race and class. But the movement was instrumental in helping to shape (in a society dominated by religious belief and culture) a more positive view of women's sphere. Involvement in mission, especially in the field, but also at home, had the practical effect of transforming the lives of many women, without necessarily transforming their consciousness. With notable exceptions, mission women consistently applied western evangelical standards of womanliness as the goal for the work, and their criterion for judging its success. The need to serve that cause provided the rationale for training and qualification in teaching, nursing, medicine and social work. So missionaries were among the first truly professional women. But unlike the 'New Woman' of the late 19th century who in the popular view had cast off her femininity to compete with men, the missionaries (notwithstanding acceptable images as eccentric old maids) placed qualities of altruism and self-sacrifice at the centre of their work. Missions offered all the opportunities of an independent career, with the added glamour of adventure and travel (and potential dangers too), but without condemning agents to the fierce criticism reserved for women whose personal ambition was seen as a fundamental threat to the ordered spheres of society.

In fact, a gendered separation of roles could work to their advantage, even as that separation was surreptitiously undermined or abandoned. Missionary women were able to claim credit for the initiation and completion of their own distinctive work, and this gave them confidence and authority. Many at home learnt new skills in administration and advocacy, and began to overcome traditional self-perceptions of helplessness in any other than domestic situations. The movement made an impact on the church, not, on the whole, by directly challenging or contradicting men, but because women gradually assumed for themselves and understood the implications of greater responsibility.

In many respects foreign missionary work formed a continuum with other expressions of female agency. What made it distinctive, and offered women the chance to live and witness in ways which went far beyond traditional limits, was the exposure to a beautiful yet disturbing world beyond familiar horizons. Some missionaries thrived on situations which offered both opportunity and danger, while others retreated into the safe familiarity of religious and cultural certainty. The geographical and psychological spaces they found for themselves had the potential to offer real liberation – for individual missionaries, for the women they worked among in the field, and, by association and example, for the wider Scottish female public. The number of presbyterian women who served as missionaries did not exceed, in total, more than a few hundred during the period under consideration. The overall impact of the movement on Scottish society must therefore be judged largely on the impression which it made on public attitudes and actions. The foreign missionary movement was tremendously significant at many levels for Victorian and Edwardian society in general, and perhaps for women in particular. The growing size, importance and sophistication of their organisations was enough to establish the innovative value of the movement for Scottish presbyterian women. But foreign missions functioned also at a deep and symbolic level, helping to shape and confirm a national psyche in an age of imperialism. At the heart of this process were the unquestionably brave, complex and remarkable individuals around whom a huge hero-making industry developed. The stories of these missionaries were told in innumerable church and secular journals, and in cheap and popular biographies. They were read, not just in homes, but at countless work parties, sewing meetings, mission soirees. Magic lantern slides and dramatic tableaux also brought scenes and incidents from the field to life in church halls across Scotland. John Mackenzie has written of imperial folk heroes:

> They served to explain and justify the rise of the imperial state, personify national greatness, and offer examples of self-sacrificing service to a current generation. They were used as the embodiment of the collective will, stereotypes of a shared culture, and promoters of unity in the face of potential fragmentation.[117]

Mackenzie considers that David Livingstone, that archetypal Scottish Victorian hero, fulfilled all of these criteria. But it is also true that several female missionaries were the subjects of very positive and powerful publicity. None more so than Mary Slessor, who was really the female working-class counterpart (for the next generation) of Livingstone – a man who was her own missionary hero.

Livingstone was a Victorian hero, but Slessor was a cult heroine of the 20th century (although her missionary service began in the 1880s). Her name was invoked so often, and with such pride, in Scottish church circles, that the legendary tales of her character and exploits cannot fail to have affected thousands of men and women, girls and boys. But whatever the mythmakers did with their versions of the story, it was indubitably the tale of an active, brave, earthy and unconventional woman. While Mary Slessor would, perhaps, have found little to dispute in the poem with which this chapter began, her own work seemed to bear witness to an entirely different atmosphere of female Christian witness. She was an ideal heroine for a new wave of young women (typified by the UFC Girls Association) who were encouraged to believe that a female life of faith could be more adventurous and free, and that their own lives could really make a difference in the world. And because Slessor was a heroine for the whole church and nation, her story must have helped to counteract old notions of appropriate character traits and spheres of activity for men and women. Indeed, much of the Scottish pride in her seemed to have been associated with the image of a no-nonsense, plain-speaking, couthy individual who treated everyone alike, and did not defer to anyone, regardless of their position. These features endeared her to a public which believed she reflected back to them all that was most valuable and distinctive about the Scottish character. Described in language which emphasised a romantic individualism much more closely associated with men, she

> was seen to push human action beyond the normal bounds, to be a wanderer who became an energising force through refusing to conform with the normal patterns of life . . . was fearless, decisive and committed unto death, taking on forces, natural or human, that called forth the exercise of an indomitable will, superhuman physical stamina, and an almost miraculous courage.[118]

But there was always also the 'feminine' side of her personality – her love and tenderness, her physical frailty, her public reticence while on furlough, her efforts at homemaking and childrearing in 'darkest Africa'. Perhaps this was a real strength for those women who were inspired to emulate her. For surely if Slessor achieved recognition and acclamation for her endeavours, without being criticised for being unwomanly, so too could others following in her footsteps.

On the other hand, the popular publications which promoted the Slessor cult (and those written about other women missionaries) tended to be didactic and moralistic in tone. Those intended for children especially used the story to emphasise religious messages about humility, sacrifice, dependence upon God, and the importance of prayer. It was those elements of the missionary's life which were to be learned and copied in the midst of mundane Scottish existence, while her explorations, conflicts, building, administrative and juridical work were the elements of romance – exciting to read about, but a million miles from the real lives of ordinary Scots. It is not surprising – indeed it was probably inevitable – that missionary stories were used in this way in Sunday Schools and pulpits across the land. But for most people the value and importance of Slessor's life was at one and the same time an affirmation of all that was best in the Scottish and Christian character, and also the celebration of something truly extraordinary, which only a chosen few could hope to follow.

Another feature of biographies was their stress on the savagery and backwardness of the 'natives' among whom the missionary laboured. This served to confirm the validity, not only of religious prosyletising, but also of the whole project of the British Empire, in which church missions occupied a key (though not always acquiescent) role. And it contributed to the mental background of racialist theories which, by the 20th century were widely accepted. So the 'white man's (or even woman's) burden' was justified, and the tutelage of subject peoples was for their own benefit.

Such attitudes are evident in this extract from *Mary Slessor, The Dundee Factory Girl who became a Devoted African Missionary* (1923):

> She longed to carry the Gospel to these savages, realising the risk she ran, but fearing no danger if only the news of God's love could be told to these dusky children of Adam . . . A brawny black having applied to her for medical help she took out the castor oil. The man acted like bad children and would not unlock his lips. She gave him a box on the ear, and when he had been dosed resumed her usual placid demeanour . . . The while, busy in a thousand sordid tasks, she kept up her reading, feeding her mind and studying the Bible as the source of all her comfort, wisdom and strength. Hence she was much in prayer, and by it was made brave. Thus while traversing the forests where leopards dogged her steps she took refuge in prayer and so won courage and deliverance. No wonder that her force of character, courage, and that indescribable charm, the kind always possess, brought chiefs and even whole tribes to her so that she might settle their differences, and point out to them the right path.[119]

What really was the impact of such material on girls and women of the Scottish churches? It must have evoked a range of responses: a general sense of interest and pride in the exploits of Scots abroad; serious attempts to base personal and spiritual lives on their example; excitement that women could act with such independence and valour; a dutiful commitment to produce more dresses and dolls for the poor wee black babies; a distraction from the dreary injustice of so many working women's lives, and from the possibility of political and collective action.

The evidence from missionary paraphenalia – in women's magazines and supplements, in letters from those who aspired to mission work, in minutes and reports from local church women's organisations – does suggest an important link between the promotion of missionary heroines, and a more dynamic view of what it meant to be a Christian woman. This was of direct consequence to many who were thereby given confidence and inspiration to 'reach forth into the unknown' in their own lives, and it would not do to underestimate the power of a good model for girls and women striving for adventure.

Perhaps the more general (but not necessarily conflicting) effect of the movement and its mythology was romantic in a less focused sense. The gulf between the complicated, exhausting, frustrating yet fulfilling experience of many women missionaries, and the lives of their supporters back home, was bridged by accounts and images of noble white heroines. These could be used to challenge old conventions and prejudices at home (as when the situation in India was highlighted in support of the campaign for British women to receive medical education), but more often served to confirm dominant Scottish attitudes to race, religion and Empire: that God was in his Anglo-Protestant heaven, while his white envoys struggled valiantly to convert the heathen masses to the benefits of Christian freedom and imperial tutelage.

Notes

1. Emma Raymond Pitman, *Heroines of the Mission Field* (1880) 1

2. Parliamentary speech, 1793. See R Coupland, *William Wilberforce* (1945)

3. For changing models of missionary work, see e.g Philip Curtin, *The Image of Africa* (1964); T Christensen and W R Hutchison (eds), *Missionary Ideologies in the Imperialist Era 1880–1920* (1982)

4. Quoted by Olive Wyon in her biography of Small, *The Three Windows* (1953) 51

5. J W Jack, *Daybreak in Livingstonia* (1901) 332

6. Minutes of the UP Foreign Missions Board (1882), Appendix 18 (NLS Dep 298/70)

7. Wyon op cit 24–5

8. J B Cobb, 'Feminism and Process Thought: A Two-way Relationship' in Sheila Greeve Davaney (ed) *Feminism and Process Thought*, (1981) 37

9. Jack op cit 333

10. *Report of the World Missionary Conference*, Vol VI (1910)

11. *The Scotsman*, May 31 1884

12. The huge Church of Scotland foreign missionary archive is now kept at the National Library of Scotland. See *Catalogue of Manuscripts Acquired since 1925* (1985) Vol 6 (MS 7530–8022)

13. J Wilson, Memoir of *Mrs Wilson of Bombay* (1838) 631

14. quoted by EGK Hewat, *Vision and Achievement* (1960) 11

15. J Wilson op cit 515

16. quoted in Free Church of Scotland *Women's Work in Heathen Lands* July 1885 14

17. Minutes of the Edinburgh Ladies Association March 8 1837

18. A Swan, *Seedtime and Harvest* (1937) 104

19. ibid 63

20. *Women's Work* July 1885 6,8

21. *HFMR* (1852) 276

22. *HFMR* (1843) 67

23. C Rainy 'Our Jubilee' in *Women's Work* July 1887 11

24. quoted in 'The Story of our Madras Mission' 94 in *Our Church's Work in India* (1910)

25. quoted in 'Women's Work in Bengal' 77 ibid

26. *HFMR* (1848) 20

27. 'Zenana Missions in Bengal' *Women's Work* (1885)

28. ibid

29. ibid

30. Wyon op cit 49–50

31. *HFMR* (1876) 324

32. R Balfour and M Young *The Work of Medical Women in India* (1929) 14

33. *Free Church Monthly* (March 1889) 30–32

34. Duff wrote to Dr Burns Thomson of the Edinburgh Medical Missionary Society, 'I am not at all in favour of the movement for mixed medical classes in our universities'. see J Lowe, *Medical Missions: Their Place and Power* (1886)

178. See also W Burns Thomson, *Reminiscences of Medical Missionary Work* (1885) Ch XVIII

35. L Bean and E van Heyningen (eds) *The Letters of Jane Elizabeth Waterston 1866–1905* (1983) 127–8

36. *FCM* (1889) op cit

37. J Lowe op cit 185–186

38. *UFC Mission Record* (June 1929)

39. Balfour and Young op cit

40. Glasgow Missionary Society Summer Quarterly Intelligence (1839) 7–8

41. A Waddel, *Memorials of Mrs Sutherland of Old Calabar* (1883) 26

42. W Marwick, *William and Louisa Anderson* (1897) 410,592

43. Waddel op cit 60

44. UPMR (1852) 174

45. *Women's Missionary Magazine* (1904) 295

46. see J Buchan, *The Expendable Mary Slessor* (1980) 195

47. *Women's Missionary Magazine* (1918) 52

48. R Shepherd Lovedale, *South Africa 1841–1941* (1941) 153

49. Jack op cit 132

50. Bean and van Heyningen op cit 114

51. ibid 22

52. quoted in Mrs H E Scott, *A Saint in Kenya: Marion Stevenson* (1932) 241

53. N J Njogore, 'Women of the Presbyterian Church of East Africa, Kenya: 1891–1991' in *Reformed World* Vol 42 (1992) 129

54. ibid 133

55. E G K Hewat, *Vision and Achievement* (1960) 265

56. *Women's Missionary Magazine* (1918) 108–9

57. *United Presbyterian Mission Record* (1884) 205

58. E Raymond Pitman op cit 21–22

59. *United Presbyterian Magazine* (1895) 446

60. Report of the Committee for the Propogation of the Gospel in Foreign Parts, *Church of Scotland Reports* (1855)

61. *UPMR* (1877) 379

62. *The Helpmeet* (1891) 2

63. *Women's Work* (July 1887) 13

64. *Women's Missionary Magazine* (1918) 83

65. *HFMR* (1877) 516

66. G Gollock, *CMS Missionaries at Work* (1898)

67. *Edinburgh Missionary Conference* Report op cit

68. On March 9 1864 Govan wrote to Stewart, 'I do not think it would be advisable that the Institution should be placed wholly under a lady. It is evidently most desirable – I would say almost indispensable – that it should be presided over by a male head' (Bean and van Heyningen, 15)

69. ibid 73. The Ladies' Association office was at 15 North Bank Street, at the top of the The Mound in Edinburgh, and next door to New College and the Assembly Hall

70. ibid

71. ibid 32

72. ibid 120. See also H McIntosh, 'Contracts of Employment and the influence of class in the first thirty years of Livingstonia' in *Records of the Scottish Church History Society* XXIII (1989) 96–112

73. ibid 164, 166

74. ibid 167

75. ibid 180–1

76. ibid 265

77. Item four of plaint filed March 21 1883 in the High Court, Fort William, Bengal

78. ibid item eight

79. D Macmillan, *The Life of Professor Hastie* (1926)

80. Private Letter Book of J T Maclagan, secretary of the Church of Scotland Foreign Mission Committee, 1882–4 (NLS Acc 7555)

81. see transcript of Libel case, August 28 to September 15 1883; also *Life of Prof Hastie* 166

82. Memorandum on the Calcutta Branch of the Church of Scotland Female Mission, May 17 1882

83. Item two, Finding of the Consulting Board to the SLA, June 19 1882

84. Letter to Calcutta Corresponding Board, August 23 1882

85. ibid

86. Concluding judgment in libel case, September 15 1883. A transcript of the case, including relevant documents, is held in the NLS (*Report on the Pigot Case*, Calcutta 1884)

87. *Scotsman* May 30 1884

88. Scotsman June 2 1884

89. *Women's Missionary Magazine* (1904) 295

90. J Buchan, *The Expendable Mary Slessor* (1980) 180

91. *The Place of Women in the Church's Life and Work,* Appendix 2: 'The Position of Women in the Organised Foreign Mission Enterprise of the Church, Reports of the United Free Church (1915)

92. M Gollock 'The Share of Women in the Administration of Missions', *International Review of Missions* (1912) 674ff

93. From 'Doubts and Difficulties Dispelled' *Women's Work* pamphlet (1885)

94. *Women's Work* (July 1885)

95. D Smith Cairns, *Autobiography* (1936) 49

96. *The Helpmeet* (1900) 79

97. quoted in Wyon op cit 54–5

98. see Waddel, op cit 135–148

99. *The Helpmeet* (1896) 241

100. Report of the UP Church Jubilee Conference, 1897

101. *UPMR* (1884) 207

102. *The Helpmeet* (1900) 351

103. Foreign Mission Committee, Reports of the United Free Church (1901)

104. The Place of Women in the Church's Life and Work, *Reports of the UF Church* (1916)

105. *The Helpmeet* (1894)

106. quoted in O Wyon op cit 70–1

107. K Young, *Our Sail We Lift: History of the Girls' Association 1901–1951* (1951) forward

108. Woman's Guild Supplement, *Life and Work* (1918) 38–39

109. See *Missionary Ideologies in the Imperialist Era* (op cit)

110. *Proceedings and Debates of the Free Church General Assembly* (1884) 93

111. Extracted from the *Women's Work* pamphlet, 'Doubts and Difficulties Dispelled' (1885). There are several characters in the dialogue, each representing different attitudes and factions within the church. For simplicity, I have just used W and M to indicate whether a woman or a man is speaking

112. *Women's Missionary Magazine* (1918) 84

113. Frances Balfour, *Dr Elsie Inglis* (1918) 107

114. A Cunningham, letter of application to become a missionary, (NLS Acc 7991–2)

115. Address given at meeting of the Scottish Churches League for Woman Suffrage, March 12 1913

116. From Report of the Girl's Auxiliary Conference, 1919. *Women's Missionary Magazine* (1919) 87–88

117. J M Mackenzie, 'David Livingstone: the construction of the myth', in eds G Walker and T Gallacher, *Sermons and Battle Hymns* (1990) 26

118. ibid Mackenzie here refers to the romantic prototype as described by Jenni Calder in *Heroes from Byron to Guevara* (1977)

119. J J Ellis, *Two Missionary Heroines in Africa* (nd) 32

4

The Position of Women in Scottish Presbyterian Polity

Introduction

Previous chapters have described the growing involvement of women in the public life and service of the Scottish presbyterian churches during the period 1830–1930. I have characterised this phenomenon as the significant feminisation of an institution which was overwhelmingly masculine in tone and structure from the time of the Reformation and for almost three hundred years thereafter. The evolution of the church as focus for a range of missionary and philanthropic initiatives was inextricably linked with the growing participation of churchwomen: in home and foreign missions, in congregational organisations and activities, in education, and in moral and social campaigns. By 1930, Scottish presbyterianism had in many respects a significantly altered character and public image.

But this feminisation was essentially of service rather than of status or authority. The churches remained solidly patriarchal in structure and attitude, in spite of a series of challenges and attempts to change. These came both from within, and as the result of pressure emanating from the transformation of social, economic and political conditions available to women. The official position of women within presbyterian polity was subject to consideration and debate throughout the period, but by 1930 it remained ambivalent and subordinate. In 1928, a dissatisfied member of the United Free Church described the typical situation of female members, in her complaint about a visit by the local Presbytery to her congregation:

> The Church is a body of men and women, meeting together for worship and service. To meet seventy or eighty or even 100 men out of 1200 members, seventy per cent of whom are women, is surely to leave out of the picture one of its most important features. Are visitors satisfied to see the Church only through the eyes of men? . . . Men are in evidence when there is collecting to be done in Church – 'taking up collection' is a stately affair! But what about monthly house-to-house visiting, rain or sun, fog or snow, to gather up the

Central Fund and Missionary Subscriptions . . . there is a vast army of women keeping the great organisation at work by tireless ungrudging service in the cause of Christ . . . Women may have guilds, work parties, Girls' Association; they may organise innumerable activities in mission; they may gather in the funds and indeed make the Church a possibility – but they have no official recognition. Their work is 'appreciated' by Presbyteries and Sessions, but they are not officially part of the Church . . . Is it not time that the Churches in Scotland should make use of the powers they already have to elect women to their courts, and that they should seek for the extension of these powers to include all offices in the Church? . . . In this way only will the Church attain to its full stature and be fitted to meet the immense calls and responsibilities of the present day.[1]

This chapter considers the various efforts and campaigns to open up opportunities for official status, responsibility and authority to women. I hope to suggest some of the underlying concerns and ideologies which influenced arguments advanced for and against these goals, and some reasons why presbyterianism was unable or unwilling to accommodate this major departure from its patriarchal heritage.

'Men Lawfully Chosen Thereto by Some Kirk': Scottish Presbyterian Theory and Practice of Ministry and Office

The Scottish Reformation challenged and eventually broke the religious control exercised by the Roman Catholic Church. Papal and clerical power were denounced. Knox and his followers preached that salvation was mediated directly to each individual human being by Christ alone. But Calvinism was no charismatic sect, boldly embodying the doctrine of the priesthood of all believers in some radical experiment of earthly equality. For the Scottish reformers, the visible church consisted in the true preaching of the Word of God, the right administration of the sacraments, and ecclesiastical discipline uprightly administered.[2] The emphasis, in the pattern of Church government which evolved from this doctrine, was on order and constitutional authority. An essential feature was a rather high and serious understanding of the Ministry of Word and Sacrament. The First Book of Discipline declared,

> In Kirk reformed or tending to reformation, none may presume to preach or minister the Sacraments till orderly they be called to the same'.[3]

Vocation to the ministry required, not just the personal apprehension of a call, but election, examination and admission. As pastor – the watchman over the flock – the predominant function of the minister was to preach and teach scripture and doctrine to the people, and hence the holder of that office was to be literate and well educated. While Knox's ideal may not have been realised in his own time, and was subject to subsequent development and compromise, the image of the minister as a central public figure, expecting and receiving considerable respect and status, was at the heart of Scottish presbyterian culture.

If the minister's task was to ensure purity of doctrine within his parish, the duty of discipline was delegated to the elders. The First Book of Discipline decreed that they should reprove, correct and punish vices with which the civil magistrate did not normally deal: by private rebuke, public admonition and excommunication.[4] The powers of the Kirk Session were extensive. Mitchison and Leneman have observed that the Church exercised a formal system of social control in which

> lay activity was most conspicuous in the lowest and highest courts . . . Even by the 17th century, the Church was equipped with a far more modern system of government than the State – it is not surprising that it tended to intrude into matters of political and penal policy.[5]

But the main concern of elders was the moral (which usually meant sexual) control of parishioners:

> Disobedience to the demands of the Session entailed civil disabilities well into the eighteenth century: the sinner had to 'compeir' or lose his scanty rights of citizenship. He could be fined, he could be refused a 'testification' enabling him to live in the parish, he could be committed to the Sheriff . . . Girls murdered their illegitimate children rather than face the ordeal of being pilloried. As late as 1751 the General Assembly . . . had to order the Act against the concealment of pregnancy to be read from every pulpit.[6]

The poet Keats wrote in 1818:

> A Scotch girl stands in terrrible awe of the Elder – poor little Susannas – They will scarcely laugh – They are greatly to be pitied and the Kirk is greatly to be damned . . . I would sooner be a wild deer than a girl under the dominion of the Kirk.[7]

Although the civil jurisdiction of elders decreased in the 19th century, their ecclesiastical standing as official representatives of a congregation remained high. They were central figures in their ritual and decision-making capacities. The men who held office in the Church tended to be those whose landowning, professional or business roles in rural, small town or urban settings, gave them standing and power within the local community. Eldership was a conventional honour for the Scottish landed and bourgeois male classes.[8]

The presbyterian system of government was exercised within the juridical framework of a hierarchy of courts – Kirk Session, Presbytery, Synod and General Assembly – each of which was composed exclusively, in different combinations, of ordained ministers and elders. Of this system, Principal Martin commented during a debate in the 1915 United Free Church Assembly, 'Our Church is worked by its male members, and that as a matter of principle.'[9]

It was consistently argued that such a principle was founded in scripture, which was the predominant source of authority for the reformed Church. But there were also almost insurmountable ideological and practical hindrances (whose force was, no doubt, derived in part from the Scriptural contention) which made the idea of women exercising public and official presbyterian ministry virtually inconceivable until the end of the 19th century.

The system of formal ministry which developed in theory and practice, and which came to assume such symbolic importance within Scottish society, might be described (in a phrase used by theologian Letty Russell) as a paradigm of domination.[10] This paradigm regards authority over the community as the suitable model for an orderly church. It is characterised by actions and traits which have stereotypically been designated as masculine. And it was evident in virtually every aspect of presbyterian ministry and eldership. In a society which became so pervaded with the ideology of separate spheres for women and men, it would be literally incredible to envisage women undertaking such office. Knox, in his desire for a decorous and godly ministry, had expressed contemptous incredulity at the idea:

> We flee the society of the Papistical Kirk in participation of their sacraments, first because their ministers are not of Christ Jesus: yea they suffer women to baptise.[11]

His view of women as essentially subordinate and potentially dangerous, and therefore requiring to be controlled, implied that any dominion exercised by them (whether in Church or State) would be neither seemly nor lawful, but disorderly. Women, in the wake of the evangelical revival, came to be regarded as upholders of moral and religious rectitude. Yet in Calvinist theology they remained the descendants of Eve. Their sinful provenance and potential still made them subject to patriarchal authority in home, church and community, for it was only when subject to such control that 'true womanhood' could flourish. For evangelical presbyterians, women who did not submit to that pattern were shameful reminders of female degradation and sin. There was no question that the female sex were to remain the recipients, not the administrators, of discipline.

The language which was commonly used to describe office-bearers of Scottish churches tended to carry connotations of gender, whether hidden or acknowledged. Reverence, respect and prestige were typically accorded specifically to men. Ministers were generally regarded as 'above' their parishioners: they were moral exemplars who had pledged to live a 'godly and circumspect life', yet they were also perceived as distant from the everyday activities and concerns of the people. In 1934, A H Gray could still write of a minister's wife who told him that all the ministers she knew considered themselves to be 'the great I Am'.[12]

Of course, in a class-ridden society, which nevertheless occasionally displayed the capacity to override barriers of both class and gender, it was not only men who could inspire such reactions (whether positive or negative), and there are certainly examples of haughty and intimidating Scottish women in the annals of history and literature. But most churchwomen apparently internalised the association between maleness and the dignity of religious office. In 1931 the Woman's Guild National President wrote:

> Deep down in the hearts of many there are still traces of that age old feeling of awe and reverence associated with elders of the Scotch Kirk. Their highest act of service is identified with the Holy Table and the Sacrament; and the question arises, unbidden in many minds, 'would it make any difference to me, to the spirit of my communion, were there women elders present?[13]

The physical geography of church buildings, and the placing of ministers and elders within them, seem also to evince a paradigm of domination. Robed in black and displaying his academic credentials, the minister conducted worship from a pulpit 'six feet above contradiction' (leaving members, in the common expression, 'under Dr So-and-So's pulpit'), or from a platform where he could perform to the gallery with dramatic flourish. The elders, gathered for the rare celebration of Communion, dressed in the dreich garb of respectability and executed their ceremonial duties with a military precision. Pew rents, and the positioning of women, working- and servant-class members, were graphic symbols of the patriarchal authority believed by churchgoers to have been divinely invested in their institution. In such a setting it would require a deeply disturbing effort of the imagination to picture a woman conducting public proceedings from pulpit or chancel.[14]

The practical barriers confronting women were no less insuperable in the early- and mid-Victorian years, and they only began to be breached in the closing decade of the century. The ethos of the Kirk demanded an educated ministry, and those seeking ordination required a university degree. Since women were excluded from Scottish universities until 1892, they were simply unable to fulfil this prerequisite. Only in 1898 did the divinity faculties begin to consider the question of female students. In 1910 Frances Melville was the first Scotswoman to graduate Bachelor of Divinity, but she, and those few who followed her example up to 1930, were not 'regular' students. They either belonged to non-presbyterian denominations, or could not be candidates for ordination.[15] Throughout the period 1830–1930, presbyterian women were never in a position to have any personal sense of vocation either examined or validated.

More strictly enforced educational qualifications were an aspect of the growing 19th-century tendency towards male professionalisation. Those who entered the clerical profession were initiated into an arcane society with its own rules, language, garb and rituals. Their stipends and manses may not always have matched the material comforts of doctors and lawyers, but they were designed for the economic and social support of the minister as *pater familias*. He was the breadwinner – provider for wife, children and servants. This role was rarely countenanced for women of the middle and upper classes (though some had to fulfil it). The persona of minister as professional man and head of the household was the basis for many objections to the ordination of women.[16]

Elders likewise were generally men who had power and influence within the prevailing social and economic order. Even in largely working-class parishes, it tended to be the better-off tradesmen and artisans who sat on the Kirk Session. Women rarely enjoyed social standing independent of male relatives – even when they had to cope with the practical burdens of breadwinning. In church life, they might gradually take on many of the practical tasks which in theory had been those of the eldership, but they did not have the status to assume its formal functions with the approval of the community. In short, women were denied the power which church officials both exercised and reflected, because the qualities and attainments required were, by circular definition, male. If true womanhood was a life of self-effacement in the domestic sphere, the quintessential 'man' was a person of independence and authority, which was exercised in the public realm of church and community. It was these separate worlds which Dr Adamson of Ardrossan longed to retain when he argued against the ordination of women deacons in 1917:

We must beware of the further masculinising of women and the feminising of the Church. A woman impudent and mannish grown is not more loathed than an effeminate man! In the order of nature there is a distinction which Christianity does not destroy.[17]

In a church which had adopted such a powerful paradigm of domination as its model for ordained ministry, and in a society so defined by the domestic ideology, the phrase, 'women's ministry' would either have been an oxymoron, or would have required careful definition to accommodate prevailing understandings of both women and ministry. During this period, those who sought some kind of official position for women within presbyterianism had three basic options. They could accept and develop the notion of a distinctive ministry for women; they could challenge the underlying ideology of separate spheres and propose instead that women should be enabled to exercise office on an equal basis with men; or they could radically question the prevailing paradigm and propose alternative models of the 'living church', thus subverting questions of status and prestige while affirming the credibility of women as bearers of ecclesiastical authority.

These three options were not always discrete or clearly defined, but they were the grounds upon which the struggle was joined, whether by stealth or in open combat.

'The Hazards of Public Debate and Collision':
Votes for Women in the Free Church of Scotland

One of the most controversial and contested elements of post-Reformation church organisation was the system of patronage, whereby the hereditary owner of the right of presentation could choose the parish minister, thus compromising one of the democratic principles of presbyterianism. Apart from a period between 1649 and 1662, state legislation enforced patronage until the Revolution Settlement of 1690 eliminated the rights of individual patrons in favour of those of heritors and elders to present ministers to charges. But the Patronage Act of 1712 restored the privilege of lay patrons to appoint ministers. The General Assembly opposed the Act, but after 1729 began to back patrons in disputes, and dissatisfaction with the situation led to the defection of four ministers to form the Secession Church in 1733 – the first act in the disintegration of uniform presbyterianism. The complex story of expulsions and secessions which split the Church of Scotland need not concern us here, except in its consequences for women members.

Within the Established Church, women and men were equally subject to the imposition of ministers who were not of their choice and were likely actively to support the interests of wealthy patrons. The patrons themselves were, of course, usually men, but some women exercised considerable power and ambition. As members of the aristocracy, their class gave them access to privileges denied to other women. Lady Glenorchy of Breadalbane, for example,

> founded more churches and launched more new congregations than any private individual in Scottish history . . . she chose the first ministers for her churches and drew up the rules and regulations by which the congregations were to be governed.[18]

Among those presbyterians who seceded from the Establishment for various reasons, the right of the congregation to elect and call a minister was recognised, but the extent of this privilege was far from consistent, and one of the key variables was the situation of female members. In 1736 the Secession Church declared in its Testimony that ministers and other office bearers were to be set over congregations by the call and consent of the majority of members in full communion. However, when it was pointed out that this formulation apparently gave women the right to vote, it was explained that this was not in fact the practice. The right of call was restricted to male heads of families, while 'wives and children might take part therein by influencing with religious and rational arguments their husbands and fathers in favour of one candidate rather than another'.[19]

However, after the Breach of 1747, it appears that the Burghers generally allowed women to vote, while the Anti-Burghers forbade the practice. At the formation of the United Secession Church in 1820 the issue was one of two points over which the two groups differed, but within a few years the women's vote was universally accepted, in spite of some Anti-Burgher objections. One minister had it recorded that

> He could not help expressing his disapprobation of female members of a congregation being admitted to vote and subscribe a call, it being in his opinion contrary to the appointed rule, as well as to the law of nature manifested in the constitution of human society'.[20]

In 1834 the Ten Years' Conflict which led to the Disruption was set in motion by the passing of the Veto Act, by which the Established Church attempted to declare that no minister should be imposed contrary to the will of the congregation. Grounds for rejection were to be that the majority of male heads of families disapproved. So the Church of Scotland, while asserting its claim for democracy, framed that claim according to patriarchal presuppositions.

But for the people who came out of the Established Church of Scotland in 1843, those presuppositions themselves became a matter of contention. At the first Assembly of the new Free Church, held in October 1843, the debate about the report on the Election of Office-bearers revolved around the question of whether women in full communion with the Church could be counted as individual members with full rights and responsibilities, or whether these could be fulfilled by men speaking and acting on their behalf. In May of that year, interim arrangements had been made which stated that ministers, elders and deacons should be 'chosen by the votes of male communicants on the role'.[21] The only reference during the debate to the question of women's rights was made by Dr Guthrie of Edinburgh, who commented that

> He had no doubt in his mind at all on the subject. It would be a novelty to give female communicants a vote, and he did not wish to introduce such a novelty without the general concurrence of his brethren (hear hear).[22]

It is difficult to ascertain how much of an issue this novelty was, but there is some evidence that it was a bone of contention between May and October 1843. Several letters appeared in *The Witness* and a pamphlet was published, entitled *The Present Crisis of the Free Church, or A Scriptural Examination of the Question, ought Females to have a voice in the calling of Pastors in the Church of Christ.*
The authors summarised their argument:

> Believing that it can be clearly established that the voice of females in the election of ministers is destitute of all warrant and foundation either in reason or in the Word of God – anxious that our Church should shun the greatest calamity which could at present befall her – and apprehensive, lest finding herself no longer fettered but free, she should yield even in appearance to the temptation of being liberal in sacred things.[23]

The pseudonymous authors were laymen, but women also felt moved to address the Moderator directly. Whether they did so in support of, or opposed to their enfranchisement, they could hardly be described as radical. The 'Female Friend' who advocated the cause appealed, not on the basis of sexual equality in the natural or divine order, but as a kind of reward (along with others she proposed which hardly accorded with anti-patronage principles) for the staunch support which the Free Church received from women. She wrote:

> What we ask is not a voice in the church's legislation, not a hand in the church's government – but simply room for the expression of our choice, as members of the body of Christ, in the calling of our ministers.[24]

But were women really considered to be full members of the Church? This apparently unequivocal status was in fact the main point of dispute. The woman who (in spite of feeling 'in its fullest extent all the embarrassing novelty and peculiar delicacy' of public correspondence with the Moderator 'by persons of the gentler sex on affairs connected with the government of the Church'[25]) wrote to express her opposition to the female vote, claimed that most women were not truly converted at all. They were 'amateur religiosi' who simply exhibited the natural propensity to religion which was part of the female character. If they were enfranchised,

> Can anyone doubt that the consequences to the ministrations of the Free Church would be most disastrous – that a silly sentimentality, a drawing room theology, would come to fill our pulpits.

And she continued,

> I find nothing 'harsh or exclusive' in the Word of God – the grand charter of women's privileges – when it assigns to me a position inferior to that of my male relatives in the affairs of government.[26]

The Report which was presented to the October General Assembly removed any reference to the restriction of voting to male communicants, and declared:

> The principle has already been recognised, and should be fully and fairly acted upon, that it appertaineth to the people, and to every several congregation, that is, to the members of the congregation in full communion with the Church, to elect their minister.[27]

The fact that this statement gave rise to any debate at all, far less the conceptual difficulties expressed by some commissioners, testifies to the tension between the Protestant acceptance of individual equality among human souls, and the age-old Christian tradition of assuming male humanity to be normative, and the female version to be defective or incomplete. This tension was compounded by the intellectual tradition of the Enlightenment, which proclaimed the natural rights of individuals, but generally concluded that only male head of households had the rational capacity to participate in public decision-making.

However, Dr Robert Burns of Paisley argued that the language of the Report was unambiguous:

> I understand that in the words, 'members of the Church', female members are included, unless you are prepared to prove that female members are not members of the Church at all, and that the restriction contained in the Interim Act of the last Assembly has been blotted out.

And he continued,

> If any one thing has created a spirit of apathy and discouragement among
> adherents of the Free Church, it is the doubt . . . thrown on the rights of female
> members, and by consequence the virtual exclusion of all females from a voice
> in the election of ministers.'[28]

But James Begg, while supporting the right of women, believed that

> The advantage of the report, I think, is chiefly in this, that it does not give a
> definite opinion on the most important question . . . but leaves it entirely open
> to every Presbytery to exercise its own discretion, and leaves it to female
> members, if they choose, to claim and exercise their rights.[29]

This indeed was the practical effect of the report, which was sent down
to Presbyteries, and carried forward in the same interim form until 1846,
when it became a Declaratory Act, without being subject to the 'mature
debate' and prescriptive legislation which some 1843 commissioners called
for.

Although at one level this Act was a concession to the rights of women
in the Free Church, it is probable that a variety of attitudes, arguments and
circumstances would inhibit the claim of many to those rights. I have
already referred to the arguments from nature and culture utilised by the
'female opponent'. Others appealed to Scripture and ecclesiastical tradition.
Dr Cunningham, convener of the committee which submitted the report,
and a leading theologian of the new denomination, gave his gloss on the
casuistry of an apparently lucid piece of legislation:

> It will be competent for [a] Presbytery, or for any superior Church court, to
> hold that 'members of congregations' are to be interpreted according to the
> laws and practices of the Church as established by former precedents, and in
> that way to understand the expression as meaning merely male
> communicants . . . I think it right to say, since the matter has been mooted,
> with regard to the question that has divided us, that I am not convinced by the
> statements of Mr Begg and Dr Burns, that female communicants have a right
> to vote, as well as male communicants. Though I hold as a general principle
> that in the election of a minister, their consent and approbation must in some
> way or other be ascertained.[30]

It is in the context of the doctrine of separate spheres, so enthusiastically
promulgated in religious circles at this time, that the importance of 'votes
for women' in the Free Church should be assessed. Dr Burns' comments
suggest that many women, full of enthusiastic fervour for the new
denomination, wanted active involvement. And there were indeed
churchwomen who held strong and passionate views about religious

matters. But it would take an extremely unconventional woman to exercise her right to speak at a congregational meeting, rather than seek to exert her influence in the 'woman's sphere' of parlours and dining tables. The consequences for a woman who endeavoured to engage in the 'hazards of public debate and collision'[31] would be serious indeed, if she valued her reputation and respectability; and especially if she was aware that Dr Thomas Chalmers, the great leader of the Free Church, had no appreciation of the importance of her right of expression. He said in 1847:

> I have always looked upon this as a very paltry and distasteful question; I think that it is revolting to the collective mind of the Free Church.[32]

It is likely that most churches would in any case try to ensure unanimity and minimise the risk of dissension by the time a nominee's name was presented to the congregation.[33] But this skirmish in the struggle at least raised the principle that women, as church members, might be considered as individuals with public rights and responsibilities. Their official invisibility, and the male prerogative to speak and act for women as if they were minors or imbeciles, could no longer simply be taken for granted. Legislation which did not specifically include them was enacted, but a precedent was set for permitting an official role for women without actually enforcing it. This was far from a ringing declaration of equal rights, and betrayed a continuing tendency to regard women, not as an integral part of the Church, but as a group whose relationship with the institution was regarded as problematic and unsettled.

'Wandering, Preaching Damsels'

Whatever the significance of the Free Church policy on the enfranchisement of female members, there is no evidence that women within any branch of Scottish presbyterianism were seeking, during the early Victorian period, a substantial or public role beyond the limited (and still quite novel) parameters of woman's work in the affairs of the church. This cannot have been because they were all unaware of challenges to the traditional position of women. The 'female opponent' of voting had warned the Moderator that controversy had been stirred up over just such challenges, on the 'other side of the Atlantic'.

In America, one significant expression of evangelical Protestantism was the anti-slavery movement. Believing slavery to be a fundamental sin against God and humankind, many northern Christians pursued abolition with zeal and fervour. Women were deeply involved in the campaign, but while some confined themselves to traditional auxiliary activities, others, most notably the Grimké sisters, engaged in public campaigning work. In 1837, following a speaking tour which filled churches and halls throughout New England, the General Association of Congregationalist Ministers issued an edict to all member churches, condemning the Grimkés for their unfeminine behaviour in addressing promiscuous (mixed) audiences. The anti-slavery campaign was conducted on both sides of the Atlantic, and there is no doubt that Scottish Protestants would be informed about this novel and controversial situation. Female activists, even if they did not actually read Sarah Grimké's *Letters on Equality* (1838), were probably aware of the gist of her cogent arguments against women's subordination. These surely provided the context for the publication of a series of articles by an American minister, Rev Hubbard Winslow, in the Secession Church's *Christian Journal* 1840, entitled 'Woman as She Should Be':

> But oh! how fallen from this high elevation is she when, impatient of her proper sphere, she steps forth to assume the duties of man . . . when, forsaking the domestic hearth, her delicate voice is heard from house to house, or in social assemblies, rising in harsh unnatural tones of denunciation against civil laws and rulers, against measures involving politics and state affairs, of which she is nearly as ignorant as the child she left at home in the cradle; against ministers and churches, perhaps even her own pastor . . . expecting to reform politics and churches, and to put down every real and supposed evil in them, by the right arm of female power . . . What a sad wreck of female loveliness she is then! She can hardly conceive how ridiculous she appears in the eyes of all sober, discreet, judicious Christian men, or how great the reproach she brings upon her sex.[34]

Matters came to a head at the World's Anti-Slavery Convention, held in London in 1840, from which several American female delegates were excluded simply because of their gender. Most Scottish presbyterian abolitionists would have agreed with Rev G Harvey of Glasgow, a member of the Relief Secession Church, who claimed that the appointment of women representatives to the Convention was 'acting in opposition to plain teaching and the Word of God'.[35]

The interpretations which enabled Biblical injunctions about slavery to be overriden in favour of a general moral principle – also derived from Scripture – were not, apparently, to be extended to discussions about women in church and society. *The Scotsman* newspaper, in spite of its reform credentials, simply omitted any report of the embarassing 'woman question'. But some of the female delegates embarked on a tour of the British Isles after the Convention.[36] The support they received in Scotland came almost exclusively from Quaker and Unitarian activists. The schism of anti-slavery societies in Scotland, 1840–41, split the movement into camps which were for and against the radical William Lloyd Garrison. His support of equal rights for women was just one of a raft of policies which were condemned as heretical by orthodox presbyterian men and women (see Chapter 5). The events of 1840 sowed the seeds of organised American feminism in the 19th century, as the excluded women were instrumental in organising the Seneca Falls Convention of 1848.[37]

In America, the Garrisonian women were anathema to Calvinist ministers, and even the liberal sects were not always welcoming or supportive of their progressive stance. In spite of their evangelical roots and ardour, many feminist abolitionists departed the institutional church and attempted to live out a practical religion, free from doctrinal restrictions and clerical disapproval. In Britain, even women who supported Garrisonian policy on abolition were quite hesitant about accepting the theoretical or practical connections between anti-slavery and women's rights, although many were subsequently involved in the range of reformist campaigns which constituted the later Victorian Women's Movement. There was a particular reluctance among British Protestant women to engage with the theological challenge presented by feminism to institutionalised Christianity. In Britain, during the 1840s, it was not anti-slavery campaigners who put themselves beyond the pale by embracing that challenge in public, but Utopian Socialists.

Barbara Taylor's fascinating study of feminism in the Owenite movement of the early 19th century has revealed the importance of this radical tradition in the development of feminist thought and action. Taylor discusses the religious origins of militant infidel women, 'whose radicalism was simultaneously a product of their puritanism and a reaction to it', and argues that 'the point from which various styles of Socialist feminist heterodoxy originated was the concept of women as a moral vanguard'.[38] Although Taylor deals mainly with English women and English events, she says enough about Scotland to suggest that there were female propagandists who made some impact during a period of major social unrest. Most of the women she writes about had fervently evangelical non-conformist backgrounds, and she claims that the tensions inherent in the ideology of women's special mission made it inevitable 'that the churches should begin to breed a female opposition'.[39]

Did the Scottish presbyterian churches, which shared much with, and yet were distinctive from, English evangelicalism, breed such opposition? Elspeth King mentions two Scottish female socialist lecturers – Agnes

Walker and Mrs A S Hamilton – who asserted, in no uncertain terms, sexual equality, and the complicity of the churches in the oppression of women. But what their background was, and how many other Scotswomen engaged in similar activity, is yet to be determined. However, King quotes a report of Mrs Hamilton's activities in the *Glasgow Free Press* of 1834, which is revealing about the extent to which internicine presbyterian rivalry threatened to overshadow every other controversy during this volatile period:

> Her first lecture, which was on Church and State Reform, was delivered on Thursday evening and lasted an hour and a half. The Established Church, or, as she quaintly denominated it, 'the Old Lady', came in for a principal share of vituperation; a course of proceeding which, she says, she finds highly useful in opening to her the doors of the Voluntary Churches in many parts of the country, the managers accepting this redeeming quality as a sufficient expiation for the other heresies which she attempts to propagate.[40]

Although Utopian Socialism was never a mass movement, it attracted considerable working-class interest: especially when there was the novelty of a woman on a public platform. One of the most prominent of female socialist freethinkers, Emma Martin, embarked on an extensive Scottish tour during 1844–5. She was anything but coy about her targets and tactics. *The Movement* newspaper announced her intent:

> Mrs Martin is determined that despite of St Paul, the voice of woman shall be heard within the churches.[41]

In Paisley and Glasgow such determination was not to be thwarted. At the end of her Paisley meeting, Emma Martin told her audience she was going to a church where an address on 'Home Missions' was to be delivered:

> In another, nay, in the same minute, the audience were pouring down the stairs and along the street'. In the church, above a rabble of religionists and socialists shouting at each other, Emma tried to speak, while ministers attempted vainly to remind her that 'women are not allowed to speak in the church'.[42]

In Glasgow she was arrested when over three thousand people followed her into a church in the Gorbals; and in Edinburgh, she and her young daughter were physically attacked by a stoning mob.[43]

Although the picture of socialist feminism in Scotland is sketchy, two things are clear: first, that during the 1830s and 1840s, people in many parts of the country had the opportunity both to hear radical doctrines about sex equality, free marriage and other gender issues, and to see them made manifest in women who militantly rejected religious injunctions to stay silent.[44] And second, that the orthodox religious establishment, led by the clergy, demonstrated a fear and loathing of such women, who were subjected to mysogynistic abuse for presuming to step beyond male-defined boundaries.

But in the mid-Victorian period there was another challenge to the conventional religious role of women, and this was firmly located within the boundaries of evangelical Christianity. The first manifestations of a second religious awakening in Britain occurred in Ulster in 1859, and included 'public prayers and preachings' by women. Between then and 1873, when the Edinburgh campaign of the Americans Moody and Sankey ushered in a new phase of revivalism, female preachers were a distinctive feature of the popular religious landscape, especially in working-class areas where the simple arminian message made the most impact. Olive Anderson, in her pioneering essay, 'Women Preachers in Mid-Victorian Britain' (1969), defines the phenomenon as

> The deliberate undertaking by women of evangelical, spiritual instruction or exhortation in mixed public assemblies held for that purpose, with no attempt to disguise the nature of the activities or audience.[45]

One of the most successful was Jessie Macfarlane, a presbyterian by upbringing, who began preaching in Edinburgh in 1862. She was encouraged by Gordon Forlong, a member of the Plymouth Brethren who defended female preaching, in a pamphlet published in 1863. He and Macfarlane were at the centre of a controversy in the city when she took the platform of the Music Hall in 1864 during a presbyterian mission meeting. Jessie Macfarlane preached extensively throughout East Scotland, the Midlands and London until her death in 1871.

Anderson associates the phenomenon of female preaching with pre-millennialism: the belief that the public ministry of women was one of the signs of the 'last days' prophesied in Joel 2:28–29. That was certainly the position of one of the most renowned preachers, Isabella Armstrong. She was Irish, and converted during the 1859 revival in County Tyrone. Thereafter she began preaching to relieve those men who were exhausted by the unusual demands of the revival. Armstrong first preached in Scotland in 1863 at Newmains Assembly in Lanarkshire. This congregation of seceders from Wishaw Evangelical Union Church was at the centre of a new wave of enthusiasm which swept through Scotland in 1866. In that year, Isabella Armstrong published a pamphlet, 'Modern Prophetesses', to argue the case for women preachers against those who believed the practice to be unscriptural. During her seven years of public ministry she had borne the brunt of much criticism, disapproval and ostracisation. And although she claims to honour 'diversity of opinion', the context from which she writes is obviously an impatience with men who are more concerned with outward form, status and education – those who obstruct women 'labouring in the Gospel':

> While all the time souls are perishing, iniquity prevailing, scepticism increasing . . . and the coming of the Lord is drawing nigh.[46]

Armstrong does not dispute that the usual sphere of women is domestic, but she is clear that, according to Scripture, women are not created inferior to men, and Christ is unfettered in who he chooses to be the instruments of his salvation:

> That prophetesses were called of God cannot be doubted; that their mission was to men as well as to women we know for certain; that their office was public as well as private is clear; and that they taught with an authority no female now, so far as I know, desires or contends for, is evident. How Christian women can now be charged with 'unsexing themselves' and a host of other appellations sometimes freely used, I am at a loss to know.[47]

There is a spirit of urgency and freedom in Armstrong's writing characteristic of those Scottish assemblies which, in the wake of revival, were drawn into the Brethren Movement. Their premillennialist enthusiasm during the first years of expansion, enabled this small community (which was strongest in Lanarkshire and North East Scotland) to accept women preachers, who were powerful and productive in evangelisation and church planting. For the women and their supporters, such success was vindication that their gifts were fruits of the Holy Spirit, such as those given to women at Pentecost (Acts 2). But if the Brethren were the only Christian community to accept female preaching, and if presbyterians were amongst some of the most vehement denouncers, there were also those who offered practical and personal support. The Free Church Presbytery of Brechin, meeting on April 9, 1867, minuted:

> It having come to the knowledge of Presbytery that, lately on a Sabbath evening, a woman was allowed to conduct Public Worship and to preach in one of their churches within the bounds, the Presbytery record their disapprobation of that conduct, and their injunction that it be not repeated.[48]

And in October 1869, *The Watchword*, a Free Church journal, reported:

> We are glad to see that the Free Church Presbytery of Orkney have condemned [female preaching], which must have been admitted inadvertently. Females have a most important position in Church, but their sphere is not in the pulpit. We

hear much of women's rights in those days, but too little, we suspect, of women's duties.[49]

The surprise is not that both presbyteries rejected the legitimacy of female preaching, but that there must have been ministers and Kirk Sessions who allowed women to use their premises, (even at the risk of reproval by higher courts), and who by implication sanctioned the self-appointed ministry of those women. This indicates that presbyterian attitudes about the appropriate sphere for women were not totally monolithic; but it is important to recognise the nature of the challenge to orthodoxy which female preaching presented. As an element of popular revivalism, these women were part of an essentially lay movement which emphasised personal holiness and obedience. Their 'striking indifference to clerical status and pastoral functions . . . and intense hostility to sacerdotalism'[50] obviously constituted a provocation to the role and prestige of the parish minister. But female preachers were not themselves seeking to become ordained presbyterian ministers, with all the formal status and power that would entail. Isabella Armstrong clearly had little time for the pomp and rank associated with ordained ministry:

> Instead of Christian forbearance, I have met with worse treatment than I might expect if I were an evil-doer . . . when I have met those who, in clerical finery unknown to the Apostle, clamoured loudly in the pulpit, and extended my hand as one Christian to another, it was not accepted . . . Where God's servants stand, while they deliver their message of love and salvation, is of no importance; but for ease and comfort . . . it is of great advantage to have an elevation, call it what you please. But to believe females must not occupy a pulpit, because it is more holy than many other places, or that a female member is less holy than a male member, is surely blind and absurd to no common degree.[51]

In no sense did their actions constitute an equal rights campaign conducted from within Calvinist orthodoxy. As Armstrong admitted:

> I am not contending that women ought to form churches and preside over them, ruling however diligently, and exercising official ecclesiastical authority, however wisely and moderately. But leaving this field clear, we have ample margin to prophecy.[52]

Female preaching, as one aspect of a religious phenomenon which was culturally and geographically rather marginal in Scottish life, did not necessarily constitute a severe or direct challenge to customary and religious ideologies of womanhood. For although Armstrong and her colleagues were eloquent and direct, both in their preaching and in defence of their personal rights as women, their focus was on the expected coming of Christ, and not particularly on challenging the existing structures of church and society (although in later years Armstrong did lecture on behalf of temperance and female suffrage).

The Watchword (a Free Church magazine which defended orthodox Calvinism, and was edited by James Begg) reported in its issue dated June 1, 1867, an encounter between a woman preacher and a minister. It seems that the conservative presbyterian establishment regarded female preaching primarily as a defiance of church law and good order, which was assumed to include the maintenance of boundaries between appropriate activities for males and females, and against which claims of charism carried little weight:

> There is much rage for novelty at present. The apostles commanded that the gospel be committed to 'faithful men who should be able to teach others also', but not a word of women. Women have a most important and useful sphere of Christian duty, but it is not in the pulpit. Christ employed women, but had not female apostles, and Paul would 'not suffer a woman to teach'. One of these wandering, preaching damsels lately came to a worthy minister and demanded his pulpit. When refused, she said she was compelled to preach by love to Christ and could not refrain. The minister replied, 'True love is the fulfilling of the law, but your love is the breaking of the law.'[53]

Dr William Cunningham, in his influential *Historical Theology*, compared the work of chiliastic revivals and sects in his own time, with that of Montanism, which was a heterodoxical charismatic movement of the patristic period:

> In both there was the same great and offensive prominence of women as the chief possessors and exhibitors of supernatural endowments, and the same perversions of the same passages of Scripture to countenance these pretensions.[54]

By the early 1870s the women preachers were becoming less acceptable even within their own Brethren Community. Other periods of church history have witnessed times of religious freedom and expectation, when the public preaching and teaching of women has been accepted, but as churches have become more settled and institutionalised, the ministry of women has been renounced and excluded. So it was with the Scottish Brethren Assemblies, as Neil Dickson has shown. During the 1880s, Rhymie Assembly in Aberdeenshire resisted the prohibition of women preachers, and was ostracized by other Assemblies.[55] Some of those who had exercised ministry used their gifts in other, more welcoming arenas. Armstrong became a renowned lecturer with the International Order of Good Templars, a temperance organisation which was particularly popular in

Lanarkshire, and which was committed to equal rights for women and men. Other working-class women made their mark with the Faith Mission, which was founded in 1886. But here a similar pattern prevailed – women's gifts were acceptable for converting and forming missions, but when these became more concerned with order and formality, the public participation of women was forbidden. The Salvation Army's female officers also made an impact in urban working-class communities, and were referred to by Charteris and others as a challenge to the presbyterian churches to develop their own, more ordered and acceptable forms of female ministry.[56]

Helen Lockhart Gibson of Kirkcaldy, who experienced conversion in 1859, probably represents the extent of female public ministry which was acceptable for a woman remaining under the jurisdiction of presbyterianism. She visited and exercised spiritual authority over many individual men, most of them working class; but most of her public work was with meetings of women. She was a member of the Free Church (although with a Baptist background), and after intimating a meeting she was to address, a Highland probationer minister felt obliged to add:

> I wish you to understand that she, who is to conduct the meeting, is not a woman-preacher, but just a woman, who wants to speak to women about their souls.[57]

Olive Anderson concludes that the shock of female preaching

> probably provoked dismay and thus stimulated the provision of less disturbing, more controlled outlets for female zeal. But it might be that the recognition of a women's sphere of religious activity might have led to the decline or transmogrification of female preaching, which from the 1870s assumed more discreet forms.[58]

One of the ways in which women's gifts of spiritual counsel and direction were widely used during the 1870s was in the 'enquirers rooms' for the anxious who attended the Moody and Sankey revival meetings which took Scotland by storm during their 1873–74 campaign. Those who were involved in this were usually Biblewomen, female missionaries, and others who already had some experience of Christian public service.[59] But in this novel setting they no doubt enjoyed a renewed sense of their own purpose and power as agents of the Gospel, in the midst of a campaign which had a telling influence on Scottish Christian life. Dwight Moody preached a simple message of salvation available to all through Christ's saving power, and the possibility of new life for the believer. His message cut across the doctrinal debates and denominational divisions of Scottish Protestantism, and had nothing to say about ecclesiastical order and discipline, although he worked along with the institutional churches. For women who were subject to the authority and restrictions imposed by their denominations, participation in the campaign, whether as helpers or hearers may have been a personally liberating experience, which remained with them as they tried to live out their new or quickened faith in the parishes of Scotland. Ira Sankey's melodious songs also made a profound impact, and inspired a major change in attitude to sacred music and instruments in Scottish churches. Many women were enabled to develop their gifts of singing or playing as a valid ministry in church and mission gatherings after the visit of Moody and Sankey. And the campaign probably alerted many – both ministers and laity – to the potential of women's work in the service of an evangelism which cared little for the niceties of Calvinist dogma and church order.

It is surely no coincidence that Scottish campaigners for organised women's work in the churches became more vociferous and successful during the 1870s. They were responding, not only to the to the burgeoning Women's Movement, but also to a range of female ministries which had been exercised in Scotland since mid-century. The challenge they saw for the presbyterian churches was to recognise and utilise appropriate models for women's work, while rejecting what they believed to be the misguided and unwarranted experiment of female preaching. So a correspondent wrote to the Church of Scotland Mission Record in 1877:

> In all other departments of work the conviction is gaining ground that men and women were meant to stand side by side – that while they have different and distinct qualities, both are equally needed for the work to be done in God's world. Are our churches to be the last to say that woman's work, as well as man's, should enter in their calculation? Is there no place for organised Christian service, unless they retire into sisterhoods and convents, or force their way into the pulpit?[60]

'A Sentimental Priesthood'

In her book, *Wrestling with the Church* (1992), Mary Levison, whose endeavours during the 1950s and 1960s were instrumental in securing the admission of women to ordination in the Church of Scotland, surveys the developments which preceded her own struggle and comments:

> I do not like the term 'woman's ministry' . . . If it refers to a ministry different from that of men then question it because this will almost certainly mean an inferior ministry prescribed by men for women.[61]

There is nothing to suggest that 19th-century Scottish presbyterianism was willing to consider or countenance the extension of ordination or office-bearing authority to women. Nor did it reassess the prevailing paradigm of domination. Instead, the churches responded to various challenges – popular evangelicalism, the Women's Movement, the Social Question – by attempting to utilise more fully the lay resources at their disposal. In particular, they looked for ways to exploit the goodwill and energy of women in church-sanctioned activity which extended their service and reputation for righteousness, but maintained and formalised their exclusion from the courts of the church.

Since the 1840s there had been some public debate about the appropriate form for such full-time female service. In her 1843 letter to the Moderator, the Free Church supporter of women voting in a call also suggested that deaconesses should

> find a place under the new administration, sharing in the work of visiting and superintending the poor in parochial districts . . . Let women act for themselves, carry through the part they undertake, or avail themselves of the assistance of men, without suspending the use of their own faculties, and throwing up their responsibility.[62]

But her call went unheeded. In 1848 an article by John Ludlow, entitled 'Deaconesses or Protestant Sisterhoods' appeared in the *Edinburgh Review*. The same author wrote two articles for the religious journal *Good Words* in 1863, as a result of which the Free Church Presbytery of Strathbogie overtured the General Assembly concerning the 'Romanising Tendencies' of the articles. In order to repudiate this charge, Ludlow published a book entitled *Woman's Work in the Church*. Among his conclusions were that the early church:

> set its seal upon the ministering functions of women, by the appointment of a Female Diaconate strictly excluded from functions of public teaching and worship, but nearly co-equal with the male diaconate in active charity.

He also argued that a deaconess should be attached to the service of a particular congregation, and that Deaconess Institutions (which seemed to presbyterians to reek of unhealthy Roman conventualism) must be

> under the direction of a man, and that one who is, or at least has been, a husband.[63]

Such Institutions had begun to flourish, though without any official church connection, on the Continent and in England, and provided interested Scots with some examples of a form of woman's ministry which was ostensibly Biblically based. It was the development and acceptance of this concept in a Scottish context which justified and institutionalised a paradigm of subordination for women who chose to work for the church. By far the most influential Victorian protagonist of lay ministry in general, and woman's ministry in particular, was Dr Archibald Charteris, Professor of Biblical Criticism at Edinburgh University 1868–98, and convener of the Church of Scotland's Christian Life and Work Committee, which began its work in 1869 by gathering information about activity in parishes across Scotland, with a view to reporting on the best means of furthering evangelistic efforts in the Established Church. In the next thirty years the Committee originated the *Life and Work* magazine, the Young Men's Guild, Mission Weeks, Deputations to Fishing and Farm workers, and the Woman's Guild, including the Order of Deaconesses. These were all part of Charteris' grand campaign to breathe new energy into the moribund insititutional life of the church.

Few men of his era matched Charteris' theoretical or practical commitment to an enlarged role for women in presbyterianism (and in other aspects of life – he was a consistent supporter of middle- and upper-class women in higher education, medicine and so on). But in spite of the changes he strived for and was instrumental in achieving, he was theologically, socially and politically conservative. As a Calvinist, he sought to preserve constitution and good order in both church and society. Although he was genuinely concerned to extend the potential of women, the model of ministry which he persistently advocated was located firmly within the patriarchal framework of separate spheres.

Charteris engaged in a systematic investigation of the principles and practice of women's work. That he did so, not only in the light of contemporary events, but also as convener of an enthusiastic General Assembly Committee which had provided evidence of the extent of female congregational activity[64] made his conclusions (which he incorporated into his 1887 Baird Lectures) timely. He recognised that in the period up to AD 100, the 'absolute freedom of the Church' allowed Christian women to fulfil many functions and earn respect and honour. This he attributed in part to the

> earlier and better principles under which officials of the church were men and women discharging sacred functions along with the duties of daily life.[65]

Charteris was keen to revive the practice whereby ordinary church members were more involved in religious work in addition to their daily tasks, so that the church and its mission would be less passive and reliant on the full-time professional minister. He believed that the work required to be to be defined and allotted according to gender, and this was the basis for his proposal to establish both a Young Men's, and a Woman's Guild. He also accepted the principle of full-time vocational service to the Church. He pointed to the evidence of deaconesses in the early undivided church, their absorption into monasticism under Roman Catholicism, and their increasing sacerdotalism, leading to decline, within Eastern Orthodoxy. He argued that early deaconesses took no lifelong vows, but were women of experience who were set apart and ordained to work within the Christian community, and accorded honour and status. He wrote:

> There is no ground to doubt that when the 'whole church' was assembled to vote . . . women as well as men were constituent members of the Assembly.

But as time went on,

> The element of independence in the position of the Deaconess made her, especially in the West, troublesome to male ecclesiastical authorities . . . Councils disputed their ordination and doubted their right to official seats in view of the congregation . . . Popes found it easier to govern nuns than deaconesses . . . The Diaconate was too free an Order – of too miscellaneous usefulness – to be under the dominion of men and it disappeared.[66]

While these features might have suggested a charter for decision-making status and freedom for female church officials, Charteris also seems to have approved of historical evidence that deaconesses were subordinated under male ecclesiastical control:

> When women were subject to one another abuses crept in and fair opportunities were lost . . . women administered baptism and ordained one another, as an *imperium in imperio*. If women are to be part of the corporate church, they must be subject to it and owe to it their standing and power . . . The orthodox church forbade women be bishops or priests and so prevented confusion.[67]

Charteris was obviously interested in, and sympathetic to, the notion of women exercising official ministry in the early Church, and found in this both warrant and example for his own proposals. But the conclusions he drew from his investigations were first, that such women should be confined to the diaconate: 'an order and ministry of *service* for which they are specially qualified.' [my emphasis][68] And second, that the diaconate would be exclusively a female ministry, so that certain tasks and functions would be virtually restricted to women. The duties associated with this order of ministry (which was not confined to women in the apostolic church) were those which evangelical Protestantism claimed to be the joy and privilege of womanhood. Charteris' proposal to revive the order specifically placed these full time officials at the peak of his pyramid model for the organisation of women's work. Deaconesses were to be both exemplars and leaders for other women, whose Christian work, done in the context of their family life, should follow the same pattern of servanthood. So, as Mary Levison observes,

> From the beginning, there was tension built into the conception of the Order of Deaconesses – they were an integral and leading part of the women's section, but also holders of a New Testament office.[69]

Levison has herself endeavoured in the last forty years to get the Church of Scotland to recognise that the diaconate is not necessarily just a female ministry, but a form of service open to both men and women: 'a catalyst to enable the diakonia of the whole – not inferior but different'.[70] She has had to struggle against the weight of tradition, firmly stamped with Charteris' imprint, that the Order was the one and only recognised avenue of official ministry for women in the Church: that a woman with a vocation would enter the diaconate, just as a man would enter the ministry of Word and Sacrament.

The ethos within which the Order of Deaconesses was established, as a constitutional feature of the Established Church, was a paradigm of subordination. Although deaconesses were envisaged as the apex of the hierarchy of organised women's work, the theory and practice of this form of ministry were imbued with that paradoxical combination of elevation and subjugation which characterised the domestic ideology. Deaconesses were the models and leaders for other women, precisely because they made a full-time, usually lifelong, and often unpaid commitment to self-sacrificial work on behalf of the church. In as much as they exemplified Victorian ideals of woman as loving carer of body, mind and spirit, they were deemed worthy of honour. Rev Wallace Williamson of St Cuthbert's Church, Edinburgh, typified this romanticised view of the ministry of women. In a sermon preached at the setting apart of deaconesses in 1892, he chose for his text 1 Cor 11:7, 'the woman is the glory of the man':

> Only the service of Christ will preserve womanly influence and keep it fresh to the end . . . To Christ you owe all. He has raised you from darkness and shame, placed you in the light and glory of immortal hopes, and called you to be a fellow-worker with Him. Your true life is not for self, but for Him . . . Come and unite yourselves in a Holy Guild of womanly service . . . The true sphere of woman is wherever woman can do good. Arise then. Join the fellowship of service, and crown your womanhood with the grace of true devotion.[71]

And Charteris made it clear that his own vision of the organisation of women did not spring fully formed from the pages of early church history, but from the reality, as he perceived it, of his own time:

> I wonder if any woman ever did a more abiding work than Florence Nightingale when she turned the tenderness and aptitude of womanhood to the work of nursing, as at once a science and a Christian occupation for life . . . It is from meditating on the progress which nursing has made . . . that I have come to think that women's work in the Church of Scotland would make better progress if organised. 'Lady-Visitors' are often much in want of training. [There is] no attempt to give the moral support of conscious union in purpose and practice with others in the land. It was not so in the early Church . . . Many women had a definite official position in the apostolic age.[72]

The practical and symbolic endowment of nursing skills was at the heart of Charteris' concept of the diaconate, and Deaconess Hospital in Edinburgh was opened as early as 1894 to provide a central element of the training programme. Other aspects of the instruction offered at the Deaconess Training Institute reflected the desire to develop and systematise the kind of church work which was already associated with women. Apart from the programme of classes in Bible study and home mission work, practical experience was gained in the slums of Edinburgh's Pleasance district – home visiting, sick nursing, work with the inebriate; Guilds and Bands of Hope; prayer and evangelistic meetings were organised in kitchens and at stairheads; services were conducted for children, mothers – the 'deaconettes' got involved in anything except the solid, respectable, Sabbath worship which was the exclusive preserve of ministers.[73]

The resistance of presbyterianism to any hint of diaconal authority beyond the strictly defined parameters of women's work was indicated by the challenge made to the 1887 proposal that deaconesses should be 'set apart' by presbyteries. Edinburgh Presbytery complained that this seemed to place women above the ruling elders and deacons who controlled local parish affairs. In 1888, Charteris defended his original plan:

> Deaconesses have no official ruling power in the Church . . . The Deaconess is to be set apart by Presbytery and not by the Kirk Session. This is in accordance with the custom of the early Church . . . Elders and deacons are appointed – not to work, but to deliberate and rule . . . To indicate the difference between the official of the congregation and the servant of the Church (who, however, must exercise her office under the authority of the Kirk Session) may remove some possible misconceptions.[74]

However, an alternative set of regulations was presented to the 1888 Assembly, and the majority (not being persuaded that women would humbly accept their assigned lowliness) voted in favour of setting apart by Kirk Sessions.

The subsequent development of the Order suggests that a number of women found scope for initiative and responsibility which extended well beyond parish boundaries, and what had previously been available to churchwomen.[75] But its emergence as a gender-specific, distinctive ministry which was always ultimately subject to male control seriously compromised its potential as a source of real challenge and opportunity. And as I have suggested in Chapter 2, the original and persisting conception of the Order as an alternative vocation for unmarried upper- and middle-class women of private means scarcely made it a viable or attractive career choice for women who were unable or unwilling to conform to that image. Alice Maxwell, who was the first Principal of the Deaconess Institute, wrote in 1904 about the extension of opportunities available, but in fact revealed the confines of class and gender into which the Order was boxed:

> When first used in connection with women, [the Diaconate] was met with an indulgent smile. Now, the Order speaks for itself. The spheres of work in which women may serve the Church are on the increase, and new doors are opening: Parishes, visitations in prisons and poorhouses, deputy work for the Woman's Guild, work with fisher girls . . . The charge of our Institutions . . . Thus, spheres of service for women grow wider and more varied. Will those of means who are free from home ties think of those openings calling for workers . . . offering with consecrated hearts their time, strength and means for the building up of the Church?[76]

For all its limitations, the Order of Deaconesses at least offered some status, recognition and community to a few Church of Scotland women. Other arrangements for the employment of female labour were rooted in the unquestioned belief in distinctive women's ministry, but were even less adequate in terms of recognition and reward. The hiring of Biblewomen was unsystematic, unregulated, and subject to no official guidelines about pay or conditions. The introduction of Parish Sisters (who worked under the Established Church's Home Mission Committee from 1893), and of women workers under the United Free Church Women's Home Mission, (who were officially granted the title of Church Sister from 1916), represent the churches' rather half-hearted (and always underfunded) attempts to standardise the conditions under which women were employed to do battle with the perplexing 'Social Question'. Recognised training and qualifications were never compulsory for these positions, the pay was poor, and the workers had no place by right at any level of the churches' decision-making hierarchy. And yet, presbyterian men in the new century congratulated themselves on throwing open opportunities for the ministry of women, and made noble pronouncements about their place in the scheme of things:

> There is in Christian thought no rivalry between men and women. Their ministries are different (even as their constitution is), but there is no question of superiority and inferiority, for both are needed by Christ.[77]

Such men seemed baffled and disappointed when so few women took advantage of these opportunities. But women were disappointed too, and questions about superiority and inferiority; about ordination and subordination, began to be raised. At the 1914 General Assembly of the United Free Church, Professor James Young Simpson of New College moved an addendum to the Christian Life and Work Report, that:

> In view of the varied and invaluable services rendered by women to the Life and Work of the Church, and advantages that would accrue from more definite recognition of their place in Church life and work, the Assembly remit to the Committee to consider how this could be best effected, and report to the next General Assembly.[78]

In support of his motion, he argued:

> There is much in the conditions under which women's work is carried on in the Church which is a virtual contradiction of the Church's belief [in equality] . . . Disillusionment and disappointment is suffered in many cases on entering into Church work . . . It seems to be standing for something which dissipates the spirit of equality . . . There is a great hesitation to provide untrammelled opportunities for the exercise of all gifts.[79]

'The Thin Edge of the Wedge'

During the first decades of the new century, a generation of middle- and upper-class women who had enjoyed the intellectual, social, and sometimes economic benefits of access to higher education provided a significant minority of energetic, committed and increasingly organised agents for change within society and the Church. Idealistic and confident young women who had experienced some measure of co-operation and comradeship in student societies such as the Student Christian Movement, and who believed in their own power and right to be social activists, were indeed disillusioned by the lack of scope within the institutional church. They were joined in their frustration by older women – veterans both of church work and of the fifty-year struggle for political suffrage which had entered its militant phase (in which a significant number of churchwomen participated – see Chapter 5). Such women were increasingly willing to express dismay at the exploitation of female goodwill and labour in the Church.[80] Indeed, many had benefited directly from the advocacy of women's rights, responsibilities and capabilities in the teaching offered at the United Free Church Women's Missionary College – an education in female community and assertiveness which derived some of its power from the liberating effects of critical perspectives on scripture and theology. In America, there were liberal feminists from the evangelical tradition, like Elizabeth Cady Stanton and Matilda Gage, who developed critiques of Christian religion based on iconoclastic hermeneutical principles. But while their radical conclusions would have certainly been unacceptable to most Scottish presbyterian women, some of the issues they stirred up would not have been wholly shocking or alien to those exposed to the 'higher criticism'. Stanton's *The Woman's Bible* (1895, 1898), for example, raised questions about the Jewish Pentateuch:

> Why should the customs and opinions of this ignorant people, who lived centuries ago, have any influence in the religious thought of this generation?[81]

The extent to which Biblical injunctions could or should have influence on current religious thought and practice was one of the central issues in the debate about women in the church.

All of this was fertile ground for seeds of female dissent in the Church, and the leading article in the April 1914 issue of the *UFC Mission Record* acknowledged as much:

> Let us take the claim of women to greater recognition in public life. Everywhere we see them bursting the bonds and conventions that have dominated them since the beginning, rising above the old narrow ideas of sex, and desiring a position as co-workers with men in the task of governing the world . . . There is the more reason for directing attention to this question because the claim of women is now beginning to make itself felt within the Church . . . The assumption is that they will wish some sort of say in the government of the Church.[82]

Discussions by men about the role of women in the church were not, of course, new. But the debate instigated in 1914, which rumbled on until Church Union in 1929, and beyond, marked a new phase in the controversy. For the first time, presbyterian courts were forced to grapple with a suggestion which would have had Knox and Calvin birling in their graves: that even a modicum of official authority might be removed from the exclusive possession of men. And if these men, moved by the spirit of the age (and also by the absence, caused by war, agnosticism, antagonism and apathy, of male sufficiency) chose to accede to that departure from hallowed tradition, would women gain direct entry into the citadel, or be told to exercise their charisms from within an 'equal but different' female order of ministry?

A committee of fifteen men, under the convenership of Prof J.Y. Simpson, was set up to consider the matter. In 1915 it reported that it had met seven times, and had consulted with women of the United Free Church and of other denominations. The Committee acknowledged the 'importance and urgency' of the subject. It noted the revolutionary changes in the position of women in the community within two generations and called for action by the Church to meet these new conditions, claiming that there was an 'imperative need to reconsider its organisation and methods of work'.[83]

If women were encouraged by this honest assessment and generous recognition of the need to make changes, to hope that the Committee would make proposals commensurate with its analysis, they were in for a disappointment. The Report introduced its proposals thus:

> Some incline to the view that all offices be open to women on the same terms as men . . . But opinion is not yet ripe for consideration of far-reaching change involving such difficult questions as the ordination of women to the ministry of Word and Sacrament, and the constitution of higher courts.[84]

That cautious rider proved to be a more accurate preamble than the fine words which opened the Report. The proposals of the Special Committee did not indicate that a fundamental or critical assessment of organisation and methods of work had prevailed. They were:

> 1. To draw the attention of congregations to the eligibility of women for election to all congregational committees, including Boards of Managers, and Committees of Management, and further, that the Assembly declare women eligible for appointment as members of Deacons Courts.

> 2. That women be associated with Kirk Sessions for consultative purposes and for the discharge of certain duties of a pastoral kind.

> 3. That there should be an office for suitably trained women – Church Sisters, held by voluntary or paid workers who shall be set apart by prayer.

> 4. That Foreign Mission, Colonial and Continental, Jewish, Life and Work, Home Mission, Highlands and Islands, Youth, and other Committees as determined by the General Assembly, may co-opt women members up to one sixth of the total membership. Presbyteries be also authorised to add women to committees as they may see the need.

> 5. The Foreign Mission Committee to ascertain whether the time has come for women missionaries to be represented on Mission Councils for all except presbyterial powers.[85]

These proposals (with the possible exception of Number 5) offered cold comfort to seekers of real change, and grist to the mill of opponents. Principal Martin of New College, who called for adequate time to consider the constitutional issues at stake, recognised that the proposals attempted to bypass such questions, and identified their basic weakness:

> To suggest that all offices be opened to women would have been revolutionary, but at least the issue would have been plain. Instead, accommodation is now proposed . . . An adjustment and not a solution – a partial and imperfect adjustment – of an inherently difficult and delicate problem.[86]

But perhaps, despite the militant mood abroad in the country and the dearth of equality within the church, United Free churchwomen were not looking for a revolution. In his reply to the 1915 debate, committee member J.H. Oldham mentioned that

> The Committee devoted two full sessions to consideration of opening all offices to women, and quite deliberately came to the conclusion that this was not the time to raise an issue affecting the fundamental constitution of presbyterianism . . .There is no general desire among women that the question should be raised at this time.[87]

Certainly, the questionnaire which was circulated to the four Women's Mission Committees of the Church, and to 160 individuals (of whom 85 replied), did not indicate a great longing among many to assume the duties and privileges of ordination. Although most respondents agreed that 'the service of women is carried on under limitations, which prevents them from making, through the Church, their full contribution to the work of the Kingdom'[88] only a small minority declared themselves in favour of opening all church offices and courts to women. Most seemed happy at the prospect of what was suggested in the Committee's proposals, although some sought a kind of modified eldership for women. This would give some status and authority to the work of visitation and mild social control which women already engaged in, but reserved the administration of the sacraments for men only. Clearly, women still had difficulty envisaging themselves occupying the inner sanctum of religious symbolism and prestige, although they acknowledged their fitness to perform most of the practical tasks and responsibilities of church life. Responses to a question about the specific nature of the limitations on women indicate frustration and grievances based on practical experience of work already done in the Home and Foreign Mission Associations: 'Even those who are generally opposed to change feel the anomalies and difficulties here'.[89] They resented the inability to represent their views on church courts; the lack of any share in planning congregational or Church work; the dearth of paid jobs (made worse by the fact that the women's associations had male secretaries, and their Assembly Reports were given by male conveners); the fact that all initiatives were under the ultimate control of bodies of men. A particular annoyance to women, upon whom the Church relied for fundraising and collections, was the lack of spending control, and the inadequate assignment of legacies to funds for women's work. When asked about the causes of these limitations, at least some respondents showed familiarity with contemporary feminist insights, and applied them to the church situation. They cited:

> Custom; conventional views of women's sphere; a diehard belief in the subordination of women; Protestant reaction to conventual type service, which allowed women of capacity to become abbesses; misinterpretation of New Testament teaching about women; failure to understand the limitation of time and circumstance to Paul's precepts; failure to realise the change in woman's educational, social and economic position, a change that demands "that while showing womanly virtues of gentleness, sensitiveness, purity, quietness of spirit, delicacy of touch, women should also develop courage, initiative, broad-mindedness, independence, justice". The Church has denied woman "the capacity to become".[90]

Several women who belonged to denominations and organisations which had done more to affirm that capacity were also consulted. One member of the Society of Friends commented 'These questions seem to me to refer to a state of things which must of necessity pass away'.[91] But in the meantime, the UF Churchwomen (or at least those who were asked) seemed satisfied with the partial and piecemeal proposals. In 1916, each of the Women's Associations, and the female missionaries serving abroad, gave them their approbation. Perhaps more radical women had already given up on the church in favour of the political suffrage movement, which was sometimes, in the pre-war years of militancy, characterised as an 'alternative religion' for women.[92] Or perhaps they believed that a policy of gradualism was the best strategy for breaching the patriarchal monolith of their church's constitution, in preparation for more fundamental changes. Writing in 1916, Florence Mackenzie, then Principal of the Women's Missionary College, certainly responded very positively to what she perceived as a wind of change:

> Some of us have felt in the past few weeks that a new spirit is arising in our midst. For long we had been bound down to the conviction that what is, must be . . . Recently, however, different things have shown that there is a willingness to face change . . . My confidence is based upon the spirit of progress which

has shown itself in the life of the Church. Discussions on the 'Recognition of the place of women in the Church' have come to a very wonderful issue . . . In speaking to us at the House Guild last Friday, Mr Oldham said that he was proud of his Church.[93]

Interesting and suggestive as the opinions of women might be, they were as marginal to the final outcome as the women themselves – consigned to the Assembly Hall gallery to observe, with a combination of anticipation, bemusement and boredom, the debates in which the same few men participated over a three-year period.[94] But commissioners, Presbyteries and kirk sessions were all given the opportunity to respond to and vote on the proposals. The suggestion which met with universal approval was that which formalised the acceptable principles and practice of a distinctive female ministry: Church Sisters would constitute no threat to male preserves of power. The same was generally true for the suggestions that committees should consult with women – either by including a token number as members, or by setting up Women's Advisory Committees, although from the traditionalists there were some perfectly legitimate criticisms that the presence of co-opted women on Assembly Committees would be constitutionally irregular:

> By this decision, a group of women, not elected by congregations, but selected by a kind of disguised patronage, were raised to a position from which [deacons, managers and congregational boards] were rigidly excluded. It was an undoubted anomaly, but presumably those who created it were of the same mind as the Philistine MP pilloried by Matthew Arnold: 'That a thing is an anomaly I considered no objection whatsoever.'[95]

Indeed, the courts of the Church seemed happy to accept that anomaly if it enabled them to offer women a semblance of co-operation, without having to deal with fundamental issues.

There were some churchmen who were willing to contemplate such questions, and to come up with revolutionary answers. Rev James Barr of Govan spoke for the radicals when he said in 1916,

> I am astonished at the timidity of the Church on this question. I am in favour of opening up all offices whatsoever in the Church to women on the same conditions as to men (applause)'.[96]

That was a minority view, either because it was perceived that the Church was not ready for such a transformation, or because most commissioners simply excluded the ministry of Word and Sacrament from any consideration of the role of women. Yet there were many who genuinely sought deeper, richer and more serious scope for the gifts and resources of women. Professor Mackintosh of New College commented in 1916 that the women he knew through the SCM

> bring a freshness of vision which is not given to every man. Their minds are unjaded and enterprising and unrestrained by many of the conventional fears and anxieties that beset us. The minds of many of us men have been formalised and stereo-typed by centuries of committees

and he continued

> A large number of women are passing through universities and colleges for whom we must find some other sphere of action in our Church than merely the sewing meeting. These women have alert and in some cases most reasonably radical minds, and we must give them some elbow room in which to work.[97]

And in 1915 the church historian, Professor McEwen, who was that year's Moderator, left the Chair to make a rousing plea that tradition be disregarded for the sake of present needs:

> Do not let us waste time. Our work needs to be energised without delay . . . Let us thank God that the position of women is not what it was in New Testament times. Dr Henderson is quite right in saying that the Reformation gave women no place in Church life. The Reformers, including Knox, thought that the regimen of women was "monstrous" and held to the old domineering idea of the authority of males. But in this they were utterly wrong (laughter and applause) and it is fantastic to appeal to them as arbiters.[98]

For a church leader to make comments which audaciously challenged the authority of both scripture and the heroic instigators of the reformed tradition, indicates the extent of the intellectual and psychological transformation which had been wrought by critical scholarship within theology, and reform movements for social change. However, a significant group of traditionalists believed that there was nothing fantastic about such appeals, and that in making them, they were acting as guardians of Scottish presbyterian heritage. Their spokesman, who seems to have felt honour bound to speak against the extended role of women at every opportunity, and at great length, was Dr Archibald Henderson of Crieff. In 1915 he objected particularly to the proposal that women be eligible for ordination to serve on deacons' courts, claiming that there was no legislation recognising the entitlement of women to be elected to take part in ecclesiastical procedure. He led a large group who registered their dissent from the deliverance 'on the grounds that the Report contained statements affecting the law of the Church, which were not in accordance with the law.'[99] But the report was duly sent down to presbyteries for comment.

By 1916, when returns had been received from around the country, it was clear that, apart from a few presbyteries who saw no reason to change the *status quo*, or who wished consideration to be delayed until after the war, there was general consensus that proposals 2–5 were acceptable. But there was considerable disquiet about the constitutional and ecclesiological implications of making women eligible for ordination as deacons. The Committee, which had wanted to avoid 'difficult questions' could not dodge some theological debate, although the level, depth and context of that debate was far from satisfactory. The 1916 Report included three memoranda on ordination, on the basis of which it maintained that

> The difficulty does not . . . lie in regard to the 'ordination' of women to such offices as they may appropriately fill; the only question to determine is that of the office to which women may fittingly be set apart.[100]

The proponents of change argued their case on functional grounds. The Deacons' Court was not an essential element of presbyterianism, but just one of the instruments of administrative and financial management which the United Church had inherited from its old constituent parts – and the eligibility of women to serve on Congregational and Management Boards had already been affirmed by the Assembly Arrangements Committee. The concern was to give to women

> Some direct part in the charge and disposition of funds which they do so much to collect, and to which in many instances they so largely contribute.[101]

It was also to make up for the increasing lack of suitable men for these positions – a problem exacerbated during the war years. But Simpson and Oldham were compelled by their opponents to adduce Scriptural and historical backing for their scheme. In doing so, they hedged their bets as to whether it would be an innovation. On the one hand they cited New Testament and apostolic evidence for the ordination of female deacons, but they also emphasised the possibility of Spirit-led change and development in women themselves, and in social conditions, as a compelling reason for innovation, if indeed it was such. As J H Oldham contended:

> Even if there is no Scriptural precedent, I would say that it does not belong to the nature of Scripture to furnish precedents for dealing with social, political or economic conditions, which were not existent at the time of writing . . . Christianity, because it is a religion of the spirit, has been able throughout history to adapt itself to changing circumstances in a world full of change.[102]

Dr Henderson was opposed to every element of the proposers' argument, and in particular their attitude to scripture:

Scripture must be accepted as it stands, and the Church has not the power to develop according to changing conditions and experiences . . . Before Paul comes to the question of public service or office in the Church, he deals with the question, what men may do and what women may do, and he bases distinctions upon their nature as God created them . . . It is easy to pooh-pooh ancient views as reactionary. I am not ashamed to say that I accept the teaching of Scripture as to the position of men and women in relation to the public offices of the Church.[103]

The debate on women deacons may have provided a forum for the exchange of liberal and conservative theological positions, but the outcome was a victory for the pragmatists who wanted to utilise the talents of women but were unwilling to countenance anything like ordination. The overture (which included the power of veto vested in ministers and kirk sessions) was sent down to presbyteries under the Barrier Act. Thirty-four voted in favour of ordaining female deacons, twenty-five opposed. Of the kirk sessions which expressed an opinion, 351 were in favour and 137 were against. Meanwhile, Glasgow Presbytery overtured the 1917 Assembly that deacons might be appointed for a fixed term, rather than ordained for life. In spite of a warning that

To evade the issue by giving office without ordination, would be like allowing women to take medical classes in university and forbidding them to take degrees or practice[104]

the Assembly apparently shared the relief of Aberdeen's Principal Iverach:

If you give some of the best ladies of a Congregation an opportunity, and give ministers the opportunity of welcoming them, you will be doing a great service to the Church. I think that a way may be found along the lines of the overture from Glasgow, whereby you may secure the splendid service of women, and not burden people like myself who hold views of ordination which I shall continue to hold as long as I live.[105]

In 1918, the Assembly Arrangements Committee proposed that the office of deacon should be tenable either by men ordained for life, or by men and women, appointed for three years. This was finally enacted in 1919.

So, five years after the debate was initiated with rousing references to revolution and equality, and in the wake of a devastating war, the United Free Church had allowed a small breach in the walls of its male bastion. A handful of women were appointed to those Assembly Committees dealing with issues which, according to the men, were susceptible to womanly insight. In theory, women might be invited – by men – to share in certain kirk session and Presbytery deliberations. And they were now entitled to take on financial and administrative duties – not with the traditional seal and dignity of ordination, but through the backdoor of expediency.

Dr Jerdan, the Assembly Clerk, had maintained in 1916 that 'the nature of woman is such that . . . she is not intended for public life . . . the sphere of our women is domestic'. By 1917 he was feeling threatened by the method of change he called 'the thin edge of the wedge'.[106] On the long view, he was surely right, since the only subsequent changes in Scottish presbyterian polity in relation to women have extended their rights, to the point of complete official parity by 1968.

But the crack which had been forced in the door of opportunity was a less than fulsome endorsement of those women who had enjoyed four years of war work and wages, the prospect of political enfranchisement, and in many congregations *de facto* responsibility for roles usually occupied by men. There was actually very little to intimidate the 'diehard believers in the subordination of women'. The Church claimed to recognise the transformation which the war years had wrought in the lives of women, and acknowledged that

> The difficulty may be that many of the finest women with special aptitude may be lost to Church service because of demands elsewhere for competent and well paid workers.[107]

But it was decidedly reluctant, in most departments, to make use even of the limited permission of right it had granted to women. Granted, there was no mass movement of women pressing to be allowed such rights, but there was a substantial number who longed for new opportunities to exercise, test and extend their gifts in the service of the church. Many were particularly disappointed that, despite the majority vote from both presbyteries and kirk sessions in favour of ordination for female deacons, in the end the Church could not bring itself to introduce that symbolically important change – especially at a time when the State had finally recognised the legitimacy of female political enfranchisement.

The Established Church also raised the issue of the role of women in its work and counsels. The question appeared on the Church's agenda in the aftermath of the First World War, rather than in the immediate context of suffrage agitation. And it emerged from the Report of the Special Commission on the War, which met 1916–1919. As part of its work, the Commission surveyed a group which consisted mainly of middle-aged, professional laymen, about 'The Life and Efficiency of the Church'. Alongside clarion calls for hymns to be 'strong and virile, not sugary, weak and non-masculine',[108] some respondents also commented to the effect that 'women's work should be developed more, and they should be given some say in the councils of the Church'.[109] In its editorial conclusion, the Report to the 1919 Assembly, calling for greater democracy within the Church, suggested:

> To this whole question, added importance and even urgency has been given by the striking advance in the position accorded to women in the social organisations and public services of our country . . . One cannot doubt that the Church will be more than ready to overhaul its machinery with the purpose of embodying that recognition in an outward, visible and adequate form.[110]

However, as in the United Free Church, worthy sentiments seemed to promise a good deal more than was eventually delivered. At the 1919 Assembly, the deliverance on the War Commission resolved to appoint a new Committee on Church and Nation, and an amendment called for its agenda to include the question of the position of women in the Church's work and councils. In 1920, Dr John White, who was joint-convener of the new committee, published an article about the role of women within the Church, expressing the view, which he continued to promote throughout his life, that the extension and development of the Order of Deaconesses was the most suitable way to expand female ministry.[111]

The interim report on the position of women, which was prepared for the 1920 General Assembly, bears White's hallmarks of extreme ecclesiological caution and pragmatism. It does not enter into any discussion about scriptural or theological principles, but quotes quite extensively from the Church of England Report on the Ministry of Women (1919), and includes a cursory summary of the development of organised women's work within the Church of Scotland, and the recent changes within the United Free Church. It then records that in 1919 both the Foreign Mission Committee and the Committee on the Religious Instruction of Youth were given leave to appoint women as associate members, with the right to speak but not to vote. The one suggestion made was to formalise and extend the right of Standing Committees to co-opt a number of female members. The Report betrays the characteristic official response to women as presenting a difficulty to the church, rather than being considered an intrinsic part of the church, by commenting that the proposal:

> Does little more than acknowledge that we have a problem to solve . . . It is a step that must lead to another sooner or later. [Women] will ask for a place in the Councils of the Church, and it is not easy to see how their demand can be withstood.[112]

At the 1920 Assembly, there was no debate about the issue. Interventions were to do rather with legal restrictions which prevented women from acting as elders, or in management roles within *quoad sacra* parishes. It was agreed that the Assembly's General Committee should assess whether the Sex Disqualification (Removal) Act of 1919 had any bearing on the latter question.

The 1921 Report added nothing new, except to note, apparently with approval, a resolution adopted at the 1920 Lambeth Conference to give canonical recognition to the order of deaconesses 'as the one and only order of ministry for women which has the stamp of apostolic approval'.[113] The Church and Nation Report complacently observed:

> The Church of Scotland has recognised the Order of Deaconesses as part of its regular organisation. Should any other question arise as to women's pastoral ministry, it will no doubt have to be dealt with by the extension and development of the Order of Deaconesses. Meantime the Committee have no recommendation to make with regard to the work at present being undertaken so successfully and extensively.[114]

Having ascertained that there were no legal restrictions, it was firmly recommended that women should be eligible to serve on Assembly Committees. It was also reported that the Sex Disqualification Act did not remove the limitation of lay management functions to men, and that new legislation would be required to alter constitutions and enable women to serve and vote. A suggestion to this effect was made to the special committee which had been set up to review *quoad sacra* constitutions.

Once again, the Assembly engaged in no discussion of any fundamentals, although Rev W Main of Edinburgh observed the anomaly which had affected the UFC legislation, and which was bound to be a factor whenever 'the role of women' was treated as a problem or a special case, requiring 'the Church' (i.e. male office bearers) to make concessions or adjustments:

> He wanted equality of the sexes. If women could become members of standing committees, so should membership be open to men who were not elders. On the other hand, women should be eligible for eldership, and certain of them might after evidence of qualifications be admitted to pulpits.[115]

Rev James Francis of Cartsburn deserves recognition as the mover of the first attempt within Scottish presbyterianism to gain official parity for women. On behalf of his congregation, and in the interests of 'justice, equality and commonsense', he asked the 1921 Assembly to agree

> That the necessary steps be taken so to alter the laws, regulations and constitution of the Church that they might apply equally to women as to men.[116]

But his unprecedented action apparently did not warrant serious consideration. Although the seconder claimed that 'it would be deplorable if the Church which has done so much for women would not open the door wide to them', the Joint Conveners of the Committee exercised a deft scissors movement to cut short any debate. Lord Sands commented that the proposal would mean a complete revolution in the Church [and whenever did the Established Church condone a revolution?], while Dr White, cautious as ever, declared that 'delay in this matter was the surest way'.[117] Only a handful supported the overture.[118]

So by 1922, the Church which, it had been confidently predicted, would be 'ready to overhaul its machinery' in order to give outward, visible and adequate recognition to the position and claims of women, had made provision for no more than 15 per cent of Standing Committee membership to be co-opted women. The highest court had shown itself unwilling to discuss or contemplate any substantial change in either machinery or ideology.

Although the issue emerged and was dealt with in different ways within the two presbyterian denominations, the outcome in each was remarkably similar. Within both Churches, there were women who felt frustrated and alienated by the lack of opportunity and consultation, and they were supported by a small number of men who sought significant change. But their advocacy proved unable to effect anything but minor concessions, in spite of continued warnings that able and faithful women would seek challenge and fulfilment elsewhere.

There was one more attempt to introduce reform before the Union of Churches in 1929. In the sneering tone which it pleased him to use whenever commenting on any aspect of women's rights, G D Reith, in his *Reminiscences of the United Free Church General Assemblies* (1936), recalled the events of 1926:

> Elated by their partial success in the matter of the diaconate, some ardent feminists in the Church overtured the General Assembly, through four Presbyteries, anent the eligibility of women for ordination to ministry and eldership.[119]

It was not so much 'ardent feminism' which lay behind this move, but rather the presence of a few women in the Church's theological colleges. In 1926, Elizabeth Hewat (who had a notable pioneering career as missionary, ecumenicist, church historian and activist) became the first to graduate BD from New College in Edinburgh. However, all women were registered as 'irregular students' – barred from the receipt of bursaries and prizes, and the opportunity to be trained and tested for licence and ordination. The concern was that, without such opportunity, such students would not be fully equipped for their vocation to serve the Church, abroad or at home. As Professor James Young Simpson remarked during the 1926 Assembly debate:

> They had in their College in Edinburgh that winter a young woman who had beaten all the men in her class. It was going to be extremely difficult to have to say to that young woman or other young women like her: 'You have gone through your course in this admirable way, you are giving your life to service in the foreign field, and yet we cannot put you on the same level as the men.'[120]

The events of 1926 illustrate the difficulties for a Church which was thirled, structurally and culturally, to the ideology of separate spheres, but which had to deal with the consequences of creeping and piecemeal breaches in the barrier between men and women. Those who argued in favour of ordination were able to point to the *de facto* developments in the Church, which suggested that women were now able to fulfil the practical criteria for ministry. They could no longer be excluded from the education deemed appropriate for candidates, and in other fields had entered into professions. Missionaries, Church Sisters and others had proved their capability for the teaching, pastoral, leadership and administrative functions of Church office. A few had even ventured into pulpits. Proponents supported these developments as Spirit-led, and suggested that ordination would simply be due recognition and consecration of God-given gifts which could now be discerned in women. The supporters of the motion denied that Paul's injunctions about women were authoritative for their own time and situation, for these specific rules were overriden by the universal dictum, that in Christ Jesus there is neither male nor female (Gal 3:28).[121]

However, conservatives disputed that interpretation, and used their own understanding of Scriptural material to bolster a paradigm of domination which would, by circular definition, continue to exclude women from the ministry:

> When such a phrase as 'in Christ' was used, they were speaking *sub specie aeternitatis* . . . But this was a question concerning God's moral government in this world . . . They got that from the only authority on the Church, the apostle Paul . . . In 1 Corinthians 11 he said 'But I would have you know that the head of every man is Christ, and the head of the woman is the man, and the head of Christ is God' . . . Every woman now present was wearing on her head a sign of authority – *exousia* – delegated power, delegated by whom? . . . He refused to believe that the Holy Ghost was going to go against his own productions.[122]

That assumption of super- and sub-ordination, divinely decreed for all time as the proper basis of relationship between men and women was used on this occasion, as so often before, to give dignity to objections which seem based on something suspiciously resembling custom or prejudice:

> The admission of women to the ministry would increase that scarcity [of candidates for the ministry], for it would discourage a certain class of men of virile type from entering the profession. (hear, hear) . . . The difficulty arose at once as to whether the woman-minister was to be single or married. Let them suppose a young woman settled down in the manse, and then married the local doctor or teacher or tradesman; did he become the head of the manse? Then if she was to resign on marriage, what became of the ordination *ad vitam aut ad culpam*?[123]
>
> It would mean the introduction of a celibate order into the Church. A woman's supreme heritage was motherhood, and any movement away from that high heritage could not be justified even in the name of the Church. A great deal of modern feminism was pathological.[124]

It is easy to sympathise with the *UFC Record* reporter who commented, 'It is rather pitiful to have such a question treated as a mere problem of marriage, and debate as to who is to rule in the manse'.[125] But these apparently superficial remarks indicate the deep roots of patriarchy in the Scottish presbyterian ethos.By 1926, the primary concern of these men (and their many female supporters) was not function, but status and symbol. The institutional Church had shown its willingness to accommodate and utilise the voluntary and paid labour of women in an ever widening range of capacities, and had no qualms about the practical celibacy imposed on Church Sisters and female missionaries (who were still not permitted to retain their paid employment if they chose to marry, although it was quite acceptable to continue their work in an 'honorary' capacity). But the conservative majority would not countenance the idea of women in positions of public leadership and oversight as an alternative life option to a husband and domesticity. Still less could they envisage the possibility that a woman might seek to exercise the male prerogative of choosing both profession and marriage. According to the still potent doctrine of separate spheres, a woman must either fulfil or sublimate her maternal vocation; she must not usurp male authority in home or Church.

The overture, as even its proposers admitted, was unlikely to get anywhere: the two presbyterian churches had become increasingly preoccupied with the impending Union, and with racist anti-Catholic scaremongering, to the exclusion of major social and political concerns in the Church and in a nation riven by the Depression. The motion was withdrawn in favour of an amendment that the present time was not opportune for taking any steps.

As 1929 approached, then, the two main presbyterian denominations had negotiated pressure to include women in decision-making and official bodies. Neither had shown the collective willingness required to contemplate or introduce the incorporation of women – on an equal basis – into existing structures of power. Both evidently preferred the relative safety of an expanding 'women's ministry', from which separate place small numbers of delegates and ambassadors might be invited to give the benefit of their much vaunted special feminine gifts and insights to 'the Church'.

In pre-Union negotiations, the Church of Scotland succeeded in persuading the United Free Church of the advantages of a unitary organisation, binding together all aspects of approved women's service in the Church. So the Woman's Guild became, in the United Church, the focus for home and foreign missionary work; for temperance activity; for historical commitments to the conversion of Jewish women, and educational work in the Highlands. The system of Presbyterial Councils and a geographically representative Central Council emphasised the parallelism of women and men in the Church: they were more or less separate, but decidedly unequal. By 1930, nearly 70,000 women belonged to the Guild, under whose auspices six Associations operated. Each was under the ultimate control of an Assembly Committee. There were twenty-eight such Committees, and of a total membership of 1752, 160 were women. There is little evidence that the extremely limited gender-neutral opportunities in Church employment and management were made available to women to any significant extent. It is not surprising that the point made plainly by the 1928 *UFC Record* correspondent whose letter is quoted at the beginning of this chapter, was alluded to (with the graciousness which men apparently so admired in women) by Mary Lamond, Woman's Guild President, at the 1929 Union Assembly:

> The women workers of the Church of Scotland thank the Assembly for recognition of their services . . . I would say they are quite worthy of any encouragement. Perhaps they are also worthy of a greater share in Church counsels than you have yet given them.[126]

The response of the newly united establishment to this suggestion was predictable. Dr P D Thomson of Leith warned:

> The Church must not allow itself to drift into action in this direction which might prove hurtful to existing honoured customs and institutions. Whatever

may be done to enlarge the sphere of womanly service and influence must be done deliberately, and with open eyes.[127]

The Fathers and Brethren had some reason to prescribe caution, for the unthinkable was beginning to happen on their own doorstep. In May 1929, Vera Findlay of the Congregational Union (though a presbyterian by upbringing) became the first woman to have her ordination to the ministry of Word and Sacrament recognised by a Scottish denomination.[128] And the small group of dissenters who refused incorporation into the 1929 Union, and became the continuing United Free Church were about to take a similar step. Their leader James Barr, who had already demonstrated his commitment to women's rights, later wrote:

> I at least will always have it as a proud memory that, when our Church had to reorganise in 1929, we had among us men of vision, broad mind and fearless purpose, who brought forward far-reaching resolutions accepted by almost unanimous vote in two Assemblies, and so passed into the law of our Church:
>
> 1. The Assembly declare that, the Church having the right to the services of every member in the Church who is in full communion, such members may be called upon to serve on Committees of General Assembly, Synods, Presbyteries and Congregations, and may so serve.
>
> 2. Any member of the Church in full communion shall be eligible to hold any office within the Church.[129]

Further afield, the ordained ministry of women had become a live issue in most Protestant denominations. By 1927 there were around 100 women ministers in a number of Congregational and Methodist churches in the USA. In England, Constance Mary Coltman was ordained by the Congregational Union in 1917. Maud Royden, an Anglican feminist, was called to the pastoral ministry at the City Temple in London, which caused a furore in Church of England circles. The Baptist Union of Britain and Ireland, in theory, permitted the admission of women from 1918 (although the Scottish Baptist Union has not yet allowed the ordination of women). The English Presbyterian Church accepted the principle of women ministers in 1921, although it was another 30 years before the first was ordained. In 1922 the Methodist Church convened a committee 'to consider the whole question of admission of women to the ordained ministry, to the work of Deaconesses, and kindred service'. And the Church of England, as already mentioned, had published an important report on the Ministry of Women in 1919.

The Scottish presbyterian denominations were somewhat less progressive than their nearest relations within the reformed tradition (i.e., English and North American presbyterians, Congregationalists and some

Baptists). The Church of Scotland and the Methodist Church debates on ordination for women extended over a similar period to successful outcomes in 1968 and 1970. The Anglican Church, with its ecclesiology of episcopal succession, concern about catholic unity, and different conception of priesthood, ratified the ordination of female priests in 1992.

A comparative study of church responses to calls for women to be eligible for official ministry reveals the remarkable similarity of issues, arguments and consequences across the main British protestant churches.[130] This strongly suggests (as indeed the Scottish presbyterian discussions acknowledged) that the matter was related to wider social trends, and not predominantly to internal theological issues. It is evident that all mainstream churches were forced to consider the official position of women during the first thirty years of the 20th century. The period when the United Free Church of Scotland, and the Church of England, were deliberating and preparing reports, followed on immediately from the pre-First World War highpoint of the women's suffrage movement. The Church of Scotland and the Methodists first considered the issue during the 1920s, in the aftermath of the War, and the partial enfranchisement of women. This was a period when feminist activists were regrouping and evaluating strategies in the light of their new political power. The churches, like political parties, had to assess the collective strength and organisation of women, and adjust their structures accordingly. As the 1920s progressed, churchmen, like politicians, perhaps felt they had got the measure of women activists. The post-war wave of enthusiasm and confidence in the power of womanhood had subsided somewhat, and the concerns of women were dispersed in a wide range of social, political and employment activities. (see Chapter 5)

Smaller liberal churches had an ecclesiology and a freer relationship to the state, which made it less difficult (relatively speaking) to sanction the innovation of female ministers. It is interesting that the Congregational Union of Scotland, and the continuing United Free Church both did so just after the time when women gained full political enfranchisement in 1928. Larger denominations, especially those which had an official position as national churches, were more likely to reflect the attitudes of society at large. And by 1930, the political authorities were defensive and conservative across a spectrum of social and economic issues, although there had been some legislation which reflected the agenda of the women's movement.[131]

It was in the context of a powerful prevailing ideology of motherhood and family that the Church of Scotland, the Methodists, and the Church of England considered the ministry of women. The influence of that ideology was evident during the 1926 United Free Church debate. Although the subject remained a matter for periodical consideration after 1930, the momentum was lost until the 1960s, when the final decisions to permit female elders and ministers in the Church of Scotland were taken in the context of a progressive era which witnessed the rebirth of the women's movement.[132]

The dust had barely begun to settle on the 1929 Union when, in 1931, the Marchioness of Aberdeen and five other prominent churchwomen appeared at the bar of the General Assembly on behalf of 335 petitioners. They requested that:

> The barriers which prevent women from ordination to ministry, eldership and diaconate be removed so that the principle of spiritual equality for which the Church stands be embodied in its constitution.[133]

But that is another story!

Conclusion

At the beginning of this chapter I suggested that in the struggle to achieve a more substantial position in the official life of the church, presbyterian women and their supporters might pursue any or all of three options. In conclusion, I want to consider the extent to which each was espoused, its strategic success, and the consequences (both practical and ideological) for women and the church.

The Development, in Theory and Practice, of an Essentially Separate 'Women's Ministry'

Notwithstanding a few diehard conservatives who believed that Christian women had no role or function outside the home, this approach had achieved widespread support by 1930. Upon its premises was based the whole gamut of officially sanctioned female work and service. Although financial backing was never adequate, and the small band of paid employees had many difficulties, these realities barely impinged on the consciousness of church members (men and women alike) who accepted the rhetoric that selfless devotion should be the primary distinguishing characteristic (or at least the aspiration) of women's ministry. Traditionalists acceded to it as a useful extension of the essentially auxiliary place of women in the Divine scheme of things, and encouraged the exploitation of those qualities conventionally associated with women. In theory, a distinctive female ministry did not undermine their adherence to the literal authority of scripture or the historical practice of the Church Universal. It corresponded with their view that the roles of men and women were not interchangeable, and that ultimately it was the task of men to rule and of women to obey. Some of those who took up employment or service according to the principles of 'women's ministry' conformed admirably to these principles. Their glorious mission was conducted with more or less aptitude and success; they were inoffensive, and safe, and complained to no one. Others used their limited opportunities with enthusiasm and imagination to explore the challenges and interests of unknown territory, They discovered in themselves and in others that which the theory expressly denied: that their gifts and qualities were not confined within the boundaries of 'woman's sphere', but intruded into the erstwhile male arena of public affairs, organisation, preaching and leadership. In 1891 Elsie Inglis, the pioneer doctor, was living in Glasgow YWCA during her training. She wrote to her father:

> The amusing thing about women preaching is that they do it, but as it is not in churches, it is not supposed to be in opposition to St Paul. They are having lots of meetings downstairs; every single one of them is addressed by women. But of course they could not give the same address in a church and with men listening![134]

By the time of church union, the official response to this development was to concede that women could indeed be competent in these ways, (and in mixed company!) but not that they should have the opportunity to demonstrate their competence on equal terms with men. Instead, they were offered a combination of tokenism and the vague prospect of developments within the Order of Deaconesses. John White, the prominent inter-war churchman, consistently advocated what might be described as a subordinate parallelism whereby women would be organised within a structure which mirrored the courts and offices of the church. Thus excluded from membership of the core structure, they would have no effective power or responsibility outwith that parallel organisation (and not always much within it). Their influence − even that of those few who became members of Assembly and presbytery committees − would be as representative women, not as capable individuals in their own right. The opportunity to transcend the sectional interests of gender had no part in this scheme of things.

Archive material makes it clear that White had no difficulty, on grounds of scripture or history, with the principle of women holding church office. He would not contemplate practical equality because unity, custom, and the traditional pre-eminence of the male sex were favoured over the claims of justice. His well-worn slogans were repeated with the irritating familiarity of a scratched record. Any change in the position of women in the Church must be made:

> Without doing hurt to honoured features in its life and constitution, and without creating fresh cleavage in a Church whose wounds are so recently healed . . . Any recognition of the ministry of women must not be a part substitution of women for men . . . To admit women to the ministry and eldership would mean an equal number of men dispossessed from the ministry and eldership'.[135]

Perhaps one of White's *obiter dicta* gives the clearest insight into his attitude:

> We deprecate generally the wish of a section of that sex to compel womanhood to become a pale and inferior ditto of manhood, not helpmeet, but ineffective rival and outclassed competitor . . . The sexes were not put into the world to compete with one another, for in competition the weaker must always go to the wall, but to help one another by diversity of function.[136]

Equality of Opportunity Not Limited or Circumscribed by the Ideology of Separate Spheres

Throughout the period 1830–1930, this position was held by a minority of Scottish presbyterians, and actively pursued by less. Its origins lay partly in the individualism which was at the heart of reformed theology – the equality of each human soul before God. It also derived some force from the tradition of liberal feminism espoused by such as Mary Wollstonecraft, Harriet Taylor and John Stuart Mill – especially in asserting the ontological similarity of women and men. Those who pursued this line of argument claimed that, since there could be no distinctions drawn between moral and rational faculties according to gender, individuals ought to have the opportunity for education and occupation as befitted their gifts and potential. They sought amendments to the existing church structures which would allow people of merit and ability, regardless of gender, to occupy positions of responsibility and leadership. The perceived inadequacy of the church was not analysed in terms of its patriarchal or class structure, but as an absence of individual freedom.

However, to state the case in such simple terms does not do justice to the theoretical and practical ambiguities of the 'equal rights' movement within Scottish presbyterianism. For although the basic premise of the argument was that individual freedoms were being restricted, there was also the recognition that the denial of rights was on the ground that the person belonged to a group 'which comprehends half the human race.'[137] That implied a structural inequality which had actually been accepted and strengthened by the classical Enlightenment theorists, who either explicitly endorsed or simply adhered to the assumption that sexual inequality was natural and ought to be preserved in civil society. Such a society was the creation of consenting men, who were abstracted from the private and domestic realm. In that realm, they retained domination over, and indeed legal possession of their wives. The property basis of liberal theory was gradually eroded during the 19th century, but the idea that women were represented by the men of their family was tenacious. Married women had the least claim to the status of 'individual': the contract they entered into imposed economic dependence and legal non-personhood in return for 'protection'. As Anne Phillips has written,

> It is no accident that women were for so long excluded from those who consent; it may indeed prove intrinsic to liberal democracy that it cannot acknowledge women as citizens in the fullest sense.[138]

There are strong undertones of a theoretical inability to accept women – especially married women – as individuals with equal rights and opportunities, in the 1926 UFC debate about the incompatibility of marriage and ordained ministry for women.

There were other tensions in this uncomfortable liaison between Calvinist, liberal and feminist worldviews. Granted, the individual was equal before God, but that God required above all obedience to his will, as expressed in scripture, which, on a traditional reading, gave backing from both Old and New Testaments for the denial of certain civil and ecclesiastical rights to women. And few secular or religious proponents of equal opportunity refuted the argument (whether appealed to from Nature or Divine purpose) that women, as a group, had a special calling to the domestic sphere, which compromised their status as individuals with other rights.

Nevertheless, the pursuit of a liberal view of justice for women did make some impact on the Church – not least because the absence of justice was periodically blamed for the apathy, disenchantment and departure of women members. In 1843, it was the equal status of women as church members which was claimed as grounds for allowing them to vote in a call, against the traditional political and ecclesiastical practice of assuming that male heads of households spoke on behalf of their entourage. After that, even as the reformist Women's Movement of the Victorian era was gaining momentum, with the active involvement of churchwomen, there was no equivalent movement for internal change in presbyterian polity until the Great War years and after. Although there is some evidence of dissatisfaction among certain female activists who felt they were treated as second class members, most progressive women were absorbed in exploring the possibilities of separate development within the women's mission and service organisations which flourished from the 1880s. Personal experience of the limitations imposed by a peculiar women's ministry; involvement in the struggle for social and political equality; achievment in higher education; a growing knowledge and utilisation of critical hermeneutics in the study of scripture – all of these factors contributed to the pressure which got the issue of women's rights onto the churches' agenda from 1914 and culminated in the 1931 petition. Most of the leading female advocates were also prominent in the suffrage movement – Lady Frances Balfour, Lady Aberdeen, Eunice Murray, Frances Simson *et al*. Frances Melville and Elizabeth Hewat believed they were called to the ministry and fulfilled the academic requirements for ordination. It is possible to distinguish two strands in the 20th-century equal opportunities' movement – those who were impatient with the notion of separate gifts and spheres; and those who did not oppose the view that women were endowed with special qualities, but believed that these could and should be exercised by granting them full access to the various levels of Church courts and ministry. Frances Melville was a forthright exponent of the the former belief:

> Personally, I can never get an answer to the question – What is this inherent incapacity of women to serve the Church equally with men? My own answer is that it is prejudice, nurtured by custom, which prevents their claims from being met . . . I hold strongly that there should be no bar to women holding any office in the Church so long as they are fully qualified and have a desire to do so . . . [I simply want] that women as well as men should be given full power by the Church to employ their gifts in its service. We have seen the light. There has been of late a great advance in the body politic, and this is the last citadel remaining for women to take.[139]

Eunice Murray, who was a leading figure in the militant suffrage organisation, the Women's Freedom League, agreed that chauvinist obstruction was the main factor in denying women their rights:

> Are our ministers still under the influence of Mr John Knox, are they too conservative to march with the times, or are they too prejudiced to concede this act of justice to women? They do not care so much for advancing the cause of Christ . . . as they care to keep this one last profession for their own sex. This profession, which should have been the first, is the last to capitulate to the demand for sex equality.[140]

The other view, that women and men were innately (and importantly) different, is evident in the 1915 Report of the UFC Committee on

Recognition of the Place of Women in the Church's Life and Work:

> The argument for increased co-operation does not rest on any minimising of
> the difference between the two sexes . . . But just because the differences are
> deep and real, it must conduce to the best and most efficient work, that the
> distinctive and complementary gifts of men and women should be made
> available for understanding the difficult and complex problems of our time.[141]

Although this Report declares its awareness of, and sympathy to, the
claims of women for justice, its adherence to fundamental distinctions of
gender means that there is always a principle beyond individual human
rights to which it can appeal. In spite of its enthusiasm for wider scope for
women, the Report was unable to provide the impetus for anything very
different from the tokenism of John White. Without the rigour required to
reach a logical conclusion, the compromised justice position collapsed back
into a 'separate spheres' solution.

Even among women who publicly advocated equal rights, there was a
willingness (whether as a matter of tactics or conviction) to accept a
truncated version. In a 1932 memorandum relating to the 1931 petition
for ordination Lady Aberdeen states that she would have regarded the
petition 'granted in essential points' if women elders and a development of
deaconesses which would 'put them in the position of Assistants to ordained
ministers' had been accepted. She even declared herself 'greatly attracted
to Dr White's alternative scheme', which was a prototype (rejected by the
church) of his parallelism.[142]

From a rather different perspective, the tension between liberal
individualism and the notion of female distinctiveness was also apparent in
the position of those who believed that the characteristic attributes of
women were the very ones required to transform church and world and
usher in a Golden Age. They emphasised their superior qualities as the
means by which social and political as well as domestic and religious life
could be infused with the values and morals which they had long been
told were uniquely female. Especially in the aftermath of the Great War,
and in the light of national and international crises, men as individuals,
and more particularly their old, tired structures, were seen as practically
exhausted and morally bankrupt. The Enlightenment confidence in abstract
male rationality and conscience, they thought, had been shattered by
overwhelming evidence of tyranny, social ills and war. 'Feminine' qualities
which had been belittled and privatised – intuition, co-operation, altruism,
nurture – were proclaimed as essential for a sweeping cultural regeneration.
Those who wanted to recast the mould of society were, in their zeal,
unlikely to be satisfied with the simple incorporation of individual women

into essentially unchanged institutions of church and state. They were more likely to argue for, or at least to dream about new ways for the community of women and men in the church to live and witness in a changing world.[143] While it is possible to perceive real differences in the starting points and conclusions of those who had at least a foot on liberal ground, they were (not surprisingly) united in rejecting the absolute and literal authority of scripture. Individual interpretations differed, but two general principles are observable. First, that within the Bible, certain universal revelations and insights carry more weight, and can override, other more specific codes and injunctions. So the New Testament was favoured over the Old; Jesus' attitude to women over Paul's; Galatians 3:28 over I Corinthians 11. Second, that Christianity is foremost a religion of the spirit, not of the letter. So the church might discern signs of the Holy Spirit renewing and reforming human relationships and institutions as history proceeded towards the perfection of God's Kingdom on earth. It is interesting that these hermeneutical tools were applied so openly and enthusiastically on this issue; and that they were used both to affirm the foundational reforming character of presbyterianism, and at the same time to counter the attitudes to women of the Reformation leaders.

The one branch of presbyterianism to have introduced equality of opportunity by 1930 – the continuing United Free Church – formulated the required legislation in terms of individual rights and without any reference to gender. And Elizabeth Barr, who was the second woman to receive ordination in that Church (and became its Moderator in 1960), did not reflect on her entry into the ministry as the outcome of a feminist or structural struggle. The opportunity was made available, and as an individual she acted in obedience to God. A mould-breaker she may have been, but Barr was true to her liberal, evangelical presbyterian heritage:

> I respect the opinion of those who do not approve of women in the ministry. I have no doubt about myself. The UFC, in which I was brought up a member, opened the way in 1930 and Christ called me as surely as he called Saul of Tarsus. I was not disobedient to the heavenly vision, and for all my failings, my sins, his grace has been sufficient for me, his strength made perfect in my weakness.[144]

Challenges to Existing Paradigms of Office and Ministry, and the Development of Alternative Models

It did not occur to the great majority of Scottish presbyterians, male or female, to challenge the paradigm of domination which shaped the official life of the church. In the Victorian era those who shocked the establishment by scorning age-old caveats to be silent and submissive, either rejected organised Christianity altogether (for example the utopian socialist feminists like Mrs Hamilton and Emma Martin). Or, like Jessie Macfarlane, Isabella Armstrong and other female preachers, they left the presbyterian church for sects like the Brethren which (for a time at least) encouraged their public ministry, but which did not seriously confront the national and parochial framework of presbyterianism. Their challenge to the dominant institutions of Christianity was moral and charismatic. Their intention was not to reform existing church structures, but individual believers.

Within the three main denominations, women who began to affirm their right to participate in public lay ministry, rarely analysed or criticised the presbyterian ethos itself, to which they were bound by tradition, affection, and their sense that it contained potential for enabling a much more expansive role. They usually expressed great and undying loyalty to the church, although they were also sometimes bold enough to voice frustrations. As the organisations for women's ministry and service developed into the twentieth century there certainly developed *de facto* alternative models of ministry which were neither confined to the mythical separate spheres image, nor simply aped the already existing male structure. The personal accounts of missionaries, deaconesses, Church and Parish Sisters, evangelists and educators tell stories of creative and often liberating ministries practised by women in a variety of circumstances. But these were exercised alongside and subordinate to the authority of the male courts and ministries, which rarely demonstrated the imagination, humility or wisdom to appreciate that the way some women worked might have relevance for reforming the whole church.

However, there were women of perception and intelligence who viewed the establishment with a fresh and critical eye. They suggested that, for the church to be lively, faithful and responsive to the changing times, more was required than simply the presence of token women in unchanged structures and attitudes. And so a few voices – sceptical, passionate, visionary – disturbed the complacent consensus.

It is not surprising that some of the most penetrating challenges to the *status quo* came from women with foreign mission connections. They, after all, often had personal experience of high responsibility, more informal faith communities and the need for cultural sensitivity and adaptability. They were able to view Scottish presbyterianism with some detachment, and in comparison with Christian practice elsewhere. And they were among the first women to benefit from the rigour and excitement of higher education.

Perhaps Annie Small was the most radical in confronting ossified conventions and structures. Her biographer, Olive Wyon, notes the enduring influence of India on Small:

> She hated the spirit of dullness and stagnation. 'So-and-so has sat down' she would say with an exasperated smile.[145]

The expression originated from a journey she made on a cart pulled by a pair of bullocks. They sat down in a deep muddy river bed and

> presented the perfect image of obstinate immovability . . . I never meet anyone who has 'sat down' — mentally, morally or spiritually . . . without seeing again that pair of bullocks. What is unfulfilled promise? What are our ruts and habits, our easy phraseologies, catchwords and maxims, our conservatism and reactionariness? What but the signs that vision and hope, the joy of new adventure and the purpose to carry it through, are failing: very soon we shall, quite firmly, SIT down . . . The diehards block the way!'[146]

In the light of this attitude, it is not surprising that Small was discouraged when she returned to Scotland:

> I had, naturally enough, idealised Scotland, especially religious Scotland . . . I was disappointed and disillusioned in almost every direction. Scottish Church life seemed isolated from that of greater Christendom.[147]

She found churches cold and unwelcoming, riven by petty jealousies, with unappealing worship and an official disregard of women which bordered on contempt. In her life and work she showed a practical commitment to overcoming such failings, divisions and lack of fellowship with an integrated faith which heralded some of the insights of modern Christian feminism. In the Women's Missionary College community; in her visits and friendships across the sectarian divide in Ireland; in her love for Iona and the Celtic dimension of the Scots heritage; in her refusal to recognise a division between sacred and secular; in her scholarship, creativity and toleration, she consciously attempted to develop new models of Christian living which would be of relevance to men as well as women. She was well aware of the Reformation legacy for women, and began her contribution to a 1931 *Life and Work* symposium on the Ministry of Women with this bold assertion:

> It is a simple fact that there is no single word in the Gospels which would forbid the admission of women to the ministry of the Church. I suppose it is universally acknowledged that Paul, divided in his own mind between personal regard for women friends and traditional orientalism in matters of sex, decided

in favour of the latter, and delayed by a millennium that natural evolution for which the Gospel had prepared the way.[148]

There can be no doubting Small's commitment to equal opportunity; and yet, at the conclusion of her article, she hints at an alternative which goes beyond the limits both of subordination and of official equality:

Is the way of amendment the way of ordination to the ministry as presently constituted in the Church? Would women not tend further to conventionalise an already conventionalised system? Should we not serve Church and world better by becoming explorers, possibly discoverers, of lines of spiritual ministry which shall supplement rather than compete? . . . Yet we cannot doubt that in due time the Church must realise that true and perfect comradeship must inevitably express itself through true and perfect colleagueship.[149]

Annie Small looked beyond the struggle for formal equality of status, to the need for women to challenge the very stereotyped, hierarchical nature of institutional religion.

Elizabeth Hewat received three theological degrees from Edinburgh University (BD, PhD, DD), and on each occasion was the first woman so to do. Her academic record may have been exceptional, but she typified several churchwomen of her generation in that she simultaneously worked within the separate sphere of female organisations, campaigned for equal opportunities, and argued for new ways of working together. Like Small, she had missionary experience to refer to:

What takes place in the East cannot but have reverberations in the West. In China, women speak freely in Churches, are trained in the same Theological Halls as men, and sit in the Manchurian equivalent of the General Assembly . . . When young Churches look at the practice of the home Church in this matter, may their reaction not be one of dismayed surprise that the customs of the West are so far at variance with what they have been taught is the Spirit of Christ?[150]

Hewat, like Small, believed that her presbyterian heritage was not irredeemably tied to the old models of authority and exclusion, and warned the church of the consequences if it refused to contemplate change:

The ideal arrangement of the future would seem to lie along the lines of colleagueship, in which ordained men and women work together in one congregation – equal in status and education. The growing complexity of congregational work – not to mention the needs of those outside the church – are fast rendering one-man ministry in the city an impossibility . . . Establish the basic principle, and one can trust to the light and leading of God's Spirit . . . If there are dangers and risks in moving ahead, there may be still greater risks in standing still and doing nothing.[151]

The three options for women in the struggle for recognition and responsibility co-existed and overlapped in individual opinion and official policy, especially from the turn of the century. But it was the development of a distinctive female ministry within an essentially unchanged paradigm of male authority which prevailed in official Scottish presbyterian polity up to and after 1930. Women who believed they had a vocation had no offical channel of expression except the diaconate and women's organisations. Excluded from ordination, they were also barred from the ruling courts of the church.

By then, the church had probably lost the active involvement of a number of aware and radical women.[152] There were several factors responsible for driving Helen Crawfurd of Glasgow out of Christianity – a process which was extremely painful for her as a minister's wife and church worker. But she was disgusted by some of the Old Testament stories of cruelty to women, and resented the Pauline demand that women should remain silent in church. However, her husband simply condemned her criticisms as blasphemy, and she had little support from within her local Christian community for her developing feminist and socialist views. She found the purpose, challenge, respect and meaning which were increasingly absent in her experience of the church, in political and peace movements during and after the First World War.[153]

The loss of momentum in the Women's Movement and the conservative backlash in the church in postwar years left proponents of women's ordination, and those who hoped and dreamed of alternative Christian communities, stranded on the margins of influence, in spite of their continuing leadership of women's work. Elizabeth McKerrow, who later became National President of the Woman's Guild, described the effect which the situation had on women:

> The barrier [to ordination] stops the natural flow of women's activities into the mainstream of the Church's life and makes it a lop-sided organisation. Women within the Church are over-organised. Mere committee work takes up too much time . . . They become women-members and guildswomen instead of Church members and Church women. We are apt to view ourselves as 'the women's organisations' and not sufficiently as an integral part of the Church.[154]

Frances Melville's gloomy prognosis – that the most able young women were leaving, while those who remained 'are becoming old, mentally as well as physically; dulled, quiescent, sitting in half-empty pews'[155] was based on her wide experience of the church, and especially of women in higher education. She had lectured at Edinburgh University, been warden of

University Hall in St Andrews, and from 1909–35 was Mistress of Queen Margaret College in Glasgow. Her warning was too readily discounted or ignored by a church which had (with some honourable exceptions) demonstrated its unwillingness seriously to address the challenge of the Women's Movement, far less its ability to 'direct and inspire' it.[156] By 1930, presbyterian women remained defined and confined by their gender to official subordination in an institution which was increasingly reliant on their service, money and goodwill.

Notes

1. *United Free Church Record* (1928) 40

2. John Knox *et al*, *First Book of Discipline* (1560) see J Burleigh, *A Church History of Scotland* (1960) 163–176

3. ibid

4. ibid

5. R. Mitchison and L. Leneman, *Sexuality and Social Control, 1660–1780* (1991) 16

6. Willa Muir, *Mrs Grundy in Scotland* (1936) 49

7. ibid 113

8. see e.g P Hillis, 'Presbyterianism and Social Class in Mid-19th Century Glasgow' in *Journal of Ecclesiastical History* vol 32 (1981) 47–64

9. *United Free Church General Assembly Proceedings and Debates* (UFCGAPD) (1915) 216

10. see L Russell, 'Women and Ministry: Problem or Possibility?' in J Weidman (ed), *Christian Feminism, Visions of a New Humanity* (1986)

11. John Knox, The First Blast of the Trumpet Against the Monstrous Regiment of Women (1558) in M A Breslow(ed) *The Political Writings of John Knox* (1985)

12. A H Gray, *About People* (1934) 148

13. Mrs Meredith, *Life and Work* (1931) 146

14. The presbyterian church does not consider the minister to be an icon of Christ – in particular during the sacrament of communion – and has not utilised the Catholic argument that in this representative capacity the celebrant requires to be male. However, many personal comments addressed to or about women ministers suggest that ancient ideas of female uncleanliness and fertility contaminating 'holy places' were atavistically powerful for some presbyterians.

15. Frances Melville (1910) and Elizabeth Hewat (1926) were the first presbyterian Scotswomen to graduate in divinity before 1930. Olive Winchester from USA was first to graduate BD in Glasgow (1912). She was ordained to the ministry of the newly formed Pentecostal Church of Scotland, and returned to the States to work for the Nazarene Church. Vera Findlay was awarded a BD from Glasow in 1929, and was ordained in the Congregational Union of Scotland – the first Scottish female minister.

16. ee, for example, the debate in the United Free Church General Assembly, 1926.

17. UFCGAPD (1917) 313

18. See chapter on Lady Glenorchy in P D Thomson, *Women of the Scottish Church* (1985) 122

19. See R Small, *History of the Congregations of the United Presbyterian Church,* Vol I App V 711–716

20. ibid

21. *Free Church of Scotland General Assembly Proceedings and Debates* (FCSGAPD) (1843) 139ff

22. ibid

23. *The Present Crisis of the Free Church* (1843)

24. ibid See Appendix B

25. ibid

26. ibid

27. FCS Reports, October 1843

28. FCSGAPD (1843) 132

29. ibid 131

30. ibid 136

31. ibid 140

32. Parliamentary Papers (1847) XIII 133

33. The guidance given on rules for the election of office-bearers makes it clear that the desire and expectation was that there would be no public controversy over the name of a nominee. Candlish also placed his remarks on the particular problem of female voting in the context of general procedure: 'There is difficulty felt by many as to the way and manner in which females should be asked to signify opinion, when the question comes to a hard run and close division . . . with all the technicality of "roll called and votes marked" . . . The whole subject of determining questions in Christian assemblies by vote demands reconsideration.' (FCSGAPD, 1843, 143)

34. *Christian Journal* (1840) 17

35. Quoted in C Midgley, *Women Against Slavery: The British Campaigns 1780–1870* (1992) 160 Elizabeth Cady Stanton recalled in her *Reminiscences*, 'The clerical portion of the convention was most violent in its opposition . . . in agony lest the women should do or say something to shock the heavenly hosts . . . Deborah, Huldah, Vashti and Esther might have questioned the propriety of calling it a World's Convention, when only half of humanity was represented, but what were their opinions worth when compared with those of Revs G Harvey, C Stout or J Burnet, who, Bible in hand, argued women's subjection, divinely decreed when woman was created' *Eighty Years and More* (1898) 81

36. Lucretia Mott and her husband James travelled extensively in Scotland. Her diary notes that she was not allowed to address a meeting of the Glasgow Emancipation Society, but spoke in the Society of Friends meeting house. (See A D Hallowell, *James and Lucretia Mott*)

37. E Cady Stanton wrote, 'As the convention adjourned, the remark was heard on all sides, "it is about time some demand was made for new liberties for women". She and Lucretia Mott 'resolved to hold a convention as soon as we returned home, and form a society to advocate the rights of women'. The proposed meeting, held at Seneca Falls, inaugurated the beginning of organised feminism in the United States.

38. B Taylor, *Eve and the New Jerusalem* (1983) 129

39. ibid 128

40. See E King, 'The Scottish Women's Suffrage Movement' in *Out of Bounds: Women in Scottish Society 1800–1945* eds E Breitenbach and E Gordon 121ff. Barbara Taylor also mentions Mrs Hamilton, who 'delivered feminist harangues against the clergy from a pulpit, dressed in "official white robes"' op cit 129

41. Quoted in Taylor 150

42. ibid 152

43. ibid 152–4

44. The utopian socialist view of marriage opposed the contract whereby a woman in legal wedlock thereby renounced all rights over property, her own person, her children. She was also subject to the double standard which allowed her husband to commit adultery with impunity, but if she was adulterous, she lost all maintenance rights and was liable to be abandoned. The Owenites believed this state was a form of slavery – domestic, sexual and civil. They promoted instead free unions of love, mutual independence and respect, and argued that these were not possible until the economic and personal dependence of women was eliminated. Their solution was the development of communities which would collectivise and remove the sex-division of domestic labour and childcare. They campaigned for immediate

marriage reforms in society, and also for communal family life within their own 'utopias'. See Taylor, 32–48

45. Olive Anderson, 'Women Preachers in Mid-Victorian Britain' in *Historical Journal*, (1969) 468

46. Isabella Armstrong, *Plea for Modern Prophetesses* (1866) 62

47. ibid 39

48. Minutes of Brechin Free Church Presbytery, April 9 1867

49. *The Watchword*, (1869) 328

50. O Anderson op cit 478

51. I Armstrong, op cit 23

52. ibid 20

53. *The Watchword* (1867) 92

54. W Cunningham, *Historical Theology Vol I* (1870, 3rd edition) 162

55. see N Dickson, 'Modern Prophetesses: Woman Preachers in the 19th century Scottish Brethren', in *Scottish Church History Society Records* XXV, I (1993) 89ff, and especially 109. Many writers have made the general point about periods of openness to the public ministry of women, followed by institutional retrenchment and exclusion. See eg K Armstrong, *The End of Silence* (1993), J Field-Bibb, *Women Towards Priesthood* (1991), R Radford Reuther, 'Prophetic Tradition and the Liberation of Women' in *Feminist Theology* 5 (1994) 58–73

56. Mary Coutts, one of the interviewees in Anne Smith's collection, *Women Remember: An Oral History* (1989), recalls being converted by a female Faith Mission preacher in the North East of Scotland in the 1910s. Within the Salvation Army, Catherine Booth, co-founder and the best known female preacher of the 19th century, is a good example of public activity in spite of personal trepidation. The editor of the *United Presbyterian Magazine* (1893) wrote an article about her: 'Mrs Booth had come forward as champion of women's rights to preach the gospel, though it was only after a severe struggle with her own unwillingness and fear that she ventured, under what she felt to be divine compulsion, to open her lips in public [in 1860] . . . When once her power as a speaker asserted itself in the teeth of ingrained timidity, her labours increased a hundredfold, and the record is scarcely less than marvellous of her indefatigable energy, her well-nigh ceaseless activity' (166ff). The tone of the whole article is one of enthusiastic approval, in keeping with Dr Corbett's support for women's rights in church as well as State.

57. Rev J Gibson, *Not Weary in Well-Doing* (1888) 117

58. Anderson op cit 481

59. *A Consecutive Narrative of the Remarkable Awakening in Edinburgh* (1874), which is a contemporary account of the Moody and Sankey campaign, edited by Mrs Peddie, mentions that up to three hundred waited behind after evening meetings in Broughton Place Church, and 'that the persons who conversed with the perplexed and inquiring were ministers, elders and deacons, and qualified private members of our various churches; and also Christian matrons and Bible-women, as far as their valuable services could be secured' 18

60. Church of Scotland *Home and Foreign Mission Record* (1877) 424

61. M Levison, *Wrestling With the Church* (1992) 135

62. *The Present Crisis* . . . op. cit. App B

63. J Ludlow, *Women's Work in the Church* (1865) see 214, 301

64. See Church of Scotland Christian Life and Work Committee Reports 1870–1884

65. A H Charteris, *The Church of Christ: its Life and Work* Ch 7 & 8 (Baird lectures, delivered 1887, published 1905)

66. ibid 144

67. ibid 163

68. ibid

69. Levison, op cit 32

70. ibid 161

71. Rev A Wallace Williamson, sermon preached in St Cuthbert's Church, October 16 1892

72. *Life and Work* (1884) 33

73. See *Alice Maxwell, Deaconess*, (1917) by Mrs Horatio Macrae, for details of deaconess training

74. *Church of Scotland Year Book* (1888)

75. The Woman's Guild institutions, publications and organisation offered scope for the development of personal skills and responsibility. Some of the more prominent early deaconesses included Katherine Davidson, Ella Pirrie, Dr Mary Dodds, Mary Lamond

76. *Life and Work* (1904) 106

77. Rev D Butler DD, address to the Scottish Churches League for Woman Suffrage, March 12 1913

78. UFCGAPD (1914) 230

79. ibid

80. For example, Annie Small: 'Conditions of church service at home amazed and shocked me . . . The great proportion of work in many congregations

was being done by women, silently and unobtrusively with little acknowledgement, without even a pretence of comradeship . . . ' (*L&W* 1931 143). Eunice Murray: 'Without women the Churches would be in a sorry plight . . . They have worked in the background, unrecognised and often unhonoured and, of course, unpaid. They have freely offered their service, love and money. Now that those who feel the call are asking for recognition, is it not ungenerous and disloyal to the teaching of Christ to deny the right to women?'(Women's Freedom League pamphlet 1923)

81. E Cady Stanton, *The Woman's Bible* (1895) 71

82. *UFC Record* (1914) 151

83. Report of the Special Committee on Recognition of the Place of Women in the Church's Life and Work,UFC Reports (1915) XXVIII

84. ibid

85. ibid

86. UFCGAPD (1915) 216

87. ibid 282

88. 1915 Report, op cit Appendix I

89. ibid

90. ibid

91. ibid

92. The militant suffrage organisations in particular used quasi-religious language, symbols and methods. A note in the June 1914 *UFC Record* observes, 'The article on 'Women and the Church' (April) has drawn a number of letters remarkable for their deep feeling . . . One writer says that the Movement has become the religion of many women. Tens of thousands of pounds donated to the Women's Movement must affect the funds of the Church'. See chap 5 section 5 for more on the connections between religion and the suffrage movement.

93. Women's Missionary College House Guild Letter (1916) 22 94 The *UFC Record* (1916) included the following observation in its report of that year's Assembly:'The Moderator's gallery was crowded with ladies who, with grim tenacity, had waited throughout the day for the debate . . .When the doctor [Henderson] finished, one woman turned to me and said with a sigh, "What is it all about? he has never reached the real question at all."'

95. G M Reith, *Reminscences of the United Free Church General Assemblies* (1935) 95

96. UFCGAPD (1916) 335

97. ibid 324

98. UFCGAPD (1915) 281

99. ibid 283

100. Report of the Special Committee on Recognition of Women, UFC Reports (1916) XXVIII 7

101. ibid 6

102. UFCGAPD (1916) 324

103. ibid 325f

104. Rev R Forgan, UFCGAPD (1917) 308

105. ibid 307

106. UFCGAPD (1916) 336, (1917) 313

107. *UFC Record* (1918) 79

108. Church of Scotland, Report of the Special Commission on the War (1919) 649

109. ibid 666

110. ibid

111. *Glasgow Herald* May 20 1920

112. Church of Scotland, Church and Nation Committee Report (1920) App II 511–524

113. Church of Scotland, Church and Nation Committee Report (1921) 574–8

114. ibid

115. *Church of Scotland Layman's Handbook* (1921) 151

116. ibid

117. ibid

118. James Francis continued his forthright advocacy of equal rights for women. In 1933, he pursued this intent with a long and witty speech, prefaced by a declaration that he was 'insistent, persistent and consistent', and including a description of John White as a 'malevolent fairy'! (see Church of Scotland Acts, Proceedings and Debates (1933) 325

119. G M Reith, op cit 292

120. UFCGAPD (1926) 228

121. ibid 224–230

122. Dr J Knight, ibid 229

123. Rev R Adamson, ibid 226

124. Rev T Napier, ibid 226

125. *UFC Record* (1926) 311

126. CSAPD, October 1929

127. ibid

128. Vera Findlay MA BD had an illustrious school and university career. She attended the Scottish Congregational College 1926–28 and her preaching so impressed the deacons at Partick Congregational Church, Glasgow, that she received a call before completion of her BD. She was ordained there in November 1928, and in May 1929, the Congregational Union of Scotland carried an amendment to make 'Minister' apply equally to men and women. Findlay was subsequently admitted to the Union without opposition. The main difficulty she faced with regard to acceptance of her ministry was when she married, and in particular when she had a child. See A Escott's article about her, 'True Valour', in McCarra and Whyte, eds, *A Glasgow Collection: Essays in Honour of Joe Fisher* (1990)

129. J Barr, *The United Free Church of Scotland* (1936) 269

130. For comparative studies of the struggle for official recognition in different denominations, see J Field-Bibb, *Women Towards Priesthood: Ministerial Politics and Feminist Praxis* (1991); R B Edwards, *The Case for Women's Ministry* (1989) K Armstrong, *The End of Silence: Women and Priesthood* (1993)

131. Between 1918 and 1929, Parliament passed 21 pieces of legislation which might be construed as responding to the claims of the women's movement. These included equal terms for divorce and guardianship, and the introduction of widows' pensions. However, in other respects, women's votes failed to make an impact. The Sex Disqualification Removal Act (1919) did not stop discrimination against women, not just in churches, but in terms of equal pay, the Marriage bar, and other areas of concern. But there was a definite retreat from pro-women legislation after 1928.

132. From 1931 until 1968, there was a succession of commissions, committees and reports which dealt with the role and ministry of women in the Church of Scotland. From the 1930s, their recommendations were in favour of extending the eldership to women. In 1944, in response to the Baillie Commission, Presbyteries voted to accept this, but most unusually, the 1945 refused to adopt and make the Act a standing Law. Consultation with Kirk Sessions and Congregations led to a reversal of the proposal. In 1959 a study document on The Place of Women in the Church was published. In 1960 the Panel on Doctrine was asked to consider the whole question, but in 1962 it reported that it did not expect to take up the remit concerning women in the Ministry 'for some time'. In 1963 Mary Lusk petitioned the General Assembly to have her call tested and, if satisfied, to proceed to her ordination. To cut a long and complicated story short, in 1966 the General Assembly agreed to open the eldership to women, and in 1968, women became eligible for ordination to the ministry of Word and Sacraments on the same terms and conditions as men. Mary Lusk (Levison) tells her own story in *Wrestling with the Church* (1992).

133. CSAPD (1931) 63

134. Lady Frances Balfour, *Dr Elsie Inglis* (1918) 87

135. John White, MS notes for speeches, papers etc. See John White Papers, Box 93, 'Women in the Church'. In the extensive collection of material held in New College Library, Edinburgh, there is little evidence of any thought processes or development in White's ideas about women. The same phrases, word for word, are repeated over and over again – sometimes even on the same page, during a period of more than twenty years. Perhaps the words of James Weatherhead, (from a memorandum in support of women ministers prepared for the 1931 Committee) are apposite: 'I am not disturbed by the somewhat dilapidated maxim that equality of status does not necessarily mean identity of function. To urge it here is simply to reveal a mind ready to grasp at any straw to support a prejudice.'

136. John White papers Box 93

137. John Stuart Mill, *On the Subjection of Women* (1869)

138. A Phillips, *Engendering Democracy* (1991) 31. A growing body of research gives evidence from individual Enlightenment theorists, and for the philosophical movement in general, of a deeply embedded male disposition. Genevieve Lloyd has written: 'The maleness of the Man of reason . . . is no superficial linguistic bias. It lies deep in our philosophical tradition . . . Our trust in a Reason that knows no sex has been largely self-deceiving . . . Our ideals of Reason have historically incorporated an exclusion of the female, and that femininity itself has been partly constituted through such processes of exclusion.' *The Man of Reason* (2nd edition 1992) preface xviii. See also LMG Clark and L Lange, *The Sexism of Social and Political Theory* (1979)

139. *Life and Work,* (1931) 143

140. Eunice Murray, lecture delivered in Govan, 1923 and published by the Women's Freedom League (of which Murray was Scottish President)

141. 1915 Report on Recognition of Women op cit

142. Memorandum prepared for Committee on Place of Women in the Church, 1932. (Among John White's papers, NCL)

143. See 'Beliefs concerning citizenship' – article by an 'Edinburgh Churchwoman' in *UFC Record* (1918) 87

144. *Reformed and Presbyterian World* (1960) 185 A conversation with Miss Barr confirms that she was not self-consciously 'feminist' before or throughout her ministry, though always aware of and concerned about the importance of opening doors of opportunity.

145. quoted in Olive Wyon, *The Three Windows* (1953) 37

146. ibid

147. ibid

148. *Life and Work* (1931) 143

149. ibid 144

150. E Hewat, ibid 139

151. ibid

152. Zoe Fairfield, who worked for the Student Christian Movement (which was influential in the lives of many progressive Christian women), recognised this in her 1913 book, *The Woman's Movement*. She wrote: 'There has been so little sympathy between leaders of the Church and Women's Movement leaders, that very few have realised their common purposes. Many of us whose lives, for what they are worth, are given to distinctively Christian work, have until lately often turned to those outside organised Christianity for sympathy and understanding about women's questions. Many women have been conscious of an attitude of disapproval, and of prejudice in many quarters, and have found very little serious attempt to understand what they believed and desired. So many women go to Church, that the absence of others is not much noticed, but it is doubtful whether the absence of men is much more general than that of more thoughtful and stronger women.'

153. See Helen Crawfurd's unpublished autobiography (nd)

154. Elizabeth McKerrow, *Perfect Love Casteth Out Fear*, Pamphlet 5 of series published by The Fellowship of Equal Service in the Church. This organisation was formed after the 1929 Union, bringing together supporters of women's rights from both wings of the reunited church

155. *Life and Work* (1931) 145

156. *UFC Record* (1918) 87

5

Women Campaigning for Change

Introduction

In 1851, the liberal feminist Harriet Taylor observed, in an article entitled 'The Enfranchisement of Women', that:

> To be accused of rebelling against anything which admits of being called an ordinance of society, [women] are taught to regard as an imputation of serious offence against the proprieties of their sex.[1]

It is one of the ironies of 19th-century history that so many Victorian women, who were educated, socialised, and otherwise pressured to avoid assertion, independent thought and public activity at all costs, embarked with vigour throughout the century upon a range of campaigns directed at change in society and in their own lives. By 1930, women had expressed their moral agency by playing a central part in the transformation of social and political life, including their own roles and positions. The domestic ideology which cast them as guardians of religious values and the *status quo* was in fact utilised by them to justify and extol female challenges to political, social, legal and economic practices and institutions. Throughout the period 1830–1930, Scottish women expressed concern about, and sought reform of many aspects of their society. There was female involvement in anti-slavery action, anti-Corn Law agitation, the Chartist movement, temperance, the Social Purity campaign (against the Contagious Diseases Acts); and campaigns for women's rights to property, divorce, higher education, fair working pay and conditions, and enfranchisement. The diversity (and incompleteness) of this list is matched by the diversity of class, circumstance and motivation of the women who were involved in these movements. The basis and extent of activity, the goals and strategies adopted, also varied considerably. But there were certain key elements which Scottish women seeking reform shared. First, they all desired change of some kind, and were prepared to give public expression to that desire. Second, their views led them (however tentatively, and sometimes militantly) to collaborate with others in some form of organised action. Third, they conducted their campaigns in the theological and cultural context of Scottish presbyterianism and British imperialism. Fourth, their gender was always a basic factor in their own and other people's perceptions of what constituted acceptable and appropriate behaviour. The influence of religion, in conjunction with conventional views of 'womanhood', served to confirm a traditional assessment of 'woman's sphere' for many evangelical females who accepted that their moral task was to be undertaken simply as auxiliaries to activist men. Others felt challenged to define and declare a distinctive sense of self in opposition to, or as a significant modification of, that stereotype. Fifth, the zeal for reform, the pursuit of justice and the collaboration required to engage in action for change, offered potential for the development of feminist perspectives and associations. As Philippa Levine cautions in her book, *Victorian Feminism*, 1850–1900:

> The definition of feminism in the historical context is, of course, fraught with difficulties. We must be wary of determining it by our contemporary evaluations and thus deny its particular context . . . None the less, women's positive identification with one another in the context of political struggle suggests that the use of the term feminism is not anachronistic.[2]

Certainly the word was in currency by the closing decade of the 19th century, and while its meaning was subject to diverse interpretations and experiences, it conveyed then, as now, at least the idea of a collective commitment to change and improvement in the situation of women. Theresa Billington-Greig, who was one of the key figures in the Scottish and British suffrage movement, gave her definition of the feminist project in 1911:

> I seek [woman's] emancipation from all shackles of law and custom, from all chains of sentiment and superstition, from all outer imposed disabilities and cherished inner bondages which unite to shut off liberty from the human soul borne in her body'.[3]

That goal of emancipation (however defined) was not always discerned and was sometimes rejected by women seeking change, but its gradual acceptance and pursuit led to the growth of a phenomenon which was highly successful in its own terms, but also limited, partial, and containing the seeds of its own demise. It may be described as the reformist Women's Movement, which began around 1860 and had fragmented by 1920. While in the past twenty years, a considerable body of research has been undertaken about this Movement as it developed in America and England, its connected yet distinctive history in Scotland has only very recently begun to receive serious attention;[4] (and indeed some historians make the unforgivable error of writing as if anything which happened in Scotland may be subsumed under England; or as if 'Britain' equates with England!) Richard Evans, in his important study *The Feminists*, claims that one of the most striking contrasts in the Western world of the 19th century was that between countries with a Roman Catholic and those with a Protestant culture:'the one a major obstacle to feminism, the other an almost essential precondition of its emergence'.[5] In this chapter it is not my intention to consider fully the development and activities of the reformist Women's Movement in Scotland, or alternative forms of female struggle. Instead, I shall examine several campaigns conducted at different stages throughout the period 1830–1930 by focusing particularly on the ways in which Scottish people, policies and practices were influenced by the presbyterian church and culture – and vice versa. What was the extent and depth of female rebellion against the ordinances of society, and its consequences – both radical and conservative? I shall consider Evans' claim in the context of this Protestant country, where the vision and language of feminists was infused with religious imagery, and a supporter of female suffrage could declare:

> We are to make this world a city of God, and women, who are near God, ought to have the direct means of incarnating their ideal on the politics of their time.[6]

The conjunction of liberal and evangelical influences in the social and economic climate of Victorian and Edwardian Scotland served to extend the positions and opportunities available to bourgeois women, while largely confirming the limitations and oppressions of working-class women. For increasing numbers of upper- and middle-class women, the tensions between the ideal of feminine perfection, and the too frequent reality of tedious and apparently purposeless existence were worked out in a process of personal change from stoical quiescence to their male-defined role, through assertion of individual selfhood, to action for change in many aspects of life. So, for example, Frances Stoddard, born in 1843, wrote in 1867:

> My own view is – that if you have a strong mind and force of character it is a misfortune to be a woman, and no voting papers, or removal of disabilities will compensate for the mistake.[7]

But later in the same year, under the influence of her American feminist aunt, she reflected,

> Here, [Boston] as at home, I find a woman is better not to have too decided views on any matter, literary, historical, social, reform or politics, if she wishes

to be a man's favourite . . . Well, Mamma dear, I would rather have the brains than live on empty compliments the plaything of any man.[8]

And in 1917, looking back on her era, she wrote to Eunice Murray, her suffragette daughter:

> I have been reading a clever article laughing at the Victorian age. Though clever it is very false. I have lived through that age, and in spite of convention and narrow evangelism and puritanical morality, Britain developed in that time in a truly marvellous way . . . In my young days the aim of a mother was to make her daughter pretty and attractive and sufficiently accomplished to let her marry well. Few other careers presented themselves to women. The Victorian Era burst through this bondage, and now we have schools and colleges for girls and women, and everywhere women are distinguishing themselves.[9]

But most proletarian women were unlikely to have regarded the era as one of great liberation. The opportunities presented by higher education and the vote (on the conditions granted in 1918) were, by and large, not for them; changes in property and divorce legislation were rendered largely meaningless by their poverty, and equality of pay and employment opportunity in the industrial world were never seriously countenanced. While bourgeois reformers systematically and deliberately appealed to the notion of separate spheres to extend the 'purifying and elevating' influence of women into the world, the same ideology was utilised consistently – by reforming women and male trade unionists as well as men of the ruling classes – to ascribe to working women only one legitimate and honourable situation: as wife, mother and thrifty homemaker. As Eleanor Gordon rightly argues:

> The evidence suggests that women's experience of waged labour was mediated by these ideologies and not determined by them . . . the recognition that it could not always be achieved meant that separate spheres were interpreted to include work for women, provided it did not encroach on men's province or usurp men's prior rights to work, and was compatible with women's culturally prescribed role.[10]

It is important not to assume that working women were passive and apathetic in accepting the limitations and hardships of their circumstances – many experienced pleasure and freedom in pursuing justice and self-determination (and also in the faith and practice of their religion). But their personal and political struggles for meaning, independence and fulfilment were largely contested in different, and sometimes opposing ways to those of their well-meaning social 'superiors'. The Scottish Women's Movement was more inspired by the individualism than by the potential egalitarianism of its religious heritage. It utilised both the 'natural rights' arguments of liberalism, and also a 'social reform' ethos which had strong theoretical and experiential links with the evangelical 'women's mission'. These roots did not readily facilitate analysis of class or patriarchal structures as causes of female oppression. Within the socialist movement, many women accepted the argument that the class struggle had to be won before women could be emancipated, and did not campaign for female suffrage. There were some activists within the reform movement who were inspired by a combination of Christianity, socialism and feminism.[11] But in spite of their efforts, they remained a marginalised minority within all three communities: the church, the Labour Movement and the Women's Movement. The romantic idea of female solidarity could on occasion inspire a truly united endeavour to improve the personal and corporate lives of women. Too often it meant in reality that one class of women (with the best intentions) saw fit to speak and prescribe for women of a different class. While we should certainly honour the courage, energy, intelligence and positive female sense of identity of those who constituted that Movement (which was not as thoroughly bourgeois as some have asserted), there were contradictions and limitations in their means and ends. As in the presbyterian church, so in wider society, the social and political Establishment made some concessions to the demands of women. But by 1930 its patriarchal structures were adapted, adjusted, but fundamentally preserved.

'We Have a Great Battle to Fight' – Scottish Women in the Anti-Slavery Movement

The movement for the abolition of the slave trade and the institution of slavery was one of the great moral crusades of the early 19th century. For many converts to evangelicalism in the English-speaking world, it was the fundamental proving ground in their battle against human sin and for Christian righteousness. It also played a pivotal role in the development of the movement for women's rights – especially in the United States, where a small number of female activists perceived and argued the connections between the need for emancipation of black slaves and of themselves. For women like the Grimké sisters, Lucretia Mott and Abbey Kelly, this awareness inspired public words and actions which went well beyond the acceptable boundaries of female behaviour, and invoked much wrath and condemnation, especially from clerical upholders of religious and social propriety. As mentioned in the previous chapter, the experience of American women in the anti-slavery movement and the bonds of friendship formed, directly resulted in the 1848 Seneca Falls Convention which marked the start of organised feminism in the United States.

The involvement of women in the Scottish movement for abolition at a time of social upheaval and religious passion, provides a fascinating source for studying the interplay of gender roles, organisation and Christian ideologies in a movement for change. Although the Scottish women shared much with their American sisters – religious conviction, social class, urban location, personal contact and friendship – their experiences and actions were also distinctive in crucial ways. As in America, abolition was one of a series of interrelated concerns which were referred to as the 'benevolent empire'. Evangelicals on both sides of the Atlantic constructed an edifice of organisations into which converts could throw their energy and money as an expression of gratitude for the gift of grace, and a commitment to do battle for good against evil. In America, the religious anxiety created by the political and economic institution of slavery was acute and focused. In Scotland, after legislation prohibiting British involvment in the slave trade, the issue was rather more abstract. Nevertheless, as C Duncan Rice argues, the upheavals of the Industrial Revolution, and its greatly unsettling impact upon the Scottish middle class, provided the local context for engagement with this most fundamental manifestation of social evil which members of the benevolent empire perceived all around them:

> Anti-slavery was an important symbolic response to both the spiritual and social shortcomings of early industrial Scotland. Middle-class philanthropy was a response to signs that society had become irreligious and atomised. In Scotland, the home and foreign benevolent empires expressed the same concerns and were supported by the same men and women.[12]

It was in this milieu that female societies were formed to support the 'sacred cause' of abolition. Their function was to engage in action within women's own 'sphere of influence' – fundraising, distributing literature, and 'imbueing the rising race with an abhorrence of slavery',[13] these being tasks which they could perform 'without violating that retiring delicacy which constitutes one of [women's] loveliest ornaments'.[14]

The Glasgow and Edinburgh Emancipation Societies were founded in 1833. They were both dominated by members of dissenting presbyterian denominations and other voluntary churches. In Edinburgh, the Smeals and Wighams – Quaker families with English roots – were leading lights. Most abolitionists were actively opposed to religious Establishment, but also theologically and socially conservative. Female supporters, from the same background and families, joined the Edinburgh Ladies Emancipation

Society and the Glasgow Ladies Auxiliary Society, and both cities were important anti-slavery centres in the 1830s and 1840s.

The splits which had emerged in the American anti-slavery movement precipitated a major division in Britain after the 1840 London World's Anti-Slavery Convention, when the question of women's rights polarised the delegates. William Lloyd Garrison refused to take his seat as a gesture of solidarity with the women who were denied the right to do so:

> After battling for so many long years for the liberties of African slaves, I can take no part in a convention that strikes down the most sacred rights of all women.[15]

After the event, some the female delegates embarked on a tour of the country to rouse and consolidate support. Lucretia Mott, a Quaker from Philadelphia, commented on the status of female anti-slavery campaigners in Britain:

> [Women] had hitherto most submissively gone forth into all the streets, lanes, highways and byepaths to get signers to petitions, and had been lauded long and loud for this drudgery, but had not been permitted even to sit with their brethren, nor indeed much by themselves in public meetings – having transacted their business, as we were informed, by committees . . . In vain we endeavoured to have a public meeting called for women – although a few did all they could to promote it.[16]

But in spite of the apparent deference of women, there were some, especially in Scotland, who were not afraid to act independently as the British movement divided in the wake of the Convention, and the pro- and anti-radical tours. Mott wrote in her letter to Maria Weston Chapman of Boston, 'Wm Lloyd Garrison will tell you what glorious meetings they had in Scotland'.[17] But in 1841, following the visit of the Garrisonian John Collins, the male Edinburgh Emancipation Society remained loyal to the conservative British and Foreign Anti-Slavery Society, while the Ladies (who were led by Jane Smeal Wigham and her step-daughter Eliza – the wife and daughter of the EES leader John Wigham) – declared their support for Garrison. The ELES subsequently became one of the main sources of British support for American radicals. In Glasgow, however, the Ladies Society took the opposite position:

> They argued that to seat the female delegates would have been in opposition to divine teaching, and would have obscured women's feminine character, 'a quality . . . as natural to half the human race, as masculinity is to the other.[18]

Apparently, the Ladies Auxiliary thereafter lapsed, and John Collins converted the radical remnant into the Glasgow Female Anti-Slavery

Society, which issued an *Appeal to the Ladies of Britain*, urging support for the Garrisonian American Anti-Slavery Society. Just how much of a remnant it was is suggested by the Dublin activist RD Webb, who commented in a cynical letter to Maria Weston Chapman decrying the lack of Anti-Slavery Support in Britain, that:

> C L Remond told me that when he was in Glasgow he could find no trace of the Ladies Society formed by J Collins, nor of Mary Welsh, who signed the address.[19]

But Welsh certainly did exist, and her small group in Glasgow, with their Edinburgh counterparts, continued to provide crucial moral and financial support to the radicals – particularly by sending boxes of goods to sell at Maria Weston Chapman's Boston Bazaar, which was a major fund-raising and public relations exercise. By maintaining their forthright support of a group whose views were well known through their publications and pamphlets (especially Garrison's paper, *The Liberator*), these Scottish women were clearly associating themselves with the feminism which had precipitated schism in the movement, and which was central to the radical position. However, in their own lives and actions they were not inclined to adopt the public strategies of their American sisters. Nor did they address the women's rights' question in the context of their anti-slavery campaigning. In 1845, on a visit to Scotland, the American radical Henry C Wright, commented about the Glasgow group's annual public meeting:

> Though it is a female society, they cannot act as president . . . read reports or make remarks . . . Men must do all.[20]

As dissenting and non-conformist Protestants, they were much more concerned, throughout the 1840s, to challenge Scottish presbyterian accommodation with slavery. The Established Church had never been a fertile source of support for the movement, but in a decade of passionate religious controversy, the two newly formed evangelical presbyterian denominations – the Free Church (1843) and the United Presbyterian Church (1847) – were both castigated by the radicals. Since members of these churches had previously vaunted their anti-slavery credentials, the disagreements of the 1840s seriously weakened the Scottish movement, including the women's groups.

In the Free Church, the dispute concerned money which had been donated to the new denomination by the Southern Presbyterian Church of America, which included slaveholders among its membership. A 'Send back the Money' campaign was launched. In April 1844, Mary Welsh wrote of a spirited meeting held in Glasgow:

The friendly and faithful resolution, relating to the Free Church in this country taking money from slaveholders in America was good, if they could have been induced to send back the money with friendly remonstrance to the American church' . . . The [male] Emancipation Society of Edinburgh exists only in name . . . they were quite afraid to offend the Free Church, and by some stratagem or other they slipp'd the business into the hands of the Town Council.[21]

By December 1845, Welsh herself was in Edinburgh, and the ELES was acting where their male relations had failed to do so. She sent a letter to Maria Weston Chapman accompanying the Bazaar box:

Our influence here is steadily expanding and it is to us a source of unspeakable pleasure thus to aid the cause of the oppressed . . . Henry C. Wright was here last week and we expect him again tomorrow, he is giving the Free Church no rest [but] their leading men have gained so much influence over the people that they may do anything they choose, be it good or bad the people will bear it. I am sick of this world's religion.[22]

Wright was one of a series of Americans, including Lloyd Garrison and freed slave Frederick Douglass, who came to Scotland to attack the Free Church. The crusade reached its height prior to the 1846 General Assembly, which the ELES petitioned as part of its orchestrated campaign of anti-Free Church propaganda. Welsh wrote to Chapman on May 17 1846:

We have had a set of glorious meetings here against the FC and are to have more this week. GT, FD, JB and HCW have done wonders in opening the eyes of the public to the enormous iniquity, never was there such excitement created as at present, and there is no doubt but that great good will be the result.[23]

But the Assembly would not allow discussion of any external petitions, and antipathy between the ministers and the radicals increased. In fact, the presence of Wright did nothing to aid the women's cause. He was a notorious Christian anarchist and polemicist, and his attacks against religious orthodoxy ran directly counter to the prevailing climate in presbyterian Scotland. Catherine Paton of Glasgow expressed the growing isolation and frustration of the radical anti-slavery activists, in November 1846:

The clergy with their supporters who left the Society are still as alien as ever and thus we have continually to combat with their opposition . . . Of all observances in Scotland [the Sabbath] is most reverenced and national prejudice strongest, it was a bold step by HCW to attack it . . . We are a very bigoted people in our religious opinions . . . to be members in a church and assent to an orthodox creed is with many all that is necessary to Christian character.[24]

From this time, the anti-slavery movement was increasingly polarised and deflected by the association of the principle of immediate abolition with the dangerously unorthodox views expressed by Garrison and his supporters. The women – mainly of Quaker background (including Priscilla Bright MacLaren, wife of the dissenting Lord Provost of Edinburgh, and Elizabeth Pease Nichol from Darlington, who married a Glasgow professor in 1846) – who remained loyal to the radical American organisation increasingly perceived their action as a fight against rising Scottish clericalism:

> We have a great battle to fight here now, and we are fully determined to gird on our armour, and never yield one inch to the enemy these Clergy, they are our greatest enemies . . . however we don't fear them a bit. Our hearts have been refreshed and gladdened by that noble man WLG.[25]

Meanwhile, there was growing unease among other women – many of them related to dissenting presbyterian clergy – who were happy to ally themselves to the radical position on immediate abolition, but who were decidedly queasy about being associated with the views increasingly expressed in the *Liberator* and elsewhere. Matters came to a head in 1850, when a number of women withdrew from the Glasgow society, issued a pamphlet, and declared their intent to establish a new society. The document made clear their priorities:

> Of late we have been surprised and grieved, by the discovery that many zealous labourers in the country have – by resolution adopted, and speeches and letters published – been making powerful efforts to propagate infidel notions . . . We will yield to none in the strength of our religious desires to see the slave emancipated, and elevated to the highest privileges cherished by the whole population; but we will not consent to sacrifice any part of written Revelation for this or any other benevolent object – we will not abandon Divinely-instituted ordinances – nor while resolved to have no connection with Slave-holding churches, will we allow ourselves to be mixed up with infidel attacks on the Christian church.
>
> . . . Our contributions have hitherto gone to support of the society connected with the National anti-slavery bazaar, at Boston; and Christian friends have long regarded our connection with them, as an indication rather of ill-judged generosity, than of Christian discernment . . . and thus the anti-slavery Cause has become exceedingly weak in this country . . . We feel ourselves justified in terminating co-operation with the Boston Society . . . But we would not cease from well-doing in this field of benevolence; and we earnestly solicit the attention of our friends to the objects of 'The Vigilance Committee of New York'.[26]

RD Webb in Dublin criticised the Glasgow women, and urged them to think again:

'Pardon me if I say that it seems to me a virtual abandonment of the Anti Slavery cause, and diversion of your efforts into a channel which has nothing whatever to do with the abolition of slavery.[27]

But there was no going back, and the New Association remained active throughout the 1850s. In 1853 it donated £400 to the non-radical Vigilance Committee (out of its total income of £711.10.6), which was was five times greater than the income of its Garrisonian predecessor. Freed from the unorthodox taint of their old allies, the women apparently felt able to throw themselves into 'respectable' work in keeping with their presbyterian beliefs and social status.

In Edinburgh, the ELES, much to the chagrin of the Wighams, also resolved to withdraw its support for the Boston Bazaar at a meeting on August 1, 1850. However, even the loyal remnant were unhappy with the American position. Eliza Wigham wrote:

We are much grieved that you should have brought forward arguments and sentiments in your advocacy of questions which we deem unnecessary, inexpedient and dangerous – we think they weaken our hands, for where did our enterprise ever stand so firmly as when faithful WLG placed it in 'the Bible and the Bible alone'?[28]

In both Glasgow and Edinburgh, most of the anti-slavery campaigners belonged to the United Presbyterian Church, which in 1847 had brought together various strands of voluntary presbyterianism. A new controversy arose in 1854 when it became known that the UP Mission in Old Calabar, West Africa, was accepting local slaveholders into communion – a move against which the 1855 UP Synod was not prepared to act. The New Glasgow Associations – both male and female – were in the hands of UP members who had considerable financial and emotional investment in Old Calabar, and in spite of their involvement in the 1840s 'Send Back the Money' Campaign, they were unwilling to challenge their own church on this matter. In Edinburgh, a new male society had been formed in 1854, with Duncan MacLaren as president, and including both Free Church and UP clergy on the committee. In 1856, the old ELES was left completely isolated when an Edinburgh New Ladies Anti-Slavery Association was formed, by female presbyterians, as an avowedly 'Christian' society. Mrs Agnes Renton became President of the new group, and her son had no doubt as to the reason for the split:

To no cause had she throughout life been more staunch and ardent in her attachment than that of the Abolition of Slavery; but when an influential organ lent its columns for the diffusion of infidel sentiments, she objected to the Ladies Society, with which she was connected, continuing to lend it their support.[29]

Her biography includes a letter she wrote to her daughter on March 7, 1856:

I met Mrs M'Crie, one of the ladies who first formed the Anti-Slavery society! I told her that our meeting was to be next day . . . It was a full meeting, and the different views were spoken to on both sides. Mrs McL was there and made a very pretty speech. But when the votes were taken there were only Mrs P, Miss S and myself in the minority; so we all rose and left the room. Mrs McC and her sister left with us, five in all. I am thankful I was able to withstand so much fine speaking. But it was all to gloss over the ___ party. I am glad that Miss G was not in Edinburgh, for they seem to think that she was at the bottom of all this, which she is not. I love the committee that I have left, but I mourn over their blindness in crying 'Peace, peace', where there can be no peace with the enemies of our Lord Jesus Christ.[30]

'Miss G' probably refers to Julia Griffiths, who worked as the agent of Frederick Douglass – a moderate campaigner. She founded a bazaar in Rochester, New York, to raise funds without the taint of Garrisonian infidelity. During 1855–56, she visited Britain and set up at least fourteen women's groups to support Rochester. Notwithstanding Agnes Renton's disclaimer, it was the new bazaar which the evangelical presbyterians of Edinburgh supported from 1856. Meanwhile, Eliza Wigham was clearly aggrieved at their desertion, and the imputation on the Christian character of the remnant:

They are forming a Christian anti-slavery Society in Edinburgh, and leaving on the left-hand our poor _____ society which in truth has been innocent enough.[31]

C Duncan Rice's assessment of the new Association is that it was

built principally upon the suspicion of radical infidelity. It was also helped by the anxiety of the UPC to maintain clear anti-slavery credentials without the taint of extraeneous issues. The rest were members of the Free Church of Scotland who were trying to recover anti-slavery face after the events of ten years before: women who were 'glad to show their anti-slavery in opposition to a troublesome association like ours.'[32]

By this time, the radical abolitionist position had been well and truly superseded by societies and activities which were more acceptable to the mid-century mood in Scotland. The sentimentalism of Harriet Beecher

Stowe; the sympathy offered to individual freed slaves; the new outlets for expressing general abhorrence of slavery, without having to engage in difficult and rigorous critique of the contemporary social, political and religious *status quo*[33] – these responses were in keeping with the more settled, established, bourgeois character of evangelical presbyterianism. The upheavals of the 1830s and 1840s were in the past, and for the time being, the window of opportunity for feminism, which had opened to let in a chink of light, was closed.

However, although women in Scotland may not have passed directly from anti-slavery involvement into campaigning for women's rights, circumstantial evidence suggests that the movement was very important as a training ground for forming and testing independent thought and action among Scottish women. For a small number of non-presbyterian women, the significance of autonomous action was clear: their decision to support the Garrisonians set them in opposition to male members of their own families, and to the clerical establishment of the day. Their reluctance to express that autonomy in, for example, public speaking or campaigning specifically for women's rights is perhaps understandable. Like their American counterparts, they belonged to small Christian sects in which the attitude to the role and rights of women was relatively more enlightened than that of mainstream denominations – perhaps they had less personal reason than others to perceive their own oppression. Unlike the American women, their sense of distinctiveness was compounded by being a tiny minority in a country where social, political and religious life was infused with the power of the presbyterian establishment. If they had combined their radical attacks on the clergy with 'unwomanly' behaviour like that of the Grimkés, Mott and Cady Stanton, their ostracisation from female colleagues and society at large would have been complete. The effectiveness of their anti-slavery campaigns – already tainted by association with the American radicals – would have been totally negated.

For the presbyterian women, anti-slavery activity might be explained as a largely conservative phenomenon. It was certainly justified and encouraged as part of the womanly task to effect moral transformation in the world, and neither style nor tactics presented any major challenge to the developing ideology of separate spheres. But abolitionism at least exposed women to a theory of justice which was understood in terms of equal value and human rights. And the transatlantic nature of the movement, the events of 1840 and their consequences, meant that there must have been an awareness among women of the feminist ideas which were being expounded. Their priority was commitment to religious orthodoxy, which precluded any serious consideration of these ideas on their own merits, and the institutions and journals of Scottish presbyterianism were active protagonists of an anti-feminist domestic ideology. But at least that ideology was not completely uncontested. And while Catherine Paton of Glasgow castigated faint-hearted clergy, whose vocation gave them great scope for 'leading captive silly women'[34] perhaps we might at least give some women credit for the courage, if not always the content, of their religious convictions.

The anti-slavery movement, in spite of the difficulties and divisions it encountered in Scotland, did give women a sense of purpose and achievement, and some indication of the mechanics and power of sustained pressure-group tactics. The value of these, and surely also the assimilation of notions of women's rights, became apparent by the 1860s, when many anti-slavery women – including Eliza Wigham, Elizabeth Pease Nichol, and the extended MacLaren clan – got involved in a new wave of campaigns. Barbara Taylor argues that middle-class feminist reformism became possible when the decline of working-class Chartism and utopian socialism erased the relationship between feminism and radicalism.[35] For female evangelical Protestants, the demise of Garrisonian abolitionism was surely also a factor in helping to eradicate the damaging assumption of connection between women's rights and religious infidelity, thus allowing women to voice new demands for their gender without total loss of respectability.

'A Great Woman's Question': The Temperance Movement

In 1829, very permissive legislation and the low duty on alcohol enabled Scots to get through an astonishing 5,777,000 gallons of spirit in one year. That marked the high point of consumption in a country which had become increasingly noted for the manner in which drink was central to the social and cultural life of all classes. It also precipitated the first public expression of concern, and determination to do something about the abuse of alcohol. Throughout the previous century the connection between drinking, conviviality and hospitality was never seriously challenged. The Scottish church was part of that consensus – church office-bearers and ministers were themselves often noteworthy drinkers, and rarely used their authority to confront others for whom drink may have become a problem.

But in 1829 John Dunlop, a Greenock lawyer, was instrumental in establishing societies which initiated the first general temperance movement in Britain. From the outset, Dunlop was supported by William Collins, an influential evangelical Glasgow publisher. In 1834, Collins expressed the radical nature of the task which temperance campaigners had set for themselves:

> So much has spirit drinking become associated with the customs and practices in Scotland, that there is scarcely an event in life, scarcely a circumstance that occurs, not a transaction can be effected, with which spirit drinking in not associated . . . It struck its fibrous roots into everything so deeply, that to tear up the spirit-drinking practices is like tearing up the whole social system of society.[36]

This call to embark on a social revolution went even further as the 19th century progressed. The crusade, which began by campaigning for moderation and against consumption of spirits, quickly sought total abstinence, and then prohibition. However, the Temperance Movement was not one unitary campaign, but a plethora of groups, committees, agencies and organisations which pursued a range of goals using many tactics and methods. By the turn of the century it was a genuine mass movement which directly and indirectly affected the lives of millions of Scots – men, women and children. Those who dismiss the movement as a curious or archaic attempt at pious social control seriously underestimate its power and complexity as a factor impinging in different and sometimes contradictory ways on the economic, political, religious, social and personal development of the country over a one hundred year period. From 1830, alcohol consumption declined in almost every decade until 1930. From 1900–1930, the reduction was remarkable: by 1930, the amount drunk was only 25 per cent of that consumed in 1900.[37]

Legislation played an important part in this, but so too did a widespread change in attitudes, and in the social fabric of the country. Churches and women were significant players in the character, growth and decline of temperance activity. The churches were at first equivocal about the importance of the issue, and suspicious of what they saw as the lay, radical and proletarian impetus of the new movement. However, by mid–century, evangelicalism began to change the personal habits of church folk, swinging the institutional clout of the dissenting denominations in particular into action for the cause. And during the years when the 'Social Question' greatly exercised the church, temperance activity, (much of it conducted by women) was perhaps the main bridge between organised religion and the 'unchurched masses'. None of the attempts to make contact with, evangelise, or provide entertainment for the poor failed to include some reference to the evils of drink.

The movement was of particular importance to women. They were early identified as among the sorriest victims of male alcohol abuse, and therefore those who had most to gain from abstinence. They were invited and exhorted to play their part in bringing about reform by using their personal influence in the family home, and, if part of the ruling classes, to set an example to their social 'inferiors'. By the latter half of the 19th century, temperance, in spite of the major social implications of its goal, was seen as a most appropriate and seemly cause for Christian women – a noble opportunity for them to use the much vaunted female powers of moral suasion to improve the tone of Scottish society.

The campaign against drink was on the one hand an essentially conservative assertion of the reality and importance of separate male and female spheres. It emphasised the importance of domestic competence, and reserved special condemnation for women who failed in that sphere, as well as those who were degraded enough to display themselves in the public world as drinkers or barmaids. But it also offered women (and children too) a range of opportunities to expand and enrich their experience beyond the home, and to assert a measure of pride, control and self-determination.

Is it reasonable to suggest that temperance truly became a mass movement? Callum Brown argues that in fact the growth of political initiatives to control alcohol consumption, after 1880, reflected the inadequacies of the moral campaign, and its rejection by the working class.[38] However, from that time, and especially into the 20th century, temperance activity (whether in campaigning organisations, friendly societies, the provision of 'counter-attractions' and important and enjoyable social networks) was central to the lives of huge numbers of women and children. For them, surely the experience was indeed of belonging to a mass movement: though one which was engineered much more effectively by dedicated voluntary and para-church organisations, than by the traditional church institutions. In assessing its significance for Scottish women, the key question is not whether the movement was effective in transforming national drinking habits, or forcing through prohibition, or even how many of them stuck to the pledge, lightly or solemnly made. The question is about how involvement in temperance activity affected the personal and collective lives of participants. This movement throws into sharper focus than other campaigns for change, the complex nuances and contradictions of the domestic ideology in times of change.

It is easy to see the attraction of temperance to the earnest evangelical Christians of 19th-century Scotland. They saw all about them devastation, cruelty, squalor and crime. Vast consumption of alcohol by the new proletariat seemed to be connected with all the evils of industrial society, while the social life of other classes (including clergy) was habitually lubricated with drink. And so they posed this question:

> How can we combat this evil? How are we to meet this giant stalking through our fair land, wasting homes, wrecking lives, making the garden a desert, the smiling land a desolation?[39]

The solution to this apparently apocalyptic national disaster was to convert individuals, transforming them from violent, criminal, frightening and uncontrolled drunkards, into sober, respectable, hard-working and upright people. For evangelicals, only the power of the gospel was sufficient to overcome a condition which was associated with feeble mindedness, weakness of will and, of course, personal sin. All the crises and wickedness of society were explained by the alarming national propensity to succumb to the temptation of intoxicating liquour, which, even if indulged occasionally, was 'quite alien to the perfect sobriety and command of mind and action, which God's children are bound to maintain'.[40] The evolving notions of fitting behaviour for men and women were an integral part of the reform of national character which was sought. Men who drank were not fit to assume their patriarchal duties as breadwinner and protector of house and family. In yielding to temptation, they betrayed their divine calling to responsible and self-reliant headship over their women and children. Instead, they drank away their money and treated their wives with violence and neglect. Temperance reformers regularly highlighted this male degradation of character and dereliction of duty. Rev W Reid of the Scottish Temperance League, in his 1860 pamphlet, *Woman's Work for Woman's Weal*, recorded this first-hand account among many others:

> I have seen me on hearing his foot on the stair put my infant on a pillow underneath the bed, and go in there to suckle it. Do you see these marks on the door? These are the marks of the poker when he was attempting to break the door to get out for whisky, and when I stood between him and the door, and told him he would only get out over my murdered body. I felt a razor at my throat, and lifted my child and fled as from a murderer.[41]

Reid commented:

> Remove, then, this disturber of the peace of homes, extinguisher of domestic joys, this source of waste and want and woe, and social intercourse will be purified and extended . . . What is there worse than a bad husband, and what husband so bad as a drunkard?'[42]

But women, too, were guilty of sin if they fell short of the model of female behaviour which was so assiduously promoted by the churches, whether by failing to provide an adequate level of domestic service for their husbands, or by drinking themselves:

> Many a husband has been driven to drinking by the negligence of an inconsiderate wife. Is it to be wondered at that a man should prefer the clean fireside of a pub, to the cold, dirty apartment at home? Or that he should turn from an ill-cooked meal to the dramshop for relief?[43]

The 1877 Report of the Free Church Temperance Committee to the General Assembly was much concerned with the connections between women and drinking, and in moving its adoption, Dr James Begg remarked:

> that they had heard a great deal about the rights of women; he was the last man to deprive them of any just rights, although there was no man who had a greater dislike to see an unsexed woman pushing herself into undue prominence either in the pulpit or otherwise. He should like to hear, in addition to women's rights, a good deal more about women's duties. He had noticed the evil consequences arising through many working class wives having no previous domestic experience, and as bearing on the employment of girls in warehouses, shops and factories, he urged the importance of cookery instruction. he would almost go to the length of saying that before marriage every young woman should stand an exam, and should not be declared eligible unless found competent to occupy the position of a wife.[44]

If incompetent wives raised the indignation of churchmen, women who drank in public revolted them. In a city like Dundee, this practice seemed to be one of the more horrible manifestations of working women usurping the natural order of things: acting like men and denying the quiet, domestic modesty which should have been their feminine grace.[45] A woman who lived near the young Keir Hardie in Hamilton during the 1870s could 'drink, smoke, swear and fight like a man',[46] and among those with whom the trainee deaconesses in Edinburgh worked in 1891 was a 15-year-old girl who 'appeared to most people fallen and degraded beyond hope. She seemed to have supernatural strength, and would struggle through the Pleasance and stand with her arms akimbo ready to fight man, woman or child that offended her'.[47] Public houses were regarded as nothing more than drinking dens (despite Reid's rather enticing image of a clean fireside), into which no woman who valued her delicacy or respectability would dare to venture. As the movement grew in militancy, women who worked in the licensed trade were forced out, on the grounds that they seduced working class men into their establishments.[48] So Scottish women were systematically excluded from a part of the public domain which, whatever the campaigner's objections, played an important role in social and cultural life. One effect of the temperance campaign was surely to widen the symbolic and spacial gulf between male and female behaviour – public drinking of alcohol became more closely connected with the self-image of proletarian men and their use of leisure time, while for working-class women who cared about their respectability, such meagre leisure hours as they could save from the gruelling round of domestic and waged work were more likely to be spent, not in a pub, but at meetings and entertainments provided by organisations with a temperance dimension.[49]

If women who drank in public were objects of disgust, those who did so in the privacy of their own bourgeois homes were more to be pitied:

> It cannot be overlooked that as they are subject to greater variation of feeling, and to more frequent mental depression, they are liable when alone, to resort to a means so effective in affording speedy relief. Man has the busy world to occupy his mind and divert his thoughts; but woman in her retirement has often no better companion than the ghosts of her own gloomy imaginations. Do we need to wonder then at the frequency of secret indulgence?[50]

For Reid, as for most religious Victorians whose thinking was saturated with the assumptions of the domestic ideology, the solution for such women was not to challenge the lifestyle which condemned them to lonely boredom, but to use their influence for temperance:

> A cause which aims directly at preservation of female virtue, and at the rescue of the fallen, cannot fail surely of commanding their countenance and aid. It provides for that sad deficiency in so many women's lives, the want of some specific aim.[51]

If one of his readers, fired up with enthusiasm for this cause, sought Reid's advice as to how she could help, his answer would be familiar to generations of churchgoing women whose moral labour was required as a sign of gratitude for their elevated status as Christians: they were to abstain, and use their great influence to encourage family and friends; they were to collect funds for the movement; and they were to visit the dissipated to seek their reformation.

William Reid's appeal to women was made in 1860, because few were actively engaged in temperance work. From the 1860s, a number of organisations (both mixed and female) recruited women into a movement whose public image was transforming from a moral campaign associated with radical political causes, into a spiritual crusade known as gospel temperance. Largely through American influence – especially the militant actions of Mother Stewart in the Ohio Whisky War – the Band of Hope, the Blue Ribbon Association, the International Order of Good Templars, and the British Women's Temperance Association (Scottish Christian

Union) were established in Scotland, and drew on the active support of increasing numbers of women of all denominations. They all required total abstinence as a minimum commitment of Christian profession. The presbyterian denominations had, as institutions, been pretty lukewarm: especially about the politics of prohibition. But a new generation of clergy were emerging from the divinity faculties, having been influenced by propaganda funded by the Collins family. And the churches began to realise that they were in danger of losing out to other groups and denominations in directing an increasingly important movement and pressure-group within Scottish society. So the evangelical language and precepts of gospel temperance carried increasing weight within the presbyterian establishment. One manifestation of this change was the attempt to draw on the active support of churchwomen.

Temperance Committees, by different names, were operational in the three main denominations by 1866, although these by no means represented unanimity of belief or practice, especially in the Established Church. But churchwomen, as such, were not organised before the 1880s. In 1882, a Church of Scotland Women's Association for Temperance was formed, on a basis 'broad enough to include every shade of temperance opinion', declaring that 'the work they desire to do is unobtrusive and womanly'.[52] By 1886, it had been decided to link it with 'other forms of work which are more or less directly connected' in a Women's Association for the Promotion of Temperance and Home Mission Work, thus embodying the almost universal belief that drink was at the root of most social evils. The Association, which attempted to encourage educational work among children, and dabbled in the provision of counter-attractions to drink, was soon overtaken by the Woman's Guild (1887), and the Women's Association for Home Mission (1893), which both practised temperance work. In 1924, as part of the general reorganisation of women's work, the Women's Temperance Association was revived as an auxiliary to the Church's Temperance Committee.

Both the Free Church and the United Presbyterian Church had Manse Ladies Total Abstinence Societies. The former was set up by Helen Lockhart Gibson and Mrs Blaikie in 1882, who:

> Feeling that the influences of the Manse are very powerful and far reaching, resolved to form a Total Abstinence Society, composed of the wives and daughters of Free Church ministers, in the hope that united efforts and personal example might be greatly blessed to the people among whom they live and work.[53]

By 1900, when the United Free Church was formed, the united number of the two societies was two thousand. In the new church, temperance activity was conducted under the auspices of Women's Home Mission.

It was during the first decades of the twentieth century that alcohol abuse was emphasised as 'the great force of evil to contend with',[54] and a range of practical initiatives, both centrally and locally organised, were undertaken. All over Scotland, coffee rooms, barrows, New Year cafés and temperance tents were organised to provide working people in different contexts the option of liquor-free refreshments. Women addressed Sunday schools, Bible Classes and Mothers' Meetings on temperance. Social meetings for slum- and lodging-house dwellers aimed at moral and spiritual reformation – they offered refreshments, concerts, an address or presentation on an improving theme, and sacred solos and hymns. Contemporary accounts convey a general impression that the United Free Church women were more directly involved, with greater enthusiasm, than those of the Established Church. However, the Woman's Guild organised a number of initiatives, including a cottage for inebriate women. In reports of these activities, great emphasis is laid on the warmth, the attractiveness, the good taste and neatness, and the wholesomeness of the food which women provided for body, mind and spirit. Churchwomen were engaged in offering the comfort, refuge, solace and pleasant environment which so many women, affected directly and indirectly by poverty and drink, could not or would not provide for themselves or their men. As the Woman's Guild Supplement of the *Life and Work*, 1903, put it:

> Surely we Guildswomen, whom God has blessed with happy homes and many safeguards, might hold out a helping hand to some of these sorely tempted sisters sinning so often, against their own weak will and better judgement.[55]

In this respect, the church-based women's temperance movement was nothing if not a genteel and patronising endeavour which passed judgement on the perceived failings (for whatever reasons) of their proletarian sisters. Indeed, it is debatable whether a real campaigning movement truly existed within the presbyterian churches, in spite of all the counter-attractions and exhortions against drink. To be sure, the cultural consequences of the temperance crusade told on the personal lives of churchwomen. In 1930, the secretary of the Church of Scotland WTA wrote:

> It cannot be said that abuse or even use of alcohol is usual among church women. The majority are total abstainers.[56]

But she also lamented the indifference of these women to the wider issue, which they regarded as of minor importance. The pages of the Women's Guild Supplement of the *Life and Work*, and other journals throughout the period 1880–1930 reveal an ongoing concern that most women did not care to take any active part in temperance work, or to be associated with total abstinence and prohibition campaigners. It is likely that most middle- and upper-class churchwomen regarded temperance simply as an instrument of home mission work. As the direct involvement of these classes in such work decreased during the 20th century, so too did their interest in a crusade which was becoming much more overtly political.

By 1907 the Guild leadership was calling for legislation, not just for prohibition, but to

> Distribute wealth more equally, so that all may have some leisure and some means to spare for the innocent pleasures and amenities of life.[57]

And in 1919 the female organisations of the churches made a real attempt to prepare and educate women on the duties and responsibilities of their citizenship, expressed both in the accession of six million women onto the British voting roll, and in the forthcoming voting on the Local Option provisions of the 1913 Temperance (Scotland) Act, which gave local communities the right to veto licences in their area. It was widely hoped and anticipated that women would use their new powers for the sake of temperance measures above all other social questions. Clerical support for the enfranchisement of women was most often expressed in precisely these terms. The *Supplement* tried to rally support in April 1920:

> On June the first, an Act comes into operation whereby all duly qualified electors will be able to decide how the liquor traffic is to be conducted in Scotland . . . It is a great woman's question and it falls to Temperance workers in the Woman's Guild to identify with this magnificent opportunity.[58]

But in spite of the campaign, only 584 polls took place, with 508 voting for No Change, 35 for Limitation and 41 for No Licence. There were several reasons for the lack of mass popular support, including the restrictive conditions attached to polling, and the might of the licensed trade. But the churches were clearly disappointed at the lack of impact made by female voters. The 1921 report of the Church of Scotland's Life and Work Committee acknowledged:

> It cannot be denied that the result of voting in the recent Temperance Act Poll (1920) was disappointing to Woman's Guild Temperance Workers. It was perhaps

too confidently expected that women would do more than they were evidently able to do.[59]

During the 1920s, temperance enthusiasts in the Church of Scotland struggled against the odds to generate active commitment to the cause. The minutes of the Women's Association for Temperance in the years before and after the 1929 Union suggest an organisation casting around for a *raison d'être*, on the margins of Guild life, with even the old coffee stalls and barrows no longer much needed or used.[60] The United Free Church, which had a higher percentage of total abstainers in membership, and was more firmly rooted in the Scottish temperance tradition, tended to encourage participation in the movement through affiliation to non-denominational organisations. It was in such groups and their activities that Scottish women of all classes were more likely to find enjoyment, opportunity and pride. The gospel temperance movement was not located within the traditional framework of the large presbyterian denominations, but cut across them and spilled over into a populist evangelical ethos with which many bourgeois churchwomen were personally uncomfortable.

The organisations which were of greatest significance to Scottish women were the International Order of Good Templars, the Band of Hope, and the British Women's Temperance Association. Earlier groups, including the Rechabites and the Sons of Scotland, which were Friendly Societies for abstainers, had sections for women. But the Good Templars, which was quasi-masonic with secret rituals and regalia, was the first to practice gender equality in admission and organisation. It was introduced to Scotland from America in 1869 and, as Elspeth King points out, it spread like wildfire:

> It had an immediate and evangelical appeal; its uncompromisingly prohibitionist aims, its firm stance on the communion wine question, its admission of women on equal terms with men and its extensive provisions for juvenile lodges and education served to give it unprecedented popularity . . . and by 1876, there were 1131 lodges spread between Orkney and the Borders, with a total membership of 83,717.[61]

It may seem extravagant to claim, as Tom Honeyman did in his history of the Order in Scotland, that

> No organisation has done so much for the women of Scotland during the past sixty years as the GTO. It was first to recognise and utilise the power and influence of women as a social force. Placed on absolute equality with men, entitled to the same rights and privileges, they have triumphantly justified the experiment.[62]

But where else in the 1870s were women welcomed and invited to participate in the official life of a public, mixed organisation? Apart from the opportunity women had to hold office, engage in public speaking (based on Parliamentary procedure), and take part in parades as persons accorded authority and respect, the ethos of the order counteracted much of the ideology which was driving men and women into separate social worlds:

> One special charm about Lodges is that they aim constantly to overthrow drinking habits by supplying a means of social intercourse under conditions where it can be seen and felt, that both sexes can meet, and . . . be mostly more happy without the use of drink than with it. They seek that kind of education that may be called social culture.[63]

The Order also brought together people from different classes and circumstances, and provided a clear context for political discussion. Keir Hardie, among other early socialists, was a keen Good Templar, and one biographer claims of the movement, that it was 'not quaint or puritanical, but where many learned their first political lessons'.[64]

However valuable mixed organisations were, the fact that women and children had so much to gain personally from the reduction of alcohol consumption, and the spirit of sisterhood engendered by the evangelical female culture, impelled the foundation of a global women's temperance association. In 1873, Mother Stewart, a veteran Civil War nurse from Springfield, Ohio, began a confrontational campaign of direct action against the American drinks trade. Many of the women who joined her experienced a 'baptism of fire': conversion not only to religion, but also to highly public and controversial activity. Women in Scotland responded to the Ohio campaign by forming Prayer Unions for the cause, and in 1875, Margaret Parker of Dundee met Mother Stewart at a Good Templar Convention in Chicago. Through this contact, a tour of Britain was arranged, and Stewart's six week visit, including large public meetings and hymn singing outside pubs, made a tremendous impact on the public. The gospel temperance movement had truly arrived. On April 21, 1876, at the request of the American Women's Christian Temperance Union, the British Women's Temperance Association was formed at a conference in Newcastle. There were delegates from throughout Britain, and Margaret Parker of Dundee, who was elected President, expressed the fervour of the new movement in her opening remarks:

> We trust that it will be the means of gathering and utilising the now scattered forces which already exist; and that by prayer, and effort, and purpose, such a

fire may be kindled in our own hearts as will never die out until God shall wipe away from this land the evil of intemperance. We believe that there is such a power and might in the influence of women, that if it were exercised aright would shake the Kingdom to its centre on this important question.[65]

By 1879, 21 already existing and newly formed groups had become branches affiliated to the Scottish Union of the BWTA. The organisation was non-denominational, and at least one Jewish woman was a leading member, but from the outset, it was known as the BWTA – Scottish Christian Union (SCU). Mrs Blaikie, wife of Rev Professor W Blaikie, was the first SCU president. Other prominent members were Mrs G A Miller, daughter of Duncan McLaren MP; Mrs D McKinnon, wife of the minister of Dumfries UFC; Mrs Kirk of Edinburgh; and Eliza Wigham, the Quaker who had been so involved in the anti-slavery movement. Indeed most of these women were connected with a range of reform movements and campaigns, as well as their own churches. As with other religious and philanthropic activity, the SCU gave able and ambitious women the opportunity to develop skills, experience and confidence in public speaking (at a time when such activity by women was still looked at askance) administration, journalism and pressure group politics. And likewise, it called forth gifts in women who, though initially horrified at the prospect of moving beyond the private domain, were driven to do so simply by the strength of their commitment to the cause. In 1890 Miss Wallace, a minister's daughter from Glasgow, was appointed as organising secretary, and from 1896 an official organ, The *Scottish Women's Temperance News*, was published. In 1902 district unions were established to train local speakers and workers, to devolve responsibility, and to make the Scottish Executive fully representative. So the SCU enabled women at different levels to engage in public campaigning. Most of this work was done through letters and petitions – to politicians, publicans, ministers and other key figures – and by distribution of literature. But the BWTA SCU did adopt some of the more direct tactics of its American counterpart, including visiting pubs in pairs to challenge publicans and customers about the impact of alcohol abuse on family and community life. Such action cannot have come easily, but 'it was God's way of leading them out, often unwillingly and fearfully into the strife'.[66]

By 1908, there were 332 branches of the BWTA SCU, and over 80,000 members. From 1892, the BWTA affiliated to the Women's World Christian Temperance Union (WWCTU), co-ordinated by the redoubtable social gospel pioneer, Frances Willard. In 1900, the Biennial Convention of the WWCTU was held in the Assembly Hall in Edinburgh, and thereafter, the

SCU decided to assert its independence by affiliating directly, instead of as part of the BWTA. The scale and scope of the work undertaken by the SCU after it adopted Willard's 'Do Everything' policy in 1893 is indicated by the different departments of the organisation: evangelism; youth (including Band of Hope, White Ribbon Bands etc); legal, parliamentary and municipal campaigns; bureau of speakers; education; anti-opium; counter attractions; infantile mortality; non-alcoholic communion wine. These are just some of the twenty departments operational by 1908. In that year, after being vetoed for many years, a suffrage department was added.

The BWTA SCU, then, was an important training ground and forum for women who were keen to engage with what they perceived as the major public issue of their time. But with the impetus of an international movement which included some of the most radical women of the day, that issue was not defined in a narrow or parochial way. The 'Do Everything' policy counteracted the rigid division of life into private and public spheres and recognised that alcohol abuse had consequences for the whole of life, personal and political. The SCU saw nothing strange or contradictory in seeking individual conversion, good family life, better social conditions, anti-drinks legislation, and (latterly) the vote for women as empowerment for more effective action. Nevertheless, it seems that evangelism took pride of place, and that gospel temperance was regarded as the most basic and important element in the Union's work. A whole panoply of meetings, groups and social events were the instruments used to communicate gospel temperance to the people of Scotland, and it was these which gave the crusade its character as a mass movement. The Band of Hope, like other groups for children and adolescents, was pivotal to the strategy of attracting people to the cause at an early age. It was introduced into Scotland in 1871, and was central in the lives of women – both the thousands who (through church or BWTA) helped to run Band of Hope groups around the country, and those who grew up with strong and fond memories of youthful involvement. Callum Brown and Jayne Stephenson have gathered some fascinating oral testimony about the role of the Band of Hope in the lives of working-class women:

> The Band of Hope was organised either in congregations or in separate branches. Its tenor was strongly religious, and . . . was often the beginning of a youthful career in temperance organisations in which secular entertainment became an enticement as girls entered their adult years. Mrs H.[3](1902) recalled: 'The Band of Hope – well you used to have hymn-singing, and you used to get magic lanterns . . . And different things. Yes, we had a good time at the Band

of Hope . . . [It] was on through the week. The same as what the [Good] Templars were, and we used to have some good nights there too . . . Enjoyed them, dancing and all the rest of it.'[67]

Many of Brown and Stephenson's Stirling respondents recall the Band of Hope as one group on a spectrum of religious activity which provided their social life in the early years of this century. Much of it was organised by evangelical denominations and independent religious bodies, and its flavour – characterised by the Moody and Sankey songs which were so often sung – was quite different from that of the predominantly staid and respectable mainstream presbyterian worship. The tensions between different brands of protestant Christianity and the activity they sponsored, plus the importance of the temperance movement as a provider of genuine pleasure and opportunity for working-class girls and women, preclude any assumption that the movement was primarily an exercise in presbyterian bourgeois hegemony. Helen Crawfurd, the notable suffragette and communist activist who began life in a strict evangelical Glasgow home, recalled the 1890s:

> At that time, the temperance movement was also active. It catered for the youth by giving concerts and soirees, but these mother thought dangerous. There was dancing at these temperance functions, and this was something that might lead to worldly associations. How I wished to learn dancing![68]

Caroline Benn points out:

> Nor was temperance a renunciatory or negative experience. Quite the contrary, it was often highly celebratory and provided a strong social network for people of all ages . . . The miners' social life was divided between those who went to pubs and races . . . and those who socialised in the temperance world . . . It was at temperance dances and outings that [Keir Hardie] met his girlfriends. Girls came to all temperance events on their own, without the tedious shackle of a male escort required so scrupulously in more refined circles, or at the universities.[69]

In assessing the radical and liberating potential of this movement for Scottish women, it would be wrong to underestimate the permission it gave to seek greater personal and social happiness. In a country where it was commonly assumed that women would uncomplainingly endure poverty and hardship, and where violence was too often the currency of family relationships, temperance offered affirmation and support in the struggle for dignity and control. It encouraged women and children to assert their right to a fair share of meagre family income, and to the time and affection of men who were too often brutal or absent. And it recognised the importance of fun and excitement in austere and dreary lives. The anti-drinks campaign also presented an analysis of the deeper social and economic malaise afficting Scotland, and encouraged women to consider their right to political power as a means of changing lives for the better. I have already mentioned the disappointment felt after the first round of local polls in 1920. But there were signs that women could make an impact by flexing their political muscles.

James Barr, convener of the UFC's Temperance Committee, reported to the 1918 General Assembly the results of some plebiscites on prohibition. Where voting was in favour, the proportion of male voters was two to one; that of women was nine to one. In the 1920 Local Veto Polls, some small towns and residential city areas did vote for prohibition and limitation, no doubt with considerable female support. Working-class areas where the worst problems existed remained heavily licensed, but the temperance movement still clung to the hope that enfranchisement of working-class women would be decisive for the cause. Certainly the election of Britain's only Prohibitionist MP seemed a hopeful portent: Edwin Scrymgeour's millenarian labour sect drew its support from the mill-girl culture of Dundee, and in 1922, with his slogan, 'Vote as you Pray', he defeated Winston Churchill. In 1929, Scrymgeour polled over 50,000 votes – an increase of 71 per cent. It was no coincidence that the number of female voters on the register had gone up by 77 per cent after the 1928 enfranchisement of all women over 21. But by then, prohibition was already a lost cause. It had been seen to fail in America, and Scrymgeour's 1923 Bill, although supported by Scottish socialist MPs (including Rev James Barr and James Maxton) was massively defeated on its second reading. The great decline in alcohol consumption during the first thirty years of the 20th century had been achieved neither by moral suasion nor by mass support for prohibition, but mainly by the increase in duties on spirits, and changes in working-class social and recreational life. And despite the personal commitment of most prominent socialists to abstinence, the labour movement increasingly regarded the temperance organisations as anti-working class. This was at least in part because these organisations had become so closely associated with the church, which in turn had virtually abandoned its pre-war social agenda. A number of social historians have pointed out that the growth and diversity of recreational opportunities which became available to the working class, and enabled them to desert the evangelical offerings of churches and sects, served mainly boys and men.[70] Women continued to rely much more heavily on religion and temperance organisations as purveyors of non-domestic or work activity (although Eleanor Gordon's research into women and the labour movement corrects any impression that these were the sole providers of social and recreational opportunities). As a focus for the changing role and importance of women in Scottish society, temperance was firmly rooted in the domestic ideology. It emphasised the centrality of women to the preservation and improvement of the nuclear family: their transcendent functions as moral guardians and agents of purity, and their more practical housekeeping tasks. Apart from providing a social environment for men and women to mix freely (as in the Good Templars), the movement did not deliberately challenge the doctrine of separate spheres. In a study of the American Women's Christian Temperance Union, B L Epstein argues that:

> The WCTU can be seen as having pushed the women's culture of the time to its limits. The politics of the WCTU demonstrate not only the possibilities but the limits of a culture that accepted the structure of the nineteenth-century middle-class family and, by extension, the subordination of women.[71]

It is doubtful whether the BWTA SCU, which largely eschewed the more radical and confrontational methods of the WCTU, could even be said to have demonstrated all the possibilities of that women's culture – the suffrage movement was more successful in that respect. Although the temperance movement included many women who were unconventional pioneers and agitators in church and society, there is little evidence that the crusade itself radicalised the attitudes and actions of the mass membership. It certainly identified one of the main manifestations of hardship, poverty and inequality in women's lives. But it tended to suggest that alcohol actually caused every misery and distress from pauperism and crime to lunacy.[72] And it focused on the responsibility of girls and women to transform the vicious habits of the menfolk in their own families. The emphasis of the BWTA, Band of Hope and other groups on individual conversion to purity and sobriety through gospel temperance largely failed (despite late adoption of the 'Do It All' policy) to offer women analyses and alternative strategies for changing unjust social or economic structures; and the commitment at all costs to preserving the nuclear family ignored the roots of domestic violence and abuse in male power and control over women and children. Women who suffered at the hands of their partners were extended sympathy, certainly. But without challenging prevailing class and gender relations, temperance campaigners had only one solution to their plight. If the man of the house continued to drink, or if sobriety did not end poverty or violence or female subordination, his partner was expected simply to bear her lot and get on with her domestic duties as wife and mother.

The pivotal role of religious temperance in the lives of Scottish women during the 19th and early 20th centuries was complex and is worthy of further study, as the initial work of Brown and Stephenson indicates. They conclude that the movement was a source both of personal self-esteem, and of social control.[73]

> The message had complex implications . . . [it gave women] a sense of pride and self-worth perhaps denied them in other spheres of activity. The pageantry of the parades and meetings, and the solemnity of the pledge-signing ceremony, could be a beacon in an otherwise bleak and perhaps mundane experience.[74]

The centrality of women to the temperance movement was largely based, as Rev W Reid perceived in 1860, on society's conviction

> that its safety depends more on the moral tone of its women than it does on either legislative enactment or well-disciplined armies . . . We implore her to become guardian of our virtue and promoter of all that is good and holy.[75]

'The Day of Mental Daubing is Over': The Campaign for Higher Education for Women

In a recent article, Lindy Moore has demonstrated that there was tension throughout the Victorian period between the idea that education as intellectual development was *per se* a religious blessing, and the notion that domestic training for one's station in life was most important for girls. She concludes:

> Those . . . familiar with the tradition of a democratic, classless, co-educational Scottish education may be struck by the evidence that many Scots actually supported a class- and sex-specific education intended to restrain, rather than provide opportunities for, the 'lass o' pairts.'[76]

The campaign for admission to the full range of higher educational opportunities was one of the most significant elements of the Victorian Women's Movement in Britain. As the aristocratic doyenne of the Movement, Lady Frances Balfour, wrote in her autobiography:

> In the Women's Movement there were always three great fights going on. First Education, then Medicine, then the Suffrage of Women.[77]

The struggle for access to higher education was conducted with vigour and eventual success (according to the demands of the protagonists) in

Scotland from 1867 until the opening of universities to women from 1892. Although there were many points of contact with the English campaign, national religious and educational differences influenced the means and ends of the crusade in the two countries. However, I believe that one crucial similarity was the militant class basis of the campaign: for it was undertaken almost wholly on behalf of upper- and middle-class women. It had no place in its vision for those of the 'lower orders' – the girls and women of the labouring classes, many of whom provided crucial ancillary support, as servants, in facilitating the bourgeois Women's Movement. Those involved in the campaign debated whether higher education for women was important for its intrinsic or professional benefits, but it was a rare voice indeed which ventured that the new horizons of intellectual formation might be aspired to by a working-class girl. The successes of the movement should therefore be considered in the general context of educational and social developments in late Victorian and Edwardian Scotland, which resulted in a more formal and wider stratification of the options available to girls and women of different classes. A look at the general provision of education for Scottish girls, and the role of the presbyterian churches in determining its ethos, content and availability, will provide a framework for understanding the nature of the campaign for higher education. Presbyterianism was deeply involved in the process of class and gender socialisation: a process which, as Moore suggests, has been concealed beneath the potent mythology of a distinctively Scottish meritocratic system of education.

'For the Business of Life and the Purpose of Eternity'

It was an 18th-century presbytery which defined the education of children as 'for the business of life and the purpose of eternity'.[78] For the Scottish reformers, the goals of education were not primarily intellectual or personal cultivation, but doctrinal understanding and Biblical literacy, which were considered to be essential prerequisites for a godly life and a redeemed after-life. John Knox held that children were born 'ignorant of godliness', and the reformers' *Scottish Book of Discipline* described it as 'utterly necessary' that 'children and rude persons should be instructed in the chief points of religion'.[79] A system of parish and burgh schools was proposed which would ground them in the elementary disciplines, provide Latin and grammar, and prepare able scholars for a higher, classically based education in colleges or universities. Although post-Reformation education was neither free nor compulsory, legal and fiscal policies were available, under the supervision of kirk sessions, to provide schools in every parish. Scotland,

unlike England, did not have to rely on the caprices of profit or charity. By
the 1820s:

> The benefits that followed for Scotland, according to the apologists, included a
> love of learning among all classes in the population, opportunity for everyone
> who had talent to make his way in the world, however humble his origin, a
> relative absence of social tension due to the easy mixing of children of all classes
> in the schools, and a literate and intelligent working class.[80]

This quotation from TC Smout's *History of the Scottish People* reflects the
linguistic and conceptual ambivalence which has effectively rendered
females invisible in general discussions about education. The juxtaposition
of generic words and male pronouns is both revealing and concealing. It
reveals that higher opportunities, where available, were strictly confined to
boys, and a tendency for male experience to be considered the norm by
which education in presbyterian Scotland should be assessed. It conceals
the distinctive attitudes and experiences which shaped female education
before and during the period 1830–1930. Although elementary literacy,
with the Bible as textbook was in theory to be equally available to boys
and girls, in practice many factors militated against even the most basic
female education. By 1820 the parochial school system was breaking down
under the pressure of huge demographic changes brought about by the
industrial revolution. In 1818, nearly two-thirds of Scottish children were
outwith the publicly financed institutions. Those living in urban squalor
or Highland poverty were especially unlikely to be receiving formal
education. And the chance to go to school was even more remote for girls –
if precious pennies were to be used for anyone to be educated, it would be
the boys of a family. From the 1820s, the Church of Scotland's Education
Scheme sought to supplement parochial schools with sessional and General
Assembly schools. After 1843, the energetic devotion of Free Church
adherents led to the establishment of many more new schools. But in
practice, public indifference to the value of female literacy, and the
competing claims of rural and industrial labour for child time, made the
elementary education of girls highly precarious. In 1857, fewer than 50 per
cent of five- to ten-year-olds in Glasgow attended any school. Between
1857 and 1862, male child labour in Clackmannan increased by 53 per cent;
female child labour increased by 78 per cent.

By the 1860s, educational provision was fragmented and without
coherence. In 1864 there were 4450 schools in Scotland. Nearly one
thousand were private 'adventure' or dame schools, with abysmal standards
of accommodation and for the most part, of teaching. Another thousand

were parochial or side schools. There were a number of ragged and industrial schools run by mission and philanthropic agencies. The remainder were denominational, belonging to one of the three main presbyterian churches, or to the Roman Catholics or Episcopalians. Less than 150,000 pupils were under government inspection, and only one in seven children attended school at all (this ratio varied between one in four, and one in thirty, depending on area). It took the Argyll Commission on Scottish school education in the 1860s, and the 1870 Act for England, to pave the way for the 1872 Act, which removed the privileged position of the parochial schools, and established a national system of elementary ducation under elected school board control.

How did these developments affect girls? Parochial schools, and denominational schools which operated on similar principles, did not exclude girls. There are biographical and anecdotal accounts which confirm that many girls (especially from middle-class families) received perfectly adequate basic education. But girls were less likely to get to school in the first place. If they did attend, it was for shorter, more interrupted periods of time. Parochial and denominational schools tended to have much higher numbers of male pupils. In the North East, education was generally supposed to be of a high standard, because the Dick Bequest provided for university-educated masters, and relatively good social conditions prevailed. In his 1864 Report to the Bequest, the inspector, S S Laurie, gave evidence that there were 154 parochial schools, and 554 other schools in the counties of Aberdeen, Banff and Moray. At the former, the average enrolment was 118.9; average daily attendance was 71.4. Of these, 52.1 were boys, and 19.3 were girls. 44.9 children attended for more than 150 days during 1864, and most of these were boys.[81] The disparity between male and female attendance widened where the overall educational facilities and social conditions were much poorer – in the Highlands and Islands, and in the cities and towns of the industrial Lowlands.

During the 1840s and into the fifties, General Assembly reports and church journals began to give evidence of presbyterian concern about the state of female education. What exercised church people was not the inadequacies of intellectual formation, but the need for girls to learn how to cook, clean, sew and keep house properly. This requirement for girls of the labouring classes was closely allied to a concern for their moral and religious instruction. In an era when the churches were assiduous in promoting a rigidly hierarchical and conservative social order, working-class females who (according to their 'superiors') did not know or fulfil the tasks and responsibilities of their allotted sphere were regarded as a powerful demoralising influence. John Caird (future Principal of Glasgow University) wrote in 1854 when he was parish minister at Errol, Perthshire:

> There is no existing means of female education apart from the common parish school. The result is that girls grow up utterly ignorant of the commonest sorts of household work, are unfit for domestic service, even of the rudest kind, and are still more unfit to manage their own houses when they marry. They have no habits of personal neatness, no taste for order, cleanliness, domestic comfort; they never aspire to anything beyond the mere eking out of their coarse, scanty, comfortless life, and their only pleasures are sensual indulgence and scandal. What a life! . . . I seldom return from a day's visiting in our village without feeling my moral tone lowered by breathing in such an atmosphere.[82]

In 1849, an Elders' Daughters Association was founded within the Established Church to raise funds to set up dedicated female schools of industry. These separate schools were to combine basic literacy and numeracy with an emphasis on domestic education and religious instruction. The movement for such provision received impetus from the 1860 resolution of Parliament's Privy Council (which awarded state grants to denominational schools), that provision of teaching in sewing for girls in all mixed schools was henceforth to become an indispensable condition of masters receiving their augmentation. A letter from Downing Street to the church committees stated:

> My Lords have evidence before them, from persons well qualified to judge, that the education of females among the labouring classes in domestic industry is defective, and might be promoted to a much greater extent than is at present the case.[83]

However, both Free and Established Churches were alarmed at this, and sprang to the defence of the traditional mixed schools. Robert Candlish of the Free Church expressed a commonly held view that domestic work was something girls could and should learn at home, and that it was an inappropriate subject for the school curriculum.[84] But the Revised Code, which restructured government funding and priorities in the 1860s by enforcing concentration on basic literacy and numeracy for the working classes, made money available to schools which employed women teachers for industrial education. Both denominations (which were directly involved in training a growing number of female teachers at their Normal Colleges) employed many more mistresses during the 1860s. Not to do so would have jeopardised funding of existing schools and training institutions. In addition, there was internal pressure from influential churchmen who argued, not only for domestic education, but also for the greater separation of boys and girls throughout the whole educational sytem, in order to improve the feminisation and moral tone of working-class girls. By 1873 there were 130 sewing schools attached to Church of Scotland Assembly Schools, and over sixty separate female schools. The latter were less numerous than might have been expected, according to the 1866 Education Committee Report, because heritors were unwilling to take on the permanent burden of a mistress's salary. But although, as Lindy Moore suggests, the situation varied considerably throughout the country, the general opinion was against the imposition of an 'English' emphasis on separate and domestic schooling for girls, especially at the expense of academic standards for both children and trainee teachers. In fact, both denominations were quick to see the economic and practical advantages of attaching a female teacher to their existing schools, not just to give industrial instruction, but to relieve the master:

> On the one hand it enables the Mistress to teach or rather to train a class of the population who have never yet received their fair share of attention in our schools – infants . . . On the other hand, it enables the Master to give an hour a day to an advanced class of Latin, Book-keeping or practical Maths. The Mistress overtakes all her literary instruction in the early part of the day while the senior girls are with the Master, and is then free for industrial work. Sewing and the cognate arts thus receive much more prominence and attention than they could receive in any other way.[85]

The assumption here was that female teachers were not fit to impart general education to older children. Certainly the course of instruction received by women at Normal Colleges concentrated on elementary, infant and industrial education, and omitted altogether the classical and mathematical subjects which Scots thought of as higher branches of learning. Under the Revised Code, there was an increased emphasis on domestic training, and by 1872 three of the presbyterian Normal Colleges had hostels for women, within which students were encouraged to reside. In the hostels, the inmates (for as such they were known) were required, in addition to their academic work, to 'receive systematic instruction in Cookery, Ironing and Household Work', and to submit to a lifestyle of close control and drudgery.[86] Male students, on the other hand, were not subject to the severe restrictions and chores of residential life. As the Free Church Committee commented:

> We prefer the good old Scottish plan, which has nothing in it of the monastic, or hospital character, crowding the persons under discipline into one artificial household, and subjecting them to one uniform martinet domiciliary routine.[87]

The distinctions between the training and socialisation developed for prospective male and female teachers reflected the traditional Scottish attachment to the Dominie, even when the education system was moving away from old patterns and priorities. In spite of the influx of female students, and their better overall performance in leaving exams, the churches did everything they could, including special arrangements and highly preferential bursary terms, to encourage male candidates to enter the profession. Following Simon Laurie's recommendations to the Argyll Commission, from the 1870s men were able to combine College with University education: an option closed to women, for whom Laurie believed the limited form of Normal School training would be adequate. So until women had access to university education, the effect was to increase and formalise the distinction between male and female training and jobs. The mixed school, with master in charge and assistant mistresses, was to dominate post-1872 educational provision. But although the idea of separate female schools failed to attract sufficient financial or ideological support, middle-class churchmen and women continued to promote the value of segregated training to inculcate the domestic ideology. Simon Laurie, who as secretary of the Church of Scotland Education Committee, a schools inspector, and first Professor of Education at Edinburgh University, was one of the most influential shapers of 19th-century Scottish schooling provision, argued its benefit as the most effective means of inculcating the practical and moral 'business of life' for working-class girls:

> While the actual facts acquit the mixed school system of being a positive cause of one of the prevailing vices of Scotland, it is a negative cause. To the improved demeanour and elevation of a more purely womanly class of girls, we must look for the amelioration of relations between the rustic youth of both sexes in Scotland, and this cannot be attained without surrounding the girl with gentler and softer influences than those to which she is subject when sharing with boys an education expressly arranged with view to the special need of the latter . . . The deficiencies of "mistresses' grammar" are far more than counterbalanced by the prominence given to industrial skill – itself both a womanly accomplishment, and exercising a feminising influence on the learners.[88]

After 1872, when schools passed under the control of elected school boards, church people maintained an active involvement through membership of these. Ministers were prominent, although their main concern was to preserve traditional religious education, based on scripture and catechism, in the non-sectarian schools. They were instrumental in ensuring that the ethos of the new public schools was presbyterian. Middle-class women were also eligible for election, and a small number (of whom Flora Stevenson from Edinburgh became the most renowned) had illustrious school board careers. Although they were pioneers of women's rights, in their board capacity they focused on the distinctive requirements and goals of girls in elementary education. They supported the founding, during the 1870s, of Schools of Domestic Economy in Edinburgh and Glasgow. And they argued for the teaching of domestic subjects in board schools, believing that it was in the interests of working-class women to maintain, and equip them for, their supremacy in the home. While domestic education did not become universal in elementary schools until 1914, for financial reasons, ministers and other churchmen did support the theory. But it was for women that the issue was central. Helen Corr has shown that there was considerable resistance from working-class women and female teachers to domestic instruction, and that female board members falsely assumed that their gender alone could act as a unifying factor in this campaign.[89] Their brand of feminism failed to understand or respond to the class tensions exposed in their approach to education for household management. They sought a full range of educational options for their own class, but thought that the best way to raise the status of working-class girls was to elevate the teaching of domestic economy to academic respectability. For all their genuine concern and hard work on behalf of female elementary schooling, they confirmed the notion that its business was primarily preparation for a narrow life.

One of the main reasons for the tensions between middle-class board members and those directly involved in post-1872 state education as teachers and students, was that there was an increasing divergence of female educational experience and provision along class lines. Before 1872, Scottish burgh schools were open to girls, although those in Edinburgh, Glasgow and Aberdeen remained exclusively male. Most of the girls who attended them came from the less elevated professional and commercial sectors of their town's society. Ayr Academy, for example, had pupils belonging to

> the usual classes attending a burgh school or academy where the fees exclude the lower classes, while the mixed education of boys and girls . . . has its effect in keeping the very highest from the school.[90]

However, by mid-century there was a growing tendency to segregate girls from boys, especially during adolescence. Some of the burgh schools organised separate classes or 'Ladies Departments', in which the quality of education offered mostly reflected current views as to what was appropriate or possible for middle-class girls to learn. Jane Waterston, the Free Church missionary who was born in 1843 and attended Inverness Academy, was certainly disparaging about her own experience there. She later argued that female education should 'do away with the old, scrappy, tinselly, slovenly kind of stuff that used to be thought enough for a girls' schoolroom'.[91]

In fact, in spite of the presence of girls in some burgh schools, the general standard of middle- and upper-class education for girls was lamentable – whether under governesses at home, or in Ladies' boarding and 'finishing' schools. By the 1860s its deficiencies were becoming more widely publicised, as indicated by the absence of endowments:

> Our forebears attached so little importance to the higher education of girls as to have thought it unnecessary – probably a waste of means, to make any provision to give free or assisted education to daughters.[92]

The general purpose of the education provided had been to make the girls sufficiently compliant and accomplished in conventional mode to marry well, since that was their vocation in life. The view that rigorous intellectual training was inappropriate to such an end, was effectively supported by the spurious medical and scientific claims about small female brains and the threat of sterility for girls who exercised those brains in academic disciplines for which they were not designed. However, there was growing recognition that some middle-class daughters had no choice but to work for a living, and that even those whose goal was marriage deserved something better than the desultory provision available. In 1863 a new 'College for the Daughters of Ministers and Professors' opened in Edinburgh. The founder, Rev David Esdaile, explained its purpose:

> A large proportion of ministers' daughters must depend upon their own exertions in teaching or some other mode of employment. And society, as a whole, is interested in whatever tends to elevate their intellectual status and practical uses . . . It may be reasonably expected that some will manifest a desire to be employed by the Church as missionaries.[93]

The school was well subscribed, but remained modest in its educational outlook until the 1890s. In the early days, 'young ladies begged the Council to be allowed to give up Arithmetic.'[94] More substantial developments took place from the 1870s. In the 1871 edition of *The Attempt* the new Merchant Company Schools of Edinburgh were welcomed. The editor criticised the high fees in private schools which had made it difficult for many middle-class families, 'especially in the department of girls' education, which has been as superlatively expensive as proverbially superficial.'[95]

Simon Laurie was behind the transformation of the old Hospital Foundations, which were charitable institutions for orphans, into large day schools for the Edinburgh middle classes. He suggested that the Merchant

Company should use the Endowed Institutions (Scotland) Act of 1869 to turn the hospitals into schools. The Merchant Maiden Hospital became the Educational Institution for Young Ladies (later Mary Erskine's), and a completely new school – George Watson's Ladies College – was established. The two new schools offered a quality of teaching and curriculum which precipitated the largely unlamented demise of the old ladies' schools. The standards attained by the Merchant Company Schools may in part be gauged by the dominance of their alumnae among the first generation of women to matriculate at university. In 1900 and 1905, of all Edinburgh University female students, over 68 per cent had attended the two schools. However, the development of such schools in Scottish cities was not enough to transform the long term professional prospects for women in Scotland. Louisa Lumsden pointed out in 1875:

> It is no uncommon thing for girls' schools in this country to be under the headship of a master; the recently reformed Merchant Maiden School is a glaring example. I have heard this practice severely and most justly condemned in England . . . It is insulting to Scotchwomen. Even in our most elementary schools there is the same depreciation of woman's work and capacity.[96]

Lumsden was one of six women who had pioneered university education for women by studying at Hitchin (the forerunner of Girton College, Cambridge) from 1869. In 1872, she and Rachel Cook from St Andrews were the first women to pass the Classical Tripos (though Cambridge did not confer degrees on Girton and Newnham students for another fifty-five years). Cook's father had been Professor of Hebrew and Ecclesiastical History, and principal of St Mary's College. His wife and daughters were at the centre of a movement in St Andrews to set up a decent girls' school, which would match the education available to the sons of the ruling classes, but using female teachers and Council members. The eldest Cook daughter, married to the minister of College Church, wrote to Louisa Lumsden inviting her to be Principal of the proposed school. It was originally planned as a day school, but some influential university men from other towns asked if their daughters could attend. It opened in 1877, and in 1882 became known as St Leonard's School for Girls. It was unusual in Scotland for its adherence to the English Public School model (for which Lumsden and many of her colleagues who had taught at Cheltenham Ladies College, had great admiration). The breadth of curriculum, and the attempt to encourage personal responsibility rather than the harassment and spying which were common in old-style girls' schools, aroused considerable hostility and suspicion. But it was the first opportunity for women to prove that they could organise and teach girls on the same academic and social principles as boys.

Another important development was organically connected with the vigorous Edinburgh campaign for female access to higher education. The classes which the Edinburgh Ladies Educational Association (ELEA) organised were very popular, but exposed the weaknesses of preliminary learning among members. In 1876, the ELEA suggested that women ought to prepare for and sit the Edinburgh University Local Exams before engaging in more demanding study. A class was organised, meeting in St George's Parish Church Hall, to work towards the local exams. Over the next ten years, the St George's Hall Oral and Correspondence Classes became the centre of a movement to promote purposeful work and testing for middle- and upper-class women and girls throughout Scotland. For some older women this was the chance which had been denied them in their youth:

> To look back is to recall wasted school days . . . There was no visible goal to be reached, no real prize to be won, and so I followed hither and thither the bent of my own foolish fancies . . . The possibilities for women appeared to be very small; for, in the range of my wildest fancy, no striving, however unwearied, seemed capable of opening a career for me. My brothers went out into the world to seek their fortunes; I stood on the threshold and said goodbye.[97]

For girls still at school in villages and towns across Scotland, it held out new possibilities which, even in the 1870s, were habitually denied:

> I lose my local pupils just when they come to an age to appreciate their lessons – either because of the idea that they must 'finish' under masters, or because parents desire their society at home. Education is not valued as it deserves . . . I doubt if even half a dozen subscribers (to a local bursary for girls) would be found in this neighbourhood.[98]

But the organisers of St George's classes did manage to raise bursaries and prizes which enabled and inspired girls to study systematically with a view to university standard education, and the possibility of a career. By 1883 there were 215 students attending in person, and 835 corresponding. In 1885, Mary Walker, the superintendent of the Classes, consulted with Professor Calderwood and Professor Laurie of Edinburgh University about setting up an institute to train women teachers, and they assured her that there was a gap for training 'of a grade above those of Normal Schools'. St George's College duly opened in 1887, and remained in existence until 1940. The success of its training depended on access to proper teaching practice. They were distrusted by Board Schools for not having been through the usual channels as pupil–teachers and Normal School students. In any case, they were preparing themselves to teach a different social class. So in 1888 a day school for girls was opened. It flourished, with the support of the solid Edinburgh middle classes. Between ten and twenty per cent of all Edinburgh women attending the university from 1900 to 1910 were former pupils of St George's.

By 1900, the reform of secondary education for girls was well under way. The new private and endowed schools (and fee-paying Board schools, like Glasgow High School for Girls) were by no means free from assumptions about female behaviour. The feminist writer Rebecca West recalled her time at George Watson's, to which she won a scholarship in 1903:

> I saw in my own education some of the things which eat the power out of women. My fellow pupils and I were not deterred from preparing to earn our livings, because it was evident that for the most part our parents would refuse to support us in idleness; but it was tactfully suggested to us that, rather than attempt to storm the world by genius and personality, we had better court it by conformity to convention and 'lady-likeness'.[99]

Nevertheless, they did provide a hitherto unattainable level of accredited academic achievement, and a measure of official encouragement. Those who wished to become doctors, mistresses in private schools, or take up one of the other careers opening up to women, could now do so – as long as they belonged to the right class. Provision after 1872 brought new possibilities for middle-class girls, but effectively closed off opportunity for all but the most persistent, able, well-supported and lucky working-class girls. The middle- and upper-class women who became increasingly active, vociferous and critical in church and society now had their own and their daughters' educational needs met outwith the State system. There was no need, it seemed, for the pioneer female school board members to argue for such provision within the free state sector. As post-elementary schooling developed after 1900, the rigid division of 'academic' and 'non-academic' children at the age of twelve militated against girls from working families. Home and economic pressures, and tenacious prejudices against book-reading females, conspired to limit the aspirations and opportunities of most. Those who, against the odds, received the benefits of a full secondary education were almost invariably channelled into a teaching profession which offered them a poor salary, low status and little career development as rewards for their commitment and capability.[100] For those in the private sector, there was some small chance of promotion and rank. For the legions of female teachers in the State system, there was always a man blocking the way. The development of female education in Scotland was based largely on the patriarchal view that the business of women's lives was essentially to provide an adequate domestic environment for men. The presbyterian churches' lack of fulsome support for the establishment of separate female industrial schools during the 1850s signified more their indifference to girls' needs than any strong commitment to equal scholarly opportunities, and although the traditional ethos of Scottish education preserved some measure of equality in a co-educational environment, prominent men like Simon Laurie were apparently willing to sacrifice academic standards in pursuit of well-trained and womanly working-class wives formed in the bourgeois image. As a matter of more direct and personal interest, churchmen supported separate education for girls of their own social class. In doing so, they by no means rejected their fundamental beliefs about the nature and function of women, for the professional ideal promoted by private secondary education was circumscribed and channelled into work which would reflect the 'natural' vocation of women for service and sacrifice. Laurie was a true representative of his generation and his church when he declared:

> The truth is that the intellect of woman is a very difficult growth and that it is interwoven with imagination, affection and moral emotions much more intimately than in man. What the world wants is not two men, a big one in trousers and a little one in petticoats, but a man and a woman.[101]

But at least, for and among middle-class women, there was some discussion of education both as personal challenge and as intrinsic right; and from 1870 there was a systematic campaign to extend equal provision of opportunity to that class. One of the earliest and most distinguished beneficiaries of that campaign was Frances Melville. She attended George Watson's College, was one of the first women to study at Edinburgh University, became the first Scottish female graduate in divinity, and was Mistress of Queen Margaret College in Glasgow from 1909–1935. She was acutely aware of the clash of interests between domestic and professional ideals in education, and believed that these were not in any sense inevitable, but the result of basic injustice:

> We hear much in educational talk of the great organic differences between the sexes determining the education of each, but so far many of the difficulties have been artificially imposed. What woman cannot or ought not to do in life, and therefore, what is useless to include as subject of her education, is not yet known, and cannot be known, until she has had entirely free play, and opportunity to find herself . . . The end of education is to fit a complete human being for life.[102]

Melville showed some appreciation of the desirability of this educational goal for girls of all social classes. However, in the preceding generation, her foresisters in the struggle for higher education generally subscribed to the view that location within the social hierarchy was an *a priori* factor in determining appropriate education. A contributor to the *Edinburgh Ladies Magazine* of 1879 at once alluded to and undermined the myth of universal Scottish education:

> North of the Tweed, the principle was early conceded that the best education should be free as air and sunlike to all alike . . . The question therefore becomes – what, for all classes, really is the best? and the answer seems obvious: that which best trains them for their respective position and duty in life.[103]

Working-class girls were to be trained for their position which was to service their own families and those of a higher class. Representatives of that class were beginning to assert their right for training which would cultivate their intellect, and prepare them for duties which were certainly moral and domestic, but might also be professional.

'Their Souls' Salvation'

On January 16, 1868, David Masson, Professor of Rhetoric and English Literature at Edinburgh University, gave the inaugural lecture of the newly formed Edinburgh Ladies Educational Association. He began:

> Ladies – one of my earliest recollections is of an old clergyman settled in Northern Scotland . . . Among notions of a kind uncommon at that time and in these parts which he used to ventilate from the pulpit, was the following: 'It is a shame that there are not the means for the Higher education of Women as for that of men. I do not see why ladies should not receive a thorough university education' . . . It is now the established conviction of a large number of people, that the time has come for a united effort to hoist the institutional means for the education far above the highest level they have yet reached. Until this is done, we persevere in the guilt of a great injustice, and we dawdle on as a nation at but half our nobleness and strength.[104]

Although public opinion may indeed have been moving in this direction, it was nevertheless a courageous venture, strewn with many obstructions, upon which the ELEA embarked. The Association was formed largely through the efforts of Mary Maclean Crudelius, a young English woman of Scottish parentage who married a Leith-based merchant. But she would have had a yet more daunting struggle without the existence of a small network of like-minded people, and especially the Edinburgh Ladies Essay Society (later Debating Society) which was founded in 1865 by Sarah

Elizabeth Siddons Mair, and which met once a month (usually in her house) until 1935. It took an active interest in issues affecting women: education in particular featured regularly in the debates. The Society had a journal (*The Attempt* 1865–75; *The Ladies Edinburgh Magazine* 1876–80) which provided a forum to record and disseminate information and discussion about the campaign. There was, of course, a significant overlap in membership of the two bodies, and many of the women involved were from prominent presbyterian families in the city. The other main source of support for the ELEA came from influential professional men, headed by the Principal and many professors from Edinburgh University. This was vital, because the whole purpose of the ELEA was to offer courses of lectures which would be equivalent to those provided by the university, and taught by the same people. The first prospectus stated:

> It is not the aim of the Association to train for Professions; but its promoters desire, in the education of women, to give them the advantages of a system, acknowledged to be well suited for the mental training of the other sex. This they have endeavoured to accomplish by securing the goodwill and co-operation of the Professors and Examiners of the University, and of others interested in the higher education of women.[105]

Two hundred and sixty three women signed up for the first course, exceeding all Mary Crudelius' expectations. Over the succeeding years the number of subjects on offer expanded as the Association endeavoured to match the requirements of the Arts Degree. While numbers fluctuated, and the level of commitment ranged from simply attending a few lectures, to producing all the essays and exams required of male university students, there were enough steady and high performing workers to impress lecturers and provide solid evidence that women (despite the inadequacies of their schooling) could cope with the rigours of higher education.[106] From 1873, certificates instituted by the university could be awarded to those who were examined in at least three subjects, based on the standard required for an MA. In 1879, the name was changed from ELEA to the Edinburgh Association for the University Education of Women.

There were also developments in the other university towns of Scotland. In Glasgow, 'lectures for ladies' had been offered since 1868. In 1877, a formal Association for the Higher Education of Women was formed, with Principal John Caird as President and Janet Galloway as honorary secretary – a position she occupied (unsalaried) with the Association and later Queen Margaret College until her death in 1909. Largely through her exertions, the Association was incorporated as Queen Margaret College in 1883, under a governing body of twelve men and nine women. In 1884, three women students were awarded MA degrees, though they had to be withheld since the College had no legal power to grant them.[107]

In St Andrews, instruction had also been offered to women by professors, in college classrooms, and under the auspices of a Ladies Association, but they were rarely examined, and were limited to the very small number of upper- and middle-class women who lived around St Andrews. In 1877 the Senatus agreed to supplement these lectures with a scheme designed to test education (however it had been acquired). The LA (Literate in Arts, later changed to Lady Literate in Arts) certificate proved popular because it offered a title: some formal recognition of achievement. Local exam centres were set up around Scotland, and much further afield. By 1896, there had been 9375 entrances, 7638 passes in one or more subjects, and 1542 had received the LLA title and diploma. From 1884, those with honours in three subjects became eligible for Headships of schools in Scotland, without requiring further examination. However, there were questions raised about the academic status and value of the LLA. Christina Struthers of Aberdeen wrote in 1883:

> There is something almost pathetic in the eagerness with which women have realised that half a loaf is better than no bread, and have rushed to adorn themselves with the only available academic fragment. But it is not enough — the LA cannot rank with established and well understood traditional degrees.[108]

But in spite of the inadequacies of the LLA, it did offer something practical for women who wanted recognition and a career — and not just for those who happened to live in a University town. The LLA Committee, convened by Professor Knight (a parish minister in Dundee before he took up the Chair of Moral Philosophy), also raised money for a bursary fund, and planned the building of a Hall of Residence for women for the hoped-for time when they would be admitted to the university. So they were aware of, and committed to the ideal of equal access. There was also an element of opportunism about the St Andrews scheme. The university had fallen on hard times and was almost moribund, with a very small student population which was in residence for only five months of the year. Knight and his colleagues hoped that by becoming a focus for the academic aspirations of women, the institution might be rejuvenated with new funding and personnel. St Andrews was often cited as the ideal place for a separate women's college or university, because it was small and quiet and the students could be under close supervision and discipline. Such a development might serve the whole of Scotland, thus leaving the bastions of male tradition untainted.

In Aberdeen, Professor Milligan of the Faculty of Divinity agreed in 1868 to give a series of lectures on the New Testament to women. He suggested that they had every right to pursue academic study according to their interest, and the local press quoted his remarks with approval. Milligan also lectured in the YWCA. In 1877, a group of male graduates of the university founded the Aberdeen Ladies Educational Association to establish a scheme of courses similar to those offered elsewhere. It enabled some favourable comparisons to be made between students and male undergraduates, and in 1882 the Aberdeen University Higher Certificate for Women was introduced. But most women with professional aspirations went to centres with larger and more developed opportunities, (especially Edinburgh, Oxford, Cambridge and London) or worked at home for the LLA, and by 1886 the ALEA was formally wound up. Whereas in Edinburgh, the Association was a focus for the campaign to open up universities on equal terms, Lindy Moore argues in her helpful study of the Aberdeen movement that the demise of the ALEA actually led to a groundswell of support for admission.[109]

In addition to organisations in the four university centres, there were ladies educational associations in other towns, such as Perth and Dundee, and many other more or less formal groupings of women petitioned or otherwise made known their desire for higher education to university standard.

The changes wrought by the Scottish Education Act of 1872 gave practical force to the more abstract arguments in favour of higher education. Male teaching students were entitled and encouraged to take part of their course at university, and Christina Struthers claimed in her 1883 pamphlet that it was the preponderance of women in the teaching profession which gave the movement such weight:

> It seems impossible to escape the conclusion that, whatever opportunities our Universities may offer to teachers, must necessarily be open to women equally with men.[110]

In 1889, The Universities (Scotland) Act and its subsequent Ordinance 18 provided for universities 'to admit women to graduate in one of more faculties, and to provide for their instruction' in separate or mixed classes. On October 5 1892 the first women entered Edinburgh University. Because of their advanced studies through the EAUEW, eight were able to graduate the following year. In 1894 Marion Gilchrist (who was a doctor and later a militant suffragette) became the first women to receive a degree from Glasgow University. Although prejudice against the idea of women engaging in academic study continued, and the early students were subjected to considerable scorn and abuse, formal restrictions had finally been removed, and the first generation of Scottish women were able to learn alongside (and test themselves in comparison to) their male peers.

However, it was one thing to open academic doors, but quite another to consider that women might want to make use of such opportunities to develop professional, renumerated careers. The aims and objectives of bodies such as the EAUEW disclaimed such aspirations: they knew that the professional men of the Victorian age guarded their privileges jealously, and observed in their own city the controversial and apparently fruitless struggle of Sophia Jex Blake and her seven colleagues for the right to study, and sit exams for medical practice. In 1883, Christina Struthers clearly thought that the Edinburgh campaign from 1869–74 had damaged the cause of access to universities:

> Our Scots Universities have for long been not only places of general culture, but also schools of professional training, and it is impossible to ignore the fact . . . that we must meet the question of [women's] admission to the professions, and here it must be acknowledged as very unfortunate that years ago, the battle for admission to universities was in Scotland fought first from the side of medical education, as a host of difficulties and prejudices was thereby created that have greatly retarded our advance.[111]

In fact, the struggle for medical education had been brought to Scotland as early as 1862, when Elizabeth Garrett (who was the first British woman to get her name on the Medical Register, by a loophole which was immediately closed) arrived in St Andrews and matriculated for study. Although her registration was annulled, despite legal appeals, she remained in Scotland to continue private study and practical work with the support of lecturers in both St Andrews and Edinburgh.[112]

However, it was the later endeavours of Sophia Jex Blake which really raised public awareness throughout Britain. A complex person, she was nevertheless publicly perceived and pilloried as that Victorian bogey, the stereotypical strong-minded woman. Many observers, both at the time and subsequently, judged that her militant image and the tactics she employed actually set back the cause for which she strived with considerable courage, energy and perseverance. This is not the place to enter into that debate, but it should be said that the entrenched bigotry and protectionism of her chosen profession and the academic establishment meant that nothing would have been acceded gracefully under any circumstances. In 1869 Jex Blake and seven other women took separate classes specially provided by teachers in the medical faculty of Edinburgh University. On November

18, 1870, the antagonism of male students (and some faculty members) erupted in a riot at Surgeon's Hall. In 1872 the Senatus passed a resolution to exclude women from the university, and in 1873, the Court of Appeal withdrew the hard-won right Jex Blake had established to enter the Royal Infirmary for practice, and to sit exams. She returned to London to continue her battle from there, but came back to Edinburgh in 1878 as a qualified doctor to practise, and later set up a women's medical college in the city.[113]

The medical controversy was raging during the formative years of the ELEA, and Mary Crudelius in particular was concerned that the Association should not be tainted by connection with any hint that women sought university education primarily for professional purposes. But those at the centre of the Edinburgh network were by no means unsympathetic towards Jex Blake. A review of her chapter in *Women's Work and Women's Culture,* (edited by Josephine Butler) in the 1867 *Attempt* found that:

> She proves in the most satisfactory way that the study of medicine was formerly very usual with women . . . the whole tone of the essay is just and high minded and thoroughly ladylike.[114]

And in 1871, the editor commented:

> It seems fated that the study of medicine should be a lasting source of persecution to the sex . . . All the old objections seem merged in the objection that the education of medical ladies would ruin the University, both in prestige and popularity; but we may well doubt whether failure to perform distinct obligations undertaken by the University may not be equally unworthy of its high honour and yet more withering to its celebrity.[115]

The same writer (Helen Reid, who later became secretary of the Church of Scotland's female missions) nevertheless seemed to believe that it would be much more seemly and appropriate for women to receive a medical education in a separate women's college, which would 'render unnecessary the undoubtedly odious incongruity of indiscriminate University teaching'.[116]

In the second annual Report of the ELEA, which was published in March 1870, the distinction between professional training and general higher education was again clearly made, in seeking the support of the university for supplying a faculty for women:

> We feel that our hopes have a certain logic to justify them, for the University has gone considerably beyond our requirements, by opening its doors to women for the study of medicine. It would not be fitting in this report to say much about this concession to women. Opinions vary extremely among

members on the subject; and this is no inconsistency, since to approve of high general development and attainment is one thing, and to approve of professional training, gone through with a view to its natural industrial outcome, another.[117]

As this acknowledges, there was no unity of opinion on this important issue within the Association. In particular, Katherine Burton, who edited the *Memoir of Mrs Crudelius*, was committed to linking education with professional opportunity, and argued her case forcefully throughout her involvement with the ELEA.[118]

This issue exposes the tensions inherent in the presbyterian ideal of education as conditioned by Victorian dogmas of class and gender. The ideology of separate spheres rested on the presumption that women would have no personal ambition or desire to earn their own living. Within the patriarchal family their work was domestic, moral, religious – but not economic. At least that was the theory. For men of the dominant classes, however, the role of breadwinner was to be assumed as both duty and pleasure. The increasing male professionalisation of the Victorian age was closely linked with the role and mystique of the universities, and Christina Struthers was right to insist that their educational and professional dimensions had to be considered together. During this period, there were three general positions adopted concerning women and higher education. First, there were the conservatives of both sexes who believed that females neither could nor should benefit from intellectual discipline: their physiology was designed for other purposes entirely, and it was pointless and dangerous for them to go against nature and God. Women who engaged in learning beyond that which would prepare them for their station in life desexed themselves and were accused of being infidels.[119] Second, there were many who believed that the frivolity and ennui which characterised the lives of so many middle- and upper-class girls were a denial of those virtues preached from presbyterian pulpits: hard work, self-improvement, discipline, serious and purposeful activity. They were convinced that girls and women would benefit from exercising these qualities in study and learning, which would make them better helpmates and mothers for Christian husbands and children, and fit them for philanthropy. But intellectual activity and book-learning could never be an end in itself for Christian women: that would be self-indulgent, whereas the essence of true womanhood was self-denial. And third, there were those who strived to break down all barriers of law and custom which prevented women entering into professions and employment of their choice. For them, access to special lectures, courses, and even female colleges simply was not enough, because the issue was one of power and formal equality, not just personal culture and learning. Women who sought such rights seemed to many to be in open revolt against the ideal of womanhood. By asserting their entitlement to choose and to exercise authority over their own lives, in open competition with men, they offended the modesty and subordination which were the crown of femininity. In short, they were asking to be considered as individuals with distinctive responsibilities and talents – to be freed from the category 'woman' which assumed that their life and role was determined and exhausted by their sex.

In England, although campaigners for higher education received active support from individual clergy, the Established Church as an institution was opposed to the movement, which was attacked in religious press and sermons, especially in the 1880s. By then, female students were regarded as the antithesis of Christian womanhood, and a threat to the political power of the Church, particularly in Oxbridge.[120] Perhaps the more overtly hierarchical ecclesiology and less democratic ideals of literacy within Anglicanism also militated against support for the higher education of women. The many notable achievements of English pioneers tended towards single sex institutions set up in spite of, rather than with the blessing of, the Established Church. In Scotland, there is no evidence of a concerted campaign by the churches against the movement. It was rarely mentioned in religious journals, until developments were well under way, and then there was advertisement and encouragement in female supplements rather than editorial comment. In all four centres of learning, individual university churchmen were actively involved in promoting the cause: William Stewart, John and Edward Caird in Glasgow; Milligan in Aberdeen; Tulloch and Knight in St Andrews; Charteris and Calderwood in Edinburgh. The Edinburgh men were among six members of the Senate who publicly protested against the 1872 resolution to exclude women from the University. In their statement they claimed:

> We should individually feel ashamed of appearing as defenders in such action, and should account any public appearance by us in the character of opponents to women desiring to enter an honoured and useful profession, a matter to our discredit.[121]

Edward Caird recalled in a memorial of his brother John:

> He felt a deep interest in the movement for the higher education of women, and took every opportunity of pleading publicly for extending to them all the privileges of Glasgow University . . . Perhaps I may venture to recall the fact that many years ago, before my brother was Principal, I had the pleasure of voting with him in Senate, in a minority of two, in opposition to a proposal to

petition Parliament against some Bill that favoured the admission of women to medical degrees.[122]

Charteris also used his position as a financial contributor to the Royal Infirmary of Edinburgh to propose a motion that women should be allowed to enter the hospital for teaching purposes. Many years later, he wrote to Sophia Jex Blake:

> I am glad I was always a steady, if humble adherent to the side of justice before its cause was popular.[123]

One of the factors which certainly increased the popularity of the medical cause was the realisation, by the 1880s, that female physicians would be a great asset to the missionary work undertaken by the churches, especially in India (see Chapter 3). A few pioneers (Jane Waterston, Letitia Bernard, Matilda MacPhail *et al*) had trained in London, but by 1884 the Edinburgh Extra-Mural School was seeking incorporation into the University. Jex Blake wrote in November:

> The Free Church are also willing to move, and they wish to memorialise the Privy Council direct, and to request that any charter granted may not exclude women, but make it at least optional for the College to admit them.

The Free Church requested that Jex Blake draft the memorial on their behalf.[124]

The enthusiasm of the churches was significant in a society where, as Jex Blake's biographer observed, 'piety paid, and an interest in missions was a great help to success in practice'.[125] It helped remove the tarnish of personal ambition from the desire to become a doctor, and replaced it with the aura of noble self-sacrifice. It is not surprising that a large proportion of Glasgow's first female graduates in medicine became missionaries.[126]

The university presbyterians may have argued for women's educational rights as a matter of justice, but a growing number of Scotsmen, among whom ministers and teachers were prominent, had more practical reasons for supporting the cause. For them the ideal that they should provide for all the female dependents in their family conflicted with the reality that they simply did not have the means to do so. Daughters could be a source of great anxiety to fathers who saw little prospect of them making 'good' marriages at a time when the female population significantly outnumbered the male. Lack of private means beyond the stipend; illness or death; business failure: all of these were factors which could make it imperative for young women to earn their own living. Jane Waterston had painful personal experience of this. Her banker father was impoverished by economic depressions, and she had to support herself plus her mother and four sisters. In a speech on the higher education of women which she gave at St Andrew's Church, Cape Town in 1885 she pleaded:

> Would it not be better to spend some of our money in giving daughters an education, trade or profession, that would enable them to work for a living? . . . We will leave you the jellies and sweets, gentlemen, if you will share with us the beefsteaks . . . We do trust and hope that the day of mental daubing is over, and that the era of mental training and development has begun for us women.[127]

Or, as Louisa Lumsden put it in an address on the same subject:

> The mistake is to regard paid work as derogatory to the dignity of a lady . . . as if work were not a blessing, and idleness and dependence a curse.[128]

This necessity, combined with the evangelical sense of responsibility and service, and the presbyterian heritage of respect for literacy, propelled many earnest young women into higher education as a prelude to paid employment – almost always in jobs which were considered suitable extensions of the female caring role. Three of the first eight women to graduate from Edinburgh University were ministers' daughters, and others were deeply involved in the church. Most of them developed careers and remained single.[129] In St Andrews Professor Knight claimed, in support of the proposed female residence, that:

> The class who may be expected chiefly to avail themselves of such university education and residence are those girls who intend to enter either teaching or the Medical Profession, and who often come from remote manses and School Houses.[130]

The daughters of Dr John Campbell, minister of Kirkcaldy Old Kirk, were abundant illustration of the point: there were eight of them; all graduated from St Andrews, and four became doctors. Moore's statistics for Aberdeen also show the predominance of ministers' daughters in a university which was perhaps less socially exclusive than Edinburgh or St Andrews. They were disproportionately represented in the social and activist elite during the first years of female admittance. Between 1898 and 1910, 50 per cent of ministers' daughters went into teaching, and 22.8 per cent into medicine. 86.4 were in paid employment: a higher than average proportion of female graduates unmarried and working.[131]

Among the first generation of university women in Scotland there is little evidence that exposure to learning opened the floodgates of unbelief, as many opponents had feared. Christian societies in the universities were among the first to become mixed, and there were also Christian Unions for female students. The background and aspirations of so many women were commonly understood and described in religious terms, and even where there may not have been deep personal faith, these pioneers were anxious to deflect and defuse the criticism which they knew their adversaries would make, given the slightest opportunity. The topics and votes of the small but important Edinburgh University Women's Debating Society (founded in 1893) indicate that a generally liberal and progressive tendency prevailed among the members, but there is absolutely no suggestion that the church or Christianity were questioned or denied *per se*.[132] Indeed, in her 1885 speech, Jane Waterston suggested that it was the thwarted spirit of endeavour and call to blind obedience which might turn a woman away from the faith of her parents:

> When she expresses the desire for work, she is told that she has no need for work, and that she should be content and happy . . . Is it a wonder that in some cases she begins to question the Bible itself. 'Can it be true? Can God have given me talents and then expect me to bury them in the earth?' . . . Is it any wonder that sometimes she joins that dreary sect that believes in nothing beyond the grave, and casts off all social bondage and restraint?[133]

So the leaders of the presbyterian churches came, by and large, to accept the right of women to higher education – for their own class; and professional training – for unmarried women seeking religious or philanthropic employment. But what about their right to theological education, and its professional aftermath, the ordained ministry? According to pioneer doctor Elsie Inglis, the *Glasgow Herald* was horrified at the implications of Ordinance 18:

> The G.H. seems to think this is the beginning of the end, and will necessarily lead to woman's suffrage, and will probably land them in the pulpit; because if they are ordinary University students they may compete for any of the bursaries, and many bursaries can only be held on condition that the holder means to enter the Church! You never read such an article, and it was not the least a joke but sober earnest.[134]

Apart from the spectre of women in pulpits, conservatives abhorred the idea that females, whose faith was supposed to be simple, sound, elevating and decidedly non-intellectual, might wrestle with the turbulent theories which were disrupting the calm pools of dogma and biblical interpretation at this time. No doubt most academic theologians would have agreed with Dr Dickson of Glasgow University, who spoke at the meeting to set up the Glasgow Ladies Association in 1877,

> Telling us that he was a little startled at such revolutionary theories [higher education for women]. However, he said that when the ladies were ready, he did not think that they would find his colleagues or himself backward in doing their share of the duty. He said all this the more cheerfully, as he did not think they would want, for some time, a full course of Dogmatic Theology.[135]

But there were at least 141 Edinburgh women who, in 1873, wanted a course in Biblical Criticism. The request, made to the ELEA in 1871, caused considerable controversy within the organisation – because it belonged within a 'professional' faculty, and because it introduced a religious element into an association which was non-sectarian. New rules were drawn up, allowing the class to be held on the understanding that it would have to be specially requested anew each session, and that it was strictly an 'outside subject', which was not doctrinal but educational. When Professor Charteris introduced his course, it brought a huge influx of new members into the ELEA (which was the main reason the committee agreed to accede to the request). The class lists for the three sessions he taught make interesting reading. That so many of those who belonged to the city's network of campaigning women enrolled suggests a lively, enquiring commitment to the Christian faith, and a hunger among many women to deepen their understanding, but also for access to new critical tools.[136] It is debatable whether Charteris, for all his worthy commitment to the cause, was the person to stimulate much excitement for his subject. His powers of oratory and intellect were not in the same class as his organisational skills. The *Ladies Edinburgh Magazine* takes up the story:

> He warned his students that academic lectures on Biblical Criticism were very unlike those prelections of a hortatory and expository sort which are frequently delivered to the ladies of a congregation by their pastor, and hinted that the history of codices and versions, and discussions concerning disputed authorship and doubtful canonicity, might not prove at all to the taste of the majority.[137]

Although many fell away, a committed core continued into the second session, and impressed Charteris with the quality of their work. In 1875, he had no time to take the class,

> although a knot of students professed themselves altogether free from any preconceived bias as to the authorship of Hebrews, and eager for a full discussion of its canonicity and exegesis.[138]

In each of the other centres, lectures and courses were run by members of the divinity faculties, and were credited in the LLA and other exams. One might have thought that the general interest in biblical studies and theology would lead to significant numbers of women studying for the

Bachelor of Divinity degree. In 1892 the University Courts of Aberdeen and St Andrews resolved to open classes in all faculties, including divinity, to women, where professors were willing to teach them. In 1897 Charteris instigated a discussion within the Edinburgh faculty about admitting women to classes. After consultation with the other divinity faculties, they all agreed in principle to a resolution which would allow women to be instructed 'in any instance in which a Professor is willing to conduct a class or classes to which women may so be admitted.'[139] However, very few women took advantage of this dispensation. Opinion about the ministry of women was by no means advanced enough to encourage many to hope, as Frances Melville did when she graduated BD in 1910, that such preparation might soon lead to ordination. The whole concept of ministerial formation and practice was laden with patriarchal assumptions which would have made it extremely difficult for any but the most determined women to broach the threshold of that world. And contrary to the *Glasgow Herald*'s prediction in 1891, the legal restriction of bursaries and scholarships to men who were candidates for the ministry practically exluded most woman who might aspire to theological education for its own sake. Only in 1933 did the Edinburgh Faculty secure from the Educational Endowments Commission the right to consider women as candidates for bursaries. By 1930, just a handful of women had graduated from the Scottish faculties of divinity. The experience of Doris Webster Havice, an American who was sent by Henry Sloane Coffin of Union Seminary, New York, to New College in 1930, so that she could 'find out what it is like to live in a man–made world', perhaps illustrates why. On her first day in Edinburgh, she went for lunch in New College and sat down between two men:

> I was startled to see them both rise, pick up their plates, and go to the side of the room where they stood up to eat.

She continues her sorry tale:

> Each professor opened his class saying, 'I am verra (sic) sorry that there is a young woman present, but I assure you that she will not be permitted to disturb the class.'

She could not speak in classes, except for that of Professor H.R. MacIntosh (who had argued the case for extending the role of women, during the UF debates in 1915). However, his commitment to female rights did not extend to the Friday class on Homiletics:

> The implication was that no woman could contribute to a class on preaching . . . I moved through New College like a disembodied spirit. There

was avoidance of all contact. It was silent except on one occasion when the professor announced that he and his wife would like the gentlemen to come to tea on the following Sunday. It was clear where I stood.[140]

Things improved somewhat for Doris when she came top in each class, and this was announced on the first day of the second term:

> Suddenly I was included in the class and in invitations to professors' homes; even in conversations with other students. As one of them put it, 'Since you are so smart we don't think of you as a woman any more.'[141]

Perhaps in that final comment lies the essence of the presbyterian response to women's struggle for higher education. There were many aspects of the campaign which could be regarded as reflecting the protestant spirit of Scotland. It was a revolt against authority – variously that of parents, churches, universities, the law, and of received wisdom. It reflected and encouraged the growth of individualism, and it emphasised the importance of education for the development of ethical and religious life. Protagonists like Christina Struthers cited their religious heritage in support of the cause:

> If women resolve to face the dangers supposed to beset the path of university study, it is contrary to the spirit of the time to hinder them by arbitrary exclusion, and they must be left, as our Catechism says, to 'the freedom of their own will'.[142]

Women involved in the struggle believed that self-improvement was a moral duty. That conviction, derived from the tenets of Calvinism, imbued their enthusiasm for educational opportunity with an existential seriousness. Frances Melville contended:

> If women are to gain their soul's salvation they must learn to be individuals once in their lives, not constantly seeking for a prop on their weakest side.[143]

The movement also urged the recognition and use of talents for the greater good of humankind. In all of these ways the struggle was not an alien imposition on Scottish presbyterian culture, and many individual church members recognised the justice of the case, though the institutional clout of the church was rarely exercised on its behalf. But to accept that these principles might apply to women required a major readjustment of the double standard which invoked them for gifted boys and men, while assuming that the female duty was primarily to create the right environment for males at all stages on their intellectual journey.[144] The higher education campaign was a major arena for testing and proving the late Victorian flexibility in understanding 'women's sphere', but it by no means destroyed the concept of separate spheres. I believe that the extent of its success was due largely to an eventual ideological and pragmatic acceptance by the ecclesiastical and educational authorities that the protestant work ethic, expressed in both intellectual and economic labour, might apply also to women. It was compromised by a dual failure to accept the implications of equal opportunity: a failure among men to countenance that women might compete and succeed in what had once been male preserves, without being de-sexed (either metaphorically – as expressed by Doris Webster's fellow student, or literally, as exemplified by the widely held belief that intellectual effort would make women infertile). And there was a failure among most of the women who took part in the campaign, to imagine that other classes than their own might be in a position to benefit from higher education. For them, working women provided the domestic services which facilitated their achievements, just as their own foremothers had been largely confined to servicing the ambitions of men. A story told by Beatrice Welsh, in her 1939 account of St George's Training College in Edinburgh, illustrates the point:

> We had a little maid called Jane . . . She had her headquarters in the dressing-room, housemaid's pantry, coal cellar apartment. Here, when not otherwise engaged, she might be found washing the dishes or reading, or even trying to do both at once – with indifferent results as regards the teacups. She took, however, a lively interest in all our proceedings, and knew the timetable as well as we did ourselves . . . Frequently she was found trying to peer through the door of the lecture room to see what we were about, or applying her ear at the other side to hear what was going on. One of our number said she thought Jane, had she been born in a higher social stratum, would have led the intellectual life. Had she belonged to the present generation I am sure she would have been found, with the assistance of a Carnegie Bursary, sitting on the University benches, where I hope her scholarship would have proved better than her housemaiding, which was very indifferent.[145]

In spite of the efforts of a few pioneers to show that women should not have to choose between profession and marriage, others believed that higher education would be a blessing primarily as a way of improving the culture and wisdom of 'feminine and womanly' middle- and upper-class women, whose lives would continue to be dominated by the requirements of domesticity, rather than economic necessity or freedom. In so doing, they fostered the bourgeois model of family life and tended to disclaim any connection between their own struggle, and that of working-class women to make ends meet. Mary Crudelius wrote to Professor Masson in 1868:

Societies for the Employment of Women don't aim high or straight enough . . .
Let them fulfil their duties as register offices for the lower classes, which is about
all that they are, but don't let them interfere with and be a drag upon efforts of
a different kind.[146]

Although women like Christina Struthers and Frances Melville were
prepared to argue against exclusivity in higher education, most of their
contemporaries believed that there was a self-evident and qualitative
difference between what should be available to their own class and to the
'lower classes'. But the underlying social axiom was that girls should be
educated to fulfil their pre-ordained womanly functions according to their
station in life, while those few who avowedly pursued intellectual
excellence and professional parity for personal satisfaction could no longer
truly be considered as women, but were to be barely tolerated under
disdainful epithets. The religious institutions and culture of the time did
nothing to challenge these fundamental parameters of gender and class as
they shaped the educational options and experience of Scottish women.

The Women's Suffrage Movement

In June 1838 a female weaver from Glasgow, describing herself as a 'real
democrat', addressed the women of Scotland through a Chartist journal,
the *Northern Star*. She called on them to join the movement, and maintained
that it was 'the right of every woman to have a vote in the legislation of
her country'.[147]

Ninety years were to elapse before that right was granted to all women
over 21 in 1928. Throughout those years, there were always Scots who
argued for the enfranchisement of women. But from around 1870, and
especially in the first decades of the 20th century, the clamour grew and
was organised into a major campaign. During 1903–14, the militant suffrage
movement revitalised the issue, which became a major political question
in pre-war Britain. Both Elspeth King and Leah Leneman, who have
written about the suffrage movement in Scotland, have acknowledged the
importance of the Scottish church as a key public institution, and the
significance of its opinions and actions (or inaction) to those involved in
the movememt. Leneman in particular has revealed the extent to which
the issue was forced onto the agenda of institutional presbyterianism at the
height of the campaign.[148] What follows is a consideration of the
connections, differences and departures between suffrage activists and
presbyterianism. I want especially to look at these factors in the context of
the doctrine of separate spheres and natures – an ideology which was

malleable enough to be utilised, in different forms, by moderate suffragists, militant suffragettes and anti-suffrage campaigners. But it was also deliberately attacked and subverted by numerous women, who presented a substantial threat (sometimes from an overtly Christian standpoint) to the ideological hegemony of religious or social patriarchy. That threat was largely neutralised, despite the concession of partial and then universal suffrage to women. The vote did not prove to be the golden key to a glorious new age, as some of the millenarian pronouncements of its protagonists had predicted.

'They Forget to Think of Them as Human': The Victorian Suffrage Movement in Scotland

Throughout the Victorian era, Scotswomen were involved in a range of campaigns and actions which constituted a Movement seeking reform in female options and lifestyles. A network of women met, discussed, analysed, organised and took practical steps which were aimed at extending justice and emancipation to beleaguered people: and by mid-century there was a growing awareness among them that the female sex was the largest oppressed group, both at home and abroad. I have already mentioned the influence of Chartist, Utopian socialist, evangelicalism and anti-slavery activists on currents of thought in the early Victorian decades. In that turbulent era seceding and disrupting presbyterianism also contributed to the flux of ideas concerning individual and collective rights, and whether those were restricted by social position and gender. The connections in Scotland between this early period and the Women's Movement which emerged in the mid-1860s await proper exploration, but the individuals who pioneered that Movement were more directly associated with the evangelical and religious currents and organisations, than with the proletarian and freethinking ones. It was only when women's rights were free of the taint of earlier subversion that the middle-class reform movement could develop its 'moral mission' without abandoning respectability.[149] In 1843 a book was published in Edinburgh by Marion Reid, about whom little is known, except that she was married to a businessman and had attended the 1840 Anti-Slavery Convention. However, *A Plea for Women* was widely distributed and read, and made a reasoned and moderate case for extending the Parliamentary franchise to women.[150] In 1851, a Female Political Association in Sheffield, comprising women with Chartist and Quaker/anti-slavery backgrounds, presented a petition to the House of Lords, and in the same year, Harriet Taylor published an essay in the *Westminster Review* entitled 'The Enfranchisement of Women'. Taylor, who was a major influence on her second husband, John Stuart Mill, expounded a confident liberal humanist argument for the rights of women, and refuted the notion that separate spheres were essential, rather than the result of custom and prejudice.[151]

So from various sources, there were tributaries of support for female suffrage as one aspect of emancipation, flowing through Scotland and Britain. The small group of middle- and upper-class women who formed the Edinburgh Essay Society in 1865 were aware of it. In 1866 (and periodically thereafter) they debated the issue.[152] In November 1867, in the wake of the defeat of J S Mill's women's suffrage amendment to the Reform Bill, a Women's Suffrage Society was formed in Edinburgh, with Priscilla McLaren, her step-daughter Agnes, and Eliza Wigham as office-bearers. Duncan McLaren, the radical Edinburgh MP and United Presbyterian churchman, voted in favour of Mill's amendment, declaring 'I don't see how a man who had a good mother can do otherwise'.[153] In 1870 and 1871 public meetings in favour of women's suffrage were held in a packed Edinburgh Music Hall. At the latter, Mill himself was the main speaker, and he argued:

> Men are so much accustomed to thinking of women only as women, that they forget to think of them as human (Hear hear). Give women the same rights as men, and the same obligations will follow.[154]

Edinburgh was certainly in the vanguard of support for the cause – all the MPs, the Town Council and many academics and ministers were in favour. And the Ladies Debating Society provided a forum and a journal for discussion of the issue. Societies also began in other towns and cities, and the main lobbying method was the petition to parliament. Between 1867 and 1876, over two million signatures were collected in Scotland. Support was also sought at public meetings. Jane Taylour, Agnes McLaren and Jessie Craigen went around Scotland, and reports often mentioned that meetings were held in church halls, and had ministers in the chair or on the platform.[155] In 1882 and 1884 large national meetings of those from around Britain who supported women's suffrage were held in Glasgow and Edinburgh and attracted thousands. Churchmen occasionally declared their enthusiasm for the cause. In 1884, the year of the Third Reform Act, the *United Presbyterian Magazine* noted:

> The Government's refusal to include women householders within the sweep of enfranchising proposals has aroused the irritation and activity of a very formidable organisation. Leaders of the female franchise movement are women of conspicuous talent and high moral tone; and their plea that Parliament, after having conferred the educational and municipal franchises on women

householders, has acted inconsistently as well as unjustly in withholding the parliamentary franchise, commands very general sympathy.[156]

And in 1885, in the context of a debate on the Contagious Diseases Acts, Mr Paton of Dalbeattie declared at the Free Church General Assembly:

> I do not know exactly the opinion of the members of this House regarding female franchise, but I most earnestly desire it; and one of my chief reasons for it is, that when the ladies have votes, they will be on the side of social legislation, and for sweeping away such obnoxious acts.[157]

In 1895 a book was published which included articles on the subject by religious leaders. John Marshall Lang (later Principal of Aberdeen University), Principal T Lindsay of Glasgow Free Church College, and Dr Cameron Lees of Paisley Abbey and St Giles' Cathedral all declared themselves in favour of women's suffrage.[158]

It is apparent, then, that a significant number of presbyterian women either actively or passively supported enfranchisement during the mid to late 19th century, consistent with their advocacy of extended rights and opportunities, especially for women of middle and upper classes. And there were also many men who shared those views; some of whom were willing to declare them publicly. However, they were far from being generally accepted, or even taken seriously. As the *Ladies Edinburgh Magazine* noted in 1880:

> It is the fashion among many people to laugh at this movement, to turn it into ridicule, and to sneer at its advocates as strong-minded, unfeminine etc'.[159]

Lady Frances Balfour, who was a prominent consitutional suffragist, joined the movement around 1887. She criticised the Church of Scotland for its lack of support of women's rights, claiming that 'it did its best to alienate all thinking women from Christianity', and commented in her autobiography that

> No-one ever spoke to me on the subject [women's rights] except as 'shocking, Ridiculous' – something wicked, immodest and unwomanly . . . The influences of my time and society were all without exception against the freedom of women.[160]

It is against this background that the struggles of the reformist Women's Movement for educational, legal and political rights should be appreciated. The franchise movement has seemed to some historians to have run out of steam after the 1884 failure, but many women by then were engaging in other forms of educational and political activity, and a new generation of activists, who were very much alive to the importance of suffrage, were

already enjoying the first fruits of the Women's Movement's success. Along
with some of the old campaigners, they were (consciously or otherwise)
preparing for the next stage of the struggle, which marked a qualitative
change in the attitudes of women to themselves, as well as in strategy and
tactics. Teresa Billington-Greig wrote in 1911:

> The suffrage movement had been a ladies movement, conventional and
> punctiliously observant of a high and narrow code of honour . . . [It] failed to
> realise that the old practice of petitioning was played out . . . It stood in great
> need of the revivification which militancy brought . . . A change from the
> policy of appeal to the policy of antagonism.[161]

'Building the New Jerusalem': 1903–1914

In 1903, Emmeline and Christabel Pankhurst formed the Women's Social
and Political Union (WSPU): a new suffrage organisation which was
initially linked with the Independent Labour Party. In October 1905,
Christabel was arrested after the WSPU disrupted a Liberal meeting, and
thus began the militant phase of the campaign. In Scotland, the first years
of the new century witnessed the establishment of many branches of
organisations affiliated to the National Union of Women's Suffrage
Societies (NUWSS), leading up to the 1905 General Election. The new
government was formed by the Liberal party which had a huge
Parliamentary majority, based largely on its strength in Scotland. The
WSPU's declared aim was to force the government to concede the vote,
and in 1906, Teresa Billington (a lapsed Catholic from Manchester) was
sent to Scotland to establish the organisation and form branches. Among
many others inspired by her, Helen Fraser was converted to the cause, and
the two women were instrumental in arousing and capitalising on militant
fervour around the country. The WSPU purpose was warmly supported
by Tom Johnston who, as editor of the Glasgow socialist newspaper, *Forward*,
devoted considerable space to coverage of the movement's aims and
activities. In June 1907, a Scottish Council of the WSPU was constituted,
with Billington-Grieg (she married Glasgow businessman Frederick Greig
that year and thereafter often referred to herself as 'TBG') as honorary
secretary, Christian socialist Mrs Bream Pearce as treasurer, and Helen Fraser
as paid organiser. The tactics of the WSPU were confrontational and
disruptive, and designed to raise the public profile of the cause. Harassment,
police brutality and imprisonment out of proportion to the offences
committed by suffragettes won them sympathy and inspired new recruits.
They also organised major meetings and events which gave thousands the

opportunity to hear powerful and persuasive female speakers. In 1907, however, TBG, who was increasingly concerned at the autocratic and centralist organisation of the WSPU, was instrumental in creating a schism. A breakaway group objected to the cancellation of the annual conference which was to debate a democratic constitution. Instead there was a call to pledge unquestioning loyalty to the Pankhursts and fellow leaders the Pethick-Lawrences. The rebels established a new militant association, which, however, renounced the more extreme violent direct action espoused later by the WSPU. The Women's Freedom League (WFL) was disproportionately strong in Scotland – in part, no doubt, because many had been brought into the movement by TBG rather than the Pankhursts. However, the WSPU retained many able Scotswomen (including committed socialists, in spite of Christabel's rejection of all original ILP connections and her ever-narrowing focus on the vote). In Scotland, the WSPU and the WFL co-operated, or at least enjoyed peaceful co-existence, to the extent that many women belonged to both. Indeed, until the final phase of the campaign, the constitutional groups associated with the NUWSS did not express public antagonism towards militancy, and especially in the years of truce while the Conciliation Committee was meeting (1910–11), there was shared action across the spectrum to a greater or lesser extent in different parts of the country. Presbyterian (and other) churchwomen were deeply involved in both constitutional and militant suffragism. Among those who espoused the former, Lady Frances Balfour and her sister-in-law Lady Betty Balfour, Lady Ramsay, and the Marchioness of Aberdeen were prominent aristocratic supporters: as office-bearers in NUWSS branches, and as busy public speakers. Dr Elsie Inglis was an executive committee member of the NUWSS, and secretary of the Scottish Federation of Woman's Suffrage Societies. Inglis was one of five Edinburgh graduates who, having been refused voting papers to participate in the election of a university MP, took the case to the Court of Session in 1906. The others were Margaret Nairn, Frances Simson, Frances Melville and Chrystal MacMillan – all practising Christians, and later members of the Scottish Churches League for Woman Suffrage (founded 1912). The case went to appeal before the House of Lords in 1908, and MacMillan spoke for several hours. Leneman observes:

> Although defeated by the law, the women's perseverance must have caused many to ponder that the Lords were denying the vote to women while admitting them competent to plead a complex legal case before the highest court in the land. Chrystal MacMillan became a heroine to all three suffrage organisations in Scotland.[162]

One of MacMillan's school friends from St Leonard's was Eunice Murray. She has already been mentioned in a previous chapter as an ardent supporter of the ordination of women. She belonged to the WFL from the outset, and was Scottish secretary for 'scattered members', which involved considerable organisation, and an exhausting routine of speaking tours. Murray was a highly effective propagandist, in person and in writing. A letter to the *Glasgow Herald* in July 1913 described the impact she made during one of the WFL 'Clyde campaigns':

> Once I heard her convincing, eloquent and logical speech I was quite delighted, and feel persuaded if people had the opportunity of hearing her, and if cabinet ministers had that privilege, the vote would be won without delay.[163]

By this time, Eunice Murray was the Scottish president of the WFL.

Within the ranks of the WSPU, some of the most interesting participants had strong religious convictions and connections with the institutional church. Mary Dickie, daughter of Rev Alexander Kennedy DD, and wife of the minister of New Kilpatrick, Bearsden, served as Scottish Provincial Local Secretary. Agnes and Elizabeth Thomson were involved in the first recorded arson attack in Scotland, when an attempt was made to burn down the new grandstand at Kelso racecourse in April 1913. They were already veterans of the campaign, having been in Holloway prison in 1911. But they were veterans in another sense, because they were aged 67 and 65 and had worked for some time as missionaries in India.

May Grant was also an ex-missionary, and daughter of the minister of St Mark's Parish Church in Dundee. She was a skilled publicist, and after imprisonment under an assumed name in Aberdeen in 1912, she revealed her identity at a public meeting after arousing great curiosity in her home town:

> Some of her hearers, she thought, had known her since she was a little girl, as the daughter of a clergyman, and as having taken part in mission work. Now she appeared on the platform as a gaol-bird! Perhaps some of them had not heard the call of the oppressed, sweated, betrayed women. Nothing but political power would give their sisters the help they needed in the struggle for existence.[164]

Helen Crawfurd was brought up in a strict evangelical atmosphere, and as a young woman married the much older minister of her church – Brownfield Parish – in Glasgow. By a long, slow process, she began to question and then to challenge the subordinate role of women in church and society. Although she later became a committed communist, she was steeped in religious culture, and her speeches retained a rich element of biblical imagery. At the time of her involvement with the WSPU, she worked with the United Evangelical Association, and described herself as a Christian socialist. In 1912 she travelled to London to take part in a window-breaking action, for which she was arrested and sent to Holloway. In her unpublished autobiography she recalled:

> On the Sunday before making up my mind to undertake the job, I went to Church and prayed that I would get a message in the sermon. Little did my husband realise what he was doing . . . His sermon was about Christ making a whip of cords, and chasing money changers out of the temple. This I took as a warrant that my participation in the raid was right. If Christ could be Militant, so could I.[165]

Dorothea Chalmers Smith was another minister's wife who took a leading part in the final phase of militancy. She was one of the first women to qualify in medicine from Glasgow in 1884. She married the minister of Calton Parish Church in 1889, and had six children. In 1913 she was imprisoned for attempted arson, went on hunger strike, and was subject to the notorious Cat and Mouse Act.

Her husband was a traditionalist in his attitude to women, and she later left him.[166] But there were other ministers and churchmen who offered moral and practical support to the movement, including a group of Glasgow clergy who appeared on the platform party when Mrs Pankhurst addressed a meeting in St Andrew's Hall on March 13, 1913. They were roundly condemned by correspondents to the *Glasgow Herald*, but on March 25, James Gray of Berkeley Street UF Church wrote in their defence:

> We are men and citizens as well as ministers and must be allowed the ordinary right to think and act for ourselves . . . the Women's Movement is, in my mind, the greatest question of the day, and the first practical attempt in this country to realise the kingdom of God on earth.[167]

At a meeting held in Edinburgh on March 11, 1912 'to express recognition by the Churches of the spiritual equality of the sexes, and the justice of the principle of their political equality', a Scottish Churches League for Woman Suffrage was constituted. Lady Frances Balfour was President, and the Vice-Presidents were Rev C M Black, Rev Robert Craig DD, Rev RJ Drummond DD, Rev C M Grant DD (May Grant's father), Rev John Hunter DD, Very Rev P McAdam Muir DD, Miss S E S Mair (founder of the Debating Society), Louisa Lumsdem, and Lady Ramsay. The names of a number of prominent ministers and female activists appear on the list of the General Council.[168] The SCLWS distributed literature to church guilds and societies, arranged special services and meetings, and sent resolutions to politicians.

These indications of support from the religious community were welcomed by suffrage campaigners, but they by no means represented a consensus within the churches. There were many anti-suffrage church ministers and members, both male and female. Some were content to grumble about the disreputable actions of suffragettes, and the fact that 'respectable' church women could be mistakenly identified as such.[169] Others got involved in the Scottish League for Opposing Woman Suffrage, or used their position to denounce 'such disruptive influences'. William Knight of St Andrews was a prominent opponent – proof that involvement in one women's campaign (higher education) was no guarantee of support for others.[170] The attitude of the church as an institution was almost wholly negative. Although the suffrage question was one of the major issues of the day, the Edwardian denominational press scarcely referred to it, even obliquely or in passing. General Assemblies of the main presbyterian denominations did not debate it, although the UF Church did not hesitate to eject the suffragettes who interrupted the fathers and brethren when they discussed women's work in 1914. In the context of his account of this disturbance, Rev G M Reith betrays a mindset which was probably shared by many of his contemporaries:

> A minor political trouble was vexing the country at this time – the extraordinary behaviour of certain women who were clamouring for equal privileges with men, as they put it, especially for the parliamentary franchise and the right to sit in the House of Commons . . . Something like a bitter sex war might have developed if the national peril had not opened another channel for their undisciplined energies, and if post-war sentimentalism had not yielded the claim.[171]

Leah Leneman's research has revealed that efforts were made to have the issue aired in the Assembly Halls. In the autumn of 1913 the Northern Men's Federation for Women's Suffrage (in which the moving force was actually the actress and businesswoman, Maud Arncliffe-Sennett) wrote to every Church of Scotland and United Free Church Presbytery, asking them to pass a resolution in favour of women's suffrage, and to overture the Assembly to do likewise. Some local constitutional societies also approached their own presbyteries. In the Established Church, only Glasgow and Irvine expressed sympathy with the cause and agreed to send overtures to the Assembly (although there is nothing in the official records which confirms that this was actually done). None of the UF presbyteries was willing to do likewise. Perhaps the motion passed by the Church of

Scotland Edinburgh Presbytery exemplified the church's general equivocation and unwillingness to take a stand on contemporary political questions, in spite of its much vaunted concern over the 'Social Question'. The motion:

> deplored the social and economic evils from which so many women suffered, sympathising with them in their efforts towards amelioration, and expressing no opinion on the question of political enfranchisement.[172]

And May Grant spoke for many disenchanted Christian suffragists when she deplored the inaction of Dundee presbytery by recalling that women did most of the work, and raised most of the money for their churches:

> As one who is deeply, passionately attached to the Auld Reformed Kirk o' the realm, and who has served her for ten years at home and for four and a half years abroad, I protest against the attitude of her ministers – an attitude as banal as it is insulting.[173]

The WSPU, meanwhile, employed a new strategy – in Scotland, as throughout Britain, members interrupted church services to pray for women who had been imprisoned and subjected to forced feeding. This action was a fascinating combination of calculated public drama, heartfelt intercession, and a daring direct challenge to the rigidly controlled masculine ethos of public Sabbath worship. On 15 March, just after Mrs Pankhurst had been arrested in Glasgow amid scenes of chaotic violence, some WSPU members approached Dr McAdam Muir, minister of Glasgow Cathedral, and asked him to pray for imprisoned suffragettes. Notwithstanding his membership of the SCLWS, he was willing only to pray for prisoners in general, and during the service, a group of women prayed aloud, 'Oh Lord, save Emmeline Pankhurst, Helen Crawfurd, and all brave women suffering for their faith. Amen.'[174] After most of these incidents, the women involved were either left alone or went away quietly, but on one occasion women who interrupted a service at St Giles' Cathedral were arrested and found guilty of causing a breach of the peace. The WSPU distributed a pamphlet entitled 'The Appeal to God' to justify their interventions in worship, and in it, Christabel Pankhurst claimed:

> [Christ] would not question their right to offer up prayers in their own behalf at a time when men are letting great women be done to death. Worldly justice is not as yet given to women, but Divine justice is their's, and if the recognised ministers of religion will not ask it for them, then women will ask it for themselves. The appeal they make is from man (sic) to God.[175]

*'We Preach Glad Tidings of a New Gospel to Humanity': The Ethos
of the Women's Suffrage Movement*

Many historians of this campaign have noted the deep sense of spiritual
yearning which imbued its pronouncements and actions, especially in the
years immediately preceding the Great War. As mentioned in Chapter 4,
the movement was perceived in some ways to be an alternative female
religion. Clearly the passion and commitment it aroused, allied to the
personalities and organisation, especially of the militant wing, gave to many
women a deep sense of meaning, purpose and challenge in their lives, and
inspired tremendous courage and solidarity. (In certain instances it also
seemed to evoke some of the less attractive characteristics of religion: blind
devotion, personality cults, schisms, and an unwillingness to grapple with
complex questions about social and economic order). The cause also
inspired direct attacks on organised religion for its sexism in theology and
practice, and for its failure to uphold a righteous struggle for justice.[176] This
sustained willingness to confront and upbraid the religious as well as the
political establishment was, I believe, one of the significant innovations of
the suffrage movement. It was one manifestation of a new willingness to
challenge male authority; to assert discontent and anger; to display a self-
conscious irreverence. By thus contradicting the stereotypical female
attributes of politeness and passivity, many women declared in word and
deed their personal autonomy:

> The feminists found in this abandonment of the worship of propriety the great
> cause of rejoicing. Militancy interpreted itself to them not as the mere
> expression of an urgent desire for political rights, but as an aggressive
> proclamation of a deeper right – the right of insurrection . . . 'I disavow your
> authority. I put aside your cobweb conventions of law and government. I rebel.
> I claim my inalienable right to cast off servitude. I emancipate myself.'[177]

But suffrage campaigners, like socialists and members of other
progressive movements, employed Christian language, symbol, imagery and
drama in support of the cause and of their emancipation. Some did so,
having rejected the institutional church, to indicate their belief that they
were the authentic keepers of a message which had been betrayed and
misrepresented by the churches. As in the 'Appeal to God', women invoked
Divine approbation and justification for their beliefs and deeds, and
pronounced God's judgement on those who opposed or obstructed them.
This may have been partly a matter of tactics and strategy, with suffrage
leaders employing every available weapon in the fight, including the
ontological and teleological appeals with which opponents of women's

rights had concluded their arguments for centuries. But many activists were evidently committed Christians, and devoted (though often frustrated) church members, and it was a matter of great importance to them that vindication of the cause should ultimately come from the tenets, if not the institutions, of their faith. Much of the movement's literature emphasised that the struggle was not just political, but of deeper significance for humankind. So the character of the 1912 Women's March from Edinburgh to London was described as 'distinctly more religious and spiritual than political',[178] and Lady Ramsay declared at a SCLWS meeting to consider the religious aspect of the movement:

> They [women] are naturally susceptible to religious and spiritual impressions. The Divine call has reached them, bidding them rise and do the work God requires of them, and everywhere they are responding to the call.[179]

This kind of language had strong resonance for women, because the struggle for enfranchisement was, at least in part, the latest (if most acute) development of a notion which was deeply rooted in evangelical protestantism: that of women's special mission. That notion rested on an assumption which the movement in general did not refute: that men and women had distinctive natures and qualities determined by their biological capacity. Both wings of the movement drew strength from this essentialism, arguing that women were by nature more caring, religious, altruistic and moral than men, and therefore that their enfranchisement would improve the quality and tone of national political life. This represented a significant evolution of the 'Women's Mission' idea, for it fundamentally challenged the separate spheres which had previously been delineated for men and women. Earlier changes in both church and society had shown the elasticity of the concept, but now that basic distinction between domestic and public; the realm of women and of men, was denied. Sandra Holton has argued in *Feminism and Democracy*:

> British feminists insisted on both the necessity of increasing state intervention in areas which had previously been part of women's domestic preserve, and the concomitant need for women's participation in the work of the state. In asserting both, they challenged the notion that domestic and public spheres could be kept apart as separate concerns of women and men.[180]

The radical significance of these insights should not be underestimated. For generations, British society had been based on a dualistic patriarchal ideology of marriage and of the political state which, though not in total ascendancy, had largely served to confine and oppress women. It had helped to facilitate all the worst excesses of *laissez-faire* capitalism, and the social horrors which dislocated and disgraced the nation. It also placed pressures and constraints on men to conform to the requirements of 'true manliness'. To suggest that the domestic sphere might be a model and agency for change, rather than simply a place of retreat, was to take account of the possibility that compassion, relational values and high moral standards of personal behaviour might be fit precepts upon which to base legislation; that the autonomy of private and political realms was a modern development, rather than an immutable fact. And to believe that women could initiate major changes in both the style and substance of national government was potentially revolutionary. Indeed, many suffragists were committed to a millenarian belief that the old male order was almost played out, and that a Golden Age would be ushered in by 'the expansive power of woman's idealising instinct':[181]

> There has come one of those great spiritual awakenings that from time to time have carried the human race forward to a higher plane of life. The soul of woman has heard the call of destiny, has awakened and is now standing upright . . . It bids her to . . . work out the salvation of generations to come . . . It is not only political reform we are called to accomplish, but a moral revolution. We preach the glad tidings of a new gospel to humanity.[182]

For those who saw the vote primarily as the means by which women could fulfil their unique social mission, the campaign was clearly understood in religious, quasi-sacramental terms. Even the down-to-earth Elsie Inglis

> spoke joyfully of the time coming when we, the women of Edinburgh and of Scotland, would help to build the New Jerusalem, with the weapon ready to our hand – the Vote.[183]

Underlying this perspective was a matriarchal vision of social transformation which could be accomplished by strong, caring, co-operative women. It is likely that it was shaped by, but also in opposition to, the dominant Social Darwinism of the time, which was giving new impetus to a virulent strain of Machiavellianism. In political and economic life, ruthlessness, aggression and war were justified as irresistible and progressive laws of nature. As one critic has written:

> War became the symbol, the image, the inducement, and the language of all human doings on the planet. No one who has not waded through some sizeable part of the literature of the period 1879–1914 has any conception of the extent to which it is one long call for blood.[184]

But another aspect of Social Darwinist thought, utilised especially by theologians such as Henry Drummond, emphasised the evolution of the human race towards co-operation and altruism, and this was the strand which appealed to suffragists. Phrases such as 'spiritual motherhood' came into vogue, urging the importance of developing supposedly innate biological characteristics in the service, not just of one's own family, but of the whole nation and race.[185] But in this symbolism there lurked seeds of danger and sabotage for the movement. Teresa Billington-Greig became disillusioned: she shocked her WFL colleagues by leaving in 1911, and widely publicising her reasons for doing so. Some of her comments about motives and tactics were justifiably considered unfair by those she abandoned. Nevertheless, there is much perceptive analysis in *The Militant Suffrage Movement*, which she wrote that year:

> The claim that women will purify politics . . . is often based merely upon the old sickly sentiment which has survived from the days when men in search of self-approval promulgated the angel-idiot theory. There are suffragists who claim that women have a higher moral nature, and who will accept any statement, however extreme, based upon that assumption.[186]

TBG gave ample evidence to indicate that caution should be exercised by any who believed that 'The Women's Age' would actually transform the human faults and failings of political life, and criticised the potential conservatism of basing arguments on the premise of the existing domestic model:

> The customary line of argument is that politics needs the purification that women alone can bring and the home is quoted as an exemplar of what ought to be in the political world. This dragging in of the home is often a platform trick employed to awaken sentimentality in the audience, but it is as often a proof of the crude and limited rebellion that has been kindled by suffragette methods. The home of today is commonly far from perfect. From its evil traditions of women's subjection and inferiority come some of the worst of our social and economic evils. The suffragette who is content with the home as it is . . . is not a true rebel but the victim of superficial emotion. Any woman who is really a rebel longs to destroy the conventions which bind her in the home as much as those which bind her in the State.[187]

Of course there were many Scottish suffragists on both wings who were well aware of injustice and cruelty in the home, and who actively campaigned against such abominations as domestic violence. One effective debating tool of the movement was to highlight the hypocrisy of men who proposed chivalry rather than equality as the basis for gender relations, but failed to protect those women who endured exploitation and abuse as wives, prostitutes or in sweated labour. But TBG's general point was well made: without a challenging critique of the patriarchal organisation and inequity of both public and private spheres, the 'special mission' of women would pose no real threat to upholders of the established order. Highlighting widespread individual examples of abuse was important, but what was really required was an awareness of the structural conditions under which such destructive relationships were the logical outcome rather than regrettable deviations.

While reactionaries were railing against 'the unholy sisterhood', some of the men who belonged to presbyterianism's 'progressive' wing were extolling the potential virtues of enfranchised women, based firmly on the moral and religious sensibilities of their distinctive nature. The social reform minister Rev A Scott Matheson wrote:

> Woman has not turned out such a dangerous creature in any of the other provinces of her emancipation that we should be afraid to extend her electoral privileges, or even allow her to sit as a member of Parliament . . . The State is an aggregate of families, and the qualities for government of the home might fit her for the larger service of the State . . . It will not turn woman into an abortive man, but give her an opportunity to purify, soften and refine the asperities of party warfare. Especially in Social Questions, which are coming to the front as the chief political factors of the future, woman's influence will tell most happily . . . By this enlargement of her sphere, a conservative influence would be brought to bear upon the most important question of all – the future of religion in our land . . . We cannot doubt that if admitted to the councils of the nation, the cause of pure and undefiled religion would be exalted to a safer and more eminent place in the land.[188]

This, of course, was one of the arguments used by socialists to oppose the movement's aim of suffrage parity with men. William Stewart, unsuccessful Labour candidate in Glasgow Dalmarnock, complained after the 1904 municipal elections:

> In reality we did win on the men's vote. There are 1200 women voters, mostly controlled by the churches and the most of them voted against Labour.[189]

The Labour Movement, it has to be said, was (with some notable exceptions) lukewarm in its support of universal suffrage and did little to demonstrate any practical commitment to real sexual equality. It too was in thrall to the patriarchal assumption that the role of women was domestic and auxiliary, and female socialists who opposed the limited goal of the suffrage movement in order to wait for the revolution to usher in a new age of female liberation, must have done so more in hope than expectation.

The major problem with the essentialist arguments for female suffrage was that they were based on the same assumptions as those of their opponents. Bolstered by religious, scientific and medical dogmas, the anti-suffragists maintained that the highest evolution of the species depended on increasing differentiation and specialisation, and that women were physiologically unsuited to the demands of politics and statecraft. As long as individual women were subsumed under the abstract category of 'Woman', it was (as Mill had pointed out) very difficult for them to be considered simply as human beings, without all the ideological baggage of conjecture about what 'Woman' could or should do. That baggage made it very difficult for a significant proportion of the population to think of women as uniquely striving and thinking individuals, rather than in terms of a generic symbol fulfilled in physical or spiritual motherhood. Of course there was a strong element among those who agitated for enfranchisement, appealing to gender-neutral individual privileges as the basis for political freedom: whether those derived from the natural rights of social contract liberalism, or from the Christian idea that each soul is equal before God. Louisa Lumsden claimed

> The root idea of Christianity is the value of the individual, and it regards women as full individuals, setting before them equally with men, its high and stern vocation and its glorious hope.[190]

But Chrystal MacMillan, who later practised as a lawyer, recognised 'the yawning gap between 'women' and 'all human beings' [which] continued to thwart this defiant liberalism'.[191] As the main advocate for the Scottish Women Graduates, she argued in 1909:

> The House of Commons presumes to legislate for the people without having asked the consent of half the people . . . Women are only considered of value in so far as they promote the interests of men . . . This fallacy of assuming that woman is of no value in herself is the assumed major premise of much writing, legislation and judicial decisions . . . [In the Scottish Graduates Case] 'women' are not 'persons'. Here again we have the purely arbitrary setting aside of the obvious interpretation of the law. The interpretation of the House of Lords when applied to the statutes in question produces contradictions and absurdities.[192]

The problem for the suffrage movement was that these contradictions and absurdities shadowed every effort to understand, explain and promote the importance of enfranchisement. Women were caught in a double bind: in order to escape from the restrictions imposed upon them because of 'woman's special nature', they extolled the political and national benefits of that very nature. Attempts to shift the terms of the debate onto the social construction of 'male' and 'female', and the recognition of basic human rights were rebuffed in law, and compromised in public opinion by the

pervasive power of the separate spheres doctrine. For all the developments
and adaptions in that doctrine, and its effects on women's lives, the basic
question for those who held political power in 1909 was the same as for
the Free Church ecclesiastical authorities in 1843 – were women really
persons? But the intervening years had made the question seem even more
absurd, for 19th-century political reform had shifted the emphasis from
the family as basic social unit, to the individual citizen, who had intrinsic,
rather than representative political rights. Whereas in 1843 it was still
acceptable to argue, as many in the Free Church did, that male heads of
households could vote on behalf of their families, this was intellectually
anachronistic by 1909. Susan Moller Okin writes:

> Behind the individualist rhetoric, it is clear that the family, and not the adult
> human individual, is the basic political unit of liberal as of non-liberal
> philosophers. In spite of the supposedly individualist premises of the liberal
> tradition, John Stuart Mill was the first of its members to assert that the interests
> of women were by no means automatically upheld by the male heads of families
> to which they belonged. That these proposals should have appeared so
> dangerously radical in the climate of late 19th and early 20th century opinion
> is ample testimony to the limitations of previous liberal individualism.[193]

The ethos of the suffrage movement was complex and many faceted,
but strongly influenced by the protestant female culture which had developed
throughout the Victorian era. That culture endowed the movement with
many positive resources, including a powerful sense of solidarity and
commitment; of hope and expectation. These were often expressed in
language, imagery and ritual which were redolent of the Christian tradition.
Suffragists also found strength and courage in what they regarded as the
Divine affirmation of human equality, confirmed by Jesus' actions and
relationships as recorded in the gospels. This encouraged them to appeal to
a higher court of Divine support and justice in the face of institutional
obstruction – one of the fundamental and potentially revolutionary rights
asserted by the Reformation tradition. But at the height of suffrage
agitation the Scottish emphasis was less on female political rights as ends
in themselves, and much more on their importance as a means to achieve
social and moral change. Although by no means all churchwomen believed
they should have the vote, this position was a logical extension of 'women's
mission', because it was based on the premise that female moral agency
required the expansion of their familial responsibility to promote human
happiness and welfare. In this way the Movement (and women's
philanthropic work in general) made an important contribution to a
change in British political culture, from the practice of a restricted

citizenship based on rational self-interest, to a much richer and more complex view of collective responsibility and social welfare.

But there were also drawbacks in the appropriation of religious heritage. The suffragists' interpretation of scriptural sources which supported respect and equality was far from being universally accepted, though it was shared by some ministers. It was counteracted by the weight of church tradition and literal biblicism, including the pronouncements of Calvinism's founding fathers against the public rule or role of women.[194] Much of the movement (militant as well as constitutional) was deeply concerned with the need to appear respectable, womanly, not neglectful of the domestic sphere. This restricted any willingness to tackle either the religious or the philosophical commitment to (and adulation of) patriarchal marriage and family. Looking at some of the virulent anti-suffrage propaganda, which depicted suffragettes as negligent mothers and their husbands as pathetic hen-pecked creatures, it is apparent that such a critique would have been tactical insanity.

It is possible also to discern, in some of the extreme actions of the militants, some traces of a legacy which has been much criticised by recent feminist theologians: that Christian women have for centuries been socialised to accept martyrdom – renunciation of one's own wellbeing – as the appropriate mode of female religous behaviour. One hesitates to demean the bravery of militants who were imprisoned and tortured, but their actions were often an uneasy combination of the new virtue of self-assertion, and that age-old impulse for self-sacrifice. In spite of the harshness of her denunciation, there is something that rings true in these words of Billington-Greig:

> They did not seek for true cases of victimisation caused by the conditions of which we complained, but set out to create an arbitrary supply of artificial victims . . . Nothing but the enthusiasm of the few has been proved by self-sacrifice, and that has come to be looked on as an emotional craze . . . The movement is still separated from the real life of the women of the nation.[195]

In one sense the militants chose to subvert the old image of woman-as-victim by deliberately choosing martyrdom as an expression of their self-determination; but possibly, as TBG implies, that image deflected the public mind away from the real injustices suffered daily by women through poverty, violence and structural prejudice.

Whatever the complexities of the suffrage movement, it is apparent that its supporters valued the support of clergy and other church members, but perceived the institutional church in Scotland (as in England) to be either implacably opposed to their cause, or unwilling to commit itself to any constructive advocacy of it. Many Scottish women, in or out of the Church, were no longer willing to remain silent. Some were forthright in their condemnation of the Church and all its doctrines. Others tried to galvanise it into supportive action, or reflected, more in sorrow than in anger, on lost opportunities:

> The truth is that much as our movement would benefit by the co-operation of the Church, the advantage to the Church itself would be even greater. Its current decadence . . . is due entirely to the fact that it has become divorced from the great social problems of the day.[196]

In a country where patriarchal presbyterianism had been such a dominant cultural force – especially among women of the class from which so many suffrage activists were drawn – public willingness to denounce its failings was a major psychological and social innovation. This was perhaps especially true for women who did not wish to apostasise, but who felt able to criticise the church while remaining committed to the practice of their faith. It denoted an abandonment of that male (and clerical) approval which women had for so long been taught to regard as their aim in life, and a commitment to personal autonomy which was both the way and the goal for female emancipation. The writer Rebecca West was involved with the suffragettes as an adolescent in Edinburgh. The following extract from her novel *The Judge* eloquently expresses the irreverent spirit which (along with its effective deployment of drama, ritual, symbol and advertisement) must have been one of the most refreshing contributions made by the suffrage movement to disrupting the stifling conformity of pre-war culture. In this passage, the 17-year-old heroine Ellen Melville is selling *Votes for Women* on Princes Street:

> She caught sight of a minister standing a yard or two away and giggling 'Tee hee' at her. It was too much. She darted down on him. 'Are you not Mr Hunter of the Middleton Place United Free Church?' she asked, making her voice sound soft and cuddly. He wiped the facetiousness from his face and assented with a polite bob. Perhaps she was the daughter of an elder. Quite nice people were taking up this nonsense. 'I heard you preach last Sunday' she said, glowing with interest. He began to look coy. Then her voice changed to something colder than the wind. 'The most lamentable sairmon I ever listened to. Neither lairning nor inspiration. And a read sairmon too!'[197]

The Aftermath

With the outbreak of war in 1914, Scottish suffrage activists graphically demonstrated that the oft-assumed and argued homogeneity of 'women' as inhabitants of a separate culture and sphere was a myth. Women were ranged along the spectrum of responses to the conflict: from the pro-war fervour of Helen Fraser and Lady Frances Balfour, through the determined and remarkable service of Scottish Women's Hospitals, initiated by Elsie Inglis, to the active peace campaigning of Chrystal MacMillan (who was one of the key players in the Women's International League for Peace and Freedom) and Helen Crawfurd (who co-ordinated the rent strikes and mounted the Women's Peace Crusade in Glasgow, as well as being involved in the international peace and socialist movements). Personal response cut across organisational lines and required realignments. The WSPU, under Pankhurst influence, ceased activity in favour of an incredible outburst of militaristic chauvinism; the NUWSS diverted energies into all kinds of practical caring and voluntary agencies; the WFL maintained pressure on the government for the vote as well as on other women's issues. As the war progressed, it seemed that the anti-suffragists were having the rug pulled from under them as women workers demonstrated their competence in an ever-increasing range of paid and ex-officio occupations which had previously been the jealously guarded preserve of men. Elsie Inglis was surely entitled to her cynicism in June 1917:

> So the vote has come! and for our work. Fancy its having taken the war to show them how ready we were to work! Where do they think the world would have been without women workers all these ages?[198]

It certainly took the war to alert presbyterian churches to the changing position of women in society – mainly because of the threat which they perceived to their ertswhile supply of unpaid and underpaid female labour. As the war ended and the new era of female enfranchisement dawned, the fathers and brethren benevolently welcomed the six million new voters: not in belated acknowledgment of a just cause, but because they continued to subscribe to the essentialist argument that 'the female vote' would support the conservative values espoused by the churches.[199] Churchwomen, meanwhile, were seeking to inspire their sisters (and brothers) with a new vision of citizenship. One Edinburgh woman called on the church to organise and utilise the 'great latent power' of womanhood, by teaching those newly enfranchised 'how to use their citizenship to accomplish the highest spiritual aims'.[200] She probably belonged to the Women's Council of St George's UF Church, which successfully petitioned the General Assembly to authorise the Home Mission Committee:

To employ one or more temporary woman agents for the purpose of presenting the higher aspects of their electoral duty before the women electors of the Church and country.[201]

There is no evidence that women who were enfranchised under the limited terms of the 1918 Act collectively demonstrated any of the strong gender-based sectionalism so vaunted and feared by different camps in the pre-war years. Only in the interesting but hardly typical 1922 and 1929 returns of Edwin Scrymgeour as Dundee's Prohibitionist MP was the female vote apparently decisive. The general impact of women on the political scene, both numerically and in terms of issues, must be judged to have been marginal. Eunice Murray was the only Scottish female candidate in the 1918 election. Standing as an Independent in Bridgeton, Glasgow, she polled 900 votes. The Pankhursts' Women's Party folded after 1922, and the first woman MP in Scotland was the anti-suffrage Marchioness of Tullibardine, who took over her husband's seat for the Conservatives in 1923. Catriona Burness's article in the *Out of Bounds* collection: 'Scottish Women MPs 1918–45', describes the initial enthusiasm within all parties for recruiting women voters, but their ambivalence in encouraging equality of opportunity, and their unwillingness to adopt policy suggestions from their female members into manifestos.[202]

In the previous chapter I described the churches' internal response to the new demands and circumstances of women. During the same period, presbyterian ministers assumed a prominent role as spokesmen for the patriarchal family in other areas of life. By the 20th century, the teaching profession had come to be regarded as that for which academically able girls of aspiring working-class and middle-class origins were eminently and naturally suited, and thousands had taken up teaching posts. But their usefulness in the post-1872 era of State-provided school education did not negate the public attitude that marriage, home and family were the essential business of life for women, overriding all other activities. In 1915, a Church of Scotland minister on Glasgow School Board requested details of married female teachers, and proposed that a 'resign on marriage' clause be included in each contract from September 1915. He also managed to persuade the Board to introduce a means test on married women already employed, whereby those whose husbands could not support them, through ill-health or desertion, were employed only on temporary contracts. Dundee followed suit, but within seven months the Scottish Education Department urged the re-employment of married women for the duration of the war.

However, the attack on employed married women resumed with a vengeance after the war. In general, women were exhorted to return to the home and give jobs back to men, and childcare facilities were removed. The church used every opportunity to promote an exalted view of marriage and motherhood as the true vocation of women – especially for those of certain classes. The predominant presbyterian church attitude is well expressed in the Report of the Church of Scotland's Commission on the War, entitled *Social Evils and Problems* (1919). It reaffirmed the traditional understanding of the family, and warned of 'a company of sinister forces' which were attempting to 'weaken or destroy the all-important institution of the home'. In the chapter entitled 'Decline of Discipline', Rev W S Bruce cited the growth of the democratic spirit, socialism and higher criticism as causes of the perceived decline, and was nostalgic for that pre-feminist era when the man ruled supreme:

> Even fifty years ago one remembers but few families where the father did not govern with authority . . . The War has sucked into its vortex many husbands and fathers, and has deprived homes of their proper guardians . . . It is difficult to explain the recent increases in juvenile delinquency and hooliganism, and alleged drinking of wives and young women, apart from the patent absence of the head of the house.[203]

Rev Norman MacLean expressed concern about the falling birthrate in Scotland:

> It is the elements in the race that are the best and healthiest which are ceasing to multiply, while the unfit hand down in proportionately far greater degree, an heredity morally and physically diseased. The future of the race, forecasted in the light of these facts, is ominous.[204]

This article presents some statistics of baptisms in working-class, lower middle-class, and 'the best residential' congregations:

> For the Church these statistics are startling. They show that the congregations on whom the work of the Church largely depends for financial support are destined to steadily diminish. Diminishing baptisms means diminishing Sunday schools and fewer Catechumens and slowly emptying pews. The materials out of which the Church was built and by which it maintained itself are in many places crumbling away. The Church is faced with no grimmer fact than that of the rapidly decreasing birthrate.[205]

These comments hint at the extent to which the eugenics movement was infiltrating public attitudes, with its 'scientific' claims of the links between inherited inferiority and moral degeneracy. Women who belonged to the 'superior' classes were castigated for their selfishness if they wanted to enjoy the benefits of paid employment and birth control.

Maclean's suggested remedies for this 'disease of the soul' are predictable: that the Church should teach the sacredness of marriage and the sanctity of the family. Other articles in the Report berate the intellectual development of girls, when they should be trained 'for their predestined sphere as wives and mothers'.[206]

The post-war atmosphere was full of this kind of talk: of duty to the home, to the country, to the Empire, and above all to God and the church. Churchwomen who spoke with hope about their citizenship were at the same time under intense pressure (especially if they belonged to the 'superior' classes) to give precedence to their womanly duties to replenish the religious and racial stock, over self-centred greed and ambition. In this context, ministers on School Boards across Scotland, from 1922, lobbied successfully for the introduction of a marriage bar on teachers.[207]

The return of women to the domestic sphere was a crucial element in the conservatism of Church and society in the post-war years. Of course for some women there was no going back to a mythical past, and they enjoyed a significantly extended public life. But although the WFL and new Women's Citizens' Associations continued to campaign on issues of concern, their agenda was largely set by the old assumptions about female duties and responsibilities. They concentrated on seeking amelioration of the appalling conditions under which so many women performed their domestic responsibilities, and focused especially on child welfare. Seeking 'such reforms as are necessary to secure a real equality of liberties, status and opportunities'[208] receded in the face of the pressing needs of so many women. With enfranchisement, the focus and impetus of the Women's Movement was dissipated. Hopes of a Golden Age did not last long, under the weight of male protectionism, conservatism, and class divisions. After the 'War to end all wars', feminism was rapidly and roundly condemned as being petty and divisive in the face of a national crisis which was to be dealt with by devotion to old certainties and duties. After 1918, despite their 'special mission', women wanted and used their vote for different things, and those who really believed in change found that in any case it was a desperately inadequate weapon for tackling the immense social, economic and health difficulties of the time. It is likely that there were substantial numbers of churchwomen who had their consciousness raised and their consciences challenged through involvement in political and social issues. They channelled their post-war energy increasingly into specific social agencies which were, on the whole, overtly neither religious nor political, and so the collective power of their experience was not widely shared or exercised within traditional church, political or feminist institutions.

However, enfranchisement was a necessary, if not sufficient condition for liberation, and the movement was right to make it a priority. If there was a subsequent fragmentation of solidarity and loss of feminist consciousness, perhaps it should be understood, not so much as a failure of female imagination or engagement, but as a reflection of the adaptable tenacity of institutional male supremacy.

Conclusion

By 1930, the world inhabited by Scottish women was considerably different from that of their foremothers in 1830. Many more had received education and were able to pursue careers – or at least to find employment outside the home. It was possible for them to graduate from universities, and at least some of the ancient professions were open to women. There were no legal restrictions on their participation in the political arena, at local or national levels. They had more substantial property and family rights, and no doubt for many, the quality of personal and domestic life had improved because of national changes in drinking habits, and awareness of birth control. However, the benefits of these changes were not spread equally among the female population of the country. In practice, it was the women of the ruling upper and middle classes whose life choices differed most significantly from those of their grandmothers. The lives of Frances Stoddard Murray and her daughters illustrate the expanding possibilities. Frances, born in 1843, was the daughter of a Glasgow businessman, and married a lawyer. She had been educated at home and 'finished' at a ladies boarding school. As an intelligent and restless young woman, she found it difficult to accept an aimless life in her parents' home. She got involved in church and community activities, but above all she made every effort to develop her mental and physical faculties. Frances was enthusiastic and robust in outdoor pursuits, including climbing and sailing. In 1877 she attended lectures organised by the Glasgow Association for the Higher Education of Women – English Literature, Astronomy and Maths. She was a friend of Janet Galloway, and supported the establishment of Queen Margaret College. Her three daughters attended St Leonard's School for Girls; one went to Girton College. They were all involved in the struggle for women's rights: especially Eunice Murray of the Women's Freedom League. For Frances, the latent potential she had striven to develop in herself sprang to life in her daughters, for whom she was able to purchase and nurture the best available opportunities.[209]

For others, the struggle for survival continued to be the main determining factor in their experience of life. In 1917, Mary Coull, the daughter of a Peterhead fisherman and a domestic servant, left school:

> When I was fourteen I had qualifications for the Academy, but they had 21 shillings to pay for books, and couldn't afford it. But I got a merit certificate and 'Very Good' in every subject – that would have taken me into a good job. When I left school I worked in the house . . . I was a servant. I was disappointed. I would have liked to go to school for more, just general learning. What I got was 'Hing in noo Mary, grow up a big quinie and be a servant to your mother', so that was my ambition . . . There was always plenty to do at home, because we were learning to be housewives.[210]

For Mary, the change which had most affected her was enforced attendance at elementary school. She had glimpsed what might have been possible, but the realities of class and gender denied her the right to individual achievement and independence. Her life choices, in spite of a century of campaigns, were as limited as her mother's.

The new opportunities were largely won as a result of struggles which women had engaged in with hope, perseverance and fortitude. In the process, a Women's Movement emerged and developed, which inspired confidence and self-awareness, and demonstrated the pleasure and value of collective action. One of the strengths of the Movement was that it encouraged and enabled so many women to assess and assert their identity as autonomous human beings whose economic, social and spiritual existence did not depend wholly upon their relationship with men. I referred at the beginning of this chapter to Richard Evans' statement that Protestantism was almost a necessary precondition for the emergence of 19th-century feminism. In the Scottish context it is possible to identify several factors which contributed to both the strengths and the limitations of the Movement. The theological belief that each individual was directly accountable to God for his or her actions and salvation encouraged a general attitude of seriousness and responsibility. The importance of literacy and intellectual formation, though far from being desired or fulfilled by all Scotswomen, at least set the tone for the aspiration, effort and achievement of significant numbers of women throughout the period in question. The presbyterian churches were historically committed to their general foundational principle of 'reformed and always reforming': so the desirability of major change in the past, and the possibility of continuing change in the present and future was theoretically respectable. This was a significantly different religious, intellectual and cultural ethos from that of the Roman Catholic tradition. The turbulent and schismatic history of the reformed church in Scotland must surely have affected, consciously or otherwise, the attitude of those whose enthusiasm for the church was matched by their passion for change in the situation of women. And in spite of the inadequacies of institutional presbyterianism, it offered an organisational model which was unlike the blatantly conservative and hierarchical ecclesiology of Catholicism or Anglicanism. A number of female activists certainly made reference to the more democratic heritage of the Scottish church in their appeals for equal rights. Although they had virtually no access to positions within church courts, the church women's organisations did give a measure of equivalent practical and business experience to many. Those whose self-definition was strongly flavoured by their protestantism were inclined to attack the Roman Catholic Church for its 'degrading conception of women', which was unfavourably compared with their elevated status within protestant churches.[211] There were Scotswomen (especially in those religious orders which played a prominent role in the development of a distinctively Catholic education system) who demonstrated that it was possible for practising Catholic women to engage actively with issues and concerns beyond the strictly domestic. But the papacy of the era extolled, as part of a general conservatism, female saints, roles and images which exemplified the traditional feminine virtues of submission, purity and maternity. Catholic women who rejected these were more likely to come from an immigrant urban working-class milieu, where the beleaguered Catholic community struggled to maintain its social cohesion and identity, and tended to do so by exhorting strict adherence to the tenets of the faith. Questioning and radical women often chose (or were impelled) to break entirely with the Church, which remained committed as a matter of dogma to the theological tradition, rooted in Aristotle and refined by Aquinas, of congenital female inferiority.

The factors which gave a Scottish flavour to the Women's Movement interplayed with the widespread evangelical notion, so characteristic of the English-speaking protestant countries, that women had a special mission. In North America, the Antipodes, and throughout the United Kingdom, this encouraged an outward focus, a solidarity and a willingness to take organised action. It also helped foster a belief in the desirability as well as the possibility of change – even of perfectibility. This was especially true for those who experienced the contradictions between spiritual equality and female submission most acutely. It would not do to overestimate the extent of this response; for many presbyterian women (and for all sorts of reasons) the physical and emotional space of domesticity was completely absorbing, if not as satisfying as it was made out to be. So Protestantism in itself is not a sufficient explanation of the emergence of a feminist consciousness and movement. Anderson and Zinsser write, in their history of European women:

> Protestantism, while no more favourable to women in its ideology or institutions, created an atmosphere more conducive to feminism . . . [But] in every Protestant nation . . . feminist claims met with massive opposition, and women had to organise themselves to fight for their rights.[212]

The distinctive features of Protestantism also help to explain the extent to which the 'rebellion of women against the ordinances of society' was circumscribed. For the matrix of religious, social and economic factors which encouraged the development of the 'female sphere' also gave rise to a class-ridden capitalist society in which the basic division between women of different classes was between those whose men were able (by virtue of wealth and status) to secure their essentially domestic and moral role, and those who had to sell their services in the economic marketplace. A feminism rooted in evangelical essentialism and liberal humanism was inadequate to the task of constructing realistic cross-class alliances and demands. There were some women whose vision of transformation was rooted in an appreciation of the huge inequalities of experience and opportunity between women of different circumstances, as well as between women and men. But the Movement in general was constrained by an ideology which was inextricably tied up with the cultural and economic *status quo*, and it had inadequate resources to comprehend or withstand the class conflict and conservative reaction of post-war Britain. By seeking to domesticate the public sphere, or to enter the political realm as isolated and autonomous beings, the reformist Women's Movement left the pervasive patriarchal structures of home, church and state largely unchallenged.

Notes

1. H Taylor, 'The Enfranchisement of Women' in *Westminster Quarterly Review* (1851)

2. P Levine, *Victorian Feminism 1850–1900* (1987) 14

3. T Billington-Greig, *The Militant Suffrage Movement* (1911) see *The Non-Violent Militant: Selected Writings of Teresa Billington-Greig* eds C McPhee and A FitzGerald (1987) 137

4. Recent works include R K Marshall, *Virgins and Viragos* (1983); *Out of Bounds: Women in Scottish Society 1800–1945* eds E Breitenbach and E

Gordon (1992); L Leneman *A Guid Cause* (1991); E King *The Hidden History of Glasagow's Women: Thenew Factor* (1993); L Moore, *Semolinas and Bajinellas* (1991)

5. R Evans, *The Feminists* (1979) 237

6. Rev D Butler, speech made at a meeting of the Scottish Churches League for Woman Suffrage, March 12 1913

7. E Murray, *Frances Stoddard Murray* (1920) 76

8. ibid 79

9. ibid 263

10. E Gordon and E Breitenbach, (eds) *The World is Ill-Divided* (1990) 6

11. For example, Mrs Bream Pearce who belonged to the Christian Socialist League in Glasgow and was a prominent member of the WSPU. Elspeth King claims that she was 'Lily Bell' who wrote regularly for *Forward*, and developed a distinctive socialist-feminist perspective See *The Hidden History of Glasgow's Women* (1993) 94–98. Also Helen Lintell 'Lily Bell' MA Thesis, Bristol Polytechnic 1990

12. C Duncan Rice, *The Scots Abolitionists 1833–61* 34

13. Quoted in L and R Billington, 'A Burning Zeal for Righteousness: Women in the British Anti-Slavery Movement' in J Rendall (ed), *Equal or DiVerent: Women's Politics 1800–1914* (1985) 85

14. ibid

15. see C Taylor, *British and American Abolitionists: An Episode in Transatlantic Understanding* (1974) 110

16. ibid 104

17. ibid 110

18. Billingtons op cit 97

19. Taylor, op cit 157. Webb described Glasgow as being under 'a thick cloud of bigotry'

20. ibid 231

21. Taylor, op cit 217

22. ibid 245

23. ibid 261

24. ibid 298–9

25. ibid 320

26. ibid 342–44

27. ibid 344

28. ibid 347–8

29. quoted in H Renton, *Memoir of Mrs Agnes Renton* (nd) 90

30. ibid 127–8

31. quoted in Rice op cit 160

32. ibid 160–1

33. In the 1850s, most anti-slavery societies moved away from direct involvement in campaigns to end the institution, in favour of amelioratory activities, such as the New York Vigilance Committee, which organised emigration for escaped slaves in the North who, under the Fugitive Slave Act (1850), were liable to be hunted down and sent back South

34. Taylor op cit 312

35. See B Taylor, *Eve and the New Jerusalem* (1983) 275f

36. W Collins, *Parliamentary Papers* (1834) VIII 402

37. See T C Smout, *A Century of the Scottish People 1830–1950* (1986) 133ff

38. See C Brown *The Social History of Religion in Scotland since 1730* (1987) 203–207

39. Woman's Guild Supplement of *Life and Work* (1907) 86

40. *Acts of the General Assembly of the Free Church* (1858–63) 182

41. W Reid, *Woman's Work for Women's Weal* (1860) 4

42. ibid 5

43. ibid

44. Acts and Proceedings of the General Assembly of the Free Church (1877) 229

45. see *Juteopolis* esp chap 1

46. C Benn, *Keir Hardie* (1992) 12

47. Mrs H MacRae, *Alice Maxwell, Deaconess* (1917) 115

48. See N Denny, 'Temperance and the Scottish Churches' in *Scottish Church History Society Records* (1989) 217ff

49. See Stephenson and Brown, 'Sprouting Wings' in *Out of Bounds* op cit 95ff; W H Fraser, 'Developments in Leisure' in *People and Society in Scotland Vol II* eds W H Fraser and R J Morris (1990) 242–243

50. W Reid op cit 22–23

51. ibid 34

52. Reports of the Schemes of the Church of Scotland (1883) 538

53. J Gibson, *Not Weary in Well-Doing* (1888) 140. See 130–142 for details of the Manse Ladies Abstinence Society

54. Reports of the United Free Church of Scotland (1903)

55. Woman's Guild Supplement (1903) 9

56. *Life and Work* (1930) 210

57. Woman's Guild Supplement (1907) 86

58. Woman's Guild Supplement (1920) 31

59. Reports of the Schemes of the Church of Scotland (1921) 301

60. See minutes of the Women's Association for Temperance (1928–32) held in the Scottish Records Office

61. E King, *Scotland Sober and Free* (1979) 16

62. T Honeyman, *Good Templary in Scotland 1869–1929* (1929) 45

63. ibid 32

64. C Benn op cit 13

65. *The British Women's Temperance Association – Scottish Christian Union: Its Origins and Progress 1878–1908* (1908) 28

66. ibid 26

67. Brown and Stephenson op cit 105

68. H Crawfurd, unpublished autobiography, 29–30

69. C Benn op cit 14

70. See W H Fraser, op cit; C Harvie and G Walker, 'Community andCulture' in *People and Society in Scotland Vol II* 336ff;

71. B L Epstein, *The Politics of Domesticity: Women, Evangelicalism and Temperance in 19th century America* (1981) 146

72. See eg *Social Evils and Problems* (1919) Ch II, 'Intemperance', in which Rev R Menzies Fergusson wrote: 'Drunkenness has been a blot upon the fair name of our country, and, as will be seen, the noxious habit . . . has filled our prisons, poorhoouses and asylums . . . The poverty and squalor which meet the eye in slums . . . in provincial towns and country villages, are mostly traceable to drink' 49

73. Brown and Stephenson, op cit 114

74. ibid 116

75. W Reid op cit 37

76. L Moore, 'Educating for the Woman's Sphere' in *Out of Bounds* 32

77. F Balfour, *Ne Obliviscaris;: Memoir* (1930) Vol II 120

78. quoted in T C Smout, *A History of the Scottish People* (1972) 422

79. *First Book of Discipline* (1560)

80. T.C. Smout, *A History of the Scottish People* (1972) 423

81. S.S. Laurie, Report on education in the parochial schools of the counties of Aberdeen, Banff and Moray addressed to trustees of the Dick Bequest (1865)

82. see J Caird, *Fundamental Ideas of Christianity* (1899) introductory memoir by Edward Caird xxv–xxvi

83. Reports of the Schemes of the Church of Scotland (1860) Education Report 13–16

84. Reports of the Free Church of Scotland (1860) XXII 13–14

85. Reports of the Schemes of the Church of Scotland (1866)

86. see M Cruikshank, *History of the Training of Teachers in Scotland* (1970) 69

87. Acts and Proceedings of the Free Church of Scotland (1849) 259

88. Dick Bequest Report (op cit) 187

89. See H Corr 'The schoolgirls' curriculum and the ideology of the home 1870–1914' in Glasgow Women's Studies Group (ed) *Uncharted Lives: Extracts from Scottish Women's Experiences 1850–1982* (1983); H Corr, 'An exploration into Scottish Education', in Fraser and Morris op cit 290–309

90. The Argyll Commission, Quoted in R D Anderson, *Education and Opportunity in Victorian Scotland* (1983) 136

91. Bean and E van Heyningen, *The Letters of J E Waterston 1866–1905* (1983) 176

92. R Grant, *History of Burgh Schools* (1945) 530

93. *Home and Foreign Missionary Record* (1862) 181–2

94. Esdaile School 1863–1963 (centenary pamphlet)

95. *The Attempt* (1871) 27

96. *Ladies Edinburgh Magazine* (1875) 209

97. *Ladies Edinburgh Magazine* (1877) 347–8

98. Letter from Auchindoir Manse, 1875 in response to ELEA seeking entrants to the local exam. (In archive of the Edinburgh Ladies Educational Association, Edinburgh University Library)

99. *The Clarion* February 14 1913, quoted in D Spender, *There's always been a Women's Movement this Century* (1983) 52

100. There are fictional accounts of rural working class girls' attempts to secure higher education for teaching, and obstructions, in Nan Shepherd's *The Quarry Wood* (1928) and Lewis Grassic Gibbons' *Sunset Song* (1932)

101. S.S. Laurie, Report to the Merchant Company of Edinburgh (1868) quoted in E Towill, 'Merchant Maidens' in *Book of the Old Edinburgh Club Vol XXIX* (1956)

102. F Melville, 'The Education of Woman' in *The Position of Woman, Actual and Ideal* (1911) 132–3

103. *Ladies Edinburgh Magazine* (1879) 513

104. quoted in K Burton, *Memoir of Mrs Crudelius* (1877) 57–8

105. ibid 33–4

106. ibid passim: see comments made by lecturers in the Annual Reports of the ELEA

107. For information about developments in Glasgow, see *Janet Galloway: A Book of Memories* (1914); S Hamilton Women and the Scottish Universities c1869–1939 (PhD thesis, Edinburgh University 1987); G Mackie, *University of Glasgow 1451–1951* (1951) 303–4

108. C. Struthers, *The Higher Education of Women* (1883) 16

109. L. Moore, *Bajanellas and Semilinas: Aberdeen University and the Education of Women 1860–1920* (1991) 10

110. Struthers op cit 8

111. ibid 6

112. See J Manton, *Elizabeth Garrett Anderson* (1965)

113. See M Todd *Life of Sophia Jex Blake* (1918)

114. *The Attempt* (1867) 270

115. *The Attempt* (1871) 5

116. ibid

117. Burton op cit 100

118. ibid see eg 106

119. For concern about the desexing and unbelief of educated women, see Moore op cit 23–29.

120. See J Burstyn, *Victorian Education and the Ideal of Womanhood* (1980) 99ff

121. quoted in Todd op cit 360–1

122. E Caird op cit cviii

123. see Todd op cit 300. This also mentions Elizabeth Pease-Nichol, the anti-slavery campaigner, as a representative of the 'old type of Victorian womanhood', courageously arguing on behalf of female students for entry into the Royal Infirmary. A list of Edinburgh women who supported the medical cause includes many of older and younger generations who were involved in all the campaigns referred to here, and also in church work.

124. ibid 491

125. ibid 457

126. see W. Alexander, *First Ladies of Medicine: The Origins, Education and Destiny of Early Women Graduates of Glasgow University* (1987)

127. Bean and van Heyningen op cit 283

128. L Lumsden *The Higher Education of Women in Britain and Ireland* (pamphlet, nd, c1883)

129. see W Boog-Watson, 'The First Eight Ladies', in *Edinburgh University Journal* vol 23 (1967–8) 227–34 S Hamilton, op cit

130. W Knight, Circular written to solicite funds for the proposed University Hall of Residence (in 'University Hall Scrapbook', St Andrews University Library). The Residence actually attracted English women, rather than those for whom it was intended. Scots found it too expensive and snooty.

131. Moore op cit see Ch 9, 120–131 for statistics

132. The Minute Books of the EUWDS are held in Edinburgh University Library. Some of the topics debated were: Dress Reform, Are Strikes Justifiable? The Theological Novel, Should Missionaries be Celibate? Female Suffrage, Vivisection, Should Questions of the Day be discussed in the Pulpit?

133. Bean and van Heyningen, op cit 281

134. F Balfour, *Dr Elsie Inglis* (1918) 53–4

135. *Ladies Edinburgh Magazine* (1877) 63

136. Class lists are included in the ELEA archive, EUL

137. *Ladies Edinburgh Magazine* (1877) 92–3

138. ibid 94

139. Senatus minutes, Edinburgh University Faculty of Divinity (1898) NCL

140. *Union Seminary Quarterly Review* Vol XXXV (1979–80) 62

141. ibid 142 Struthers op cit 7

143. Melville op cit 124

144. This idea was persistent, even among those who were seeking equality of educational opportunity. Christina Struthers wrote, 'It seems that parents who dread exposing their sons to the dangers likely to arise from female incursions into universities, are strangely blind to the facts of life . . . when instead of sending the lad to dingy and comfortless lodgings, he might go accompanied by his sister who would share studies and, at the same time, promote his comfort, and save him from risk and sore temptation'.

145. B Welsh *After the Dawn* (1939) 26–7

146. Burton op cit 104–5

147. *Northern Star*, June 23 1838 quoted in J Schwarzkopf, *Women and the Chartist Movement* (1991) 40

148. L Leneman, 'The Scottish Churches and Votes for Women' in *Scottish Church History Society Records* Vol XXIV (1991) 237ff

149. B Taylor, op cit 275ff

150. M Reid *A Plea for Woman* (1843) reprinted 1988

151. *Westminister Quarterly Review* (1851)

152. See L Milne-Rae *Ladies in Debate* (1935) and minutes of the Edinburgh Ladies Debating Society in EUL

153. B Mackie, *The Life and Work of Duncan MacLaren* (1888) 102–3

154. Speech delivered in Edinburgh Music Hall, January 12 1871

155. See L Leneman, *A Guid Cause* Ch 1 11–31

156. *United Presbyterian Magazine* (1884) 332

157. Free Church General Assembly Proceedings and Debates (1885) 56

158. see 'The Scottish Churches and Votes for Women' 237

159. *Ladies Edinburgh Magazine* (1880) 109

160. *Ne Obliviscaris* . . . 114

161. McPhee and FitzGerald, op cit 149

162. *A Guid Cause* 69

163. *Glasgow Herald* July 17 1913

164. *Dundee Advertiser* December 18 1912

165. Crawfurd op cit 89

166. see *A Guid Cause* 159

167. *Glasgow Herald* March 25 1913

168. Material relating to the Scottish Churches League for Woman Suffrage is included in a scrapbook entitled 'Votes for Women' (NLS)

169. For instance, the Woman's Guild Supplement, 1908, carried a report of a Summer School of Mission Study: 'Each delegate received a label on which she wrote her name. Our labels . . . were rather puzzling to some of the dwellers at Bridge of Allan, one of whom was heard confiding to his friend that he thought we must be Suffragists! I do not think we took this as a compliment.' (L&W WG Supp 1908) 122

170. see *A Guid Cause* 100

171. G M Reith *Reminiscences of the United Free Church General Assembly* (1933) 152

172. Minutes of Church of Scotland Edinburgh Presbytery January 7 1914

173. *Dundee Advertiser* December 10 1913

174. see 'The Scottish Churches and Votes for Women' 243, 247–50

175. *The Appeal to God* (1913) WSPU pamphlet

176. eg Helen Fraser, during the 1907 Aberdeen by-election campaign, spoke at a crowded and noisy meeting to consider the ethical side of the Women's Movement, of 'the importance of women working for their own liberty, and of sexism in the teachings of the Church' *Aberdeen Free Press* February 18 1907

177. McPhee and Fitzgerald op cit 147

178. *Suffrage Annual and Women's Who's Who* (1913) 145

179. Speech given at meeting of Scottish Churches League for Woman Suffrage, March 12 1913

180. Holton, *Feminism and Democracy* 15

181. *United Free Church Record* (1918) 151

182. E Pethick Lawrence, *Women as Persons or Property* (1913) WSPU pamphlet

183. *Dr Elsie Inglis* 100 David Watson, leader of the social work movement within the Church of Scotland, adhered to this kind of view too. He wrote, 'One thing we may be sure of – that when she wins the franchise . . . her influence will always be cast on the side of religion and purity, temperance and peace . . . No one can doubt that she will play an important part in social regeneration, reconstruction, in bringing in the new day, the golden year. For love and pity are hers'. *Perfect Womanhood* (1905)

184. J Barzun, *Darwin, Marx, Wagner: Critique of a Heritage* (1958) 92

185. Olive Schreiner's *Women and Labour* (1911) was a highly influential feminist work written in the context of Social Darwinism. She was close to Herbert Spencer, and especially to Karl Pearson At the UFC Women's Missionary College Retreat in July 1915, 'Our meditation in Chapel focussed upon our calling as women. The crown of a woman's life is wifehood and motherhood, but that in the ordinary sense, especially in days of warfare, is denied to so many. Is what is left only a second best? Surely not. There must be a 'motherhood' open to all women, as full and rich a possession as that which is unattainable by the many . . . Miss Small reminded us of the call that comes to all . . . To be foster-mothers of the babes of Christ, upbuilder-mothers of His Church, and interior mothers, speaking from our own deep experience of the things of God.' (WMC House Guild Newsletter, 1916)

   see also E Pearson 'Spiritual Motherhood and Philanthropic Service' in *The Position of Woman Actual and Ideal*

186. McPhee and FitzGerald op cit 198

187. ibid 197

188. A S Matheson, *The Church and Social Problems* 287 (1893) see also D Watson, op cit

189. quoted in J Smyth, 'Rents, Peace, Votes' in *Out of Bounds* 188

190. Address given at meeting of Scottish Churches League for Woman Suffrage, March 12 1913

191. D Riley, 'Am I That Name?' (1988) 83

192. C Macmillan 'The Struggle for Political Liberty':address given to mark the opening of Parliament, 16 February 1909

193. S Moller Okin, *Women in Western Political Thought* (1979) 282

194. While in some respects the 16th century reformers held more positive views about women than those which had characterised Roman Catholicism, they offered no countenance to women seeking the right to public and political activity. Calvin himself was most interested in whatever would benefit the church, and believed in the freedom of the Holy Spirit to break through the 'normal' order of Creation. This, along with his affirmation of essential spiritual equality, was certainly a resource for those (in his own time and later) who longed for a more expansive religous or secular role. However, Calvin also argued that 'common sense dictates that the rule of women is defective and unseemly', and in a sermon on I Cor 11, he maintained that Paul's injunction to subordination referred to all women: 'I say this for the benefit of any unmarried man, lest he at any time abandon his privilege by nature, namely, that he is the head. Of whom? Of women, for we must not pay attention to this only within the household, but within the whole order that God has established in this world.' (quoted in D Howerda, ed, *Exploring the Heritage of John Knox* (1976). Calvin himself felt obliged to disavow some aspects of John Knox's notorious and vituperative *First Blast Against the Monstrous Regiment of Women* (1558). Even if we grant that the tract was written in the heat of trying circumstances for the community of English reformers, its tone and target is unequivocal. Knox piled up Biblical and patristic references to argue that Eve's malediction had made all women subject for all time. The place ordained by God for women was one of submission and service to men. Therefore the rule of women in any form was repugnant to the law of God, and without legitimacy or justice. Although women campaigners could (and did) argue for political enfranchisement and equality as something consistent with reformation principles, they could adduce no positive evidence from the founding fathers to counter these negative pronouncements. Their views were entirely supportive of patriarchy in home and state

195. McPhee and FitzGerald op cit 242

196. Forward, 6 December 1913

197. R West, *The Judge* (1922) 46–7

198. *Dr Elsie Inglis* 100

199. See *UFC Record* (1918) 112

200. ibid 87

201. *UFCGAPD* (1918) May 25

202. see C Burness, 'The Long, Slow March: Scottish Women MPs 1918–45', in *Out of Bounds* 151–73

203. Report of Church of Scotland Commission on the War: *Social Evils and Problems* (1919) 148

204. ibid 96

205. ibid 97

206. ibid 199

207. see C Adams, 'Teaching – a Celibate Profession: a Study of The Marriage Bar on Women Teaching in Scotland 1915–1945 (M Ed Thesis, Glasgow University 1987)

208. The third aim of the Edinburgh Women's Citizens' Association. See papers in Scottish Record Office

209. Murray, op cit 264

210. A Smith, Women Remember: *An Oral History* (1989) 131–2

211. see The Banner of the Covenant (organ of the Scottish Women's Protestant Union) November 1911 46–7

212. B Anderson and J P Zinsser, *A History of Their Own: Women in Europe from Prehistory to the Present Vol II* (1988) 255–6

6

Conclusion

> The farther away the Church gets from the ideal that in Christ there is neither
> male nor female, and that there is a glorious liberty granted to the children of
> God, the less living will its hold be on the Christianity of the world.[1]

Scottish women throughout the period 1830–1930 should not be
characterised simply as victims of, nor as absentees from, the complex
experiences and processes of change which constitute the nation's history.
They had the capacity to respond critically to their situation, and to change
it in various far-reaching and sometimes contradictory ways. The main
concern of this book has been to explore some of the ways in which
women exerted their moral agency, and to discuss evidence for this activity
in the context of the presbyterian institutions and ideologies which were
dominant cultural forces throughout the period. This concluding chapter
is a more personal assessment of the significance of presbyterianism as a
source of oppression or liberation in the lives of Scottish women.

In posing that question, and in those terms, my starting point is my own
experience as a Scottish woman in the presbyterian tradition; and my
political commitment to the freedom, equality and empowerment of
women in all aspects of human life. That is the interpretative key I have
used throughout the process of historical investigation. The language of
liberation is central to late 20th-century discourses and movements in
feminism and theology, and I admit to being a child of my time!

But it is right to ask whether such vocabulary is appropriate in assessing
the lives of women who, by and large, would not themselves have used its
terms to evaluate their experiences and aspirations, and therefore some
definition of terms is in order. As a way into this I shall consider briefly
two positions which seem to be quite clear about the effects of the
Christian religion on the lives of women, and on their position as agents
of history.

1. The related notions of 'True Womanhood' and separate spheres were
not immutable, natural truths, although they were typically described as
such, but were subject to considerable development and contestation.
However, most of their advocates would have agreed that Christianity –

and in particular western Anglo-Saxon Protestant Christianity – was responsible for the elevation and emancipation of 'Woman' from heathen degradation and brutality. This is the oft-repeated theme of most prescriptive writing about the appropriate roles and responsibilities of 'Woman'. Those few women who had the temerity to cast public doubt on the benefits of religion were condemned out of hand on both sides of the Atlantic, for they presaged

> the destruction of the domestic constitution, the prostration of all decency and order, the reign of wild anarchy and shameless vice.[2]

Writers like Rev Hubbard Winslow believed not only that in social terms their civilisation had reached its apotheosis in the recognition and elevation of women, but that, more importantly, the real issue was about eternal salvation. That was available to women, and people of every rank and station, who had faith and lived according to the precepts of the church. According to this position, the liberation of women was a function of their obedience, within a 'Christian civilisation' to the tenets of Christian religion, and this was the burden of 'women's work for women' in the foreign mission fields. If this was an unproblematic assertion, then it would be pointless for me to pose my own question about liberation. However, I hope that this study has demonstrated some of the inadequacies, as well as the merits of such an understanding, in discussing the situations and struggles of women within the domestic, ecclesiastical, educational and political structures of the times.

Writing in 1953, from a French Roman Catholic milieu, Simone de Beauvoir identified some dangers when religion creates the delusion of a liberation already attained:

> Woman is asked in the name of God not so much to accept her inferiority as to believe that, thanks to him, she is the equal of the lordly male: even the temptation to revolt is suppressed by the claim that justice is overcome. Woman is no longer denied transcendence, since she is to consecrate her immanence to God; the worth of souls is to be weighed only in heaven, and not according to their accomplishments on earth.[3]

As so many Scottish women discovered, equality and natural justice for their sex were equated with a socially subordinate and strictly circumscribed sphere, and their heavenly value, they were told, depended upon self-denial of wider personal ambition. Writing in the *Christian Journal* of 1853, one woman was happy to accept these limitations:

> When I hear females, as I sometimes do, deprecating the contractedness of domestic life, and eagerly panting after the employments and publicity of

philosophers, statesmen and legislators, I am led to think that my life, in the little sphere of my family, must be more varied than their's . . . If mere human applause [is sought], the female part would have but little opportunity to shine; and might justly complain of the narrowness of her sphere. But when it is considered that quality of actions is determined by God . . . how is the case altered? The woman, therefore, who complains of the obscurity of her condition, feels and talks like a heathen. She virtually professes to value the praise of men before the praise of God, and is likely, by impiety and folly, to forfeit both . . . The natural effect of public applause is to produce self-ignorance and deception, for the standard of morals is extremely low and defective in the world . . . O, that in humility of mind, I may ever prefer that condition which leads me to the most intimate knowledge of self, and rejoice to become nothing.[4]

However, we have encountered many other Scotswomen throughout the period 1830 – 1930 who (consciously or otherwise) could not assent to this paradoxical definition of self-realisation, and its apparent denial of constructive participation in the public historical process, in return for heavenly favour.

2. Mary Daly, a contemporary post-Christian feminist, believes that language, as interpretation and legitimisation, is central in the social construction of reality. She argues that the androcentric language system of the Christian tradition is not accidental, but has served to maintain and justify the patriarchal order. In so doing, it has erased women from history and consciousness. Daly believes that feminists must name and so create their own world. She is not interested in restoring women to history or in reconceptualising history as human. Women, she maintains, are non-beings in patriarchal culture and have been eradicated from its discourse. For Daly, only women who make an existential leap into a new 'sacred feminist space' can be historical subjects, for they

> consitute an ontological locus of history . . . in this very process women are the bearers of history.[5]

According to this position, the patriarchal Christian tradition is irredeemably oppressive, and women who live, or have lived, in this territory of 'non-being' are excluded from participation in history.

This definition of liberation implies that women must completely disown all expressions of patriarchal culture and history. It denies the experiences and struggles of women who, in spite of their absence from, or misrepresentation in the records, nevertheless were really present (and not just as victims) in that past. Elizabeth Fox-Genovese warns that feminists should not jettison all claims to the product and record of so many centuries of collective life. To the extent that men have spoken they have done so on the basis of the privileged access to history and rule, not on the basis of intrinsic personal and sexual merit. Their social representation and social institutions belong however to our collective past. The lords of creation do not exist independently of those they oppress.[6]

I repudiate both the uncritical and unqualified assertion that the Christian religion emancipated women, and also the argument that it has done nothing but turn them into non-beings with no history. Neither of these positions does justice to the paradoxical complexities of individual and collective experience. In order to undertake a fair assessment of the relationship between women and presbyterianism, a more expansive and grounded definition of liberation is required. The work of feminist theologians such as Letty Russell, Rosemary Radford Reuther and Elizabeth Schussler Fiorenza suggests several features which might be included in such a definition. Liberation includes the quest for independence, power and freedom: not understood solely in individualist but also socio-political and spiritual terms. It is rooted in the discernment of sin and oppression, which is understood as whatever denies, constrains, or destroys the space and potential to be fully human: created in the image of, and to be in relationship with, a loving God. There are two crucial elements in this – liberation is not just a goal, but a dynamic process which affirms the possibility of personal and social transformation; and that process, by demonstrating the exercise of agency, humanises those who struggle to transcend the givenness, the objectivity, the 'non-being' state of their existence.[7] William Storrar, who proposes a 'warm claes' liberation theology for the Scottish nation, describes the starting point for contextual theologies of liberation as being 'the oppression of the non-person whom Christ liberates into history and humanity', and includes women amongst those who have been relegated to the status of non-personhood by the historical models of church and state.[8] This is not the place to develop a Scottish feminist theology of liberation, but rather to describe a theological approach which helps me to interpret the historical material I have encountered. This understanding of liberation is neither all-inclusive nor complete. It certainly should not be applied dogmatically to pass inappropriate judgement on the lifestyles, beliefs and choices of women in Scotland's past. But it offers a framework for a critical analysis of Scottish presbyterianism in its function as the established religion of the dominant social order; and for consideration of resources within their religious tradition which were usable by, and supportive of, women seeking autonomy and justice. It will also help to explain why social class was a key (though never absolute) factor in determining the extent to which liberty and self-assertion would be possible for individuals and groups.

In each of the preceding chapters I have argued that institurional presbyterianism performed a crucial ideological and practical function in the development of a patriarchal system of rule in family and state. As Scottish Calvinism accommodated the evangelical revival, it (in common with other parts of the English-speaking world) became increasingly enthusiastic about 'woman's mission'. This encouraged expanding opportunities for female service, but the church felt threatened by requests for real responsibility and status. Although the presbyterian ethos was concerned to promote literacy, the fundamental religious reason for such female education as was provided was so that girls and women might read and obey scriptures which seemed to confirm their subordinate status in creation, and their culpability for human sinfulness. The main purpose of learning was not to develop independent thought and action: many individual parents, teachers and ministers did value and promote such benefits, and some of the girls and women encountered in these pages found their education (or even frustration at its inadequacies) a source of pleasure, challenge and liberation. But for many more, especially from working-class backgrounds, the effect was to cramp and confine both potential and expectations. The presbyterian denominations (notwith-standing some committed individuals) did not lead, and rarely supported, campaigns for women's rights. They were powerful protagonists of a religious and domestic ideology which, throughout the period, presented the suppression of personal ambition and growth, in favour of service to husband, family, church and God, as the approved Christian state of existence for women.

However, these chapters have mainly been concerned with presbyterianism in its socio-cultural role, as creating, adapting or resisting the conditions within which Scottish women had to act. As such it was not uniformly or simply an instrument of domination and reaction, but provided some fertile ground for seeds of change – personal, spiritual, social and political – to take root. Much has been said in passing about the scriptural, doctrinal and structural elements which, in symbiotic and ever-changing relationship with the socio-political context, give presbyterianism its identity. Now I want to look at these elements more systematically, to aid a fuller understanding of presbyterianism's potential as liability and resource for women seeking humanisation. In reality it is not always possible to separate the negative and positive manifestations of the ethos, but for the sake of clarity I shall consider first those features which have tended to act in an oppressive way, and then those which have affirmed and enabled the liberation of women.

'Denied the Capacity to Become': Oppressive Establishment Church and Theology

> During the Christian ages, the church has not alone shown cruelty and contempt for woman, but it has exhibited an impious and insolent disregard of her most common rights of humanity. It has robbed her of her responsibility, putting man in place of God. It has forbidden her the offices of the church . . . It has denied her independent thought, declaring her a secondary creation for man's use . . . It has anathematized her sex, teaching her to feel shame for the very fact of her being.[9]

Between 1830–1930, and despite schism, reunification and the social reform movement of c1880–1920, Scottish presbyterianism functioned as the national established religion: the sacred ideology of the dominant social order. It was not a sect or community on the margins of Scottish life, but a belief system (embodied in several distinct institutions) which either had a privileged situation and relationship with the political state, as the legally established church (Church of Scotland); or made claim to such a relationship (Free Church of Scotland, UF Church); or maintained a voluntary position, but was still closely related to the Scottish political world (United Presbyterian Church). The self-conscious perception of the institutional church (in its different and changing guises) was as a central player in the national ethos and destiny. William Storrar has written that

> The establishment theology of Scottish nationhood was grounded in the dominant reformation model of Church and Nation, when the former was a power in the land. It was static, institutional, exclusive.[10]

The paradigm of domination which shaped Scottish presbyterianism at local level, derived from Calvinist theology, also influenced the whole structure and culture of Scottish religous life. It affected people at the deepest emotional and psychological levels, as well as in social terms. What were the elements of this paradigm?

First, there was the patriarchal-monarchical model of God. The Reformers insisted on the absolute sovereignty of God as a monarch ruling over his kingdom and demanding total obedience and submission of will. As supreme ruler, this God legitimised other hierarchical forms of power as expressions of divine intent for the life of the world. The response evoked by this God was primarily a sense of awe, reverence, fear and humiliation.

Since he had total control over the eternal destiny of human beings, it was appropriate to feel abject dependence. It has been suggested that the Scottish adoption of ultra-orthodox federal Calvinism, with its doctrine of double pre-destination, elicited a particular lack of assurance of worth and salvation. For God was loving only towards the arbitrarily chosen elect, but not essentially in his Being.[11] The harsh twin doctrines of natural human depravity, and accountability for sinfulness, meant that many devout people simultaneously felt unable truly to change, and yet held themselves responsible for their failure. The resulting acute anxiety remained a distinctive feature in the religious experience of many Scots, even after 19th-century evangelical arminianism challenged its doctrinal supremacy. Eliza Fletcher was a Glasgow woman, apparently converted during the 1859 revival (though she rarely felt secure about the veracity of this) who was noted in the 1870s and 1880s for her inspirational Bible classes and talks for working people. In many ways she was characteristic of the style of active female evangelicalism encouraged by the idea of 'woman's mission' – a person of

> masculine intellect, yet with all a woman's tenderness and keen sensibility. We remember well her ready wit, her unselfish generosity, her courageous spirit.[12]

But she was plagued throughout her life with a desperate, even self-indulgent anxiety about the state of her soul:

> Is it a sign that God does not wish me to be saved? Am I condemned already; am I never, never to be truly saved?[13]

She attributed her overwhelming conviction that she was reprobate to the doctrine of election, and especially to a sermon she had heard in early childhood. In 1875 she wrote:

> I have never, never felt his love . . . I feel as if He was my enemy; and yet oh! I know He is so worthy of love and trust . . . It's here that dark, and stern and awful election comes in, and from my earliest childhood I've kicked at the doctrine of election. But I don't want to. I want to get to Him, but only He can bring me; and if I can't go, isn't it because I'm not divinely drawn? . . . I'm very, very vile.[14]

And in the final year of her life the sense of foreboding was tangible:

> Another thing which has been greatly overpowering me, and is still, is the almost constant and awful realising of eternity . . . I seem to be held over the edge of the world to come, and made to see its awfulness. This clouds one, and causes a sadness and depression which I cannot describe.[15]

In Eliza Fletcher's life there is something of the tension logically inherent in a theology unable to guarantee the salvation for which so many heroically strived. Her experience suggests that Calvinist doctrines held powerful sway despite the growing attractions of a simple evangelicalism which Eliza herself preached.

Mary Ann Rogerson's diary, kept from 1853–58 (when she was aged 20–25), is an example of the introspective examination encouraged by Calvinist faith. She was a farmer's daughter and wife whose own children included several ministers, and she meditated on Sabbath evenings on the sermons she had heard, and upon the condition of her soul. Her reflections too are riddled with expressions of unworthiness, guilt and shame, and with constant allusions to the 'dangers and snares' of everyday life:

> Oh poor sinful worm of the dust as I am, still I would seek to cast myself upon thy care for the future . . . My life is fast passing away and I am nearing a dark futurity . . . Oh how much reason I have to fear I am not in Jesus a new creature.[16]

Like Eliza, Mary Ann's emotional state seemed to lurch between long periods of anxiety and self-distrust, and less frequent 'seasons of peaceful calm'. Both refer often to the need of complete and passive submission to God's will; but also to the awful obligation to show evidence of holiness in well-doing. But the inner debate continues to torment, with fears that worthy actions depend too much on their own strength, and are cause for wicked pride. A battle between free will and predestination seems to rage unresolved in their souls. If the voices of these women are representative of others, then the inner life and outward actions of many Scotswomen were shaped by a troubling, paradoxical faith which counselled self-doubt and denial, and yet required long hours of introspection, the strain of which could seriously impair physical and mental health. And the outward demonstration of evangelical fervour might be accompanied by powerful feelings of despondency and hostility to God.[17] This framework, with a focus on death and its aftermath frequently verging on the obsessional, must have been at least as debilitating as it was an impetus to action, for women who sought to be agents for God in the world.

Mary Slessor, as a young girl in Dundee, began to have nightmares after she visited an old widow who took her hand and held it near the fire:

> If you were to put your hand in there, it would be awful sore. But if you don't repent your soul will burn in blazing fires for ever and ever.[18]

Slessor often said that it was the fear of hell fire that drove her into the Kingdom. For every woman, like her, who was able to transform that fear into a creative and loving life, there must have been others paralysed – inwardly at least – by apprehension and confusion. The disquiet which arose out of efforts to conform to the precepts of Calvinist doctrine affected men and women alike. But women also had to contend with the injunctions regarding the appropriate modes of female behaviour, and to square the latter with the former. In Chapter 1, I quoted Neal Ascherson's comment about the Scottish tension between self-assertion and self-distrust. His evaluation is surely based largely upon male expectations and experience. For centuries, ministers preached against the besetting human sins of pride and self-assertion, and men battled with those while striving – as they were encouraged to – for worldly success. But for many women, who had been enjoined, socialised and often coerced to accept that they were weaker, dependent and subject always to the requirements of others, the problem was not so much pride but an excess of humility and self-negation. By its very nature, the extent and effects of this phenomenon are difficult to substantiate and evaluate, because women who doubted their own value, and found it difficult to perceive themselves as having an independent identity, were unlikely to be involved in exercises of self-promotion. However, there is, I believe, some evidence that women were psychologically inhibited and disempowered by the combination of religious doctrine and cultural convention. The great diffidence of so many Woman's Guild members, for example, in relation to assuming public or leadership roles; the letters of application from prospective missionaries who, paradoxically, seemed to think that self-deprecation and disclaimers as to their right or ability to preach the gospel (except as humble instruments of God, who might use them in spite of all their failings); the constant self-reproach against forwardness and ambition found in diaries and memoirs of women; the widespread assumption (from which men undoubtedly benefited) that women would sacrifice their own interests entirely in order to serve the needs of others. These perhaps suggest that the inner tension Ascherson identifies was even more acute for women striving for a sense of their own identity and worth, than for men who were encouraged to develop singularity, control, and other active qualities associated with Christian 'manliness'. Women who displayed such qualities to any significant degree were not only exposed to conventional accusations of aping masculinity, but also had to cope with spiritual wrestling against the temptations of self-assertion.

The image of an omnipotent, distant God, whose real kingdom is other-worldly, who has the power to exclude his creatures from it, and who uses whatever means are necessary to accomplish his divine will, was rarely described as oppressive. Rather, it was seen as the natural and scriptural understanding of the relationship between God and the world.[19] But it produced, not only enervating, self-destructive anxiety (and, on the opposite pole, relief which could readily issue in arrogant self-righteousness) but also the conviction that grief, sorrow and injustice in this world must ultimately, and sometimes against all the evidence of experience, be justified and accepted as the will of a righteous God. The writer Margaret Oliphant struggled painfully with this after the death of her young daughter:

> Where are you, oh my child, my child. I have tried to follow her in imagination, to think of her delight and surprise when from the fever, wandering and langour of her bed she came suddenly into the company of angels and the presence of the Lord. But then the child was but a child and death is but a natural event; it changed her surroundings, her capabilities, but it could not change the little living soul. Did she not stop short there and say, 'Where is Mamma?' did not the separation overwhelm her? This thought of very desolation. Did she not think of the sad horror, the heart that was breaking for her? God knows. All this is fanciful, perhaps wrong, but I cannot help it . . . She is with God, she is in His hands. I know nothing, cannot even imagine anything. Can I trust her with Him? Can I trust Him that He has done what was best for her, that He has her safe, that there has been no mistake, no error, but only His purpose in all, and that He is keeping her now in the position most happy for her, that even my own human judgement, when enlightened, will approve as the best? This is the question that He puts to me and keeps putting to me through all these weary nights and days. This is the faith He demands of me.[20]

The notion that 'God's purpose' must override any human challenge or sense of injustice, and is intrinsically good, was also used to maintain social and domestic hierarchies: to close off any discussion or subversion by subordinate groups. In 1850, the *Free Church Magazine* claimed:

> For the purpose of maintaining society in a state of peace and happiness, the creator has established a variety of relations among men, principal of which are − husband and wife, parent and child, master and servant, magistrate and people . . . these are characterised by a manifest inequality. The principle is that of physical inequalities with moral compensations, lest the greater measure of power belonging to one party should become an instrument of oppression and misery to the other.[21]

Just as slaves had been told in the American South, so servants and the poor of the Scottish working classes were exhorted to accept their lowly status and lack of material comfort as divinely ordained, to be rewarded in heaven. Church publications were full of condescending articles written by ministers and 'ladies', with advice for the poor. An 1886 'talk with working girls' counselled against envy of 'superiors' and concluded:

> Be glad, then, if you have hard work to do, for it gives you the chance to do it cheerfully and please Him. Be thankful, too, if you have a crowded home, that honest hands can make it comfortable, and a loving spirit can make it happy. Thank Him for every mercy, and never forget to thank Him for the gift of life, power and loving, and the hope of immortality.[22]

And a book entitled *The High Estate of Service* (1898), dedicated to the servant members of St George's Church in Edinburgh, extolled the virtues of their position:

> I doubt if in any book the duty of serving is so emphasised as in the New Testament . . . The Bible, with its insistence on universal brotherhood, yet knows nothing of the equality which some demand and which would reduce all to a dull, hopeless, lifeless uniformity . . . Christ will make us sufficient, not for the spheres we fancy and covet, but for those He places us in.[23]

It is evident that in spite of a marked change of attitude after 1880, when some presbyterians were much more aware of, and concerned about, social inequality, others were all the more determined to maintain the class hierarchy. It is hardly surprising that Christian Watt, who came from a fishing background in the north-east of Scotland, and spent much time in domestic service, but was never less than direct in expressing her opinions of the prevailing social order, should write in her remarkable recollections:

> The kirk had become an organisation to suppress the working class . . . If you had no profession you were of no consequence to the minister, save only to fill the kirk on Sundays.[24]

If upper- and middle-class women colluded with this static paradigm of authority in their relationships with the working classes, most were also willing to submit to the consequent doctrine of female status. The reformed affirmation of *sola scriptura* made it particularly difficult to challenge a subordinate existence which was apparently enshrined in the Word of God; for to do so was regarded as defiance of God Himself, and tantamount to heresy:

> I cannot help thinking that, though the possibilities of our nature may be as great as those of man's, yet as a consequence of the Fall, our place now is one of comparative lowliness . . . But if instead of vainly struggling against all that would remind us of our position, we quietly take the places assigned us by God, not man . . . perhaps we shall one day discover that our primeval sentence is as mercifully suited to the present needs of our nature as man's is to his.[25]

The radical assertion of Elizabeth Cady Stanton, in her introduction to *The Woman's Bible* (1895, 1898) that the Bible is not a 'neutral' book, but a political weapon used against women's struggles for liberation, was hinted at in the comment by Lady Frances Balfour, that

> the ecclesiastical mind has never shaken off its belief that [women] are under a special curse from the days of Eden, and that St Paul's outlook on women in his day was the last revelation as to their future position in a jealously guarded corporation.[26]

There is no shortage of circumstantial evidence that the accumulative socialising effect on so many Scotswomen, of the Genesis stories, the Levitical codes of the Old Testament, the Household Codes of the New Testament, and other scriptural material pronouncing the inferior status of women, was to encourage acceptance of social limitations and subordination to husbands as normative. When such ideas began to be challenged, religious people were ready to leap to their defence. As the editor of the Woman's Guild *Supplement* wrote in 1906:

> It is not easy nowadays to fulfil [our divinely appointed mission as helpmeet] when the spirit of unrest is all pervading, and we are far too ready to seek 'larger spheres' and 'greater opportunities' quite outside our own little niche.[27]

But some of the patients Elsie Inglis encountered in Glasgow were in no mind (or no position) to seek anything outside their 'own little niche' in the patriarchal household. She got very angry with husbands who came into the infirmary where she worked, and insisted their wives went home to look after their children, in spite of the women's considerable pain and illness, and their need to have operations:

> I wonder when married women will learn they have any other duty in the world than to obey their husbands . . . They will come in the day before the operation, after the woman has been screwed up to it, and worry them with all sorts of things, and want them home when they are half dying. Any idea that anybody is to be thought of but themselves never enters their lordly minds, and the worst of it is these stupid idiots of women don't seem to think so either . . . They don't seem to think they have any right to any individual existence.[28]

The point of such examples is not that the decent Victorian Christians of Glasgow, or anywhere else, would necessarily have condoned such male behaviour (which many would have ascribed to the congenital moral defectiveness of the urban poor), but that some of the beliefs, traditions and structures of their religion were key contributing factors to its prevalence. Likewise, no doubt there was much sorrow when women died as the result of excessive childbearing, but the presbyterian church adhered consistently to the reformed estimation of a woman's main duty and privilege as marriage and motherhood. That duty was recast in disturbing mould during the early decades of the 20th century, under the influence of Social Darwinism and the eugenics movement. Churchmen endorsed these theories in their call to middle-class churchgoers to replenish the superior Christian stock, which they thought was in danger of being overwhelmed by a tide of breeding moral and racial defectives. Birth control; the right of women either to affirm and enjoy sexual relationships, or to choose the size of their families; were denied and abhorred almost unanimously by church courts and representatives right up to 1930. The fictional examples of Margaret Darroch and Jean Guthrie, whose husbands represent very different types of pious presbyterian men, suggest the most destructive consequences of the negative and hypocritical attitude to sexuality which patriarchal religion could foster. The creators of these characters may have had a jaundiced view of the church, but there is no doubt that plenty of real women died from the exhaustion of excessive childbearing and rearing.[29] J W Coutts of Milngavie, writing on *The Church and the Sex Question* in 1922, waxed lyrical:

> Anyone who has read a fairly representative series of 19th century biographies . . . will not fail to remember the picture made time after time . . . of an exhausted mother condemned to spend the even of her days upon a sofa, or quietly surrendering the unequal struggle somewhere about the middle span of her life . . . All of us know instances in the humbler walks of life of women whose struggle with poverty and an ever increasing family has made them take rank as among the supreme heroines of life . . . Yet among them too the exhorbitant price of such a life has resulted . . . in premature break-down or death.[30]

A central feature of presbyterianism has been a powerfully masculine language and ethos for imaging the divine, and the accompanying exclusion of women from the male chain of command from God the Father, through Christ the Son to their male representatives in the world – rulers, ministers, husbands, fathers. Theologian Sally McFague notes,

> This model could have gone in the direction of parent (and that is clearly its New Testament course), with its associations of nurture, care, guidance, concern, and self-sacrifice, but under the powerful influence of the monarchical model, the parent became the patriarch, and patriarchs act more like kings than like fathers: they rule their children and they demand obedience.[31]

The doubt already cast on the equality of human creation by certain scriptural texts and their interpretation (Gen 2–3, I Cor 11: 1–15) must, for many women, have been confirmed by the psychological experience of worshipping a male God who was represented, in all ecclesiastical positions of status and power, by men. After the Reformation, a comprehensive attack on Mariolatry and veneration of saints removed access to any female symbolism in relation to the divine. Women, by creation and intent, were secondary creatures, while maleness was the normative condition of humanity. As a woman writing in the *UFC Record* of November 1913 observed:

> We have evolved an elaborate civilisation upon the conception of a man race and a woman race; nor, even in this late year of grace, 1913, has our consciousness of the purpose of God for the social order been clear enough to prevent the reproach that only through a contest within the twofold unity of the race can ancient and grave wrongs be righted.[32]

In this context, women, subject to definitions of their role and purpose which were devised in the interests of the ruling order, had an 'otherness' and invisibility foisted upon them. They were excluded from, or failed to recognise their own experiences in, descriptions of the generic 'man'. Or they had to redefine their life and witness using masculine language and concepts. There were at least two possible consequences of this for women who struggled to become fully 'human' within the terms of Scottish presbyterian society. One was, as suggested in Chapter 5, that such efforts were interpreted (and actively criticised or patronisingly tolerated) as female attempts to become more masculine:

> The formula is very simple: once the *a priori* norms of femininity have been set up, all of the exceptions are classified as 'de-feminised'. Criticism is directed exclusively toward individuals who fail to conform; never is it directed to the assumptions of the ideology itself.[33]

The second, and connected outcome was that, since 'human' equated with white, privileged, rational, active, controlling, body-denying man, the dominant model of 'humanisation' available to women was a transcendent dualism which operated by conquest and control – of one's own carnality; of emotions; of sensual pleasures; of other classes, races and cultures; of the non-human environment. The pugilistic and triumphalist tone of so many hymns which were popular during the latter part of the period, when an imperialistic worldview was prominent, testifies to this.

There were many who participated in different ways and to different extents within this imperialist framework. The salvation they sought for themselves, and preached to others, was *from* their complex, embodied situation as women, rather than *of* women (and other subordinated peoples) as a social group. In the context of a religious masculinism (which evidently survived and thrived in the structures, language and symbols of the churches, even when perceived to be under attack from a sentimental feminisation), I suspect there were numerous women who, like Alison Cairns, experienced confusion and self-abhorrence in relation to their female sexuality and identity. Born in 1901, she was the daughter of Professor David Cairns, who was United Free Church Moderator 1923–24. For a long time she deplored having been born a woman, and expressed a general discomfort with her body:

> The Bible, Spenser and Bunyan had created for us a parabolic conception of self as triumvirate – mind, soul and heart – living uneasily together inside the body (something not quite right, but exonerated by clothing).[34]

From the myriad examples which could be cited of the ways in which a repressive and life-denying creed was used to judge and control human lives, the following strikes me as a good illustration of the poignant absurdity of so much which was solemnly believed, and exhorted in a genuine spirit of loving concern. Helen Lockhart Gibson of Kirkcaldy had a Sabbath School pupil who was fond of going dancing:

> The last time I saw her, I told her she could not have both Christ and the dance. She said, 'I can't give up the dancing'. 'Then', I said, 'you must lose your soul'. Very soon after she was suddenly cut down by smallpox.[35]

The logical coherence of all these elements in the presbyterian experience might be appreciated by placing them in the cosmic framework which Calvinism constructed. Medieval Christianity was ambivalent about the natural world. From one perspective it was a sacramental embodiment of the invisible God which was the ground of its being. But a darker tradition believed that nature was possessed by demonic powers seeking to destroy human beings through sexual temptation: women, as Tertullian had famously stated, were the gateway of the devil. Calvinist doctrine dismembered the more positive sacramental view of the cosmos with its dogma of the total depravity of nature. The first answer in the Scots Catechism proclaims that glorification and enjoyment of God are the chief ends of man (sic). But the tenets of Calvinism cast radical doubt as to whether it was possible to enjoy and glorify God in creation. Only the Word could communicate the saving knowledge of God. Beyond that, everything was fallen, unable to bear the divine presence, and subject to the devil. No natural and sensual experience or joy could truly be trusted. And for Knox and his witch-hunting successors, the nature of women remained especially corrupt and dangerous, unless subdued by surveillance and control. The psychological residue of this legacy affected women in Scotland long after the grimmer aspects of Calvinist cosmology began to be challenged.[36]

Nevertheless institutional presbyterianism was not static or unitary. Operating in the socio-political context of Victorian and Edwardian Scotland, different theological and structural expressions of the reformed tradition developed. They were sometimes in competition with one another, and often in opposition to new trends in science and politics. There were elements within the presbyterian tradition which were positive about changing and expanding roles of women in church and society. They had some influential advocates: men like Archibald Charteris, the Caird brothers of Glasgow University, Dr Corbett of the United Presbyterian Magazine, J H Oldham, Professor J Young Simpson. But the cumulative impact of presbyterian structures and ideologies did not positively advance the situation or independence of most Scottish women. Church theology presented women as culpable and subordinate. Church courts largely failed effectively to challenge the underlying factors which condemned the majority to lives of poverty, drudgery and abuse. Church practice and preaching encouraged both the real class divisions between different women, and also a facile essentialism which purported to define 'Woman' for all time. Church law denied them equal power and freedom within its own institutions. In all of these ways, presbyterianism (as a respondent to the 1915 UFC questionnaire on women's place in the church put it), denied women 'the capacity to become'.

But that was not the whole story. The presbyterianism of 19th- and early 20th-century Scotland was certainly a patriarchal religion within a patriarchal society. Helen Crawfurd described the women of the nation as being 'bound hand and foot to the Church in its various forms', and characterised the mass of women as

> so harassed and burdened with the struggle for existence, their lives so circumscribed and stunted by obsolete domestic drudgery, that they took little interest in wider issues, or were too tired to take part in the changing of irksome conditions.[37]

But such a statement, though understandable as a general desciption and criticism of the reality she observed around her in the Glasgow slums, does not do justice to the diversity of female experiences and actions, cutting across boundaries of class and time and belief. This book has told stories of women who did take an interest in wider issues, and who acted, as they could, to change conditions. The cultural power of the church was extensive, but its impact was by no means always or totally repressive.

Resistance to the dehumanising tendencies in ecclesiastical, domestic and social structures broke through in many ways: occasionally (as with utopian, socialist and suffragette feminists), and especially during periods of social flux, in conscious opposition to the church; more often in the mundane daily process of struggling to create and sustain life and hope for themselves, their families, their workmates and their communities. In that process, women drew on elements of the same religion which had provided such effective tools for their oppression.

'It is not Christ who is Barring the Way': Resources for Liberation

> We in Scotland have always prided ourselves on liberty, the facility with which we can adapt our traditions and practices to the demands of the time, on freedom from superstition and convention, on the desire to get down to foundational truth, on our willingness to follow the spirit of Christ. Are we going to betray all these in this question of the equality of women?[38]

Brown and Stephenson have noted that Scottish women, well into the 20th century, grew up and lived in a highly religious environment. They also suggest that the influence of Christianity in its establishment presbyterian form was (especially after 1870) 'diffusive rather than enforced'.[39] One way in which women exerted some independence and choice was in their personal religious lives. Brown and Stephenson give some evidence of working-class women who resisted compulsion to adhere to their local presbyterian church, or who (more commonly) supplemented its dull diet with the more engaging worship offered by smaller denominations and sects:

> The bland hymns and socially ordered snobbery of morning worship at the Church of Scotland was compensated by attendance at more evangelical, emotional and rousing evening services at minor churches.[40]

This comment, based on the experience of women in the Stirling area during the first decades of the 20th century, received assent from a group of women who were children and young working women in Linktown, an industrial part of Kirkcaldy, during the same period. They found worship in their local Established Church worthy but dull. They enjoyed accompanying each other to a wide range of populist and recreational religious gatherings – many of them held in the open air, where these oral respondents recalled a greater psychological sense of equality and independence than at public worship in the parish church.[41]

Christian Watt rejected the established church as oppressive and hypocritical, but not the Christian faith. Indeed, she believed that she had a God-given mission which gave purpose to her difficult life.[42] Also in the North East, with its strong tradition of anti-establishment pietistic evangelicalism, Mary Coull was a regular attender at the Church of Scotland, but was converted by a woman preacher of the Faith Mission:

> Now this craiter, Stir-Alice was her name, and she held meetings in the Baptist church hall. Every night I was enthralled with her speaking: there was just something about her different from the minister, and she got through to me..[That night] I walked along a lonely road myself . . . And you know this, my burden was away and it never came back . . . After that, my mother's roarings and fightings of me hadn't the same effect, for I had more strength than my own . . . That's never left me.[43]

Stir-Alice and her fellow Faith Mission preachers were part of a distinctive tradition of women following their own light to spread the good news at revival meetings. They touched and changed many lives.

But biographies, journals and other sources bear ample testimony to the fact that, not just on the fringes, but also within the presbyterian establishment there were women whose faith was not something imposed simply by force or fear or convention. They had thought, and considered objections, and still asserted the deep and personal resonance of the reformed Christian tradition with their experience. Jeanie Morison, daughter-in-law of Hugh Miller (editor of the Free Church *Witness*) wrote in 1874:

> In spite of difficulties I still believe the Bible to be indeed the Word of God. We must always fall back for the reason of our belief on internal evidence. 'The spirit witnessing with our spirits that we are sons of God'. I recognise my father's hand – in this God who reveals Himself to me in this book, the Being whom I was made to worship and to serve . . . I read my own history in its pages . . . The promise and gifts of salvation, beginning with pardon, and going on to perfection.[44]

It is important to acknowledge the strength and meaning which individual women derived from their faith, and to respect that. As Mary Coull said (and as many others would have said, if asked), 'It's my faith that's kept me going'.[45]

But there is more involved in our working definition of liberation. However significant it may have been for individual lives, a Christianity failing to challenge the conditions which impoverish and dehumanise is no more than Marx's

Sigh of the oppressed creature, the heart of a heartless world, and the soul of soulless conditions.[46]

There were many Scotswomen who confronted oppressive conditions with compassionate hearts and souls. The pages of their books and magazines and journals tell of genuine disquiet and care for others – even when their actions were motivated in part by anxiety about their own sanctification. Religious commitment encouraged numerous women beyond the conventional show of charity to demonstrate heartfelt love and service. That meant personal giving, or working for church and philanthropic organisations, or sharing what little they had with neighbours and friends. This effort was usually couched in terms of personal faithfulness or evangelical concern to save souls. But especially during the first decades of the 20th century, some perceived that Christianity called for justice, and the transformation of social structures as well as individuals. The evangelical revival of the early 19th century did inspire some Christians with a vision to transform the whole sinful world, and gave many their first experience of political activity. But the momentum of that vision was lost during the mid-Victorian period, when the evangelical emphasis was on individual salvation. It was particularly under the influence of major theological and intellectual developments in the latter half of the 19th century that some groups of Christian women sought to develop coherent self-understanding and strategies for change. For them, as for other concerned people, what brought faith into tension with the establishment religion of the *status quo*, was a new awareness (backed by scientific study) that it was no longer possible simply to blame social evils on personal immorality or the providence of God. They were influenced by

> the emergence, in the wake of the Enlightenment and Romanticism, of a new historical way of looking at life, and the rapid development of the attitudes and techniques of religious scholarship.[47]

No doubt there were many women in the presbyterian tradition who, like Jeanie Morison, were able to use their own intelligence and selective perception to 'read their own history' in the androcentric scriptures, doctrines and practices of the church, without damage to their personal integrity. But the whole 19th- and early 20th-century debate about women's mission and women's rights was generated by a perceptible shift, for increasing numbers of women, from passive acceptance (or individual transcendence) of inferior status, to active and collective challenge. They were no longer prepared to receive as immutable facts the limitations of sphere and opportunities into which they had been socialised.

The Women's Movement was part of a complex of challenges to the unquestioned authority of establishment religion, which have been lucidly discussed by A C Cheyne. In his article, 'The Bible and Change in the 19th Century', he notes the following:

> Account should . . . be taken of the heightened moral sensitivity of the Victorian age, which made it difficult to maintain that every part of the Bible was equally authoritative. A new spirit of tolerance and tentativeness which, along with a growing preference for the apologetic as opposed to the dogmatic spirit, rendered the hard-line orthodoxy of the traditionalists increasingly uncongenial, was also a factor. Most important of all was the scientific revolution associated with the writings of Charles Lyell and Charles Darwin, which provided a picture of man and his environment difficult to reconcile with the statements of Scripture if literally understood.[48]

In this context, many women developed a more self-conscious understanding of themselves as women (and not just as 'Woman'), and they became willing, in varying degrees, to use their experience and aspirations as a measure of the validity of religious dogma and tradition, rather than vice versa. There must have been some psychological release for women who were able to reflect on the more colourful utterances of the reformers in that light: like Frances Stoddard, writing to her fiancé, David Murray, in 1869:

> I thank you for the pamphlet on the women's question. I note you are their special champion. Have been reading 'Knox's blast' agin the sex; at first it produced in me feelings of pity and sorrow for such strange misunderstandings of the noble functions and capacities of my sex. Towards the end I became irritated and resolved henceforth to have nothing to do with men who award such slander to one of their kind.[49]

In Scotland, this involved growing numbers of presbyterian women in confronting 'the fact that the Reformation Churches failed completely to take account of women.'[50] It is difficult to assess the extent of this perception, and whether there emerged a systematic critique of that failure. Obviously, the exclusion of women from the faculties of divinity, from the ministry and from the courts of the church denied them the opportunity to conduct a public theological debate of the kind which raged around men like William Robertson Smith and George Adam Smith.[51] Church-women's organisations such as the Woman's Guild were by no means promoters of controversy. And I have discovered no erstwhile missing radical feminist polemics from the period of the Women's Movement and critical scholarship, to match the biting eloquence of Elizabeth Cady Stanton or Matilda Joslyn Gage in America. If moderate and devoted churchmen could be put on trial for heresy, one can imagine the kind of venom which would rain down upon any women who dared publicly to challenge the infallible truth and divine authority of the faith – especially as it pertained to their own condition. Indeed, among the dangers believed to be inherent in the higher education of women was its potential incitement to heresy and rebellion. There were anxious Victorians who presumed that, like Eve, it was the aspiration of the 'New Woman' to become like God.

However, there is some evidence that those involved in the Women's Movement did reflect upon and discuss critically the tenets of their religious heritage. The Ladies Edinburgh Debating Society, (and the pages of its journal) was an important early forum for an influential group of women to expound and test new ideas and theories. The demand for classes taught by divinity professors within the various higher education associations also suggests that theological issues were not just a matter of academic speculation, but regarded as of vital relevance in the contention over the 'Woman Question'. Even the exhortatory writing produced by leaders of the emerging female church organisations bore periodic witness to significant changes of emphasis as to what parts of Christian tradition were regarded as authoritative and persuasive for women. By the 20th century new approaches – focusing more on a 'usable past' which had specific liberating potential – emerged. Entry into universities was one reason for this: not so much the formal teaching offered, since so few women studied theology, but access to the academic environment and resources, and also involvement in groups such as the Student Christian Movement, made an impact on thinking and experience. From 1894 the Women's Missionary College, too, rooted critical reflection in a community committed to the empowerment of women. But the wider context of unrest, action for social reform and increasingly militant suffrage agitation confronted progressive women with the need to assess their beliefs in the light of compelling issues.

It is an interesting sign of the loosening of orthodox bonds on the presbyterian tradition, that by the 1870s women like Frances Murray could resolve to have nothing to do with the slanderous Knox, yet did not feel constrained to abandon the church which he had founded. No doubt there were women who remained members out of duty, habit or propriety. But on the whole, those who tried to square their feminism with their religion did not desert the church, because they did not believe that their challenges were inimical to the spirit of the Reformation. Indeed, there were some who asserted their Pentecostal right to prophecy (Acts 2:16–18) in proclaiming that they were part of a movement of the Holy Spirit to call the church back to the central truths of its reformed heritage. Among those (especially in the suffrage movement) who did cast off their church membership, the majority distinguished between the reactionary oppression of the institution, and the liberating example and intent of Jesus. But wherever they chose to draw the line, they all challenged one of the most intransigent elements of Calvinist orthodoxy – the assertion that the Bible was uniformly, infallibly inspired, and that it gave unequivocal guidance on every subject.

Historical criticism introduced the possibility of an alternative hermeneutical principle: that not all biblical statements have equal claim to truth and authority, and that it was legitimate to discern the heart of the Christian message from textual material which exhibited internal inconsistencies, by postulating a canon within the canon. A writer in the 1869 edition of *The Attempt* shows the influence of these new ways of thinking in her review of *Women's Work and Women's Culture* – a landmark collection of essays edited by the English campaigner Josephine Butler:

> There is great confusion in the minds of many as to the doctrines which Christianity really teaches. Many laws instituted by man have received the sanction of the world for so many centuries, that we have at last come to believe that they are laid down in the Gospel . . . There is an instinctive dread of letting ourselves in any way doubt their propriety. But men nowadays are beginning to break through some ancient trammels . . . and are daring to read for themselves the Gospel, not fearing to let reason shed its brightest light on the teaching therein contained. The result of this is a great widening of religious views.[52]

She then discusses Butler's argument that theories about women should be judged in the light of Christ, not just upon the exigencies with which Paul had to deal, and quotes the author with approval:

> I appeal to the open Book and the intelligence of every candid student of Gospel history for justification of my assertion, that in all important instances of His dealings with women, His dismissal of each case was accompanied by a distinct act of Liberation.[53]

In the debate about women and the Bible, most did not claim (as the *Woman's Bible* did) that the the scriptures were actually androcentric – written by and for the benefit of men – but rather that they had been mistranslated and misunderstood. In general, it was argued that the injunctions of Paul and the pastoral letters about the role of women in the early church were culturally conditioned by specific circumstances which affected the life and witness of the early church in a Hellenistic environment. This was the approach of Isabella Armstrong (who certainly believed that she stood firmly in the evangelical tradition of adherence to the Word) in her *Plea for Modern Prophetesses* (1867).[54] But Jesus' own words and example were considered to provide a standard from which universal ethical principles could be derived. In biblical studies and devotional life, the historical figure of Jesus was becoming much more central. Kay Carmichael observes:

> Victorian times saw an outpouring of what the insensitive describe as mawkish sentiment over the Christ figure. For those who needed it, and it was not only women, Jesus became the symbol of loving, tender care as an alternative to the cold, harsh, unforgiving image of God being presented in the pulpit on Sundays, week after week.[55]

But Jesus was important not simply as a private source of comfort and compassion. He was also perceived as revealing the quality of right and equal relationship between women and men. For he had defied the clerical establishment and conventions of his day, affirmed the individual character, dignity and worth of the women he encountered, and refused to regard them in terms of some symbolic, archetypal 'Woman'. Isabella Armstrong tartly observed:

> The disciples marvelled that Jesus talked with the woman at the well (John 4:27) . . . and it is evident that the disciples still marvel, that the Great Shepherd speaks so graciously to the female members of His body, though it is to be regretted that they do not evince the same circumspection in allowing Him to manifest in His own time His own God-like purposes.[56]

Mary Slessor's strong faith was rooted in the conviction that she had a direct relationship with Jesus of Nazareth, who empowered his followers so that they could engage in a life of active, loving service. She wrote once to a friend, 'Creeds and books and ministers are all good enough but look you to Jesus'.[57] Certainly her own life bore ample witness to her conviction that this discipleship relativised all other claims and conventions.

In reformed, and especially in evangelical Protestantism, Pauline texts had been paramount in shaping doctrine and practice. Christ had been significant above all in his ontological, representative character as sacrifice to atone for human sin, and as Head of the Church. The new interest in him as historical figure, seeking radical transformation of the world, brought a freedom and dynamism to the faith of many. Jane Waterston claimed in 1885:

We have read the Bible with women's eyes, and if Christianity is true at all it is a living thing, growing with the growing years, and not a lifeless form which at best can give us but dead women's clothes of fifty or sixty years after Christ. It is surely not the letter that giveth life, and yet you would give to women letter and tradition as their sole portion. Much harm has been done by false ideas of what Christianity taught concerning women.[58]

Waterston recognised that reading the Bible involves an interaction between the text and the context: that the circumstances and concerns of the reader make a difference to the message which is received. It is noticeable that during the 1880s and 1890s, much more attention was paid in religious press and publications to women. There were numerous articles and books about Women of the Bible. The content and conclusions of these articles tend to confirm traditional teachings about the nature and role of women. But they appeared as a response to the growing female self-consciousness; as an apologetic attempt to demonstrate that women were significant participants in biblical history, which therefore retained its relevance for women in a changing world.[59]

Further evidence of a paradigm shift in understanding of Christianity was the recovered importance (linked to that of the historical Jesus) of the Kingdom of God. This underpinned the outlook of those who sought to restore or enliven the church's social witness in the years c1880–1920. Under the influence of historical criticism, German idealist philosophers, and with the decline of classical *laissez-faire* political economy, the rigid scholasticism and pietism which maintained a clear distinction between sacred and secular; church and world, began to break down. The Kingdom of God was the focus for a religious commitment which no longer accepted the *status quo* as divinely ordained. Referring to the Old Testament prophets, and to Jesus' core message, (as summarised in Luke 4:16–19) a significant number of churchmen and women embarked upon a critique of structures and conditions which denied the progressive plan and purpose of God for humankind. They regarded salvation, not as an escape from the sin and misery of the world, but as the power and possibility of individual and collective transformation in the world. The protagonists of this Christian ethos argued that they were simply reclaiming the reformation heritage of seeing the whole world – spiritual and material; personal and political – as under the sovereignty of God. And they recalled that the Scottish Reformation was initially a movement of rebellion, change and concern for all aspects of human life in the 'godly commonwealth'.[60]

It would be foolish to suggest that a facile equation can be drawn between presbyterian women seeking equal rights, and adherence to this theological viewpoint. Though they belonged mainly to the respectable urban middle classes, yet there was diversity of circumstance, political and religious beliefs (as even the genteel debates of the Edinburgh Ladies Debating Society suggest). Helen Reid, for example, used her position as editor of *The Attempt* to disseminate sternly conservative views about both theology and politics, complaining in 1870

> Such are the attractions of Germanism for the Scotch mind, that free-thinking tenets walk about under the mask of liberality, to the endangerment of steady principles such as our noble reformers rooted in their country's heart.[61]

and in a 'valedictory' to 1873:

> Grave cause for anxiety is ever increasingly evident in the turmoil of class legislation, out of which have arisen those giant spectres of Trades Unions and strikes, which keep up the unfailing antagonism of capital and labour, and by propagation of a spirit of moral cannibalism . . . threaten the disintegration of that national and Christian unity which has been Britain's bulwark for centuries.[62]

But although some reacted with fear and panic to social unrest, others were inspired by a vision of the coming Kingdom of God to exercise what they had been encouraged to think of as their especially feminine powers as moral regenerators. This potent mixture was a real source of strength and confidence for a significant minority of churchwomen. By the 1920s, there was an evident disparity of theological and social perspective between the conservative men who led the postwar retrenchment within presbyterianism, and the leaders of the women's organisations. People like Elizabeth McKerrow of the UFC continued to use the vocabulary of the Kingdom to speak of the gulf between the way things were, and the way God intended them to be, to inspire their more conventional sisters:

> The Christian woman who sets herself to do her part in the building of the Kingdom of God on earth, will bring more than knowledge or service. Faith too she will bring – faith in God and His power to achieve the impossible. And what does the world need more today than just this – the certainty that in the end Righteousness will conquer Evil, Love will burn up Hate, and that Jesus shall reign.[63]

Helen Crawford lost faith in the Kingdom of God as a liberating principle for the poor, and turned instead to the communist project of scientific materialism. But she continued to acknowledge the tremendous cultural, emotional and literary power of the Bible:

> My early religious upbringing made me familiar with Biblical stories, upon which I put my own interpretation. The Lamb dumb before her shearers,

represented the uncritical exploited working class. The wonderful imagery of the Book of Revelation . . . conveyed to me a picture of the wrath of an indignant wronged working class against their exploiters, rising in revolutionary masses to deal with them. Queen Vashti, in the book of Esther refused to come in and parade herself before the King, her lord and master, and his nobles. She was my first suffragette or feminist, and a rebel. She lost her position but she kept her soul.[64]

The consultation process upon which the United Free Church embarked in 1914, when it began considering the place of women in the church, provides the earliest direct evidence I have found of presbyterian women appealing to elements of their Christian heritage specifically to challenge the church's structural inequalities. Prior to this, women were invoking aspects of religion to demonstrate that it was compatible with the emancipation of women; or (in the suffrage movement) they were critical of sexism within the tradition, and their primary concern was not the reform of the church.

But women who, after the Union of 1929, organised an official movement for equal opportunity within the Church of Scotland (The Fellowship of Equal Service), were already campaigning during the 1920s. Central to their arguments was the contention that the institutional church was actually guilty of betraying the chief tenets of its faith, and that only by being open to the Holy Spirit, at work in the world, could it avoid decay and eventual dissolution. Eunice Murray warned:

> If the Church refuses to hear the message women have to give, they will find other channels through which to speak . . . Let men ask themselves not how they can silence the legitimate demand of women for recognition within the Church, but how they can utilise the enthusiasm, talents and devotion of these earnest women who, feeling they have a call, desire to serve humanity and Christianity.[65]

And Elizabeth McKerrow, who later became President of the post-Union Woman's Guild, pointed out that the message conveyed to women by their subordination in church had wider implications:

> The Church's view of women affects the whole social fabric. The principle of the sacredness of human personality is derived from Christianity . . . Society requires both encouragement and example, and these should be found in the Christian Church. It is very difficult for the ordinary person to understand 'spiritual equality' when for man it means determining women's contribution, and for woman it means conformity or repression. Spiritual equality *involves* equal opportunity.[66]

'She Must Not Soar Too High'

This discussion about the resources of presbyterianism which had potential for the liberation of Scottish women, has largely focused on the privileged, relatively influential individuals who had access to various ways of recording their views. The working-class Stirling respondents whose oral testimony formed the basis for Brown and Stephenson's research apparently made no allusions to Jesus as subverter of patriarchy or oppression. The Kingdom of God did not offer them a potent vision to inspire rebellion against their masters in home or workplace. The recollections of women from similar backgrounds in the Linktown area of Kirkcaldy, about religion during the early decades of the 20th century, were primarily of its social and cultural role in their lives. None had derived any sense from ministers or church organisations that Christianity proclaimed a message about social justice. Most had been conscious of a general 'invisibility' as girls and women in church, based on the prominence of male figures in church organisation and Biblical stories. None could recall hearing sermons or messages offering unusual or challenging models of women, or about Jesus' relationships with women.[67] Helen Crawfurd clearly came to the conclusion that the kind of Christianity to which she believed Scottish women were in thrall did not have the capacity to offer freedom and justice. To return to the language of liberation theology, even the most courageous women and men struggling to make the church reckon with structural sin and evil, imagined a Scottish church *for* rather than *of* the poor. By 1930, their progressive and inclusive vision was marginal to the witness and preoccupations of most ministers and lay people.

One of the most characteristic legacies of the Reformation was the work ethic, and this was an important source of empowerment for many Christian women. But on examination it seems that it was experienced rather differently, depending on social class and opportunity.

An article appeared in the 1855 *North British Review* entitled 'The Non-Existence of Women', in which J W Kaye argued that that the right to work was a human right of self-definition, whereby it was possible to move from private, passive suffering, into active doing in the 'real' public sphere. The cultural restrictions on women working, he maintained, denied their human identity and declared their psychological and social non-existence.[68] This is an exposition of the idea that work liberates, through personal dignity, creative production, freeing of aptitude and capacity, economic independence, the community of sharing a common task, and the engagement of body, mind and soul. The evangelical idea of woman's mission contained all of these ideas (even, to some extent, when applied only to home duties) except, crucially, that of financial recompense. At its best, woman's mission transcended the patriarchal exploitation of female ministration: the provision of services which the dominant group in society does not wish to perform for itself, and which women were conditioned to accept as natural and virtuous. For many Christian women, the new opportunities to work (in religious, philanthropic or professional activity) were seized upon as a matter of personal decision and choice, rather than compulsion. They might describe their motivations in terms of self-sacrifice and Christian usefulness; and their hopes for success might be subverted by religious self-doubt. But the humanising value of their productive activity could be a really life-changing experience – especially when it included the possibility of transcending the psychological or economic dependence which were central features of 'true womanhood'. Perhaps, too, the daily effort to relate some of the harsher Calvinist precepts to their own situations contributed to the historical process of theological challenge and transformation.

However, let us remember to be cautious about careless use of 'women' as an inclusive category. The women who seized upon the liberating potential of such work were rarely those who already had to grind out long hours in factories and sweatshops, in domestic service and on the streets, in the exhausting struggle to maintain the basic conditions of existence. For too many, labour extracted effort which diminished and dehumanised them. It did not value and nourish gifts, but ignored minds and trampled upon individual identity and dignity. For the majority of working-class women, work violated their health and wellbeing, and was experienced to some degree as alienating and exploiting. For women of all classes, but especially the poor, the effort of domestic labour was undervalued, sentimentalised or disregarded. In discourse, such work was either stripped of its weary, backbreaking tedium and presented as the maudlin *sine qua non* of female fulfilment. Or, when domestic servicing failed to meet the requirements of husband or society, (as was so often judged, by representatives of the church, to be the case in the homes of the poor) the provider was subject to condemnation for her failure to perform adequately as wife and mother.

In work, the freedom of choice which some middle- and upper-class women were able to exercise depended on the provision of a network of domestic support by other women whose service function, it was believed, was established by the simple fact of their birth into a certain class and gender. The morality of this practice was rarely questioned by those whose own quality of life was thereby improved, even when in a general way they condemned the sufferings of their sex. Much of 'women's work for women' was devoted to social and moral progress, but it often had the effect of stereotyping and objectifying other women: of confirming their dependence and inferiority, even although the concern was genuine. The class consciousness and social snobbery of many otherwise progressive women is quite striking from a late 20th-century vantage point.

The corollary of this was that the freedom to transcend the givenness of a situation, to exercise significant life choices, was severely constrained, if not wholly denied, for most poor women. Economic and social privilege underpinned the liberal moral theories of individual freedom and responsibility by which middle-class women typically attempted self-assertion.

There were also other notable differences which were used to allege the superiority of certain Scottish women over others, and gave them the right, as they saw it, to pass judgement on the way those others led their lives. This was true of the foreign missionary movement, and the imperialist ethos which informed much of that endeavour. It should also be noted that many devout presbyterian women shared in the shameful demonisation and bitter attacks on the Scoto-Irish Roman Catholic population in which the Scottish churches indulged in the inter-war years. *The Banner of the Covenant* was the organ of the Scottish Women's Protestant Union (which counted Lady Frances Balfour and her sister Lady Victoria Campbell among its luminaries). Between 1908–24 its tone reveals a degeneration from what might be considered the legitimate (if intemperate) defence of Protestant principles (often couched in terms of women's rights) to the thoroughly unpleasant racist fearmongering which had its counterpart in the General Assemblies.[69] This book has not considered the effect of a presbyterian culture on the growing female Catholic population of Scotland, but it has surely been a major source of division in lifestyle and attitudes between women. Kay Carmichael comments:

> As a child, growing up in the east end of Glasgow in the first half of this century, the community in which I lived demonstrated significant differences between Protestant and Catholic families. It was the Protestant women who transmitted awareness of the differences . . . In my experience [they] saw themselves as in every way superior to Catholic women whose religious roots lay in the Roman Catholic areas of southern Ireland.[70]

These issues are worthy of further investigation. They are simply mentioned here to emphasise that that the experiences of women in

Scottish society were affected and conditioned by a whole range of factors – some of which I have not touched on at all – and that gender, though basic, does not operate in isolation. It is also important to recognise that hypotheses, however helpful, cannot be used exhaustively to explain and contain real lives which elude tidy categorisation. For every example given, it would probably be possible to cite a counter-example. So, for instance, the general conclusion of this chapter is that resources for liberation and agency were more accessible to middle-class than to working-class women. Yet lives are many-faceted, and women drew refreshment, strength and pleasure from various sources. Doris Webster Havice's recollections of meeting Edinburgh women from different social milieux around 1930, though anecdotal, give a quite contrasting impression of relative emancipation and restriction. She was invited to speak to a group of Newhaven fishwives:

> I found them marvellously alert and very interested in the status of women in America. They impressed me . . . as being completely untrammelled by the class structure of society. The fishwives were loud and lusty and inquiring, and we enjoyed each other very much.[71]

She continues:

> Contacts with the so-called upper class were interesting also, but not as much fun. Many of these women in difficult marital situations, and they saw me as an outsider to whom they could speak frankly. They hoped because of my theological interests that I could counsel them. The lack of communication between husbands and wives was appalling among this group. Communication between parents and children was also very inhibited. In this class the impact of 'proper' behaviour patterns had the effect of making communication very superficial.[72]

Working women could find, in the midst of their material hardships, great sustenance and enjoyment in the solidarity of each other's company: perhaps a sense of community and of humour above all had the potential to transcend the limitations of their lives, and affirm them as human beings. And there is no reason why history should not acknowledge that women could be oppressed, circumscribed, victimised – yet also (and sometimes the very same women) 'loud and lusty and inquiring'. Middle-class women who developed their own communities, as students, professionals, philanthropists, tended to be single. For them, the decision to pursue careers and independence often included a conscious choice not to marry, and to endorse the exclusion from professions of those who did. Women who were wives and mothers were often more physically and emotionally isolated. The church at least provided a setting where all women could meet, and its women's organisations offered an important basis for social intercourse, though the quality of community therein must have varied considerably in different times and places.

We should be alert to the dangers of accepting at face value so much of what was written in church circles about women. First, because far too many women – especially working class – remain hidden from history, as people who did not have the opportunity or inclination to record their thoughts, beliefs and experiences. Secondly, because there was such a tendency among those who did have access to public media, to contort reality so that it would conform to the mythological images of 'true womanhood'. After her death in 1915, the *UFC Record* eulogised Mary Slessor as 'above all a saint. Her devotion and self-sacrifice was absolute'.[73] Charles Ovens, a carpenter who had worked with her, and knew the intensely practical quality of the life she had lived, commented, 'Aye! . . . But she was nae jist a' that holy!'[74]

The struggle for women in Scottish church and society has to a great extent been a struggle to affirm their personhood (individually or collectively) in its embodied particularity, against a prevailing tendency to reduce real human beings to symbols and stereotypes: defined primarily in terms of their genetic sex and the services which they are to provide as a matter of biological destiny and divine command. The beliefs and structures of the presbyterian church have been used on both sides of that struggle. David Watson, the founder of the Church of Scotland social work movement, who claimed to support the emancipation of women, nonetheless revealed himself as an ardent fan of that 'Perfect Womanhood' which is always defined in terms of its relationship to the male sex. He wrote in 1905 of the 'defects which hinder' such perfection:

> Nothing so much handicaps a woman as oddity, eccentricity, peculiarity. Nothing assists her so much as that grace, charm and ease of manner which men everywhere and instinctively expect in women.[75]

But Jeanie Morison, like many others, asserted her characteristically protestant right to individual choice as at root a religious freedom:

> I am responsible to none but God, and my own conscience, for my opinions . . . No man can come to me and take my burden of responsibility on his shoulders; and therefore no man has a right to dictate to me in what manner I am to discharge myself of that responsibility.[76]

In the complex processes which wrought change in Scottish society from 1830–1930, women (within or outwith presbyterianism) were both agents and objects. Some felt a powerful sense of injustice or limitation, and resolved to overcome those. Others changed their attitudes and lifestyles without realising it. Yet others had changes forced upon them. The possibility for change existed in many aspects of women's lives: spiritual, relational, educational, economic, political. The extent to which that possibility could be realised was affected by the interactions of class, gender, geography, relationship, ethnicity and other circumstances. There were many for whom freedom of choice in virtually all aspects of life was effectively denied.

The presbyterian form of Christianity provided social and cultural conditions which helped facilitate and shape the processes of change. But as a patriarchal institution within a hierarchical class society, the churches' organisation showed, in relation to women, 'evidence of considerable rigidity which sometimes breaks down but which rarely yields without a real struggle.'[77] As a shaper of Scottish culture, it remained committed to a conservative domestic ideology, acting (though by no means always deliberately) to hinder the full and egalitarian recognition of personhood which has often been proclaimed as a distinctive feature of presbyterianism. As a faith, through which the deepest meaning and purpose in human life is apprehended and declared, its ambivalent potential for Scottish women is perhaps expressed better in personal reflection than academic speculation:

Notes in Church

These four stone walls, they seem too close together

What is it I hear? – strange words concerning
The souls of men – Thou Who art Love
Art thou hate also? Art Thou Revenge?
I had deemed it not so.

Is Faith here? I know that she is here
But bounded by the four stone walls
She must not soar too high
She must not hope too much
And he (God's messenger) is bounded too
And they, the worshippers, worship with placid brow
Content it is so

"Miserable sinners!" I wonder why
My lips refuse the words? I, made, and loved
And sent by God to fill a little space,
Dare I be miserable?

They stoop so low, these worshippers
But do they stoop to rise? And unto what?
Is their God bounded too?
Ye four stone walls
I dream ye'll crumble into dust
The preacher's voice be silent
But all men know their God
For His great music sounding through the world
Shall hush the discords here

Give us, O God in Christ! The wide, wide heart
That we may take each sister, brother, in –
For failing this, we hinder Its approach.

> – From *The Attempt*, 1867[78]

Notes

1. F Balfour, introduction to E Picton-Turbervill, *Christ and Woman's Power* (1919) xi

2. *Christian Journal* (1840) 19

3. S de Beauvoir, *The Second Sex* (1953) 589

4. *Christian Journal* (1853) 70

5. M Daly, Beyond *God the Father: Towards a Philosophy of Women's Liberation* (1973) 35; see also her Gyn/Ecology: *The Metaethics of Radical Feminism* (1978)

6. E Fox-Genovese, 'For Feminist Interpretation', in *Union Seminary Quarterly Review* (1979–80) 9

7. See eg L Russell, *Human Liberation in a Feminist Perspective – A Theology* (1974); E Schussler Fiorenza, *In Memory of Her* (1983); R Radford Ruether, *Sexism and God-Talk: Toward a Feminist Theology* (1983); 'Prophetic Tradition and the Liberation of Women: Promise and Betrayal' in *Feminist Theology No 5* (January 1994) 58–73

8. W F Storrar, 'Liberation and Identity: Towards a New Practical Theological Paradigm of Scottish Nationhood' PhD thesis, Edinburgh University (1993)

9. M Jocelyn Gage, *Women, Church and State* (1893, reprinted 1980) 241

10. W Storrar op cit

11. see eg articles by J Torrance in *Evangelical Quarterly* (1983) 89ff, *Scottish Journal of Theology* (1981) 225ff

12. C A Salmond, *A Woman's Work* (1890) 170

13. ibid l

14. ibid lxxv

15. ibid cxvii

16. *Mother's Diary:Sabbath Evening Meditations of Mary Anne Paterson (nee Rogerson) 1853–58* (nd privately published c1907)

17. Eliza Fletcher had a breakdown following a particularly agonising and extended period of spiritual desolation, c1876 and she went on a long trip to Australia to recover. She also wrote bitterly against God, feeling angry about the 'dark decrees' which offered no assurance, and that God was unjustly hard on her. (Chap 8 op cit)

18. quoted in J Buchan, *The Expendable Mary Slessor* (1980) 13

19. see S McFague, *Models of God* (1987) 63ff

20. E Jay (ed) *The Autobiography of Margaret Oliphant* (1990) 6–7

21. *Free Church Magazine* (1850) 298

22. *Life and Work* (1886) 80

23. I Cowan, *The High Estate of Service* (1898) 90

24. D Fraser (ed) *The Christian Watt Papers* (1983) 24

25. see *The Attempt* (1867) 145ff

26. F Balfour, *Dr Elsie Inglis* (1918) 107

27. Woman's Guild Supplement, *Life and Work* (1906)

28. *Dr Elsie Inglis* 88–9

29. see Robin Jenkins, *The Awakening of George Darroch* (1985); L Grassic Gibbon, *Sunset Song* (1932). 30 J W Coutts, *The Church and the Sex Question* (1922) 172–3. Coutts was a minister from Milngavie. He challenged Christians to take a more just and enlightened view of sex and relationships. On Birth Control, he rejected the 'snobbery and class discrimination' of those influenced by the eugenics movement.

31. see Mcfague, op cit 66. Perhaps the influence of the monarchical model made fathers act like kings!

32. *United Free Church Record* (1913) 547

33. M Daly, *The Church and the Second Sex* (1968) 113

34. L Irvine, *Alison Cairns and her Family* (1967) 76

35. J Gibson, *Not Weary in Well Doing* (1888) 29

36. I have found Rosemary Radford Reuther's critical and constructive work on the history and future of theology helpful in understanding the importance of the way humans and their religious doctrines perceive and relate to the natural world. See, e g *Gaia and God:An Ecofeminist Theology of Earth Healing* (San Francisco 1992)

37. see Helen Crawfurd's unpublished autobiography, 49, 75

38. *Life and Work* (1931) 145

39. C Brown and J Stephenson, 'Sprouting Wings' in *Out of Bounds* (1992) 99

40. ibid

41. Linktown Action Centre Ladies Group interviewed 1995

42. see *The Christian Watt Papers* (op cit) introduction and passim

43. A Smith, *Women Remember: An Oral History* (1989) 134

44. *The Attempt* (1874) 244–5

45. A Smith op cit

46. K Marx, *Critique of Hegel's Philosophy of Right* (1844) ed SB O'Malley Joseph (Cambridge 1970) 131

47. A C Cheyne, 'The Bible and Change in the 19th century' in D F Wright (ed), *The Bible in Scottish Life and Literature* (1988) 199

48. ibid

49. E Murray, *Frances Stoddard Murray* (1920) 102

50. quoted in O Wyon, *The Three Windows* (1953) 111

51. William Robertson Smith was the most celebrated of the theologians who shocked the Free Church by using critical scholarship in their teaching and writing. In 1881, his tenure of the Old Testament Chair at Aberdeen Free Church College was terminated because his work on the Pentateuch was considered to be heretical. In fact, this was the last victory for the traditionalists, and further complaints against others were dismissed. In 1892 a Declaratory Act recognised diversity of opinion on some points of the Westminster Confession, and theology was free to develop along critical lines.

52. *The Attempt* (1869) 266

53. ibid 267

54. I Armstrong, *Plea for Modern Prophetesses* (1867). She makes extensive, and quite sophisticated use of linguistic and contextual tools in her exposition of biblical passages most frequently used to impose female subordination and silence.

55. K Carmichael, 'Protestantism and Gender' in G Walker and T Gallacher (eds), *Sermons and Battle Hymns* (1990) 222

56. I Armstrong, op cit 3

57. quoted in J Buchan, op cit 13

58. speech to St Andrew's Church Literary Society, Cape Town, 1885. Quoted in J Bean and E van Heyningen, *The Letters of J E Waterston 1866–1905* (1983) 288

59. The quantity of discursive and biblical interpretation dealing with, or about women greatly increases from around 1880. In the Scottish church press, the format and perspective of the *United Presbyterian Magazine* particularly lent itself to long articles on women of the Bible, eg Phoebe (1888) 385; Hagar (1889) 453; the Woman of Samaria (1896) 529. Shorter pieces also appeared in the Woman's Guild Supplement of *Life and Work*, from 1891. There were also numerous books on the subject, eg Henry McCook, *Women Friends of Jesus* (1889). The content of these tended to affirm the newly recognised usefulness and honour of women in the service of the church, as being a restoration of scriptural practice.

60. see D C Smith, *Passive Obedience and Prophetic Protest* (1987), and contemporary books, sermons and articles (of which Smith gives some details)

61. *The Attempt* (1870) 5

62. *The Attempt* (1874) 2 The opinionated Miss Reid, the daughter of a Leith publisher, must have been in her mid-twenties when she wrote these articles. She began co-editing *The Attempt* when she was seventeen years old.

63. E McKerrow, *United Free Church Record* (1928) 209

64. H Crawfurd, op cit 49

65. E Murray, *The Ministry of Women* (speech given in Govan 1923. She also published other pamphlets: *The Power of Women in the Church (nd)*; *Women's Place in the Early Church* (1928); *Women and the Church* (nd)

66. E McKerrow, *Perfect Love Casteth Out Fear* (nd), pamphlet published by the Fellowship of Equal Service – a Church of Scotland organisation whose objective was to secure the ordination of women, and equal opportunity in all aspects of church life. The Marchioness of Aberdeen was Hon President, Mary Lamond and Frances Melville were hon vice-presidents, and Elizabeth McKerrow was hon secretary. Prof G Henderson of Aberdeen University was President. Probably founded c 1930–1

67. Brown and Stephenson, op cit. Perhaps the Prohibitionist Party, which returned Edwin Scrymgeour to Parliament in the 1920s, on the strength of the female working class vote in Dundee, ('Vote as you pray' was his winning slogan) was most effective in evoking a collective political response to millenarian religious beliefs. See W Walker, *Juteopolis* (1980)

68. *North British Review* (1855) 559ff

69. See S J Brown's discussions of anti-Irish racism within the presbyterian churches during the 1920s, in *SCHSR* (1990) 72–96, *SJT* (1991) 489–517 *Innes Review* (1991) 19–45. Surely these attitudes were deeply influenced by Social Darwinist views on race, just as ideas about women's nature and capacity were shaped by the pseudo-science of sex differentiation

70. K Carmichael, op cit 213–4

71. D Webster Havice, 'Roadmap for a Rebel' in *Union Seminary Quarterly Review* (1979–80) 71

72. ibid

73. *UFC Record* (May 1915)

74. quoted in J Buchan op cit 243

75. D Watson, *Perfect Womanhood* (1905) 101

76. *The Attempt* (1871) 78

77. *Revised Interim Report of a Study on the Life and Work of Women in the Church* (World Council of Churches, Geneva 1948) 19

78. *The Attempt* (1874) 8

Bibliography

Primary Sources

Church Records

Reports of the Schemes of the General Assembly of the Church of Scotland 1830–1930

Proceedings and Debates of the General Assembly of the Free Church of Scotland (including Reports) 1843–1900

United Presbyterian Church Synod Papers 1847–1900

Proceedings and Debates of the General Assembly of the United Free Church of Scotland 1900–1929

Reports of the General Assembly of the Uited Free Church of Scotland 1900–1929

Church of Scotland Layman's Handbook 1903–

Miscellaneous Presbytery Minutes 1830–1930

Miscellaneous Congregational Reports and Records Minutes, Correspondence and other archive material relating to the Foreign Missions of the Scottish presbyterian denominations (see NLS Catalogue of Manuscripts Acquired since 1925 (Edinburgh 1985) Vol 6 (MS 7530–8022) for details)

Miscellaneous minutes and other records relating to the Woman's Guild and other women's organisations of the Scottish presbyterian denominations
(Scottish Records Office CH1/38 and under parish classifications)

Church of Scotland Commission on the War Report: Social Evils and Problems (Edinburgh 1919)

Reports of the Edinburgh World Missionary Conference 1910 Vols IV–VI (Edinburgh 1910)

364

Other Records and Pamphlets

Minutes of the Edinburgh Ladies Education Association/Edinburgh Association for the University Education of Women (Edinburgh University Library Special Collections)

Minutes of the Edinburgh University Women's Debating Society (Edinburgh University Library)

Material relating to the LLA Diploma and University Hall, St Andrews (St Andrews University Library)

Material relating to the Suffrage Movement (National Library of Scotland)

Material relating to ordained women ministers in Scotland (in private hands)

Edinburgh University Faculty of Divinity: Senatus Minutes John White archive (New College Library)

Miscellaneous material (New College Library)

The Present Crisis of the Free Church of Scotland (1843)

Women and the Church in Scotland (1912)

E Murray *The Ministry of Women in the Church* (WFL 1923)

The Pigot Case (Calcutta 1884) Transcript of Pigot v Hastie libel case, Bengal 1883.

Papers and Journals

Christian Journal

Church of Scotland Home and Foreign Mission Record

United Presbyterian Mission Record

United Presbyterian Magazine

The Watchword

Free Church Monthly

Life and Work 1887–1931 (including Woman's Guild Supplement 1891–1924 and Women's Work Supplement 1928–1930)

United Free Church Mission Record 1900–1929

'Youth' Magazine

Eastern Female's Friend

News of Female Missions

Women's Work Among the Heathen

The Helpmeet

United Free Church Women's Missionary Magazine

International Review of Missions

UFC Women's Missionary College House Guild Letter

The Banner of the Covenant (Paper of the Scottish Women's Protestant
    Union) 1908–1924

The Attempt 1865–1874

The Ladies Edinburgh Magazine 1875–80

Miscellaneous issues of other journals as cited in text

Secondary Sources

Biographies

M Anderson, *Memories of Fifty years Mission Work in the West Parish of
    Greenock* (Glasgow 1914)

W Marwick, William and Louisa Anderson: *A Record of Their Life and Work
    in Jamaica and Old Calabar* (Edinburgh 1897)

Lady Frances Balfour, *Ne Obliviscaris: Dinna Forget* (London 1930)

Countess of Ashburnham, *Lady Grisell Baillie, A Sketch of Her Life*
    (Edinburgh 1893)

L Irvine, *Alison Cairns and her Family* (Cambridge 1967)

A Gordon, *The Life of Archibald Hamilton Charteris* (London 1912)

Helen Crawfurd, unpublished autobiography (nd) copy of typescript MS
    in William Gallagher memorial library, STUC, Glasgow

Lady Mary Richardson (ed), *Autobiography of Mrs Fletcher with letters and
    Other Family Memorials* (Edinburgh 1875)

C A Salmond, *A Woman's Work: The Life of Eliza Fletcher* (Glasgow 1889)

W P Livingstone, *Christina Forsyth of Fingoland: The Story of the Loneliest
    Woman in Africa* (London 1918)

J Gibson, *Not Weary in Well-Doing: The Life and Work of Mrs Helen Lockhart
    Gibson* (Edinburgh 1888)

F Barbour, *Dr Elsie Inglis* (London 1918)

M Todd, *Life of Sophia Jex-Blake* (London 1918)

Louisa L Lumsden, *Yellow Leaves:Memories of A Long Life* (Edinburgh 1933)

Mrs H Macrae, *Alice Maxwell, Deaconess* (London 1919)

Eunice Murray, *Frances Stoddard Murray* (London 1920)

Elizabeth Jay (ed) *The Autobiography of Margaret Oliphant* (Oxford 1990)

H Renton, *Memorial of Mrs Agnes Renton* (nd, privately published)

J Buchan, *The Expendable Mary Slessor* (Edinburgh 1980)

W P Livingstone, *The White Queen of Okoyong: Mary Slessor, A True Story of Adventure, Heroism and Faith* (London 1916)

O Wyon, *Three Windows:The Life of Annie Hunter Small* (London 1953)

E T MacLaren, *Recollections of the Public Work and Home Life of Louisa and Flora Stevenson* (Edinburgh 1914?)

Mrs H E Scott, *A Saint in Kenya:The Life of Marion Scott Stevenson* (London 1932)

A Waddel, *Memorials of Mrs Sutherland of Old Calabar* (Paisley 1883)

J Bean and E van Heyningen (eds), *The Letters of Jane Elizabeth Waterston 1866–1905* (Cape Town 1983)

D Fraser (ed) *The Christian Watt Papers* (Edinburgh 1983)

E G Murray, *A Gallery of Scottish Women* (London 1935)

D P Thomson, *Women of the Scottish Church* (Perth 1975)

General

B S Anderson and J P Zinsser, *A History of Their Own:Women in Europe from Prehistory to the Present Vol 2* (London: Penguin 1990)

K M Boyd, *Scottish Church Attitudes to Sex, Marriage and the Family* (Edinburgh: John Donald 1980)

E Breitenbach and E Gordon, (eds) *Out of Bounds:Women in Scottish Society 1800–1945* (Edinburgh: Edinburgh University Press 1992)

C G Brown, *The Social History of Religion in Scotland Since 1730* (London 1987; rewritten and updated as *Religion and Society in Scotland Since 1707*. Edinburgh: Edinburgh University Press 1997)

S J Brown, *Thomas Chalmers and the Godly Commonwealth of Scotland* (Oxford: Oxford University Press 1982)

S J Brown and M Fry (eds) *Scotland in the Age of Disruption* (Edinburgh: Edinburgh University Press 1993)

S J Brown, 'The Social Vision of Scottish Presbyterianism and the Union of 1929' in *Records of the Scottish Church History Society* (1990) 72–96

S J Brown, 'Reform, Reconstruction, Reaction: The Social Vision of Scottish Presbyterianism c1830–1930' in *Scottish Journal of Theology* (1991) 489–517

J H S Burleigh *A Church History of Scotland* (London: Oxford University Press 1960)

N de S Cameron (ed) *Dictionary of Scottish Church History and Theology* (Edinburgh: T & T Clark 1993)

A C Cheyne, *The Transforming of the Kirk* (Edinburgh: St Andrew Press 1983)

L Colley, *Britons: Forging the Nation 1707–1837* (New Haven, London: Yale University Press 1992)

J W Coutts, *The Church and the Sex Question* (London 1922)

A L Drummond and J Bulloch, *The Church in Victorian Scotland 1843–1874* (Edinburgh: St Andrew Press 1975)

A L Drummond and J Bulloch, *The Church in late Victorian Scotland 1874–1900* (Edinburgh: St Andrew Press 1978)

A H Dunnett, *The Church in Changing Scotland* (London 1934)

R Evans, *The Feminists: Women's Emancipation Movements in Europe, America and Australia, 1840–1920* (London: Croom Helm 1979)

W H Fraser and R J Morris (eds) *People and Society in Scotland Vol II 1830–1914* (Edinburgh: John Donald 1990)

A Dickson and J H Treble (eds) *People and Society in Scotland Vol III 1914–1990* (Edinburgh: John Donald 1992)

P Gay, *The Bourgeois Experience: Victoria to Freud. Vol 3: The Cultivation of Hatred* (London: WW Norton 1994)

A H Gray, *Men, Women and God* (London 1923)

R L Greaves (ed) *Triumph over Silence: Women in Protestant History* (Westport: Greenwood Press 1985)

W Knox (ed) *Scottish Labour Leaders: A Biographical Dictionary* (Edinburgh: Mainstream 1984)

J Lewis, *Women in England 1870–1950* (Brighton: Wheatsheaf 1984)

J Lewis (ed) *Labour and Love* (Oxford: Basil Blackwell 1986)

A A MacLaren, *Religion and Social Class: The Disruption Years in Aberdeen* (London: Routledge and Kegan Paul 1974)

G Malmgreen, (ed) *Religion in the Lives of English Women 1760–1930* (London: Croom Helm 1986)

R K Marshall, Virgins and Viragos: *A History of Women in Scotland 1080–1980* (London: Collins 1983)

A S Matheson, *The Church and Social Problems* (1893)

S Mechie, *The Church and Scottish Social Development 1780–1870* (London 1960)

W Muir, *Mrs Grundy in Scotland* (London 1936)

J Rendall, *The Origins of Modern Feminism: Women in Britain, France and the United States 1760–1860* (Basingstoke: Macmillan 1985)

D Riley, *Am I That Name?: Feminism and the Category of 'Women' in History* (London 1988)

J Sayers, *Biological Politics: Feminist and Anti-Feminist Perspectives* (London: Tavistock 1982)

C Smart (ed) *Regulating Womanhood: Historical Essays on Marriage, Motherhood and Sexuality* (London: Routledge 1992)

D C Smith, *Passive Obedience and Prophetic Protest: Social Criticism in the Scottish Church* (New York: Peter Lang 1987)

T C Smout, *A History of the Scottish People 1560–1830* (London: Fontana 1972)

T C Smout, *A Century of the Scottish People 1830–1950* (London: Fontana 1986)

T C Smout (ed) *Victorian Values* (Oxford: Oxford University Press 1992)

W Storrar, *Scottish Identity: A Christian Vision* (Edinburgh: Handsel 1990)

B Taylor, *Eve and the New Jerusalem: Feminism and Socialism in the 19th Century* (London: Virago 1983)

G Walker and T Gallacher (eds) *Sermons and Battle Hymns: Protestant Popular Culture in Modern Scotland* (Edinburgh: Edinburgh University Press 1990)

D Watson, *Perfect Womanhood* (Edinburgh 1905)

D Withrington, 'The Churches in Scotland c1870–1900: Towards a New Social Conscience' in *Records of the Scottish Church History Society* vol xxix (1972)

D F Wright (ed) *The Bible in Scottish Life and Literature* (Edinburgh: St Andrew Press 1988)

J D Young, *Women and Popular Struggles: A History of British Working Class*

Women 1560–1984 (Edinburgh: Mainstream 1985)

The Position of Woman, Actual and Ideal (London 1911)

A Woman's Claim of Right in Scotland: Women, Representation and Politics (Edinburgh: Polygon 1991)

Chapter 1 – Introduction

M Boxer and J Quataert, *Connecting Spheres: Women in the Western World, 1500–The Present* (Oxford: Oxford University Press 1987)

M Caird, *The Morality of Marriage* (London, 1896)

L M G Clark and L Lange (eds), *The Sexism of Social and Political Theory: Women and Reproduction from Plato to Neitzsche* (Toronto: Toronto University Press 1979)

L Davidoff and C Hall, Family Fortunes: *Men and Women of the English Middle Class 1780–1850* (London: Routledge 1992)

J Dempsey Douglass, *Women, Freedom and Calvin* (Philadelphia: Westminster Press 1986)

R Dobash and R E Dobash, *Violence Against Wives: A Case Against the Patriarchy* (London: Open Books 1980)

J Dwyer and R B Sher (eds) *Sociability and Society in 18th Century Scotland* (Edinburgh: Mercat Press 1993)

B Gottlieb, *The Family in the Western World from the Black Death to the Industrial Age* (Oxford: Oxford University Press 1993)

E Helsinger R Sheets and W Veeder, *The Woman Question: Society and Literature in Britain and America, 1837–1883* (3 Volumes) (New York: Garland Press 1983)

J Kelly, Women, History and Theory: *The Essays of Joan Kelly* (Chicago 1984)

E King, *The Hidden History of Glasgow's Women: The Thenew Factor* (Edinburgh: Mainstream 1993)

C Larner, *Enemies of God: The Witchhunt in Scotland* (London: Chatto & Windus 1983)

L Leneman and R Mitchison, *Sexuality and Social Control: Scotland 1660–1780* (Oxford: Basil Blackwell 1989)

L J Nicholson, *Gender and History: The Limits of Social Theory in the Age of the Family* (New York 1986)

L J Nicholson (ed) *Feminism/Postmodernism* (New York: Routledge 1990)

C Pateman, *The Sexual Contract* (Oxford: Polity Press 1988)

A Phillips, *Engendering Democracy* (Cambridge 1991)

M Poovey, *Uneven Developments: The Ideological Work of Gender in Mid-Victorian England* (London 1989)

Chapter 2 – 'Woman's Mission' and Women's Work

S Burman (ed) *Fit Work For Women* (London: Croom Helm 1979)

O Checkland, *Philanthropy in Victorian Scotland* (Edinburgh: Donald 1980)

E Gordon and E Breitenbach (eds) *The World is Ill-Divided: Women's Work in Scotland in the 19th and 20th Centuries* (Edinburgh: Edinburgh University Press 1990)

E Gordon, *Women and the Labour Movement in Scotland 1850–1914* (Oxford: Clarendon 1991)

G Gordon (ed) *Perspectives of the Scottish City* (Aberdeen: Aberdeen University Press 1985)

M Magnusson, *Out of Silence: The Woman's Guild 1887–1987* (Edinburgh: St Andrew Press 1987)

L Mahood, *The Magdalenes: Prostitution in the 19th Century* (London: Routledge 1990)

L Mahood, 'The Domestication of 'Fallen' Women: The Glasgow Magdalene Institution 1860–1890' in D McCrone, S Kendrick and P Straw (eds) *The Making of Scotland: Nation, Culture and Social Change* (Edinburgh: Edinburgh University Press 1989)

F Prochaska, *Women and Philanthropy in 19th-Century England* (Oxford: Oxford University Press 1980)

W Walker, *Juteopolis: Dundee and Its Textile Workers 1885–1923* (Edinburgh: Scottish Academic Press 1979)

Chapter 3 – Women and the
Foreign Missionary Movement

R Balfour and M Young, *The Work of Medical Women in India* (Bombay 1929)

W Burns Thomson, *Reminiscences of Medical Mission Work* (Edinburgh 1885)

T Christensen and W R Hutchison (eds) *Missionary Ideologies in the Imperial Era 1880–1920* (Arhus: Aros Press 1982)

R Compton Brouwer, *New Women for God: Canadian Presbyterian Women and India Missions 1876–1914* (Toronto: University of Toronto Press 1990)

E G K Hewat, *Vision and Achievement 1796–1956: The History of the Foreign Missions of the Church of Scotland* (Edinburgh: St Andrew Press 1960)

M Hunter, *The Gospel of Gentility* (New Haven: Yale University Press 1986)

J W Jack, *Daybreak in Livingstonia* (1901)

J Lowe, *Medical Missions: Their Place and Power* (Edinburgh 1886)

E Raymond Pitman, *Heroines of the Mission Field* (London 1880)

Kwok Pui-Lan 'The Image of the "White Lady": Gender and Race in Christian Mission', in Concilium 1991/6: *The Special Nature of Women?*

R Shepherd, *Lovedale, South Africa* (Cape Town 1941)

A H Small, *St Colm's College: Memories of Fifty Years 1894–1944* (Edinburgh 1944)

M Stewart, *Training in Mission* (Edinburgh: St Andrew Press 1972)

A S Swan, *Seedtime and Harvest: The Story of the Hundred Years Work of the Women's Foreign Mission of the Church of Scotland* (London 1937)

K Young, *Our Sail We Lift: The Story of the Girls' Association 1901–1951* (Edinburgh 1951)

Our Church's Work in India: UFC Missions (Edinburgh 1910)

Chapter 4 – The Position of Women in Scottish Presbyterian Polity

I Armstrong, *Plea for Modern Prophetesses* (Glasgow 1866)

K Armstrong, *The End of Silence: Women and Priesthood* (London: Fourth Estate 1993)

O Anderson, 'Women Preachers in Mid-Victorian Britain: some reflections on feminism, popular religion and change' in Historical Journal Vol xii (1969) 467ff

J Barr, *The United Free Church of Scotland* (London: Allenson 1934)

A C Charteris, *The Church of Christ* (London: Macmillan 1905)

R Edwards, *The Case for Women's Ministry* (London: SPCK 1989)

J Field-Bibb, *Women Towards Priesthood* (Cambridge: Cambridge University

Press 1991)

M Levison, *Wrestling with the Church* (London: Arthur James 1992)

J M Ludlow, *Women's Work in the Church* (London 1865)

D Havice Webster, 'Roadmap for a Rebel' in *Union Seminary Quarterly Review* XXXV (1979–80) No 1–2 70ff

N Dickson, 'Modern prophetesses: Women Preachers in the 19th century Scottish Brethren', in *Scottish Church History Society Records* XXV I 89ff

Chapter 5 – Women Campaigning for Change

Anti-slavery

L and R Billington, 'A Burning Zeal for Righteousness': Women in the British Anti-slavery Movement 1820–1860' in J Rendall (ed) *Equal or Different: Women's Politics 1800–1914* (Oxford: Basil Blackwell 1987)

D Brion Davis, *Slavery and Human Progress* (Oxford: Oxford University Press 1984)

C Midgley, *Women Against Slavery: The British Campaigns 1780–1870* (London: Routledge 1992)

C Duncan Rice, *The Scots Abolitionists* (Baton Rouge: Louisiana State University Press 1981)

E Cady Stanton, *Eighty Years and More* (London 1898)

C Taylor, *British and American Abolitionists: An Episode in North Atlantic Relations* (Edinburgh: Edinburgh University Press 1974)

Temperance

British Women's Temperance Association – Its Origins and Progress 1878–1908 (Edinburgh 1908)

N Denny, 'The Scottish Churches and the Temperance Movement' in *Records of the Scottish Church History Society* (1989) 216ff

B L Epstein, *The Politics of Domesticity: Women, Evangelism and Temperance in 19th-century America* (New York: Wesleyan University Press 1981)

T Honeyman, *Good Templary in Scotland 1869–1929* (Glasgow 1929)

E King, *Scotland Sober and Free: The Temperance Movement 1829–1979* (Glasgow 1979)

M B MacGregor, *Towards Scotland's Social Good: One Hundred Years of*

Temperance Work in the Church of Scotland (Edinburgh: Church of Scotland Publishing Committee 1948)

D Paton, 'Drink and the Temperance Movement in 19th century Scotland' (PhD unpublished thesis, Edinburgh University 1977)

W Reid, *Woman's Work for Women's Weal* (Glasgow 1860)

Education

W Alexander, *First Ladies of Medicine: The Origins, Education and Destination of Early Women Graduates of Glasgow University* (Glasgow 1987)

R D Anderson, *Educational Opportunity in Victorian Scotland* (Oxford 1983)

W N Boog Watson, 'The First Eight Ladies' in *University of Edinburgh Journal* vol 23 (1967–8) 227ff

K Burton, *Memoir of Mrs Crudelius* (Edinburgh 1879)

J Burstyn, *Victorian Education and the Ideal of Womanhood* (London: Croom Helm 1984)

M Cruikshank, *History of the Training of Teachers in Scotland* (London 1970)

J Fewell, F Paterson and H Corr (eds) *Girls in Their Prime: Scottish Education Revisited* (Edinburgh: Scottish Academic Press 1990)

J Grant, K McHutcheon, E F Sanders (eds) *St Leonard's School 1877–1927* (Oxford 1927)

S Hamilton, 'Women and the Scottish Universities c1869–1939: A Social History (PhD unpublished thesis Edinburgh University 1987)

W H Humes and H M Paterson (eds) *Scottish Culture and Scottish Education 1800–1980* (Edinburgh: Donald 1983)

W Knight, *History of the LLA Exam and Diploma for Women, and of University Hall for Women Students at St Andrews University* (Dundee 1896)

L Milne-Rae, *Ladies in Debate, Being a History of the Ladies Edinburgh Debating Society 1865–1935* (Edinburgh: Oliver and Boyd 1936)

C Struthers, *The Higher Education of Women* (Aberdeen nd)

B Welsh, *After the Dawn: A Record of Pioneer Work in Edinburgh for Higher Education of Women* (Edinburgh: Oliver and Boyd 1939)

Women's Suffrage and Feminism

O Banks, *Faces of Feminism: A Study of Feminism as a Social Movement* (Oxford: Martin Robertson 1981)

C Bolt, *The Women's Movement in the United States and Britain 1790–1920s* (New York: Harvester Wheatsheaf 1993)

D Beddoe, *Back to Home and Duty: Women between the Wars 1918–1939* (London 1989)

R First and A Scott, *Olive Schreiner* (New Brunswick, NJ: Rutgers University Press 1990)

B Harrison, *Separate Spheres: Opposition to Women's Suffrage in Britain* (London: Croom Helm 1978

S S Holton, *Feminism and Democracy: Women's Suffrage and reform Politics in Britain* (Cambridge: Cambridge University Press 1986)

E King *The Scottish Women's Suffrage Movement* (Glasgow 1978)

L Leneman, *A Guid Cause: The Women's Suffrage Movement in Scotland* (revised edition Edinburgh: Mercat Press 1995)

L Leneman, 'The Scottish Churches and 'Votes for Women' in *Records of the Scottish Church History Society* vol xxiv (1991) 237ff

J Liddington and J Norris, *One Hand Tied Behind Us: The Rise of the Women's Suffrage Movement* (London: Virago 1978)

C McPhee and A Fitzgerald (eds), *The Non-Violent Militant: Selected Writings of Teresa Billington-Greig* (London: RKP 1987)

M Reid, *A Plea for Woman* (1843, reprinted Edinburgh: Edinburgh University Press 1988)

J Rendall (ed) *Equal or Different: Women's Politics 1800–1914* (Oxford: Basil Blackwell 1987)

D Rosen, *Rise Up Women!* (London: RKP 1974)

S Rowbotham, *Women in Movement: Feminism and Social Action* (London: Routledge 1992)

D Thompson, *The Chartists* (London: temple Smith 1984)

A Wilson, *The Chartist Movement in Scotland* (Manchester: Manchester University Press 1970)

A Wiltsher, *Most Dangerous Women – Feminist Peace Campaigners of the Great War* (London: Pandora 1984)

Chapter 6 – Conclusion

L Boff, *Church, Charism and Power* (London: SCM 1985)

M Daly, *The Church and the Second Sex* (London: Chapman 1968)

M Daly, *Beyond God the Father: Toward a Philosophy of Women's Liberation* (London: Women's Press 1986)

M Daly, Gyn/Ecology: *The Metaethics of Radical Feminism* (London: Women's Press 1991)

S de Beauvoir, *The Second Sex* (London: Jonathan Cape 1953)

E Fox-Genovese, 'For Feminist Interpretation', in *Union Seminary Quarterly Review* 35 (1979–80) 5–14

S McFague, *Models of God: Theology for an Ecological, Nuclear Age* (Philadelphia: Fortress Press 1987)

R Radford Ruether, *Sexism and God-Talk: Toward a Feminist Theology* (London: SCM 1983)

R R Ruether, 'Prophetic Tradition and the Liberation of Women: Promise and Betrayal' in *Feminist Theology* 5 (January 1994) 58–73

L Russell, *Human Liberation in a Feminist Perspective* (Philadelphia: Westminster Press 1974)

E Schussler Fiorenza, *In Memory of Her: A Feminist Reconstruction of Christian Origins* (London: SCM 1983).

Index